AYN RAND'S *ATLAS SHR*

Ayn Rand's complex philosophical novel, Atlas Shrugged, *is hugely popular, yet intimidating or confusing to some people. By assembling this impressive collection, Edward Younkins has done something wonderful for both those who enjoyed the novel and those yet to discover it. Younkins and his collaborators examine many different facets of the novel, from the perspectives of a variety of different disciplines: literature, philosophy, economics, politics, history. This is sure to be a thought-provoking and conversation-stimulating anthology.*

Aeon J. Skoble, Associate Professor of Philosophy,
Bridgewater State College, USA

Edward Younkins appreciates the significance of Ayn Rand's novel Atlas Shrugged *to so many disciplines and thus he has assembled an impressive collection of essays by distinguished experts in many fields to mark the 50th anniversary of Rand's monumental work. Younkins understands the unique nature of* Atlas; *it is a great work of romantic literature, its plot shows in the concrete the importance of economic liberty and a morality of rational self-interest, it outlines an integrated philosophy – Objectivism – by which to guide one's life, and it offers a vision of the kind of life and world that this philosophy can produce. This collection is a welcomed volume for the millions who love Rand's magnum opus.*

Edward Hudgins, Executive Director, The Atlas Society & the Objectivist Center, USA

Atlas Shrugged *is a thrilling and, in my view, nearly indispensable part of courses on economics and government. Dr. Younkins's insightful collection of essays by experts in many fields will prove immensely valuable to teachers and students who use* Atlas *and to any reader who seeks deeper understanding of Ayn Rand's marvellous novel.*

John B. Egger, Professor of Economics, Towson State University, USA

A collection of this type is long overdue. Edward Younkins has exhibited an impressive vision in assembling this extraordinary book just in time for the 50th anniversary of Ayn Rand's masterpiece.

Lew Rockwell, President, Ludwig von Mises Institute, USA

Atlas Shrugged *has been called the most important novel of ideas since War and Peace. Now, more than 20 years after Ayn Rand's death, she and her great book are beginning to get the scholarly attention they deserve. This Companion is a fine example of that.*

David Boaz, Executive Vice President, Cato Institute, USA

This book is dedicated to all admirers of Ayn Rand's Atlas Shrugged
past, present and future

Ayn Rand's *Atlas Shrugged*
A Philosophical and Literary Companion

Edited by
EDWARD W. YOUNKINS
Wheeling Jesuit University, USA

ASHGATE

Published by
Ashgate Publishing Limited
Gower House
Croft Road
Aldershot
Hampshire GU11 3HR
England

Ashgate Publishing Company
Suite 420
101 Cherry Street
Burlington, VT 05401-4405
USA

Ashgate website: http://www.ashgate.com

British Library Cataloguing in Publication Data
Ayn Rand's Atlas shrugged : a philosophical and literary
    companion
    1.Rand, Ayn. Atlas shrugged 2.Objectivism (Philosophy)
    3.Philosophy in literature
    I.Younkins, Edward Wayne, 1948-
    813.5'2

Library of Congress Cataloging-in-Publication Data
Ayn Rand's Atlas shrugged : a philosophical and literary companion / [edited by]
Edward W. Younkins.
        p. cm.
    Includes bibliographical references and index.
    ISBN: 978-0-7546-5533-6 (hardcover)
    ISBN: 978-0-7546-5549-7 (pbk.)
  1. Rand, Ayn. Atlas shrugged. I. Younkins, Edward Wayne, 1948-

    PS3535.A547A9427 2007
    813'.52--dc22

                                                                        2006018030

ISBN: 978-0-7546-5533-6 (HBK)
ISBN: 978-0-7546-5549-7 (PBK)

Printed and bound in Great Britain by TJ International Ltd, Padstow, Cornwall.

Contents

Figure

List of Contributors

Roger E. Bissell, a professional musician and graduate student in psychology at California Coast University, is a writer on psychology and philosophy. His work has appeared in a number of publications, including *Reason Papers*, *Objectivity*, *Journal of Consciousness Studies*, *Vera Lex*, and *ART Ideas*.

Walter Block, Harold E. Wirth Eminent Scholar Endowed Chair in Economics at Loyola University, New Orleans, Louisiana, is the editor of a dozen books and is the author of seven more (the most famous of which is *Defending the Undefendable*, Fox and Wilkes, 1991).

Peter J. Boettke, Director of Graduate Studies (Ph.D. Program) and Deputy Director of the James M. Buchanan Center for Political Economy at George Mason University, Professor of Economics, George Mason University, is the editor of the *Review of Austrian Economics*.

Samuel Bostaph is Professor of Economics and Chairman, Department of Economics, at the University of Dallas and an academic advisor to The Future of Freedom Foundation.

Susan Love Brown, a political and psychological anthropologist and Associate Professor of Anthropology at Florida Atlantic University, is the editor of *Intentional Community: An Anthropological Perspective* and a member of the associate faculty of the Women's Studies Program.

Joy Bushnell is a writer based in Western New York currently working on two novels as well as being heavily involved in activism and charity work at the local level.

Robert L. Campbell, Professor, Department of Psychology, Clemson University, has various research interests, including theories of human development, the development of moral personality, and the nature of free will, as well as the historical evolution of moral psychology. He is Co-Editor of *New Ideas in Psychology* and the Associate Editor of the *Journal of Ayn Rand Studies*.

Bryan Caplan is an Associate Professor of Economics at George Mason University. Caplan's articles have appeared in the *American Economic Review*, the *Economic Journal*, the *Journal of Law and Economics*, *Social Science Quarterly*, and numerous other outlets.

Stephen Cox, Professor of Literature and Director of the Humanities Program at the University of California, San Diego, is the author of *The Stranger Within Thee* (University of Pittsburgh Press, 1980), *Love and Logic: The Evolution of Blake's Thought* (University of Michigan Press, 1992), *The Titanic Story* (Open Court, 1999), and *The Woman and the Dynamo: Isabel Paterson and the Idea of America* (Transaction Publishers, 2004). He is also a founding co-editor of *The Journal of Ayn Rand Studies*.

Jack Criss is the publisher and executive editor of the Metro Business Chronicle, a monthly business newspaper based in Jackson, MS. He is also author of *Ready, Aim, Right!* (Quail Ridge Press, 2004), a collection of political/philosophical essays and editorials compiled from over the past 15 years.

Douglas J. Den Uyl, Vice President of Education, Liberty Fund, Inc., has published books and articles in ethics and political theory as well as in the area of the history of philosophy. He co-edited with Douglas Rasmussen *The Philosophic Thought of Ayn Rand*, and recently published *The Fountainhead: An American Novel*. He is co-author with Douglas Rasmussen of *Liberty and Nature: An Aristotelian Defense of Liberal Order* (Open Court, 1991), *Liberalism Defended: The Challenge of Post Modernity* (Edward Elgar, 1997), and *Norms of Liberty: A Perfectionist Basis for Non-Perfectionist Politics* (Pennsylvania State University Press, 2005).

Mimi Reisel Gladstein, Professor of English and Theatre Arts, University of Texas at El Paso, currently serves as Chair of the Department of Theatre, Dance and Film Department. She is the author of *The New Ayn Rand Companion* (Greenwood Press, 1999), *Atlas Shrugged: Manifesto of the Mind* (Twayne, 2000), and *The Indestructible Woman in Faulkner, Hemingway, and Steinbeck* (UMI Research Press, 1986).

Stuart K. Hayashi is a freelance writer in Mililani, Hawaii. Stuart was an assistant editor at http://wwwmoorelies.com in 2004 and worked as a legislative aide in the Hawaii State Capitol from January 2005 to May 2006, and has been published in *TCS Daily*.

Steven Horwitz, Associate Dean of the First Year and Professor of Economics, St. Lawrence University in Canton, New York, is the author of two books, *Microfoundations and Macroeconomics: An Austrian Perspective* (Routledge,

2000) and *Monetary Evolution, Free Banking, and Economic Order* (Westerview, 1992).

Lester H. Hunt, Professor of Philosophy, University of Wisconsin, Madison, is the author of *Nietzsche and the Origin of Virtue* (Routledge, 1993) and *Character and Culture* (Rowman and Littlefield, 1997).

Jennifer L. Iannolo is the founder and Editor-in-Chief of *Gastronomic Mediations*, an international magazine celebrating food's sensual and philosophical pleasures. A lifelong entrepreneur, she has given guest lectures at New York University, Babson College, and the Culinary Institute of America. She was recently featured in the NY Times Bestseller, *Secrets of the Young and Successful*. Jennifer is also the editor of *The Atlasphere*.

Jomana Krupinski is an environmental biologist and an MBA student at Wheeling Jesuit University.

Ronald F. Lipp is a writer based in Newcastle, California. His subjects include modern culture and history. Among other works on art, he is a principal contributor to the catalog of the Alphons Mucha museum in Prague.

Roderick T. Long, Associate Professor, Department of Philosophy, Auburn University, is the author of *Reason and Value: Aristotle versus Rand* and (The Objectivist Center, 2000); *Wittgenstein, Austrian Economics and the Logic of Action: Praxeological Investigations* (Routledge, forthcoming); editor of the *Journal of Libertarian Studies*; and president of the Molinari Institute.

Spencer Heath MacCallum is a social anthropologist living in Casas Grandes, Chihauhau, Mexico. He is the author of *The Art of Community* (Institute of Humane Studies, 1970); editor of *Michael von Notten, The Law of the Somalis*; contributor to *The Half-life of Policy Rationales: How New Technology Affects Old Policy Issues* (Klein and Foldvary, eds.), and to *The Voluntary City* (Beito, Gordon and Tabarrok eds); and writes in such publications as *The Freeman, Human Organization, The Independent Review, Journal of Libertarian Studies, Modern Age*, and *Reason*.

Tibor R. Machan holds the R.C. Hoiles Chair in Business Ethics & Free Enterprise at Chapman University's Argyros School of Business & Economics and is a research fellow at the Pacific Research Institute (San Francisco, CA) and the Hoover Institution (Stanford University, CA). He has written, among other works, *Individuals and Their Rights* (Open Court, 1989), *Classical Individualism* (Routledge, 1998) and *The Morality of Business, A Profession for Wealth Care* (Springer, 2007).

Russell Madden teaches writing and communications at several local colleges in Iowa. He ran for Congress and learned just how far we have yet to go to recover our liberty. He has published in *The Freeman, Full Context, The Daily Objectivist, Laissez Faire City Times, Spintech, Suman Philosophine* and many other publications.

Karen Michalson is a writer and a musician. She is the author of *Hecate's Glory* (Tor Book, 2003) *Enemy Glory* (Tor Books, 2001), and *Victorian Fantasy Literature: Literary Battles with Church and Empire* (Edwin Mellen Press, 1990). She also writes scholarly articles and reviews. She currently studies law at Western New England College School of Law and holds a Ph.D. in English from the University of Massachusetts.

Kirsti Minsaas has been a research fellow in English literature at the University of Oslo, Norway. She has lectured extensively on Ayn Rand's fiction, both in Europe and in the United States and has published several articles on Rand's fiction and literary theory.

Virginia Murr is a philosophy major at Rockford College in Illinois. A 5th degree black belt, she is the International Executive Vice President of Toku-Kai.

Douglas B. Rasmussen, Professor of Philosophy, Department of Philosophy, St. John's University, is coeditor with Douglas Den Uyl of *The Philosophic Thought of Ayn Rand* (University of Illinois Press, 1984) and with Tibor Machan of *Liberty for the Twenty-First Century* (Roman & Littlefield, 1995). He is co-author with Douglas Den Uyl of *Liberty and Nature: An Aristotelian Defense of Liberal Order* (Open Court, 1991) and *Liberalism Defended: The Challenge of Post-Modernity* (Edward Elgar, 1997), and most recently *Norms of Liberty: A Perfectionist Basis for Non-Perfectionist Politics* (Pennsylvania State University Press, 2005).

Jennifer J. Rhodes is a graduate assistant and MBA student at Wheeling Jesuit University.

Jeff Riggenbach is the author of *In Praise of Decadence* (Prometheus, 1998). He has been a working critic of the arts (most notably of literature, music, and film) since 1972. From 1996 to 2000, he taught courses in philosophy, music appreciation, popular culture, and writing at the Academy of Art College in San Francisco.

Peter Saint-Andre works on Internet protocols for messaging, identity, and security. His essays have appeared in *Full Context*, the *Journal of Ayn Rand Studies, Liberty* and *Objectivity*.

Hans Gregory Schantz has worked with IBM, The Lawrence Livermore National Laboratory, and ITT Technical Institute in Austin, Texas. Dr. Schantz is a consulting engineer with Next-RF, Inc., and chief scientist for the Q-Track Corporation. Author of *The Art and Science of Ultrawideband Antennas* (Artech House, 2005), Dr. Schantz has more than ten patents for his electromagnetic and other inventions.

Ken Schoolland is an Associate Professor of Economics and Political Science at Hawaii Pacific University. He is the author of *Adventures of Jonathan Gullible: A Free Market Odyssey* (Small Business Hawaii, 1981).

Chris Matthew Sciabarra, Visiting Scholar, Department of Politics, New York University, is author of *Marx, Hayek and Utopia* (State University of New York Press, 1995), *Ayn Rand: The Russian Radical* (Penn State Press, 1995), and *Total Freedom: Toward a Dialectical Libertarianism* (Penn State Press, 2000). He is a founding co-editor of *The Journal of Ayn Rand Studies.*

Larry J. Sechrest, Professor of Economics and Director of the Free Enterprise Institute, Sul Ross State University, Alpine, Texas, is the author of *Free Banking: Theory, History, and a Laissez-Faire Model* (Quorum Books, 1993), as well as a number of articles in reference works, scholarly journals, and popular periodicals.

Fred Seddon currently holds adjunct professorships at four universities in South Western Pennsylvania, and is the author of *Ayn Rand, Objectivists and the History of Philosophy* (University Press of America, 2003), *An Introduction to the Philosophical Works of F.S.C. Northrup* (Edwin Mellen Press, 1995), and *Aristotle and Lukasiewicz on the Principle of Contradiction* (Modern Logic, 1996).

Gennady Stolyarov II is a science fiction novelist and Editor-in-Chief of the *Rational Argumentator*, a magazine championing the Western principles of Reason, Rights and Progress.
(http://www.geocities.com/rational_argumentator/index.html)

Edward W. Younkins, Professor of Accountancy and Director of Graduate Programs, Department of Business, Wheeling Jesuit University, is the author of *Capitalism and Commerce: Conceptual Foundations of Free Enterprise* (Lexington Books, 2002), and editor of *Philosophers of Capitalism: Menger, Mises, Rand, and Beyond* (Lexington Books, 2005).

Preface

I first read my favorite novel, *Atlas Shrugged*, in the spring of 1992 on the recommendation of Wheeling Jesuit University MBA student Jessica Lofgren (now Bedway) and my colleague in WJU's Philosophy Department, Fred Seddon. Upon entering Ayn Rand's fictional universe, I was immediately enthralled by her brilliant philosophical insights and by her striking narrative power. The plot of *Atlas Shrugged* was a model of integration among theme, story, and characters. All elements were logically connected, tied to the whole, and integrated with the novel's unifying theme. Even the philosophical speeches were integrated with the events of the story.

Here was a novel about the great minds of the world going on strike while the world is moving toward destruction. The heroes were giants of intellect and productivity who make the evil of the villains possible by their own assistance and support (i.e., their sanction). Although their minds had been restrained by government intervention and regulation, Rand showed that the great minds were themselves partly to blame because they conceded to the altruistic claims of the would-be destroyers of capitalism. Although Rand had great admiration for producers and entrepreneurs as heroic, she also displayed her disdain for their unwillingness to defend themselves.

Atlas Shrugged is appealing on many levels. It is a moral defense of capitalism, political parable, social commentary, science fiction tale, mystery story, love story, and more. The further and deeper I studied *Atlas Shrugged* the more I was able to appreciate how these multiple approaches to plot enriched one another.

This anachronistic alternative-reality allegory was both dystopian and utopian in nature. Its world was populated by giants of ability, moral character, and achievement and by productive geniuses who created futuristic inventions. The novel displayed a sharp contrast between these heroes and the villains of the story who were crooked politicians and businessmen. Both the heroes and villains were larger than life.

The story is about a revolution brought about by the heroes of *Atlas Shrugged*. It is about the fall that occurs in the world when the thinkers and creators go on strike. This is John Galt's ingenious strategy to solve society's problems. Galt creates a band of heroic men to implement this strategy. As a result, the independent minds withdraw from society to live in Galt's Gulch, an ideal community which illustrates what the world could be like.

Ayn Rand not only builds in dramatic conflict between the good and the bad (e.g., Dagny and Rearden vs. the looters), she also shows conflict between the good and the good (e.g., Galt and the strikers vs. Dagny and Rearden). John Galt drives the conflict in order to dramatize the martyrdom of the men of the mind whose own victimhood is made possible only by their own error. It is through the conflict that Rearden, Dagny, and the other scabs come to understand the nature of their mistake. Rand's fascinating story tells us how Dagny and Rearden discover the secret of the strike and are ultimately led to join it.

My idea for a readings book on *Atlas Shrugged* goes back to October of 2003. After an evening class in which I used this great novel, I was sitting at my computer in my office and thought how wonderful it would be if someone compiled such a collection. Then I thought that this "someone" could very well be me. I began emailing individuals who I knew greatly admired *Atlas Shrugged* and, in a very short period of time, I had many authors lined up. My goal was to have the book released in time for the fiftieth anniversary of *Atlas Shrugged* in 2007.

This collection of readings is an exploration and a celebration of this monumental work of philosophy and literature that is the culmination of Rand's literary life and the product of her many years of thinking and hard work. The authors of the included essays analyze the novel's integrating elements of theme, plot, characters, and so on from many perspectives and on various levels of meaning. I am extremely grateful to them for all of their fine work.

This companion to *Atlas Shrugged* is divided into the following eight sections: 1) an overview; 2) philosophy; 3) literary aspects; 4) aesthetics; 5) political economy; 6) human relationships; 7) characterization, and 8) history. The essays are grouped in categories that make the most sense to me, but many could easily have been placed in other groups. In addition, the essays do not have to be read in progression in order to be understood by the reader.

Thanks are due to Chris Sciabarra, my unofficial co-editor, who unfailingly and generously provided advice with respect to this project. I would also like to thank Tibor Machan for suggesting that I contact Ashgate Publishing Company and the editor there, Paul Coulam, for enthusiastically and quickly agreeing to publish this book. Most of all, I am indebted to my secretary at Wheeling Jesuit University, Carla Cash, for her most capable and conscientious help in bringing the book to print.

Edward W. Younkins
Wheeling Jesuit University

Introduction

Atlas Shrugged (1957), the philosophical and artistic capstone of Ayn Rand's novels, is the demarcation work and turning point that culminated her career as a novelist and propelled her into a career as a popular philosopher. This stunning intellectual achievement marvelously fulfilled her purposes and accomplished all she wanted to do in the realm of fiction. *Atlas Shrugged* has become one of the most influential books ever published impacting a variety of disciplines including philosophy, literature, economics, business, political science, and others.

In *Atlas Shrugged*, Rand presents her original, brilliant, and controversial philosophy of Objectivism in dramatized form. More than a great novel, it expounds a radically new philosophy with amazing clarity. *Atlas Shrugged* presents an integrated and all-embracing perspective of man and man's relationship to the world and manifests the essentials of an entire philosophical system—metaphysics, epistemology, politics, and ethics. *Atlas Shrugged* embodies Objectivism in the actions of the story's heroes.

Atlas Shrugged inspired both passionate admiration and violent antagonism. Over the years it has reached a large audience despite mainly negative initial attitudes of critics and intellectuals who wrote reviews savagely attacking it. Innumerable readers have affirmed and attested to the importance of *Atlas Shrugged* to their lives. It is obvious that Rand's evocative writing has enormous emotional impact with respect to the sense of life and view of man and the world that she portrays (Gladstein 2000, 19–25, 26–30).

Atlas Shrugged is a powerfully mythic work that evokes extraordinary responses. In part, its power to induce intense emotion and its mythic stature stem from the large time and emotional investment required to read Rand's nearly 1200 page *magnum opus*. For many individuals open to her ideas, *Atlas Shrugged* has become a foundational mythology that concretizes the meaning of Objectivism through the actions of the characters (Hunt 1984).

Atlas Shrugged is now being taught in colleges and universities in a variety of courses. It provides an excellent base for teaching issues in business, business ethics, economics, and political and economic philosophy. Use of *Atlas Shrugged* aids in moving from abstract principles to realistic business examples. The novel serves as a link between philosophical concepts and the practical aspects of business and illustrates that philosophy is accessible and important to people in general and to business people in particular. Reading and studying *Atlas Shrugged* helps students better understand the philosophical, moral, and economic concepts underpinning business and capitalism.

In the so-called "Bible of Objectivism" Ayn Rand created the Objectivist philosophy and inspired the origin of the modern libertarian movement in America—a movement that she strongly disavowed. Despite her rejection of libertarianism, her novel did popularize libertarian ideas along with Objectivist doctrine and showed how a rational person can function in an irrational society. For many, Rand's greatest legacy to mankind serves as a blueprint for the future and is a potential source for social change. *Atlas Shrugged* will be a force in the world for a long time and will be discussed and analyzed by thinkers in a variety of fields for many decades or perhaps even centuries (Gladstein 27–8).

Atlas Shrugged is written with conviction and precision of mind. To produce her novels, Ayn Rand became what she called a "writing engine" who exhaustingly planned, edited, and revised in order to make them better and better (Rand 1997, 48). All that mattered to her was to perform her work with solemn purposefulness until it was done properly. This is clear to anyone who reads Rand's journals and drafts which illustrate her process of continually improving this great novel (Knapp 1998).

As illustrated and described in the original archival research of Shoshana Milgram Knapp (1998), Rand was a dedicated and disciplined artist who made many additions, subtractions, and other changes. Her purposeful revisions were of both the small and large types. She would: 1) remove or trim passages to gain greater impact while maintaining precision and unity; 2) improve dialogue and descriptions to make them more concise, to the point, and more telling; 3) remove large portions of text to achieve integration and conciseness; 4) continually search for the right words to attain clarity; 5) strive to make all aspects of the novel consonant with its tone; 6) find better events to illustrate her ideas; 7) develop more precise formulations; 8) add clarifying passages; 9) substitute implicit and action-oriented scenes in place of explicit descriptions; 10) develop passages that concurrently serve different purposes and that operate on various levels of meaning; and so on.

The most extraordinary quality of *Atlas Shrugged* is its integration. Ayn Rand understood that everything that was included in a novel affects that novel. The unity of a novel depends upon necessary causal and logical connections among its many aspects. It follows that she included no random elements or events. She tied everything to *Atlas Shrugged*'s unifying theme of "the role of the mind in human existence" (Peikoff 2004).

The plot of *Atlas Shrugged* is a model of integration among theme, story, and characters. The marvelously constructed and interwoven plot is a miracle of organization encompassing multiple layers or tiers of depth. Every event, action, and character serves both dramatic and philosophical purposes. Every line is important. She presents characters in stylized form in terms of their essential attributes. Rand's emblematic characters have all irrelevancies and accidents removed. Rand probes each character's motives, connects a set of personal traits to each character's motivation, and integrates the actions of the characters with their motivation and character traits (Peikoff).

This volume addresses the philosophical, literary, and other aspects of *Atlas Shrugged*. Although the essays are fun to read and geared to general readers who are fans of this great novel, scholars will also enjoy them and benefit from reading them. While all of the contributors are enthusiastic admirers of Rand's most famous novel, this does not keep them from making some critical observations about it. The authors are from a variety of fields including, but not limited to: philosophy, literature, economics, psychology, sociology, anthropology, communications, music, and engineering. Because *Atlas Shrugged* is a transdisciplinary novel that also works on many levels of meaning, these writers' multiple approaches are able to demonstrate how the novel's many aspects enrich one another. It follows that this anthology is a compelling examination for Ayn Rand scholars and enthusiasts alike.[1]

The first section of this volume is devoted to providing an overview of *Atlas Shrugged*. In the opening essay I summarize the story and introduce readers to various philosophical and literary aspects of *Atlas Shrugged*. Chris Matthew Sciabarra's "*Atlas Shrugged*: Manifesto for a New Radicalism" then discusses how this novel provides a manifesto for a methodological radicalism upon which political and social change can be built. Next, Douglas B. Rasmussen considers Ayn Rand's view of logic and reality and the Aristotelian significance of *Atlas Shrugged*'s section titles. Fred Seddon then analyzes various tiers of meaning in the chapter titles of *Atlas Shrugged*. In his offering, Lester H. Hunt describes one of the literary methods employed by Rand in her highly intentional and integrated work. The final essay in this section consists of Hans Schantz's very detailed table of contents and outline of the events in *Atlas Shrugged*.

Part II examines some philosophical aspects of *Atlas Shrugged*. Tibor Machan begins by exploring Rand's original idea, first proposed in *Atlas Shrugged*, of the "sanction of the victim." This is followed by Roderick Long's article in which he suggests that *Atlas Shrugged* was intended by Ayn Rand to offer an enduring assessment of, and alternative to, some of the main ideas in Plato's *Republic*. Gennady Stolyarov then provides an analysis of the role, significance, and essential ideas of John Galt's speech.

The selections in Part III look at the nature of *Atlas Shrugged* as a literary work. In "Ayn Rand's Cinematic Eye" Mimi Gladstein explains that, because of Ayn Rand's experience in film writing and long history with the movies, she writes her novels with a "cinematic eye" and a cinematic mode of narration. Jeff Riggenbach then explains how *Atlas Shrugged* could be regarded as a work of science fiction as well as of romantic realism. In the last piece in this section, Kirsti Minsaas discusses how *Atlas Shrugged* recalls the epic-heroic literature of the past and how Ayn Rand reworks ancient myths in this novel.

Part IV is concerned with aesthetics. Ron Lipp discusses Ayn Rand's theory of art as expressed in *Atlas Shrugged* and her other works. Next, Roger Bissell's innovative essay expresses the idea of romantic music through a "lecture" given by Dr. Richard Halley. Then in his "Fuel for the Soul" Russell Madden explains how *Atlas Shrugged* provides the emotional fuel to stimulate one's love of existence and to motivate a person toward his full flourishing as a human being.

The next section deals with issues of political economy. Peter Boettke argues that *Atlas Shrugged* is the most economically literate work by a major novelist in the history of literature and explains that the economic principles her novel communicates include rewards for productive efficiency and innovation, the benefits of trade, and the destruction of production and the distortions in exchange relationships that result from government intervention in the economy. In his essay, Larry Sechrest suggests that woven throughout the story are elements which strongly communicate the spirit of anarcho-capitalism. Spencer MacCallum then discusses how businessman Werner Stiefel, made great strides in practically applying the principles of social organization illustrated in Galt's Gulch. Next, Sam Bostaph analyzes Ayn Rand's "Atlantis" as a free market economy. In turn, Bryan Caplan analyzes the parallels between *Atlas Shrugged* and Public Choice Theory. The essay by Steven Horwitz argues that Ayn Rand built a great number of valuable insights about money in Francisco d'Anconia's "money speech." Next, Jack Criss discusses the role of human productivity in *Atlas Shrugged.*

The articles in Part VI all examine human relationships. In her selection, Karen Michalson discusses how she wanted to be the glorious hero that Dagny Taggart was, but was not because of the lack of having Dagny's context for action in the world. Next, Joy Bushnell analyzes Dagny's search for her perfect partner. Peter Saint-Andre then investigates Ayn Rand's philosophical insights into the nature of friendships and the degree to which the relationships between the four primary characters in *Atlas Shrugged* live up to her ideal. In the last two essays in this section, Jennifer Iannolo analyzes romantic love in *Atlas Shrugged* and Susan Love Brown examines sexuality in the novel.

Part VII looks at some of the characters in *Atlas Shrugged.* Virginia Murr discusses Hank Rearden's mind-body split in her essay. In the next selection, Ken Schoolland, along with Stuart Hayashi, relates his many years of teaching to the situation of Hugh Akston. Then, Robert Campbell discusses the moral but flawed character of Eddie Willers. Next, Jomana Krupinski describes the moral evolution and redemption of Tony, the "Wet Nurse." Jennifer Rhodes then analyzes the tragic story of Cherryl Brooks, Rand's hero-worshipper.

The last section of this readings book looks at *Atlas Shrugged* in an historical context. In his article, Stephen Cox discusses the significant debt Ayn Rand owed to Isabel Paterson and the great influences that Paterson's vision of human action had on *Atlas Shrugged.* Douglas Den Uyl next analyzes the degree to which *Atlas Shrugged* reflects the essence of America. Walter Block then takes a look at individuals who he considers to be real-life counterparts of Robert Stadler. Finally,

Stuart Hayashi discusses an array of incidents in which Atlas has actually shrugged throughout history.

The contributors to this volume provide a great deal of evidence that *Atlas Shrugged* is the greatest novel ever written. Taken together these essays instill a greater appreciation for Ayn Rand's monumental achievement and show that there is much to be gained from the intellectual exploration of it.

Note

1   Interested individuals may want to read Nathaniel and Barbara Branden's *Who Is Ayn Rand?* (Random House, 1962); Mimi Gladstein's *Atlas Shrugged: Manifesto of the Mind* (Twayne, 2000); William Thomas's (ed.) *The Literary Art of Ayn Rand* (The Objectivist Center, 2005), and Robert Mayhew's (ed.) highly anticipated forthcoming *Essays on Ayn Rand's Atlas Shrugged*. Mayhew has edited collections of essays on Ayn Rand's other novels all of which have been published by Lexington Books.

References

Gladstein, Mimi Reisel. 2000. *Atlas Shrugged: Manifesto of the Mind*. New York: Twayne Publishers.

Hunt, Robert. 1984. "Science Fiction for the Age of Inflation: Reading *Atlas Shrugged* in the 1980's." In *Coordinates: Placing Science Fiction and Fantasy, Alternative Series*. Edited by George E. Slusser, Eric S. Rabkin, and Robert Scholes, 80–98. Carbondale, Illinois: Southern Illinois University Press.

Knapp, Shoshana Milgram. 1998. *Ayn Rand's Drafts: The Labors of a Literary Genius*. Two audio lectures. New Milford, Connecticut: Second Renaissance Books.

Peikoff, Leonard. 2004. *The DIM Hypothesis: The Epistemological Mechanism by Which Philosophy Shapes Society*. Fifteen audio lectures. New Milford, Connecticut: Second Renaissance Books.

Rand, Ayn. 1997. *Journals of Ayn Rand*. Edited by David Harriman. New York: Plume.

PART 1
An Overview

Chapter 1

Atlas Shrugged: Ayn Rand's Philosophical and Literary Masterpiece

Edward W. Younkins

Published in 1957, *Atlas Shrugged* presents a comprehensive statement and detailed illustration of Ayn Rand's original and perceptive philosophical ideas and inspiring moral vision. This long, complex novel has sold nearly six million copies. Respondents to a joint Library of Congress-Book of the Month Club survey in 1991 hailed the book as second only to the Bible in its significant impact on their lives. In addition, a 1998 Random House/Modern Library readers' poll placed *Atlas Shrugged* at the top of their list of the greatest novels of the century.

Ayn Rand's *Atlas Shrugged* is a story of human action on a monumental level. In it Rand skillfully ties physical actions to important human values. Although the author also deals with mental portraiture and analysis, her primary concern is with human action. She selects and integrates actions and events that dramatize the theme of the novel which is "the role of the mind in human existence" (Rand 1975, 81). *Atlas Shrugged* is a "story about human beings in action" (Rand 2000, 17). Rand thinks in essentials in uniting all the issues of the actions in the novel. Her concern is with values and issues that can be expressed in action. The story's plot action is based on the integration of values and action and of mind and body. Rand thereby shows actions supporting wide abstract principles.

For Rand, the right philosophy is necessary to create the right story. *Atlas Shrugged* embodies Rand's Objectivism and introduces readers to ideas they might not otherwise encounter. Rand uses the story of *Atlas Shrugged* as a vehicle for manifesting her ideas, bringing philosophy to life through character and plot.

A Conflict of Visions

The story takes place in a slightly modified United States. The country has a head of state rather than a president and a National Legislature instead of a Congress. The time is ostensibly the not-too-distant future in which American society is crumbling under the impact of the welfare state and creeping socialism (most other nations have already become Communist People's States). The story may be described as simultaneously anachronistic and timeless. The pattern of industrial organization appears to be that of the late 1800s, with large capital-intensive corporations being run and owned by individual entrepreneurs. The mood seems to be close to that of the depression-era 1930s. Both the social customs and level of technical knowledge remind one of the 1950s. The level of government interference and political corruption is similar to that of the 1970s (Merrill 1991, 60; Gladstein 2000, 40–41).

The story is an apocalyptic vision of the last stages of a conflict between two classes of humanity—the looters and the non-looters. The looters are proponents of high taxation, big labor, government ownership, government spending, government planning, regulation, and redistribution. They include politicians and their supporters, intellectuals, government bureaucrats, scientists who sell their minds to the bureaucrats, and liberal businessmen who, afraid of honest competition, sell out their initiative, creative powers, and independence for the security of government regulation. The non-looters—the thinkers and doers—are the competent and daring individualists who innovate and create new enterprises. These prime movers love their work, are dedicated to achievement through their thought and effort, and abhor the forces of collectivism and mediocrity. The battle is thus between non-earners who deal by force and profit through political power and earners who deal by trade and profit through productive ability.[1]

Rand's Entrepreneurial Heroes

The plot is built around several business and industrial executives. The beautiful Dagny Taggart, perhaps the most heroic female protagonist in American fiction, is the operating genius who efficiently runs Taggart Transcontinental Railroad, which was founded by her grandfather. Her brother James, president in title only, is an indecisive, incompetent, liberal businessman who takes all the credit for his sister's achievements. Dagny optimistically and confidently performs Herculean labors to keep the railroad running despite destructive government edicts, her brother's weaknesses, the incompetence of many of her associates, and the silent and inexplicable disappearance of society's competent industrialists.

As both society and her railroad are disintegrating, Dagny attempts to rebuild an old Taggart rail line. In the process, she contacts Hank Rearden, a self-made steel tycoon and inventor of an alloy stronger and lighter than steel. Rearden, Dagny's equal in intelligence, determination, and sense of responsibility, becomes her ally and eventually her lover. They struggle to keep the economy running and ultimately discover the secret of the continuing disappearance of the men of ability (Gladstein 63–9; Merrill 68–73).

Who Is John Galt?

John Galt, a messiah of free enterprise, is secretly persuading thinkers and doers to vanish mysteriously one after the other—deserting and sometimes sabotaging their factories before they depart. Galt explains how desperately the world needs productive individuals, but how viciously it treats them. The greater a person's productive ability, the greater are the penalties he endures in the form of regulations, controls, and the expropriation and redistribution of his earned wealth. This evil, however, is only made possible by the sanction of the victims. By accepting an undeserved guilt—not for their vices but for their virtues—the achievers have acquiesced in the political theft of their minds' products. Galt masterminds his plan to stop the motor of the world by convincing many of the giants of intellect and productivity to refuse to be exploited any longer by the looters and the moochers, to strike by withdrawing their talents from the world by escaping to a secret hideout in the Colorado Rockies, thus leaving the welfare state to destroy itself. The hero-conspirators will then return to lay the groundwork for a healthy new social order based on the principles of laissez-faire capitalism.

Galt, the mysterious physicist who is also a philosopher, teacher, and leader of an intellectual movement, has invented a motor that can convert static electricity into useful but inexpensive kinetic energy. He chooses to keep his invention a secret until it is time for him and the other heroes to reclaim the world.

For two-thirds of the novel, Galt exists only as a plaintive expression—Who is John Galt? He has been in hiding, working underground as a laborer in the Taggart Tunnels, while recruiting the strikers (Gladstein 65–8; Merrill 73–4).

Other Heroes

One of the key hero-characters is Francisco d'Anconia, aristocrat, copper baron, and former lover of Dagny, who prefers to destroy his mines systematically rather than let them fall into the hands of the looters. Another is Ragnar Danneskjöld, a philosopher turned pirate, who avenges the work of Robin Hood by raiding only public, nonprofit, commerce ships in order to return to the productive what is rightly theirs. The Randian view is that Robin Hood robs from the strong and deserving and gives to the weak and worthless. Robin Hood, the most immoral of all human symbols, reflects the idea that need is the source of rights, that people only have to want—not to produce, and that men have claim to the unearned but not to the earned (Gladstein 65–71).

Galt's Gulch

The men of ability fade out of the picture and are labeled traitors and deserters by Dagny and Hank, who remain fighting at their desks. Ironically, because they haven't been told of the conspiracy, Dagny and Hank are even battling their natural allies—the ex-leaders of the business world who have gone on strike.

Dagny pursues one of the deserters by plane to a valley deep in the Rockies, crashes, and accidentally discovers John Galt's headquarters—the Utopian free-enterprise community created by the former business leaders along with several academicians, artists, and artisans. They have set up Galt's Gulch (also known as Mulligan's Valley) as a refuge from the looters and moochers of the outside world.

Galt's Gulch is the hidden valley that is the Atlantis of *Atlas Shrugged.* This paradigm and microcosm of a free society consists of a voluntary association of men held together by nothing but every man's self-interest. Here, productive men who have gone on strike are free to produce and trade as long as they observe the valley's customs. In this secret free society, enshrouded by the crumbling interventionist one, each individual is unencumbered in the pursuit of his own flourishing and happiness (Sechrest 2007; Bostaph 2007).

Dagny is the last hero, except for Hank, to reach Galt's outpost. While there, Dagny listens to the logic of Galt and his associates and falls in love with Galt, who represents all that she values. Inspired by the vision of Rearden, who continues to search for her and battle the looters, she decides to return to a world in shambles. Dagny and Hank refuse almost to the end to accept Galt's plan and stubbornly fight to save the economy.

Galt's Speech

A national broadcast by Mr. Thompson, the Head of the State, is interrupted by Galt who, in a three-hour speech, spells out the tenets of his philosophy (Rand 1957, 923–79). Among his many provocative ideas is the notion that the doctrine of Original Sin, which holds man's nature as his sin, is absurd—a sin that is outside the possibility of choice is outside the realm of morality. The Fall of Adam and Eve was actually a positive event since it enabled man to acquire a mind capable of judging good and evil—man became a rational moral being. Another provocative idea is that both forced and voluntary altruism are evil. Placing the welfare of others above an individual's own interests is wrong. The desire to give charity, compassion, and pleasure unconditionally to the undeserving is immoral.

Galt explains that reality is objective, absolute, and comprehensible and that man is a rational being who relies upon his mind as his only means to obtain objectively valid knowledge and as his "basic tool of survival." The concept of value presupposes an entity capable of acting to attain a goal in the face of an alternative. The one basic alternative in the world is existence versus non-existence. "It is only the concept of 'Life' that makes the concept of 'Value' possible." An organism's life is its standard of value. Whatever furthers its life is good and that which threatens it is evil. It is therefore the nature of a living entity that determines what it ought to do.

Galt identifies man's life as the proper standard of man's value and morality as the principles defining the actions necessary to maintain life as a man. If life as a man is one's purpose, he has "a right to live as a rational being." To live, man must think, act, and create the values his life requires. In other words, since a man's life is sustained through thought and action, it follows that the individual must have the right to think and act and to keep the product of his thinking and acting (i.e., the right to life, liberty, and property).

He asserts that since men are creatures who think and act according to principle, a doctrine of rights ensures that an individual's choice to live by those principles is not violated by other human beings. All individuals possess the same rights to freely pursue their own goals. These rights are innate and can be logically derived from man's nature and needs—the state is not involved in the creation of rights and merely exists to protect an individual's natural rights. Because force is the means by which one's rights are violated, it follows that freedom is a basic good. Therefore, it follows that the role of government is to "protect man's rights," through the use of force, but "only in retaliation and only against those who initiate its use" (Ghate 2001; Gladstein 98–106; Stolyarov 2007).

The Melodramatic Climax

Galt follows Dagny back to the world and is captured by the looters. In an attempt to save the crumbling economy, they offer him the position of Economic Dictator, which he promptly refuses. They torture him, but the torture machine breaks down. Then, in a melodramatic confrontation, Galt is rescued by the Utopian entrepreneurs, and the looters are vanquished.

Galt and Dagny return to the valley, rewrite the Constitution, and add a clause stating that Congress shall make no law abridging the freedom of production and trade. At the end of the novel, just before going back to rebuild the world, Galt symbolically traces the sign of the dollar in the air.

Creators versus Looters

Ayn Rand's monumental *Atlas Shrugged*, presents the businessman in a realistic, favorable, and heroic image by emphasizing the possibilities of life in a free society, the inherent ethical nature of capitalism and the good businessman, the strength and self-sufficiency of the hardworking man of commerce, and the value of the entrepreneur as wealth creator and promoter of human economic progress. *Atlas Shrugged* shows the businessman's role as potentially heroic by celebrating the energy and opportunity of life for men of talent and ambition to make something of themselves. This great novel teaches that acts of courage and creativity consist of following one's sense of integrity rather than in blind obedience and in inspiring others instead of following them. *Atlas Shrugged* portrays the business hero as a persistent, original, and independent thinker who pursues an idea to its fruition. Rand's 1957 masterpiece dramatizes the positive qualities of the businessman by showing the triumph of individualism over collectivism, depicting business heroes as noble, appealing, and larger than life, and by characterizing business careers as at least, if not more, honorable as careers in medicine, law, or education.[2]

Atlas Shrugged aids in moving from abstract principles to realistic business examples. *Atlas Shrugged* provides a link between philosophical concepts and the technical and practical aspects of business. Philosophy is shown to be accessible and important to people in general and to business people in particular.

The only way for man to survive in society is through reason and voluntary trade. *Atlas Shrugged* focuses on the positive and shows readers what it takes to achieve genuine business success and how to create value.

Rand, like Aristotle in his *Nicomachean Ethics*, holds an agent-centered approach to morality and concentrates on the character traits that constitute a good person. Reading *Atlas Shrugged* prompts people to reflect on what is constitutive of a good life. Rand's heroes are shown to hold proper principles and develop appropriate character traits. The villains in the novel provide examples of what happens to people when they hold faulty principles (or compromise certain important principles) and fail to develop essential virtues.[3]

Atlas Shrugged illustrates that there are good and bad businessmen and that businessmen don't always act virtuously. There are two kinds of businessmen— those who lobby government for special privileges, make deals, as well as engage in fraud and corrupt activities. Then there are the real producers who succeed or fail on their own.

Rand's business heroes are independent, rational, and committed to the facts of reality, to the judgment of their own minds, and to their own happiness. Each of them thinks for himself, actualizes his potential, and views himself as competent to deal with the challenges of life and as worthy of success and happiness (Locke 2000). *Atlas Shrugged* makes a great case that the businessman is the appropriate and best symbol of a free society.

Production is the means to the fulfillment of men's material needs. *Atlas Shrugged* masterfully illustrates that the production of goods, services, and wealth metaphysically precedes their distribution and exchange. The primacy of production means that we must produce before we can consume. Production (i.e., supply) is the source of demand. This means that products are ultimately paid for with other products (Salsman 1997). Rand shows that, because life requires the production of values, people in business are heroic. The heroes of *Atlas Shrugged* find joy in taking risks and bringing men and materials together to produce what people value.

Atlas Shrugged chronicles the rise of corrupt businessmen who pursue profit by dealing with dishonest politicians. They avoid rationality and productivity by using their political pull and pressure groups to loot the producers. Rand is scathing in her indictment of these villains who would rob the creative thinkers who are responsible for human progress and prosperity.

Government intervention discourages innovation and risk-taking and obstructs the process of wealth-creation. In *Atlas Shrugged* the producers' minds are shackled by government policies. Lacking the freedom to create, compete, and earn wealth, the independent thinkers withdraw from society. This is Rand's recommended response to the bureaucratic assault of the entrepreneurial spirit.

Atlas Shrugged delineates government intervention as the great enemy of the businessman. Rand details how government intervention into private markets produces costs and unintended consequences more harmful than the targeted problem itself. Socialistic bureaucrats attempt to protect men from their own minds and tend to think only of intended, primary, and immediate results while ignoring unintended, ancillary, and long-term ones. Government-produced impediments to a free society are shown to include taxation, protectionism, antitrust laws, regulation, welfare programs, inflation, and more (Boettke 2007).

Atlas Shrugged portrays capitalism as the only system that is objective, just, and compatible with individual freedom. The reader is shown that individual freedom, private property, free markets, voluntary exchange, and a limited government produce a society that best meets the needs and preferences of, and is in accordance with the nature of, imperfect but rational beings in a finite world.

Atlas Shrugged's **Structure, Plot, Plot-Theme, and Plot Action**

Atlas Shrugged is an achievement of intricate structural composition and integration. The titles of its three major sections pay tribute to Aristotle, correspond to his basic philosophical axioms, and accomplish a thematic goal by implying something regarding the meaning of the events and actions in the respective sections of the novel. In Part One called Non-Contradiction, there is a numerous series of strange and apparently contradictory events and paradoxes with no discernible logical solution. In Part Two, Either-Or, based on Aristotle's Law of Excluded Middle, Dagny faces a fundamental choice with no middle road—to continue to battle to save her business or to give it up. Part Three, A is A, is based on Aristotle's Law of Identity. In it, Dagny and Rearden (along with the reader) learn the true nature of the events and all the apparent contradictions are identified and resolved (Minsaas 1994; Bernstein 1995). In addition, there are multiple and integrated layers and levels of meaning and implications for each of *Atlas Shrugged*'s thirty chapters. Rand's chapter titles are meaningful at the literal level in addition to being significant at deeper philosophical and symbolic levels (Bernstein; Seddon 2007).

Atlas Shrugged's plot-theme, the mind on strike, is the essential line of its events. It is the central means of presenting the theme and the main conflict of linking the theme to the action (Rand 2000, 40–4; 1975, 82–6). More specifically, the plot-theme is the "men of the mind going on strike against an altruist-collectivist society." This is the central situation that dramatizes and expresses *Atlas Shrugged*'s abstract theme.

Rand presents conflict in terms of action thus creating a "purposeful progression of events" (2000, 17). To do this she portrays strong willful characters, the creators and the looters, who are in sharp moral conflict with one another. She thereby expresses the plot conflict in action. Dagny Taggart and Hank Rearden, the primary creators, philosophically are against the looters, but in action they support them. In addition, existentially Dagny and Rearden oppose Galt and the strikers but philosophically they agree with them. The plot of *Atlas Shrugged* is a story of human action from which moral issues cannot be separated (Bernstein).

The major plot of *Atlas Shrugged* is the story of the strike (Rand 1997, 399, 416–17, 428–33). In her audio course, Kirsti Minsaas explains that Rand gradually supplies hints and clues with respect to the existence of the strike and that, through the use and emphasis of subsidiary surface plots, she is able to keep the events of the major plot hidden and to reveal the strike only in a step-by-step and retrospective manner. These secondary cover plots include: (1) Dagny Taggart and Hank Rearden's struggle to save their respective companies and industries primarily through the construction of the John Galt Line and (2) Dagny's quests to find the inventor of the revolutionary motor and to find and stop the destroyer who is draining the brains of the world. Through the pursuit of the above objectives, the main plot is revealed, the mystery is solved, the question "Who is John Galt?" is answered, and the reasons for the collapse of the railroad and of industrial society are understood (Bernstein). The plot of *Atlas Shrugged* has an inexorable internal logic in which the intellectual puzzle is acted out and solved by the heroes.

In his audio course, Andrew Bernstein observes that there are dual lines of action in *Atlas Shrugged* involving the observable and the unobservable. We perceive Dagny and Hank striving to construct the John Galt Line and searching for the inventor of the motor. We also see the looters, their policies, and the disastrous effects of their policies. What is not discernible is John Galt removing the men of the mind from the world and relocating them in Mulligan's Valley. The key link between these two spheres of action is Eddie Willers who unknowingly feeds information to John Galt, disguised as a low-level worker with whom Eddie has lunch.

Rand portrays the heroes of *Atlas Shrugged* overcoming obstacles. It is they who move the world and carry it on their shoulders. They (especially Dagny and Hank) are shown to be self-starters and the motive power of their own happiness. The producers are dramatized as self-initiated valuers who go by their own judgment and seek their own well-being. It is the self-actuating rational valuers who propel the world and sustain it. Rand's heroes are extraordinary characters who represent people as they could be and should be (Bernstein; Gladstein 63–75).

Atlas Shrugged is a study of the great producers who have the ability to see, make connections, and create what has not been seen before. It shows that the mind is at the root of the creation and maintenance of wealth. The passionate producer is the prime mover and visible hand in markets (Salsman). Production, like existence, is a primary and rests on the laws of identity and causality. Consumption comes after, and depends upon, production. According to Rand, if human life is the standard, then productive work is a major virtue and entrepreneurs and industrialists can be viewed as potentially heroic. Recognizing the integration of mind and body, Rand contended that the rational, purposeful, and creative character of human action is manifested in the act of material production.

The construction of the John Galt Line most directly depicts the mind's role in human existence. Much of the balance of the novel demonstrates the effects of the absence of the men of the mind (Rand 2000, 13). *Atlas Shrugged* teaches that prosperity and productivity depend upon the mind by showing both the presence and absence of the producers in the world.

Dramatization, Symbolism, and the Reworking of Greek Myths

The most crucial events in *Atlas Shrugged* are dramatized. The key events are shown to the reader as if they were occurring before his eyes. Rand also uses flashbacks (e.g., Eddie Willers thinking back to his childhood) to convey important information. Less critical information is simply narrated (145–60).

Rand applies her inductive theory of concept formation in writing *Atlas Shrugged*, as well as in her other works of fiction. Rand projects important abstractions dealing with values, virtues, emotions, and so on in specific concrete actions. She first presents a "visual description by means of essentials and then the symbolic and philosophic meaning of that description" (127).

Atlas Shrugged is primarily presented to the reader in a form that a person would perceive it in real life. Although Rand chooses the focus or perspective, she presents the reader with "direct sensory evidence" and does not tell him what to think or to feel. She provides information by giving the reader precise, "concrete, objective facts" and observational details. The reader is given the evidence in context and it is up to him to make a reasoned judgment (97).

Rand mainly dramatizes the meaning of *Atlas Shrugged* in action, but still effectively uses some symbolism as a supplemental technique. She typically first illustrates an idea in action and then uses a symbol to bring abstract subject matter down to the observational level. It follows that there are no "floating symbols" in *Atlas Shrugged*. Rand has the reader initially experience particular concrete actions in order to have enough information to inductively derive and understand the principle involved, and only then does she employ a symbol to capture the essence of the abstraction (Bernstein). The idea that a tangible symbol represents is something abstract. Key symbols in *Atlas Shrugged* include: (1) The Oak Tree; (2)

The Calendar; (3) The Bracelet of Rearden Metal (in the form of a chain); (4) Wyatt's Torch; (5) The Sign of the Dollar; (6) Galt's Motor; and (7) The Cigarette (Merrill 60–61; Bernstein).

Rand also effectively alters and adapts some famous Greek myths in order to tell them from an Objectivist viewpoint. These myths include: (1) Phaëton; (2) Prometheus; (3) Atlantis; (4) Atlas; and (5) Odysseus and the Sirens (as alluded to in the story of Roger Marsh). Ayn Rand's use and recasting of ancient Greek myths adds to the epic scope of *Atlas Shrugged*. By changing them, she challenges their traditional meaning and endorses them with new meaning reflecting a revolutionary worldview complete with a new moral philosophy (Bernstein; Minsaas 1994, 2007).

Characterization

Rand adeptly presents the nature of the heroes and villains in *Atlas Shrugged* in terms of their motives. Her main means of characterization are actions and dialogue (i.e., "words in the context of a character's actions"). By observing a Randian character's actions and hearing his conversations, a reader is able to grasp the motives of the character and to discern what is at the philosophical root of the character. Rand masterfully integrates a character's internally consistent actions, decisions, and words with his motives. The particular details she presents are related to wider fundamental abstractions and deeper motivations of the character presented. A man's basic values and premises form his character and inspire him to action (Rand 2000, 58–63).

In her stylized portraits of the characters in *Atlas Shrugged*, Rand presents no random details and focuses on the essentials to understanding each character. By eliminating irrelevant and trivial attributes and actions, her characters become moral projections. Rand's characters are persons in whom certain characteristics and behaviors are pinpointed more constantly and distinctly than in typical persons (Gladstein 62–3; Rand 1975, 87–9). Her method is to focus selectively on motives, traits, and especially actions that constitute character differences. Rand realizes that what a hero or villain in a novel does paints him better than what he says and enormously better than whatever the author may say about him. A man's actions always reveal key aspects of his character. By excluding superficial or accidental facets of a character's personality, Rand makes certain that attention is not averted from essential purposes and motives. As a result, the reader is able to gain clear and deep insight into her characters.

The Philosophical Speeches

The lengthy, philosophical speeches in *Atlas Shrugged* are integrated components of the plot, make explicit the principles dramatized throughout the actions of the novel, and move the story onward. For example, Francisco's "money speech" attends to Rearden's moral turmoil, frees him from his feelings of guilt, aids him in his trial, and moves him toward joining the strike.

In addition, Galt's speech on the radio ties together all the ideas previously dramatized in action in the novel, leads to Galt's capture and the story's climax, hastens the collapse, and makes the rebuilding of society easier. Galt's speech is necessary in order to understand the climax of the novel. When the looters hear his speech, they realize that he is the best thinker in the world and thus search for him in order to enlist his help in saving the deteriorating economy. It is the speech that moves Galt from mythical to concrete status in the novel. The events and actions prior to the speech provide the inductive evidence needed to derive the principle that "the mind is man's tool of survival." By then the reader and the American people in the novel have seen the men of the mind in the world, their gradual disappearance, the effects of the looters' policies, and the resulting crumbling of the world. It is through this speech that Galt demonstrates the value of the men of the mind. Galt's long speech is warranted because the detailed and complex events previously presented concretize the message given in his speech. The knowledge contained in Galt's speech is what convinced the strikers earlier in the novel to abandon their firms and to retreat to Galt's Gulch. The philosophy of the morality of life embodied in the speech is what the producers needed to hear and accept in order for them to realize their own greatness and to stand up against the looters. Galt's speech was not given until the American people were ready to hear it (Bernstein; Ghate). In large part, his Objectivist statement is addressed to the common but rational listeners in an effort to gain their support by going on strike themselves. In his audio course, Onkar Ghate explains that after a brief introduction, Galt's speech is broken into three parts: (1) the Morality of Life (i.e., The Code of the Producers); (2) the Morality of Death (i.e., The Code of the Looters); and (3) the importance of choosing the morality of life (i.e., acting as a rational human being).

A Novel of Free Will, Moral Codes, and Mind-Body Integration

A Romantic novel like *Atlas Shrugged* presumes man's free will, freedom to choose, and his ability to attain a purpose. A rational being can select a goal, act to achieve it, and discover or create the means to accomplish it. A human being can initiate and make choices about what he will do. A person's free will choice is the cause and the cause generates certain effects (Rand 2000, 19–22).

Atlas Shrugged dramatizes and explains that what is primary in studying human action is the nature of man and that man's distinctive mode of action includes rationality and free will. Rand portrays men as rational beings with free will who have the ability to form their own purposes and aims. She shows that human action involves purposeful, intentional, and normative behavior.

Andrew Bernstein explains that Rand illustrates man as a "volitional being who needs a moral code to guide his actions." She shows that the concept of value is the crucial and determining element in a man's life. The events and characters of *Atlas Shrugged* thus portray the philosophical principles that affect the actual existence of men in the world. The conflict between the looters and the creators dramatizes the struggle between contradictory values and moralities. Because human values are abstractions made from observations, the reader is given concretes in the novel in order for the abstract values to become real for him.

By including only that which is essential, Rand illustrates the connections between metaphysical abstractions and their concrete expressions. *Atlas Shrugged* is a feat of complex structural integration. The author carefully selected the details with no event, character, line of dialogue, or description included that does not further and reinforce the theme of the importance of reason. Nothing is thrown in arbitrarily. Rand was aware of the specific purpose of every chapter, paragraph, and sentence and could state a reason for every word and punctuation mark in the novel (Rand 2000, 4).

Atlas Shrugged is the systematic dramatization of a rational philosophy that includes a view of life as exaltation and of the universe as benevolent. It depicts conflict in action between whim-worshipping looters who seek power over men and the creators who accept, learn, and deal with the absolute laws of nature and existence. The secondhanders are concerned with "who makes it possible?" meaning both whom they should enslave and whom they should get to enslave them. The creators are thus shown being sacrificed to the parasites. *Atlas Shrugged* also dramatizes that the irrational looters need the assistance of rational people in order to succeed. The moral code of self-sacrifice is used against and accepted by the creators who are made to feel guilt for their achievements and wealth. This is the "sanction of the victim" moral principle. In order to get the men of the mind and other rational (or at least semi-rational) people to withdraw their sanction of the altruist ethics, Galt shows the altruist ethics' irrationality and inability to deal with reality through his persuasive arguments and the strike itself (Bernstein).

Atlas Shrugged illustrates the inextricable linkage of the mind and the body. In it Ayn Rand argues that the rational, purposeful, and creative character of the human person is reflected in the act of material production. The mind, man's highest and noblest aspect, enables him to deal with physical reality in order to create wealth and abundance that sustain and promote his practical survival and flourishing on earth. Productivity involves the use of reason to adapt nature to man's life requirements (Rand 1997, 549–51).

Likewise, *Atlas Shrugged* teaches, especially in the romance between Dagny and Rearden, that love is rooted in reason and that sexual choice is the result of a person's basic convictions and values. Sex is a "celebration of life," the ultimate form of admiration and respect of one person for another, and the physical expression of a person's spirit. Just as productive activity is the conversion of values into physical form, "sex is the means and form of translating spiritual admiration for a human being into physical action" (606–7). In an important way the romance between Dagny and Hank ties the entire story together and shows that production and sex have a mutual essence that joins them (465). The same principles used in one's creative (i.e., productive) life are applied to one's personal life.

Atlas Shrugged demonstrates that man is an indivisible entity that can only be separated for purposes of discussion. There are inextricable linkages and correspondence between one's mind, body, and actions. It follows that the values of one's mind are not disconnected with the actions of his body. Cartesian dualism of mind and matter is incompatible with true human existence. Man is an indivisible union of consciousness and matter (551).

Atlas Shrugged is a great story that helps people to understand the nature of the world in which they live. It illustrates that only a free society is compatible with the nature of man and the world and that capitalism works because it is in accordance with reality. Capitalism is shown to be the only moral social system because it protects a man's mind, his primary means of survival and flourishing. *Atlas Shrugged* is a powerful tool to educate, persuade, and convert people to a just and proper political and economic order that is a true reflection of the nature of man and the world properly understood.

Notes

This essay contains some material previously published as "*Atlas Shrugged* Revisited: Forty Years of Voicing the Philosophy of Freedom." *The Freeman* 47, 2. (May 1997): 295–9.

1   Readers interested in learning more about conflicting visions may want to read Thomas Sowell's *A Conflict of Visions* (William Morrow and Company, 1987) and those interested in learning more about the methods of the looters and creators may wish to see Edmund Contoski's *Makers and Takers* (American Library Publishers, 1997).

2   For invaluable discussions of businessmen as heroes and prime movers see Edwin A. Locke's *The Prime Movers* (AMACOM, 2000) and Ayn Rand's *Why Businessmen Need Philosophy* edited by Richard E. Ralston (Ayn Rand Institute Press, 2000).

3   For an excellent discussion of the role of the virtues in human flourishing see Tara Smith's *Ayn Rand's Normative Ethics* (Cambridge University Press, 2006).

References

Bernstein, Andrew. 1995. *Philosophic and Literary Integration in Ayn Rand's Atlas Shrugged*. Seven audio lectures. New Milford, Connecticut: Second Renaissance Books.

Boettke, Peter J. 2007. The economics of *Atlas Shrugged*. In *Ayn Rand's Atlas Shrugged*. Edited by Edward W. Younkins. Aldershot, United Kingdom: Ashgate Publishing Company.

Bostaph, Sam. 2007. Ayn Rand's Atlantis as a free market economy. In *Ayn Rand's Atlas Shrugged*. Edited by Edward W. Younkins. Aldershot, United Kingdom: Ashgate Publishing Company.

Ghate, Onkar. 2001. *A Study of Galt's Speech*. Five audio lectures. New Milford, Connecticut: Second Renaissance Books.

Gladstein, Mimi Reisel. 2000. *Atlas Shrugged: Manifesto of the Mind*. New York: Twayne Publishers.

Locke, Edwin A. 2000. *The Prime Movers*. New York: AMACOM.

Merrill, Ronald E. 1991. *The Ideas of Ayn Rand*. Chicago, Illinois: Open Court.

Minsaas, Kirsti. 1994. *Structure and Meaning in Ayn Rand's Novels*. Audio lecture. Principal Source Audio.

———. 2007. Ayn Rand's recasting of ancient myths in *Atlas Shrugged*. In *Ayn Rand's Atlas Shrugged*. Edited by Edward W. Younkins. Aldershot, United Kingdom: Ashgate Publishing Company.

Rand, Ayn. 1957. *Atlas Shrugged*. New York: Random House.

———. [1971] 1975. *The Romantic Manifesto: A Philosophy of Literature*. Second revised edition. New York: Signet.

———. 1997. *Journals of Ayn Rand*. Edited by David Harriman. New York: Dutton.

———. 2000. *The Art of Fiction*. Edited by Tore Boeckmann. New York: Plume.

Salsman, Richard. 1997. *The Invisible Hand Comes to Life: Economics in Atlas Shrugged*. Two audio lectures. New Milford, Connecticut: Second Renaissance Books.

Sechrest, Larry J. 2007. Atlas, Ayn, and Anarchy: A is A is A. In *Ayn Rand's Atlas Shrugged*. Edited by Edward W. Younkins. Aldershot, United Kingdom: Ashgate Publishing Company.

Seddon, Fred. 2007. Various levels of meaning in the chapter titles of *Atlas Shrugged*. In *Ayn Rand's Atlas Shrugged*. Edited by Edward W. Younkins. Aldershot, United Kingdom: Ashgate Publishing Company.

Stolyarov, G. II. 2007. The role and essence of John Galt's speech in Ayn Rand's *Atlas Shrugged*. In *Ayn Rand's Atlas Shrugged*. Edited by Edward W. Younkins. Aldershot, United Kingdom: Ashgate Publishing Company.

Chapter 2

Atlas Shrugged: Manifesto for a New Radicalism

Chris Matthew Sciabarra

In 1945, when Rand began outlining the work that was to become *Atlas Shrugged*, she made a self-conscious decision to create a "much more social novel than *The Fountainhead*" (Rand 1997, 390). She wished to focus not simply on the "soul of the individualist," which *The Fountainhead* had dramatized so well, but to proceed "from persons, in terms of history, society, and the world." This new "story must be primarily a picture of the whole," she wrote in her journal, making transparent the cluster of relationships that constitute society as such:

> Now, this *relation* must be the theme. Therefore, the personal becomes secondary. That is, the personal is necessary only to the extent needed to make the relationships clear. In *The Fountainhead* I showed that Roark moves the world—that the Keatings feed upon him and hate him for it, while the Tooheys are consciously out to destroy him. But the theme was Roark—not Roark's relation to the world. Now it will be the relation. (392)

Atlas Shrugged explores these relations in every dimension of human life. It traces the links between political economy and sex, education and art, metaphysics and psychology, money and moral values. It concentrates on the union of spiritual and physical realms and on the specific, concrete means by which certain productive individuals move the world, and by which others live off of their creations. It shows the social importance of the creative act by documenting what would happen if the prime movers, the "men of the mind," go on strike.

Most importantly, however, *Atlas Shrugged* provides a manifesto for a new radicalism—not a *political* radicalism per se, but a *methodological* radicalism, a radical way of *thinking* upon which political and social change is built.

A Radical Framework

"To be radical," said Karl Marx ([1843] 1963, 52), "is to grasp things by the root."

Unlike Marx, however, Rand repudiated communism and the root, "basic premises of collectivism" that it embodied. Rand's attack was *"radical* in the proper sense of the word" as she explained: "'radical' means 'fundamental.' Today, the fighters for capitalism have to be, not bankrupt 'conservatives,' but new radicals, new intellectuals and, above all, new, dedicated moralists" ("Conservatism: An Obituary," in Rand 1967, 200).

For Rand, the very notion of checking one's premises, as such, is a radical notion: it is a principle that requires one to understand the roots of a philosophic or social problem through rigorous, logical, and integrated analysis. From its debut in January 1962, Rand's regular column in *The Objectivist Newsletter* was entitled "Check Your Premises." In her first essay, she reiterated: "Objectivists are *not* 'conservatives.' We are *radicals for capitalism*" ("Choose Your Issues," in Rand 1962–65, 1). Indeed, "the future belongs to a new type of intellectual, a new radical: the fighter for *capitalism*" ("The Intellectual Bankruptcy of Our Age" in Rand 1989, 99). These "New Intellectuals must assume the task of building a new culture on a new moral foundation ... They will have to be *radicals* in the literal and reputable sense of the word: 'radical' means 'fundamental'" (Rand 1961, 54).

The analytical power of Rand's radical framework went beyond a search for roots. In seeking to understand the *system* of statism, Rand showed how various factors often mutually supported one another in sustaining the irrationality of statism. I have called Rand's orientation toward grasping the full, dynamic context of the statist social order an example of "dialectics," which I describe as "the art of context-keeping" (Sciabarra 1995; 2000). Rand is a consummate dialectical artist and scientist in her ability to trace skillfully the reciprocal preconditions and effects of these many factors across time. She does this by exploring the many manifestations of the coercive social relations at work within statism on different levels of generality and from different perspectives within these levels. Such coercive relations are at war with human beings and with life itself; they are *"anti-man, anti-mind, anti-life"* ("Is Atlas Shrugging?" in Rand 1967, 151).

Rand had embraced this orientation from her earliest journal musings. In her notes for her first novel, *We the Living,* for example, we encounter the first signs of a multilevel model of analysis. In this novel, Rand sought to grasp the dynamics of collectivism in the realms of "morality," the "political and cultural," and the "economical." For Rand, all forms of collectivism were sustained by a constellation of decadent moral, mental, and economic conditions (1997, 56–7). This multilevel approach shows up again in Rand's notes for *The Fountainhead,* where even architectural styles are viewed "sociologically" as well as "artistically" (187–8), and again, in her notes on *Atlas Shrugged,* where moral codes are grasped in terms of their "Personal" and "Social" implications (653).

As I have suggested in my book, *Ayn Rand: The Russian Radical,* Rand's mature analytical framework reaches its apex in *Atlas Shrugged.* In this work, it can be said that Rand examines a collapsing social order and its dysfunctional social relations on three distinct analytical levels (see Figure 2.1):

Level 1: The Personal. On this level, Rand explores the mystics' epistemological and psychological assault on reason and the human mind, as well as the altruistic ethical inversion that is required of each individual who submits to the edicts of statist politicians. Such submission entails the "sanction of the victim," without which the whole coercive edifice would be undermined.

Level 2: The Cultural. On this level, Rand explores the utter cultural, educational, and artistic bankruptcy of a society at war with human creativity, as well as the linguistic use of euphemism as a legitimating ideological tool of the politically privileged.

Level 3: The Structural. On this level, Rand is concerned with the devastation of economic and political structures wrought by statist regulations, prohibitions, and controls on production, which foster a tribalist war of all against all.

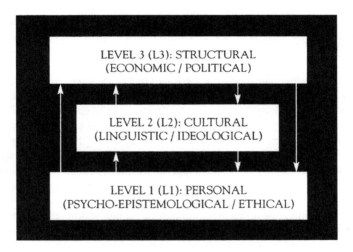

Figure 2.1 Tri-Level Model of Analysis

The novel shows how each of these levels entails relations among entities—Rand's characters, who are individual human beings acting purposefully within their given social context. In Rand's conception, the relations on these three distinct levels of generality—the personal, the cultural, and the structural—can only be abstracted and isolated for the purposes of analysis, but never reified as wholes unto themselves. The levels are *both* preconditions *and* effects of one another. This has vast strategic implications for social praxis, for the techniques of social change: A genuine revolution against the structural corruptions of politics and economics cannot succeed without a corresponding personal and cultural transformation.

Mind-Body Integration

That transformation must be founded on an integrated world-view, one that entails a total and unequivocal rejection of the mind-body dichotomy, and all the false alternatives it engenders. In her philosophic journals, Rand (1997) explains how her novel was meant to "*[v]indicate* the industrialist" as "the author of material production" (550). But underlying this vindication was Rand's desire to secularize the spiritual and spiritualize the material:

> the material is only the expression of the spiritual; that it can neither be created *nor used* without the spiritual (thought); that it has no meaning without the spiritual, that it is only the means to a spiritual end—and, therefore, any new achievement in the realm of material production is an act of *high spirituality*, a great triumph and expression of man's spirit. And show that those who despise "the material" are those who despise man and whose basic premises are aimed at man's destruction (20 January 1947 in Rand 1997, 551).

In Rand's view, the "spiritual" does not pertain to an other-worldly faculty. The "spiritual" refers to an activity of human consciousness. Reason, as "the highest kind of spiritual activity," is required "to conquer, control, and create in the material realm" (551). Rand does not limit material activities to purely industrial production. She wishes to "show that *any* original rational idea, in any sphere of Rand's activity, is an act of creation" (550). This applies equally to the activity of industrialists and artists, businessmen and intellectuals, scientists and philosophers. Each of these spheres is accorded epistemological significance—and supreme respect.

By connecting reason and production, thought and action, theory and practice, fact and value, morality and prudence, Rand intended to uncover the "deeper, philosophical error" upon which these various dichotomies were based. As such, *Atlas Shrugged* was designed to "*blast* the separation of man into 'body' and 'soul,' the opposition of 'matter' and 'spirit'" (551). Rand rejected the metaphysical dualists who had bifurcated human existence. She proclaimed in her journal that "Man is an indivisible entity." Mind and body "can be considered separately only for purposes of discussion, not in actual fact," she explains. Thus, in the projection of her "ideal man," John Galt, there is "*no intellectual contradiction and, therefore, no inner conflict*" between mind and body (29 June 1946 in Rand 1997, 512).

It was this kind of "indivisible union" (663) that Rand glorified in her exalted conception of human sexuality as a response to values. She explained in her journals that she had wanted to concretize the "*essential*, unbreakable tie between sex and spirit—which is the tie between body and soul" (6 October 1949, 609). Rand dramatizes the organic unity of body and soul in the orgasmic unity of two lovers:

The course led them to the moment when, in answer to the highest of one's values, in an admiration not to be expressed by any other form of tribute, one's spirit makes one's body become the tribute, recasting it—as proof, as sanction, as reward—into a single sensation of such intensity of joy that no other sanction of one's existence is necessary. He heard the moan of her breath, she felt the shudder of his body, in the same instant. (Rand [1957] 1992, 252)

Rand had condemned both the religionists, who had damned human beings for the sins of the flesh, and the materialists, who had divorced the mind from the natural functions of the body. Hers is a "philosophy for living on earth" ("Philosophy: Who Needs It," in Rand 1982, 12); romantic love, as expressed in the sexual act, is both a spiritual and physical celebration of life.

But Rand sought to provide a dramatic link between Level 1 and Level 3 concerns: she reasoned that those who had accepted the dualism of mind and body in the sexual realm shared the same false premise with those who had accepted the dualism of reason and production in the economic realm—or as Hank Rearden says in *Atlas Shrugged*, "that by accepting the mystics' theory of sex I was accepting the looters' theory of economics" (Rand [1957] 1992, 859). It was this sharp insight that led Rand to reject both conservatives (the "mystics of spirit") and "liberals" (the "mystics of muscle"), each of whom wished to regulate and control those social relations that they believed were metaphysically important ("Censorship: Local and Express," in Rand 1982, 228–9).

John Galt's sixty-page speech abounds with the principles of integration at the heart of Rand's Objectivist philosophy, while standing as a firm rebuke against those who would fracture human existence. In her notes while writing the speech, Rand (1997, 661–2) declared:

You had set every part of you to betray every other, you believed that your career bears no relation to your sex life, that your politics bear no relation to the choice of your friends, that your values bear no relation to your pleasures, and your heart bears no relation to your brain—you had chopped yourself into pieces which you struggled never to connect—but you see no reason why your life is in ruins and why you've lost the desire to live?

Level 1: The Sanction of the Victim

John Galt's revolution *against* human fragmentation is also a revolution *for* those who have been victimized by it and by the altruist morality that feasts on self-immolation. Throughout the novel, Rand shows how altruism is used by some (the "looters") to instill guilt in others (the "producers"), by putting the virtues of the latter at the service of the former. She argues that the altruist's demands for individual self-sacrifice to a "common good" requires the "sanction of the victim"

(Rand [1957] 1992, 454). The creators have for too long implicitly collaborated with their exploiters. That Galt grasps this principle, and that Hank Rearden and Dagny Taggart do not, sets up the main plot conflict in the novel. When Rearden begins to understand the implications of his actions, and the vast social consequences of a reckless moral code, he refuses to participate in his own martyrdom or to condone the government's confiscation of his property. He tells his persecutors:

> Whatever you wish me to do, I will do at the point of a gun. If you sentence me to jail, you will have to send armed men to carry me there—I will not volunteer to move. If you fine me, you will have to seize my property to collect the fine—I will not volunteer to pay it. If you believe that you have the right to force me—use your guns openly. I will not help you to disguise the nature of your action. (479)

By withdrawing the "sanction of the victim," the men of the mind strike out against the altruist core of statist political economy. But it is the "pyramid of ability" that explains why the strike works so effectively, by draining the economy of talent. Those who are at the top of their intellectual craft contribute the most to those below them, while those who are at the bottom free-ride on the achievements of the innovators above them. Rand does not view this as a static class pyramid, for she believes that individuals can rise to levels consonant with their developed abilities. When human beings relate to one another on the basis of these abilities, exchanging value for value, a benevolent harmony of interests becomes possible. When "need," rather than ability, becomes a criterion for the acquisition of values, it sets off a degenerative social process in which the "needs" of some place a moral claim on the lives of others. This is the evil of altruism, says Rand; it becomes a pretext for oppressing the most creative individuals in society.

Rand depicts this oppression in the novel, when a "survivor" of the Twentieth Century Motor Company tells how one factory was destroyed when it institutionalized the "noble" Marxian credo, "from each according to his ability, to each according to his need." The most talented people quit their jobs within the first week of the plan's implementation. Many of those who remained turned to alcohol, to dull their awareness of the nightmare conditions engulfing them. Individuals were driven to mutual distrust, resentment, and hatred for whatever abilities or virtues of character they possessed. In the end, only the "needy" parasites were left to run the company—with no productive hosts from which to draw nutriment. The plight of the factory becomes a symbol for the slow deterioration of a whole society, as the producers escape to Galt's Gulch, the "Utopia of Greed," refusing to act as hosts for the benefit of "looters" and "moochers."

Levels 2 and 3: Cultural and Structural Degeneration

Moral and social deterioration go hand-in-hand with cultural and structural degeneration. In the dystopian society of *Atlas Shrugged*, Rand contrasts the "symphony of triumph" (13) that is Richard Halley's "Concerto of Deliverance" (963) with the "dreary senselessness of the art shows" (875) in vogue. And yet it is the senseless that receives public adulation and government subsidies. As the literary leader of his age, Balph Eubank declares: " ... no, you cannot expect people to understand the higher reaches of philosophy. Culture should be taken out of the hands of the dollar-chasers. We need a national subsidy for literature. It is disgraceful that artists are treated like peddlers and that art works have to be sold like soap" (141). This is the same cultural figure who asserts that "Plot is a primitive vulgarity in literature," a claim like that of Dr. Simon Pritchett who tells us: "Just as logic is a primitive vulgarity in philosophy." And Mort Liddy who proclaims: "Just as melody is a primitive vulgarity in music" (134).

As another sign of the cultural and philosophic bankruptcy of the society portrayed in *Atlas Shrugged*, we are introduced to Dr. Pritchett's book, *The Metaphysical Contradictions of the Universe*, which "proved irrefutably" that "Nothing is absolute. Everything is a matter of opinion" (265). And then there is Dr. Floyd Ferris of the State Science Institute, which produces the top-secret "Project X," an apparatus of death. Ferris is the author of *Why Do You Think You Think?*, a book which declares that "Thought is a primitive superstition" and that "Nothing exists but contradictions" (340–1).

Rand makes it clear that such books flourish in this degraded society, but that their floating abstractions have actual implications: "You think that a system of philosophy—such as Dr. Pritchett's—is just something academic, remote, impractical? But it isn't. Oh, boy, how it isn't!" (265).

The ultimate concrete testament to the deadly implications of a culture that denigrates reality, logic, certainty, principles, ethics, rights, and the individual is the fatal voyage of the Taggart Comet, a train which disappears into the eternity of a tunnel, each of its passengers sharing "one or more" of the ideas of a nihilistic age (605–7).

Rand also shows that such nihilism could never triumph if its death premises were fully articulated. These ideas can gain currency only when rationalized as means to glowing "social" ends. In a way, such expressions of the dominant political "ideology" of a society in decline have a kind of Marxist sensibility about them: Rand illustrates how the use of a certain *political* language serves the thoroughly corrupt material interests of those who wield political power. "The State Science Institute is not the tool of any private interests or personal greed," we are told; "it is devoted to the welfare of mankind, to the good of humanity as a whole" (819). These "sickening generalities" and Orwellian slogans, repeated over and over again by the politically privileged, are the veneer that covers up the looting of the productive and the development of weapons of mass destruction and torture.

Every government bill, every political organization, is a study in euphemisms. Corporations slurping at the public trough, while using antitrust rulings to crush their competitors? That's the "Anti-Dog-Eat-Dog Rule" in action. Then, there are companies like the "Interneighborly Amity and Development Corporation" or the "Friends of Global Progress," who campaign for the "Equalization of Opportunity Bill," the forced "social" sharing of productive assets. "The Bureau of Economic Planning and National Resources" and other government agencies focus on "Essential Need" Projects. "The Unification Board," the "Railroad Unification Plan," the "Steel Unification Plan," the "Order of Public Benefactors," all aim for "the democratization of industry" (544). Such acts in the "public interest" destroy *private* property, genuine *social* accountability, and *individual* responsibility. Rand documents, painfully, how the destruction of the market economy and its specialization and division of labor is, ultimately, a destruction of the "division of responsibility" (29 June 1946 in Rand 1997, 507). In a statist social order, where everybody owns everything, nobody will be held responsible for anything. "It's not my fault" is the statist's credo (Rand [1957] 1992, 222).

A focus on the "structural" (what I've called "Level 3") provides Rand with an opportunity to portray, in frightening detail, the *process* by which a statist economy implodes. As the economic system careens from one disaster to another, as the "men of the mind" withdraw their sanction from a government that regulates, prohibits, and stifles trade, statist politicians attempt to exert more and more control over the machinery of production. To no avail. In the end, Directives are issued, like Number 10-289, which attach workers to their jobs, order businesses to remain open regardless of their level of "profit," nationalize all patents and copyrights, outlaw invention, and standardize the quantity of production and the quantity of consumer purchasers, thereby freezing wages and prices—and human creativity.

The "pyramid of ability" is supplanted by the "aristocracy of pull." What F.A. Hayek once called the "road to serfdom" is complete. A predatory neofascist social system, which had survived parasitically, must ultimately be destroyed by its own inner contradictions, incapacitating or driving underground the rational and productive Atlases who carry the world upon their shoulders.

Conclusion

It was Hayek who once noted that "it must be our privilege to be radical" because "[w]e are bound all the time to question fundamentals" ("The Dilemma of Specialization," in Hayek [1967] 1980, 130). Rand's radical legacy, as presented in *Atlas Shrugged*, led her, in later years, to question the fundamentals at work in virtually every social problem she analyzed. She viewed each problem through multidimensional lenses, rejecting all one-sided resolutions as partial and incomplete. Hers was a comprehensive revolution that encompassed all levels of social relations: "*Intellectual* freedom cannot exist without *political* freedom; political freedom cannot exist without *economic* freedom; *a free mind and a free market are corollaries*" (Rand 1961, 25).

As a novel, *Atlas Shrugged* is a remarkable achievement of integration. Rand had always seen the plot of a novel, its story, as a structured totality: "A STORY IS AN END IN ITSELF," she wrote to one correspondent. "It is written as a man is born—an organic whole, dictated only by its own laws and its own necessity—an end in itself ..." (Letter to Gerald Loeb, 5 August 1944, in Rand 1995, 157). And so, it is no coincidence that *Atlas Shrugged* itself is a superbly integrated "organic whole," one that fused action, adventure and sensuality with philosophy, contemplation and spirituality, incorporating elements of science fiction and fantasy, symbolism and realism. It launched a philosophical movement that has been nothing less than revolutionary in its implications.

As a manifesto for a new radicalism, *Atlas Shrugged* dramatizes the poisonous nature of predatory, coercive power across many social dimensions. Rand's magnum opus celebrates as antidote a rational and heroic conception of human freedom—and the unique constellation of psychological, moral, and cultural factors that nourish it.

References

Hayek, F.A. [1967] 1980. *Studies in Philosophy, Politics, and Economics*. Chicago: University of Chicago Press, Midway Reprints.

Marx, Karl. [1843] 1963. The critique of Hegel's philosophy of right. Edited and translated by T.B. Bottomore; foreword by Erich Fromm. *Early Writings*. New York: McGraw-Hill.

Rand, Ayn. [1957] 1992. *Atlas Shrugged*, 35th anniversary edition. New York: Dutton.

―――. 1961. *For the New Intellectual: The Philosophy of Ayn Rand*. New York: New American Library.

―――. 1962–1965. *The Objectivist Newsletter* 1–4. New York: The Objectivist.

―――. 1967. *Capitalism: The Unknown Ideal*. New York: New American Library.

―――. 1989. *The Voice of Reason: Essays in Objectivist Thought*. Edited by Leonard Peikoff. New York: New American Library.

―――. 1995. *Letters of Ayn Rand*. Edited by Michael S. Berliner. New York: Penguin Dutton.

―――. 1997. *Journals of Ayn Rand*. Edited by David Harriman. New York: Penguin Dutton.

Sciabarra, Chris Matthew. 1995. *Ayn Rand: The Russian Radical*. University Park: Pennsylvania State University Press.

———. 2000. *Total Freedom: Toward a Dialectical Libertarianism.* University Park: Pennsylvania State University Press.

Chapter 3

The Aristotelian Significance of the Section Titles of *Atlas Shrugged*
A Brief Consideration of Rand's View of Logic and Reality

Douglas B. Rasmussen

> We cannot think contradictory propositions because we see that a thing cannot have at once and not have the same character; the so-called necessity of thought is really the apprehension of the necessity in the being of things ... The Law of Contradiction is really metaphysical or ontological.
>
> H.W.B. Joseph, *An Introduction to Logic*, 2nd ed., rev.

I remember being shocked when I first learned many years ago that Ayn Rand thought that the universe is benevolent. I was shocked because I thought that believing that the universe is benevolent carried with it the belief that the universe is the product of a Divine mind or that there is a hand of Providence that intervenes in the workings of nature so that things will work out for the best. I knew, of course, that Rand as an atheist could not believe that there is a Divine mind that orders the universe or intervenes in nature. So, she had to mean something else. What I eventually came to learn is that she meant something much more profound, something that is vital to not only metaphysics but also to human life. She meant that reality is intelligible, and what she understood by this went far beyond what most metaphysicians claim.

I call this claim the reality-is-intelligible thesis. This is an ontological claim, and it thus bears upon the fundamental nature of reality. The meaning and implications of the reality-is-intelligible thesis will be the first concern of this chapter. Yet, my examination of this thesis must be very brief, highly limited, and most general, since this is not the occasion for presenting a fully developed work in ontology or even defending the claims that are herein stated. All of that must be left for some other time.

Besides explaining some of the deeper ontological implications of Rand's claim that the universe is benevolent, I will also point out something that Rand did not fully understand or keep clear—namely, the distinction between logic and reality. I will explain this distinction, its importance, and show how the failure to keep this distinction clear leads Rand to make a serious error regarding the basis for moral values. It also causes her at times to appreciate insufficiently not only the difficulties that people face in knowing reality and living a worthwhile human life but also the myriad complexities and details that are required for radical political change. More directly stated, she sometimes fails to appreciate the role of the contingent and the particular in human knowledge, human flourishing, and human liberty. But first let us consider what is involved in her claim that reality is intelligible.

Rand's reality-is-intelligible thesis has its most vivid expression in the section titles of *Atlas Shrugged*. These titles correspond to the Aristotelian laws of thought: Non-Contradiction (the Law of Non-Contradiction [also sometimes called The Law of Contradiction]); Either-Or (the Law of Excluded Middle); and A is A (the Law of Identity). For Rand, as for Aristotle, these laws of thought are not merely how we must think in order to obtain knowledge; they also describe the fundamental character of reality. These laws are thus ontological and pertain to the very nature of being. Nothing can ultimately exist or be that fails to comply with these principles. The nature of reality is such that (1) something cannot be and not-be at the same time and in the same respect; (2) something either exists or does not exist at a given time and in a given respect; and (3) something is what it is at a given time and in a given respect. What do these ontological laws mean or imply about the universe in which we exist? What does the reality-is-intelligible thesis involve?

First, it means that existence—that is, everything and anything that exists—must exist in some form or other. Nothing is without a nature or identity. To exist is to be something, to have a nature or an identity. Yet, compliance with these most general ontological laws does not dictate the specific form that an existent must take. Thus, the principle is: anything that exists must be in some manner or mode—its being must exist in some form—but it can exist in any.

Second, it means that there is no so-called metaphysical question of what it is that is responsible for the existence as such of a thing. Rather, the existence of a thing is fully expressed through whatever it is that constitutes its nature or identity. Each thing's nature or identity is the ultimate source or ground for understanding how it came to be, what it is, and how it continues to operate and exist. Unlocking the secrets of a thing's nature may not, of course, be immediate or easy. Indeed, we know that it is quite often extremely involved, but the ultimate answer to all why-questions is nonetheless a "what"—that is, the nature or identity of a thing.

Third, it means that we inhabit a universe in which what things ultimately are is not merely a matter of convention. Contradictions cannot exist because to exist is to be something, and whatever this is for any given thing, this does not change simply because we do not like it, do not see it, or choose to ignore it. Indeed, regardless of how extensively and intensely we intervene into the natures of things, whether it is to discover how they operate or to mold them to our purposes, it is still their character or nature that guides all our activities. This is, of course, the point of the maxim Rand so often cites. "Nature to be commanded must be obeyed."

Fourth, it means that existence as a whole and the entities that compose it are subordinate to law. This law is not ultimately something that has been commanded by some mind—human or Divine—nor is it merely the result of custom or convention. Rather, it is a standard or measure. The nature or identity of a thing is its standard or measure—its law.[1] The nature of a being explains what it is, its force and manner of working, and, in the case of certain beings, even for what it operates and exists. The ontological character of the laws of thought means that we inhabit a universe of natural laws. Part of realizing the intelligible character of reality is grasping that the universe is, despite its immensity, diversity, and constant change, nonetheless orderly. The universe makes sense.[2]

Fifth, though the nature of a being provides the measure for understanding and evaluating it, there can be no understanding or evaluating without a measurer. There needs to be a being with the capacity to measure, and it is the nature of this being and its faculties that must be examined if measuring is to be understood. That is to say, we need to understand ourselves as human beings, if we are to understand how it is that we do indeed come to know the nature of things. No study of knowledge can occur without an examination of human nature.

However, we need to stop here and note something that is truly basic. It is something Aristotle had the good sense to realize and never forget—namely, that the fact that we are conscious and aware already has profound implications for how we understand the cognitive process. As Rand notes in "This Is John Galt Speaking" of *Atlas Shrugged*, "If nothing exists, then there can be no consciousness: a consciousness with nothing to be conscious of is a contradiction in terms. A consciousness conscious of nothing but itself is a contradiction in terms: before it could identity itself as consciousness, it had to be conscious of something" (Rand, 1957, 1015). Consciousness is a faculty of individual human beings. It can exist and function only if it is already aware of something other than itself. It is fundamentally impossible for all the objects of human consciousness to be, in the last analysis, merely manifestations of that faculty. For consciousness to be what it is, it must ultimately be of or about something other than itself. As it is often described in the Aristotelian tradition, consciousness is an inherently relational or "intentional" activity. It is metaphysically subordinate to reality.

This relationship between consciousness and existence is fundamental, and if we are to avoid an initial deviation from the truth upon which myriad errors will be later multiplied, then, contrary to most epistemologists of Modernity, we should not begin the study of knowledge with the question "Is there anything that exists apart from our consciousness?" Instead, we should begin with the question "How do we know the nature of things?" I shall have more to say about this second question shortly. But it is crucial to understand that we do not ever really have to wonder whether we are in cognitive contact with reality—that is a given.[3] We need not take seriously, if we ever did, the stories with which so many philosophy instructors like to scare college freshmen about being trapped within one's consciousness. It is reality with which we are ultimately dealing from our first awareness to the last.

Thus, the basic meaning behind Rand's reality-is-intelligible thesis is that the things of existence have a nature or identity and that these things can be known. The universe is benevolent because it allows human beings the possibility to discover what and who they are, what their world is like, and what their lives require in order to flourish. Nothing is guaranteed; but there is nothing in the nature of reality that is inimical to human flourishing. As Rand points out, insurance companies make good profits betting against disaster. Metaphysically speaking, life is the only game in town, but it is a game that can be won if properly understood. Indeed, much is possible if we but use our minds, develop the appropriate virtues, and make sure that we establish a political/legal order that protects our liberty.[4]

The question "How do we know the nature of things?" remains, and it requires that the basic ways that human beings come to know be considered. This question is, of course, immense, and what I have to say on this question, like before, must be highly limited and most general and offered with little or no defense. I will begin with some opening observations about the relationship between the laws of thought and sense perception, and then I will concentrate on Rand's understanding of logic.

The laws of thought are for Rand, as they are for Aristotle and Aquinas, not a priori mental categories that we impose on sense perceptions to make them intelligible, as a cookie cutter gives form to dough. They are instead laws of reality and thus are present in our very first cognition of reality. These laws are implicit in what the senses themselves reveal. The reason for this is that our sense perceptions are not confined to the presentation of mere sense data, but are about things, and their qualities, quantities, and various other attributes.[5] Thus our first awareness of these laws is as laws of reality, because it is through sense perception that we have our first encounter with reality. It is only upon reflection that they become guides for our thought.

I will develop this last point when I discuss Rand's view of logic, but there is an important distinction that needs to be noted in order to see how the laws of thought and reality could be implicit in what the senses reveal. We need to realize that what is presented in sense perception is not necessarily recognized by sense perception, and it is thus possible for our senses, to paraphrase Etienne Gilson, "to carry a message that they themselves cannot interpret" (Gilson, 1983, 199). A very young child will try, for example, to obtain another piece of cake now that she has eaten the one she had and is thus aware that she cannot have her cake and eat it (as well as she cannot eat her cake before she has it). Yet, this awareness on her part is still not an awareness of her awareness of this impossibility much less an awareness of how this impossibility is an instance of the principle of non-contradiction. Those levels of awareness are only achieved by a process of conceptualization that makes what is implicitly known in sense perception explicit. So, it must be understood that the laws of thought and reality are implicit in sense perception in the following way: the child's awareness that she cannot have her cake now that she has eaten it involves grasping some of the constituents that are to be used in forming the idea of "impossibility" and later further to be used in expressing the principle of non-contradiction. The child is aware of the law of non-contradiction in the sense that she is aware that she cannot have her cake now that she has eaten it, but has of course not yet discovered that what she knows is an "impossibility" and an instance of something much more general—namely, the noncontradictory character of being. That awareness is much like the discovery that one has all along been speaking prose.

What should be clear from this is that Rand, Aristotle, and Aquinas are "concept empiricists," and this means, to quote the Scholastic maxim, that "nothing is in the intellect that is not first in the senses." All human knowledge begins in and arises from sense perception. Sense perception in general presents the data that will be integrated into concepts and then into propositions and even further into arguments. Again, as Gilson notes, "It is the whole man who knows particular things, in that he thinks what he perceives" (Gilson, 1986, 173). Human knowledge is thus a constant interplay between sense perception and reason, and though we may distinguish the conceptual from the empirical or the rational from the sensory, these are not separable when it comes to human cognition.

Rand observes in "Concepts of Consciousness," Chapter Four of *Introduction to Objectivist Epistemology*, that logic belongs to a sub-category of concepts that pertain to products of consciousness. Products of consciousness have to do with the mental grasp of reality, but they should not be confused with what is grasped—that is, the existential content. Products of consciousness, such as "knowledge," "science," "idea," etc., are not the same things as the phenomena they are about. Cognition is of reality, but it is not reality. The products of consciousness would not exist if there were no human consciousness, but what they are ultimately about would continue to exist even if there were no human consciousness. Logic, then, does not exist without human consciousness, and to study logic is not the same thing as the study of beings *in rerum natura*, that is beings that exist and are what they are independent of human cognition. Logic is not ontology. This is, however, a subtle point and sadly to say not one that Rand fully appreciates or follows, but I will have more to say about this later.

The subcategory of products of consciousness to which logic belong is concepts of method. Concepts of method designate courses of action for attaining human goals. These actions may be exclusively psychological or some combination of psychological and physical actions. Logic is the fundamental concept of method. It is the art of noncontradictory identification. Every other method depends on it; for no method—whether it is epistemology, ethics, medicine, or drilling for oil—can proceed without an identification of the relevant facts of reality. Thus, logic for Rand, as it was for Aristotle, is an *organon*—a human tool or instrument for attaining knowledge. Its crucial importance comes from its being the basic tool for knowing reality.

By stating that logic is the art of noncontradictory identification, Rand is, of course, claiming that the method of logic is defined by the laws of reality—Non-Contradiction, Excluded Middle, and Identity. In other words, these laws are not only laws of thought but also laws of logic. They not only describe the fundamental ontological character of reality (which includes the nature of thought); they also offer the method by which we are to proceed in obtaining knowledge. Metaphysics dictates fundamental method. Yet, what is it about logic, particularly its tools, that allows it to function as the guide for human cognition?

Unfortunately, Rand does not answer this question. She says very little about the nature of logic or its tools. Of course, she does make it clear that she will have no truck with those who think that the laws of logic are purely formal or merely linguistic in character. Logic's laws are neither empty nor conventional. They have an ontological basis. Nor does she seem to think that these laws of thought are merely psychological reports regarding how the human mind operates. Logic's laws may not exist without human psychology, but they are more than this. They serve a purpose. They provide the measure or standard that defines the human method of cognition. Thus, logic qua method is distinct from psychology. Yet, this still does not explain what it is about logic or its tools that permits them to be our guide in cognizing reality. Further, it does not explain how it is possible for logic to be the method to which all other methods must conform and nonetheless be distinct from reality.

Rand's failure to address these issues is one of the larger lacunae in her thought, and it is not without, as we shall see, adverse consequences. Yet, the Aristotelian tradition is not silent regarding the nature of logic and how it is both the method for human cognition and yet distinct from reality. So, very briefly, here are a few of the more central insights of this tradition[6] regarding these issues.

1) Though logic is dependent on psychological processes for its objects of study to exist, logic does not deal with actual thought processes. It is not the acts of conceiving, judging, and reasoning qua psychic states but qua signs that concerns logic.

2) Though nearly all of the activities of conceiving, judging, and reasoning have some form of linguistic or symbolic expression, it is the significatory character of these expressions that is the concern of logic.

3) Concepts, propositions, and arguments are the objects of logic's study. They are signs.[7] Their fundamental character consists in being of or about something other than themselves. They are inherently relational or intentional.

That is to say, their proper and definitive being consists in signifying and thus relating the human knower to reality.

4) Since concepts, propositions, and arguments are fundamentally intentional in nature, they cannot be considered or studied without considering to some extent the nature of the reality that they disclose. It thus is a serious mistake to abstract entirely from and disregard all questions as to what [one] thinks about, and still find that there are certain principles in accordance with which, if [one] is to think about anything, [one] will think (Joseph, 1916, 5).

Logic cannot be properly formal until one understands the fundamental character of its forms—that is to say, the intentional nature of concepts, propositions, and arguments. Pure formalism in logic results from a failure to grasp the inherently relational character of logic's basic tools.

5) It is only through considering our acts of apprehending, judging, and reasoning that we come to study concepts, propositions, and arguments. We become aware of our cognitive operations, and we learn how to connect properly our thoughts by making sure they we do so in ways that follow the fundamental character of reality. This is the way the rules of logic are formed. This can, of course, become quite involved, but a good example of how the fundamental character of reality is reflected in logic can be found regarding the proper use of the "logical words" (traditionally called syncategorematic terms). The elemental meaning of such terms as "and," "or," and "not" is expressed in the rules on how to construct a proposition. One may not construct propositions with the form "P and not-P," but one may construct propositions with the form "P or not-P." These are powerful rules, and they allow for the development of even more logical rules. We need not, however, concern ourselves with these matters at this time, but it is important to note that all of our knowledge of the rules of logic (as well as grammar[8]) is achieved through this reflective process.

6) To study concepts, propositions, and arguments is not to study psychology, linguistics, or ontology. Rather, it is to study things as they are known, as they exist in cognition. For example, though our concept of a horse must be of or about horses, this does not mean that the concept of a horse is the same thing as the horses or that the characteristics of the concept of a horse and those of a horse are the same. The concept of a horse has, for example, such features as universality, predicability, extension, and intension, while horses do not. A horse can, however, run in a race, but the concept of a horse cannot. The point here is, of course, that the objects that logic studies are not the same thing as the beings that exist and have a nature apart from human cognition. As Aquinas states, although it is necessary for the truth of a cognition that the cognition answer to the thing known, still it is not necessary that the mode of the thing known be the same as the mode of its cognition (Aquinas, *Summa contra gentiles,* II, 75).

Logic is indeed the tool for knowing reality. Our concepts, proposition, and arguments are ultimately of or about reality. Yet, there is still a difference between them and reality.

These observations are by no means complete, but they do provide a sense of the subtlety and nuance that the Aristotelian tradition brings to the study of logic. Also, they assist one in avoiding elementary philosophical errors. This can be illustrated by an example that originates in Berkeley. Consider the following claim. "Physical objects cannot be thought of as existing apart from a thinking mind." This can mean (a) physical objects cannot be thought-of-as-existing apart from a thinking mind, or (b) physical objects cannot be thought of as existing-apart-from-a-thinking mind. Statement (a) is true and obvious, but this does not mean that what one thinks about cannot exist without being thought of. There is a difference between the act of awareness and the object of awareness, and the truth of (a) does not establish (b). There is ultimately a difference between something as it exists in cognition and as it exists independently of cognition. If we ignore or try to close this gap, we get ourselves into serious trouble.

Rand gets herself into serious trouble in this regard. I will provide two examples. The first is an error of commission and concerns her account of the good. I will quote her at length regarding this matter. After noting in the preceding paragraph that she is concerned with nature of moral values, she states:

> There are, in essence, three schools of thought on the nature of the good: the intrinsic, the subjective, and the objective. The intrinsic theory holds that the good is inherent in certain things or actions as such, regardless of their context and consequences, regardless of any benefit or injury they may cause to the actors and subjects involved. It is a theory that divorces the concept of 'good' from beneficiaries, and the concept of 'value' from valuer and purpose—claiming that the good is good in, by, and of itself.
>
> The subjectivist theory holds that the good bears no relation to the facts of reality, that it is the product of a man's consciousness, created by feelings, desires, "intuitions," or whims, and that it is merely an "arbitrary postulate" or an "emotional commitment."
>
> The intrinsic theory holds that the good resides in some sort of reality, independent of man's consciousness; the subjectivist theory holds that the good resides in man's consciousness, independent of reality.
>
> The objective theory holds that the good is neither an attribute of "things in themselves" nor of man's emotional states, but an evaluation of the fact of reality by man's consciousness according to a rational standard of value. (Rational, in this context, means: derived from the facts of reality and validated by a process of reason.) The objective theory holds that the good is an aspect of reality in relation to man—and that it must be discovered, not invented by man (Rand, 1966, 14).

We can see clearly from her remarks that she means to dismiss not only the subjectivist theory, but also the view that the good is some kind of reality that exists in splendid isolation, separate and apart from human beings. She endorses the view that the good is an aspect of reality in relation to man and that it must be discovered by him. Thus, it would seem that the existence and nature of the complex reality that is the good (that is, some aspect of reality in relation[9] to man) does not depend on its being cognized by the human mind for its existence.[10] All of this is certainly something Aristotelians, or at least neo-Aristotelians, could endorse. Indeed, one need only recall Aristotle's criticism of the Form of the Good. So, I will call this claim the neo-Aristotelian objective theory of the good.

Yet, Rand also states that "the good is ... an evaluation of the facts of reality by man's consciousness according to a rational standard of value."[11] Clearly, this is a different claim. An evaluation, even a rational and accurate one, does not exist apart from human cognition. According to this claim, the existence of the good is dependent not only on (a) its being in some relation to man but it is also on (b) its being cognitively related to the human mind. Certainly (a) could be true without (b) also being true, but Rand does claim both (a) and (b). I shall call this joint claim the Idealist objective theory of the good, because if no one makes an evaluation of how some aspect of reality relates to man according to a rational standard of value, then the good does not exist. The good exists only if there is an act of human cognition. This is, of course, not something an Aristotelian, even a neo-Aristotelian, can accept.

Moreover, one wonders what the basis is for the "rational standard of value" by which the facts of reality are evaluated. What make the standard of values rational? She certainly means more than simply instrumental rationality. Rand is supposed to be describing fundamental approaches to moral values here, and so she cannot explain what a rational standard of value is by an appeal to the good because that would involve what she is attempting to explain. This would be to engage in conceptual circularity. There are serious problems with this idealist claim.

It might be objected, however, that I am not being radical enough with Rand's view and am looking at it too much through Aristotelian eyes. Possibly, Rand actually wants to make this idealist claim. Under one interpretation of her ethics, there are no ethical obligations unless one chooses to live, and one does not choose to live unless one chooses to think (or to focus one's mind). So, it might be that all of ethics depends on the pre-moral choice to live and think (or focus), and thus the good has reality only in and through human cognition. Further, it might be argued that since this choice is implicit in everything we think and do, nearly everyone must make this choice to live and think. Thus, though the good exists only in cognition, it so exists for almost everyone. As such it has some of the qualities of objects that cognitively exist. For instance, it does not vary from individual to individual and is incapable of being the source of conflicts. The good is *qua object* before the human mind the same for everyone, and there is no role for the individuative features of a person to be factored into moral decision making. This certainly seems dangerously close to a Kantian approach to moral epistemology, since the good is seen as conditioned by the form of human cognition and is hence something universal.[12]

I have elsewhere (Rasmussen, 2002) discussed some of the problems with the idea that moral obligation depends on the exercise of the pre-moral choice. Simply stated, these problems amount to this: holding that moral obligation depends on act of pre-moral choice ultimately reduces morality to a matter of subjective choice or sheer commitment. This is, of course, not a position with which Rand would want to be associated, and it is an embarrassing consequence of such an interpretation of her ethics. Yet, what I want to stress here is that such a conceptual gambit is really not necessary. If we go back to the quotation with which we started and make a small correction, Rand can avoid holding the idealist view of the good and becoming embroiled with its difficulties and embarrassing implications.

The correction envisaged is simply to say that the concept of the good is such and such an evaluation. By doing this, it can be noted that our concept of the good does indeed require an evaluative act, but this does not mean or imply that the good cannot be some aspect of reality in relation to man independently of whether it is discovered by the human mind. Indeed, the good can still be human, even individual, and not yet discovered by the human mind.

Yet, it seems clear that Rand has not integrated very well the distinction between the objects of logic and realities they disclose, especially when it comes to the realm of moral values. Further, it seems that the nature of the confusion rests in failing to distinguish complex relational realities that can exist independently of cognition from those relations that come to exist between the knower and the object in virtue of some cognitive act. Rand likes to say that everything in existence can be measured, and the act of measuring requires, of course, a measurer. But this does not mean that what is measured or the basis for measurement that a thing's nature affords only exists only if it is measured.

The second example of where Rand fails to keep the distinction between logic and ontology clear has to do with her account of the standard and purpose of ethics. Here her error is one of omission. She states:

> The Objectivist ethics holds man's life as the standard of value—and his own life as the ethical purpose of every individual man.
>
> The difference between 'standard' and 'purpose' in this context is as follows: a 'standard' is an abstract principle that serves as a measurement or gauge to guide a man's choices in the achievement of a concrete, specific purpose. 'That which is required for the survival of man qua man' is an abstract principle that applies to every individual man. The task of applying this principle to a concrete, specific purpose—the purpose of living a life proper to a rational being—belongs to every individual man, and the life he has to live is his own.
>
> Man must choose his actions, values, and goals by the standard of that which is proper to man—in order to achieve, maintain, fulfill and enjoy that ultimate value, that end in itself, which is his own life (Rand, 1964, 25).

These remarks, however, generate some vexing questions. What is it that differentiates one individual's living the life required for man's survival qua man from that of another's? What it is that differentiates living according to the standard of the life that is proper to a rational being from achieving, maintaining, fulfilling, and enjoying one's own life as one's moral purpose? Are we to assume that individuals do no more than locate the abstractly conceived values and virtues of "man's survival qua man" in space and time and add nothing to the character of that way of living? Are individuals no more than, so to speak, pin cushions in which the values and virtues that constitute the moral good are stuck?

Rand offers little or no discussion of how one is to differentiate one individual's moral goodness from that of another's. She says very little about how the contingencies and particularities of situations impinge on everyday moral decision-making, but even worse, she never discusses how the needs, interests, histories, and culture that descriptively characterize each individual make a difference to the very character of the moral life of individuals. Rand certainly understands that the human good is not some Platonic Form, and thus it is always the good of an individual human being. However, she does not fully appreciate that the human good, as it actually exists in reality independent and apart from human cognition, is itself something that is individualized. This failing is made even clearer by her omission of any discussion of the need for a virtue whose purpose is to discover what the values of living the morally worthwhile life amount to in the concrete lives of different individuals. She has no discussion of the virtue of practical wisdom.[13]

Rand is certainly not a thinker who ignores what is essential. Further, her theory of concepts makes it clear that concepts are formed only by "omitting measurements" but never by denying their existence. So, it certainly seems that she would not think that what is concretely and specifically good for one individual person is necessarily so for another. Indeed, simply because we have a concept of the morally worthwhile life that applies to every human being does not mean such a life as it actually exists is something universally the same. Yet, Rand also does argue that there can be no conflicts of interests among rational human beings. However, if the human good exists independent and apart from cognition, and if the unique identities of individuals do indeed play a role in determining the concrete character of the human good as it exists apart from cognition, then the possibility of such conflicts cannot be ruled out as a matter of principle. So, what lies behind Rand's thinking?

It seem to be this: if one focuses on the concept of the morally worthwhile life as opposed to the reality that exits in the lives of diverse individuals, then one can be moved to treat the morally worthwhile life as something universal. Yet, this is a move that is not justified by an Aristotelian view of logic and reality. Rather, it is a move that suggests an adoption of a central Kantian assumption—namely, assuming that the form of the mode of human cognition determines the form of the content of what is cognized.[14] In this case, this assumption involves treating the human good as it actually exists as a universal rather than as an individualized reality which only becomes universal when cognized. Once again, then, because of the lack of attention to the subtleties of the relationship between logic and reality, we see the specter of Kant in aspects of Rand's ethics.

Certainly, it is not my contention that Rand is an implicit Kantian. Rather, my purpose has been to show that the relationship between logic and reality is both fundamental and subtle. Rand understands the importance of the laws of logic ultimately reflecting the fundamental nature of reality. Contradictions, for example, cannot be thought and ought not to be tolerated, because the basic nature of reality is non-contradictory. Reality is intelligible, and Rand understands this better perhaps than any other philosopher. Yet, she does not fully appreciate the difference between logic and reality and as a result becomes entangled in some serious conceptual knots. It is in avoiding these confusions that the wisdom of Aristotelian tradition's account of logic remains vitally significant.[15]

Notes

1   From the Greeks through Aquinas to indeed Locke we have the idea that the nature of a thing is that thing's law.
2   Some philosophers might object that these considerations do not show that the universe as a whole has a nature and operates according to natural law. Of course, this objection raises the questions: Does it make sense to look for natural laws that govern the universe as a whole as distinct from the things that make up the universe? In what sense, if any, is the universe (or existence) a totality that can be taken as whole? Is the unity or oneness of the universe (or existence) like the unity or oneness we observe among the things that make up the totality? We must leave these fascinating questions for some other occasion, however.
3   It should be noted that the Aristotelian approach to this issue does not confine knowledge to strictly that of knowing propositions. I have used the term "cognition" here to indicate an intentional union or contact with reality. This certainly includes but is not confined to the propositional.
4   But achieving these goals is, of course, much more than just a matter of doing philosophy. See Douglas J. Den Uyl's contribution to this volume.
5   This obviously presupposes the validity of the senses, which I cannot consider here.
6   The works of H.W.B. Joseph and Henry B. Veatch are vital to understanding this tradition.
7   See Rasmussen, 1992, 1994.
8   Rand does briefly discuss some of these logical words under the topic of grammar in Chapter Four of the *Introduction to Objectivist Epistemology*.
9   I am omitting here any discussion of the nature of the relationship between an aspect of reality and a human being, but in the Aristotelian tradition this is usually explained in terms of whether it allows the individual to actualize his or her potentialities as a human being. For a discussion of this point see Chapter Six of Rasmussen and Den Uyl, 2005.

10 But this is, of course, not to say that the good can be actualized without human thought and effort.
11 It is important to realize that this claim involves considerably more than saying the good only becomes actualized through human thought and effort.
12 For an account of some of the problems with this approach to the good, see Chapter Seven of Rasmussen and Den Uyl, 2005.
13 For an excellent account of the importance of practical wisdom to ethics and its special relevance to ethical individualism, see Den Uyl, 1991.
14 This is, of course, to conflate logic with reality.
15 This essay has benefited from the suggestions of Roger E. Bissell and Douglas J. Den Uyl.

References

Den Uyl, Douglas J. 1991. *The Virtue of Prudence*. New York: Peter Lang.

Gilson, Etienne. 1986. *Thomist Realism and the Critique of Knowledge*. Translated by Mark A. Wauck. San Francisco: Ignatius Press.

Joseph, H.W.B. 1916. *An Introduction to Logic*, 2nd ed., revised. Oxford: Clarendon Press.

Rand, Ayn. 1957. *Atlas Shrugged*. New York. Random House.

———. 1964. The Objectivist Ethics. *The Virtue of Selfishness: A New Concept of Egoism*. New York: Signet Books: 13–35.

———. 1966. What is capitalism? *Capitalism: The Unknown Ideal*. New York: The New American Library: 3–27.

———. 1990. *Introduction to Objectivist Epistemology*, 2nd ed. New York: Meridian Books.

Rasmussen, Douglas B. 1992. Realism, intentionality, and the nature of logical relations. *Proceedings of the American Catholic Philosophical Association* 66: 267–77.

———. 1994. The significance for cognitive realism of the thought of John Poinsot. *American Catholic Philosophical Quarterly* 68 (Summer): 409–24.

———. 2002. Rand on obligation and value. *The Journal of Ayn Rand Studies* 4, no. 1 (Fall): 69–86.

Rasmussen, Douglas B., and Den Uyl, Douglas. 2005. *Norms of Liberty: A Perfectionist Basis for Non-Perfectionist Politics*. University Park: Pennsylvania State University Press.

Veatch, Henry B. 1952. *Intentional Logic: A Logic Based on Philosophical Realism*. New Haven, Connecticut: Yale University Press. Unaltered and unabridged reprint. Hamden, Connecticut: Archon Books, 1970.

Chapter 4

Various Levels of Meaning in the Chapter Titles of *Atlas Shrugged*

Fred Seddon

Ayn Rand wrote four novels, but she chose to give titles to the various chapters only in *Atlas Shrugged*. The purpose of this essay is to explore the multiple meanings, where they exist, of these titles.

Part I—Non-contradiction

Chapter I—The Theme

There are at least three levels of meaning in Chapter I's title. First is the theme of the novel itself, which, while not explicit in the first chapter, is certainly hinted at, to wit: The role of the mind in man's life. What would happen if the mind went on strike? In fact, the working title for the novel was *The Strike*.

The second level is the one captured by the opening line, "Who is John Galt?" This sentence is repeated throughout the novel and suggests its detective-like nature as well as the search for the man himself.

The third level is a literal one and refers to the musical theme Dagny overhears the brakeman whistling. The word "theme" even occurs four times within five rather short paragraphs (13—all pages numbers refer to the Dutton hardcover).

Chapter II—The Chain

The title has at least three meanings. The first is the bracelet made from the first heat of Rearden Metal. The second and more spiritual meaning is stated by Lillian, when she says referring to the bracelet: "A chain. Appropriate, isn't it? It's the chain by which he holds us all in bondage" (43). Yet it is really Rearden who is held in bondage, not by a physical chain of metal, but rather by the spiritual chain of altruism that prevents him from divorcing Lillian and throwing her, his mother and brother out of his home and his life. This is the third and most subtle meaning of "chain": altruism.

Chapter III—The Top and the Bottom

These two nouns each have a double meaning. The first is physical and refers to locations in two different buildings. The Top is the top of a skyscraper; the Bottom is the underground cafeteria of the Taggart Terminal.

The second sense is spiritual and refers to types of human beings: the Top being the heroic producers, the Bottom, the vicious, non-productive looters. The opening of the chapter takes place when the spiritual bottom dwellers, Taggart and his crowd, meet for drinks in the most expensive barroom in Manhattan. It is located at the top of a skyscraper, yet the description of the room makes one think of the bottom of a building, i.e., a cellar. The chapter closes with Eddie Willers talking to John Galt in the cafeteria of Taggart Transcontinental. It is an inversion of the barroom. The barroom is at the top, yet its ceiling is low and its customers even lower. The cafeteria is at the bottom, yet its ceiling is high, and so are the two who are quietly talking.

This is the first of three chapters, all occurring in Part I, whose names follow the pattern "The _____ and the _____." Chapter VII is "The Exploiters and the Exploited," while Chapter IX is "The Sacred and the Profane."

Chapter IV—The Immovable Movers

The title refers to both the producers of *Atlas Shrugged* as well as the god of Aristotle's *Metaphysics*, Book XII and *Physics*, Books VII and VIII. An explicit reference to Aristotle awaits the reader in Chapter V when, in answer to his father's question as to when Francisco had time to watch the stock market, he answers "While I was writing a thesis on the influence—upon subsequent metaphysical systems—of Aristotle's theory of the Immovable Mover" (110). Aristotle describes his god as an "immovable mover" who moves the universe without moving. He does this by being the final rather than the efficient cause of the universe.

Chapter V—The Climax of the d'Anconias

Francisco d'Anconia is the climax of a long line of productive geniuses. He tells James Taggart that, "In his lifetime, every one of my ancestors raised the production of d'Anconia Copper by about ten per cent. I intend to raise it by one hundred" (74). Rand may have also picked the word "climax" to suggest the explosive end of all of the d'Anconia copper on earth in Part III, Chapter V, pages 919–20.

Chapter VI—The Non-Commercial

On one level, the non-commercial represents the looters and the moochers. The action of this chapter takes place at a party Lillian gives to "celebrate" the anniversary of her marriage to Hank Rearden. Yet Rand lays a few land mines, so to speak. Many readers might want to put Francisco in the non-commercial category since he has seemingly given up the world of business for the life of a playboy. Also, near the end of the chapter, we meet Ragnar Danneskjöld (151). He is a pirate. A pirate is a paradigm of the non-commercial. But it seems only various People's States are after him. And we learn that he went to Patrick Henry University, the same school Francisco attended in the days of Hugh Akston and before the arrival of Simon Pritchett, the philosopher of the non-commercial.

Chapter VII—The Exploiters and the Exploited

This is a chapter in which Rand deconstructs the Marxian notion of exploitation. According to Marx, the capitalists exploit the proletariat by systematically retaining most of the value labor creates and paying labor a minimum or subsistence wage. Ben Nealy, the contractor, represents this type of view when he tells Dagny, "Muscles—that's all it takes to build anything in the world" (162). Rand shows that it is the productive geniuses like Dagny and Hank who are really exploited, while those with friends in Washington are the real exploiters.

Chapter VIII—The John Galt Line

This chapter heading is the first of several that simply indicate the action of the chapter–in this case, the building and the first run of the John Galt Line.

Chapter IX—The Sacred and the Profane

Surely the most obvious meaning of this title is the respective attitudes expressed by Hank and Dagny on the nature of the sex they had the night before. Hank regards it as vile and degrading, but as something he wouldn't give up. It's profane, but he can't help needing and wanting it.

Dagny regards the act as sacred. Since she doesn't hold any version of the soul-body dichotomy, she does not separate the values of her mind from the value of her body. She is sacred, as is are work and her sexual activities.

But the title also applies to the scene following the above. It describes the first meeting between James Taggart and Cherryl Brooks. She regards the bridge on the John Galt line as sacred, as she does any great achievement. "What else is there to look up to?" she asks Taggart (260). He regards it as profane and actually feels virtuous when he takes "his revenge upon every person who had stood cheering along the three-hundred-mile track of the John Galt Line" (267).

Chapter X—Wyatt's Torch

Here we have a title, which, like Chapter VIII above, is merely descriptive. In this case, it refers to the fact that Ellis Wyatt has quit the world. But before doing so, he set his oil fields on fire so that the looters will have a more difficult time looting his achievement. The title appears twice more in the book: once in "Account Overdrawn" and once at the very end of "The Moratorium on Brains," where the torch is the last thing the passengers on the doomed train see before entering the Winston Tunnel.

Part II—Either-Or

Chapter I—The Man Who Belonged on Earth

This title is taken from a sentence in this chapter. The context is Dagny's recalling how Hank looked during the summer of their vacation in the country. "He belonged in the countryside, she thought—he belonged everywhere—he was a man who belonged on earth" (370). In addition, later in the chapter, Dr. Stadler wonders why a genius in theoretical physics would waste his time producing a practical device such as a motor. Dagny's response to Stadler is "because he liked living on earth."

Chapter II—The Aristocracy of Pull

This is another title that refers to a line delivered by a character in the chapter it names. It occurs at the wedding of Jim and Cherryl:

> "We are at the dawn of a new age," said James Taggart, from above the rim of his champagne glass. "We are breaking up the vicious tyranny of economic power. We will set men free of the rule of the dollar. We will release our spiritual aims from dependence on the owners of material means. We will liberate our culture from the stranglehold of the profit-chasers. We will build a society dedicated to higher ideals, and we will replace the aristocracy of money by—"
> "—the aristocracy of pull," said a voice beyond the group. They whirled around. The man who stood facing them was Francisco d'Anconia. (Emphasis—mine)

What Francisco means is that under the system Taggart envisages, money will be "made" not by men of ability and industry but rather looted from the productive by those with connections in Washington.

Chapter III—White Blackmail

I have long thought that Rand should have invented a neologism for the title of this chapter, viz., whitemail. Alas, she did not. What the title means is explained in at least five different places in the book (435, 455, 465, 968), the last occurring in Part III, Chapter VII, "This is John Galt Speaking" where Galt says, "Theirs is a system of white blackmail devised to bleed you, not by means of your sins, but by means of your love for existence" (1067—italics in the original).

Originally, this chapter was to be titled "Atlas Shrugged" since the story of Atlas occurs on page 455. At that time, the working title of the book was *The Strike*. Once Atlas acquired its final title, she had to rename Chapter III.

Chapter IV—The Sanction of the Victim

The meaning of this title is actually presaged on page 455 Chapter III, when Frisco says to Rearden, "Why don't you uphold our own code of values among men as you do among iron smelters?" After hearing this, Rearden sits very still, and the words in this mind were, "the sanction of the victim."

The first two scenes of Chapter IV depict Rearden acting on his newfound knowledge. In the first scene, we see Rearden with his family, but now he is no longer willing to interact with them on the basis of their moral code. We are witness to the same action during his trial, when he refuses to accept the corrupt moral code of a system that wants to penalize him for being a productive genius.

Chapter V— Account Overdrawn

The word "account" only appears once in the whole chapter, and that is in the last scene, between Hank and Lillian. They are discussing his affair with Dagny and after Hank tells her that "nothing on earth will make me give it up," Lillian screams, "But I have a right to demand it! I own your life. It's my property ... You're the account I own!" (528–9)

The title may also refer to the fact that the country is running out of copper and, eventually Rearden metal.

Chapter VI— Miracle Metal

At first sight, this title appears to be merely descriptive; it is the name the government officials will give to Rearden metal after Rearden signs the gift certificate. But Rand's choice is no accident. To the looter mentality, the existence of Rearden metal is an inexplicable phenomenon, more of a miracle than a natural occurrence. Her use of the word "miracle," a word often associated with the pre-modern world view, also presages what is in store for the country after they handcuff the minds of the producers. Material conditions will revert to a medieval level of subsistence.

Chapter VII—The Moratorium on Brains

Here we have a backward reference to Directive Number 10–289, which was put into effect in the previous chapter, but one of whose most horrific consequences, the Tunnel disaster, is described in this one. In the previous chapter, during a phone call to Dagny, Francisco calls the directive by this chapter's title.

Chapter VIII—By Our Love

In case one hasn't guessed the meaning of this title, Rand keeps us in suspense and only reveals it on the very last page of the chapter. For all of us who have wondered how intelligent people, like Dagny and Hank, can stay at their jobs (Nathaniel Branden once said it was psychologically naïve but dramatically necessary), Dagny gives the reason when she says:

> Hank, I don't think they care whether there's a train or a blast furnace left on earth. We do. They're holding us by our love of it, and we'll go on paying so long as there's still one chance left to keep one single wheel alive and moving in token of human intelligence. We'll go on holding it afloat, like our drowning child, and when the flood swallows it, we'll go down with the last wheel and the last syllogism. (632—Emphasis mine)

Actually neither of them hang around quite that long.

Chapter IX—The Face Without Pain or Fear or Guilt

The title explicitly refers to the face of John Galt. Eddie tells the worker in the underground cafeteria, "Do you know what is strange about your face? You look as if you've never known pain or fear or guilt" (652). To readers who don't know that the worker is Galt, Eddie's statement provides another clue to the identity of the worker. Since Eddie's remark occurs on the second last page of the chapter, the reader will only get the clue if he remembers what the title of the chapter is and asks, "Why is this chapter titled after the face of an obscure track worker? Hm."

Chapter X—The Sign of the Dollar

The literal meaning of this title is, of course, the cigarettes stamped in gold with the dollar sign. Kellogg also elaborates on its two symbolic meanings. The looters use it as a sign of greed and depravity. But it really stands for "achievement, for success, for ability, for man's creative power." It also is the monogram of the

United States. In her *Playboy* interview she wrote, "The dollar sign ... is the symbol of a free mind." I think the title may remind many Christians of the sign of the cross. The allusion is even greater at the end of the book. The last words of the book are the "sign of the dollar." And the last sentence read in full, "He raised his hand and over the desolate earth he traced in space the "sign of the dollar." Like the Pope blessing the crowds in St. Peter's, but with this difference, the sign of the cross is a sign of torture and the sacrifice of "the ideal to the non-ideal," while the sign of the dollar is a sign of a free economy and free men.

Part III—A is A

Part III is unique among the three parts of *Atlas*. It is the only part in which two chapters are employed to name the same item, and Rand does it three times, with Chapters One and Two, Chapters Three and Four, and Chapters Eight and Nine. For example, Chapters One and Two name Galt's Gulch; Chapters Three and Four name the world of the looters; and Chapters Eight and Nine name John Galt.

Chapter I—Atlantis

The legendary meaning of Atlantis is first introduced into *Atlas* in Part I, Chapter VI, "The Non-commercial." In that chapter, a minor character relates the following to Dagny:

> The Isles of the Blessed. That is what the Greeks called it, thousands of years ago. They said Atlantis was a place where hero-spirits lived in a happiness unknown to the rest of the earth. A place which only the spirits of heroes could enter, and they reached it without dying, because they carried the secret of life within them. Atlantis was lost to mankind, even then. But the Greeks knew that it had existed. They tried to find it. Some of them said it was underground, hidden in the heart of the earth. But most of them said it was an island. A radiant island in the Western Ocean. Perhaps what they were thinking of was America. They never found it. For centuries afterward, men said it was only a legend. They did not believe it, but they never stopped looking for it, because thy knew that that was what they had to find. (153)

In this chapter we arrive at a place that is meant to be a literal Atlantis. A place where the productive heroes of the novel can go to escape the world of the looters.

Chapter II—The Utopia of Greed

This title is a name that is synonymous with the meaning of the previous title— Atlantis. Rand dramatizes life among the truly and properly greedy people.

Chapter III—Anti-Greed

The practice of using two chapters to name the same item continues in Chapters
Three and Four, which name the same place, vis., the world of the looters.

Chapter IV—Anti-Life

As Chapter VI will be Hank's chapter, this one belongs to the arch-villain, James
Taggart. In the opening scene, Taggart is examining his life to see what is his
motive power. With his skill for evasion, he prevents himself from discovering the
answer. Rand is setting us up for an answer that will only become explicit at the
end of Chapter IX. There we read, "He was suddenly seeing the motive that had
directed all the actions of his life ... it was the lust to destroy whatever was living,
for the sake of whatever was not" (1145). When he screams "No," in full
realization of his evil, Galt reminds him that he had already stated Taggart's
premise on the radio. Recall Galt's words, "yours is the Morality of Death. Death
is the standard of your values, death is your chosen goal."

Chapter V—Their Brother's Keepers

As the title of this essay suggests, I have limited myself to talking about the levels
of meaning in the chapter titles of the novel. But it is for that very reason that I
want to recommend Susan McCloskey's analysis of this chapter in her audio and
written essay "How to Read a Novel." This is another chapter in which Rand
deconstructs a cultural icon, viz., that we are our brother's keepers. What she does
is to show that spiritual brotherhood, e.g., that between Rearden and the wet nurse,
Rearden and Francisco etc., is of far greater value and significance than biological
brotherhood, e.g., Dagny and James, Hank and Philip, and, in the background,
Cain and Able.

    After destroying d'Anconia Copper, Frisco "greets" New York City with the
exclamation, "Brother, you asked for it." His use of the word "brother" is surely
not meant to be benevolent.

    The difference between the two kinds of "brothers" is that both biological
brothers, James and Philip, expect to be kept by their siblings; whereas the spiritual
brothers are traders in spirit and in material wealth.

Chapter VI—The Concerto of Deliverance

This title, as we find out on page 744 of the "Atlantis" chapter, refers to Halley's
Fifth Concerto. Curiously, although the Concerto is mentioned nineteen times
throughout *Atlas*, beginning with the opening chapter and ending with the very last
scene of the book, it is not mentioned in this eponymous chapter, which is devoted
exclusively to Hank Rearden and his "deliverance" from the clutches of the looters.

Chapter VII—"This is John Galt Speaking."

If Chapter VI belongs to Hank, then the following three chapters of the book have Galt at center stage. In this chapter, he delivers a 60-page talk on philosophy, covering every branch of philosophy except aesthetics. He is, of course, the "egoist" of Chapter VIII and the "generator" of Chapter XI.

Chapter VIII—The Egoist

If one were told that Ayn Rand, perhaps the world's most famous egoist, wrote a very big book about a bunch of egoists who go on strike against altruism, if one were told that in that big book the word "egoist" would not appear until page 1070 in a chapter titled "The Egoist," one might be skeptical. Yet, that is the case. In addition, one would also be surprised to find out that said chapter is the only chapter in the whole book where the word occurs, and then seven times including the title. Each use of the word in the chapter refers to only one character, John Galt. And yet all of the heroes are egoists. I can't explain any of this, but I do find it fascinating.

Chapter IX—The Generator

With this chapter, we return to titles that have more than one meaning. This chapter contains the torture scene. John Galt has fallen into the hands of his enemies, and they take him to the State Science Institute in order to torture him into taking over the economy of the country. In order to do this, they tie him to an electric generator that is designed to inflict great pain, yet stop short of killing him. When the generator breaks down during the torture of Galt, no one in the underground chamber can fix it—except Galt, the intellectual generator. Rand makes explicit reference to both of these generators in the last sentence of the chapter: "For the moment, their only certainty was that they had to escape from that the cellar where the living generator was left tied by the side of the dead one."

But there are two other generators referred to in this chapter. I have in mind Dr. Stadler and Project X. Without Stadler's genius, Project X, a sound wave generator, would have been impossible. Without Stadler's capitulation to the looters, Project X would have been impossible. How eloquent that the evil generator dies at the "hands" of the generator of death that he made possible.

Chapter X—In the Name of the Best Within Us

This title connects two passages separated by over 1160 pages. Given Rand's penchant for integration as a philosopher, let us look at the second of these references. It occurs in Arizona, where Eddie Willers is trying to get the stalled Comet started.

"Dagny!"—he heard himself crying soundlessly—"Dagny, in the name of the best within us!" ... He was jerking at futile levers and at a throttle that had nothing to move. ... "Dagny!"—he was crying to a twelve-year-old girl in a sunlit clearing of the woods—"in the name of the best within us, I must now start this train"! ... "Dagny, that is what it was ... and you knew it, then, but I didn't ... you knew it when you turned to look at the rails." ... "I said, not business or earning a living ... but, Dagny, business and earning a living and that in man which makes it possible—that is the best within us, that was the thing to defend ... in the name of saving it, Dagny, I must now start this train." (1166)

The reference to Dagny as a twelve-year-old girl can be found on page 6: "The minister said last Sunday that we must always reach for the best within us. What do you suppose is the best within us?" "I don't know." "We'll have to find out." She did not answer; she was looking away, up the railroad track.

Here ends this little study. I find that when I reread *Atlas Shrugged*, awareness of Rand's playing with the various meanings in many of the titles adds to my overall enjoyment of the book. I hope it does the same for you.

Chapter 5

Some Structural Aspects of
Atlas Shrugged

Lester H. Hunt

One of the features of *Atlas Shrugged* that makes it such an unusual book, especially for one that is so overwhelmingly popular, is how highly wrought it is. Whether or not it is true that, as the narrator of Dostoevsky's *Notes from the Underground* says, "there are intentional and unintentional cities," it is certainly true that there are intentional and unintentional books. And this is a very intentional book: every detail in it seems to mean something, to be intended to mean something. What I want to do here is to describe one of the literary methods by which Ayn Rand achieves the peculiar meaning-saturation of this book.

In the first chapter of *Atlas* there is a passage that catches the reader's eye with its overt symbolism:

> It was a symphony of triumph. The notes flowed up, they spoke of rising and they were the rising itself, they were the essence and the form of upward motion, they seemed to embody every human act and thought that had ascent as the motive. It was a sunburst of sound, breaking out of hiding and spreading open. It had the freedom of release and the tension of purpose. It swept space clean, and left nothing but the joy of an unobstructed effort. Only a faint echo within the sounds spoke of that from which the music had escaped, but it spoke in laughing astonishment at the discovery that there was no ugliness or pain, and there never had to be. It was a song of immense deliverance. (13)[1]

In the second chapter, there is another passage, near enough to the one that I just quoted that it can echo the first in the reader's mind. It is the description of the pouring of the first heat of the first order of Rearden metal:

> the first break of the liquid metal into the open came as a shocking sensation of morning. The narrow streak pouring through space had the pure white color of sunlight. Black coils of steam were boiling upward, streaked with violent red. Fountains of sparks shot in beating spasms, as from broken arteries. The air seemed torn to rags, reflecting a raging flame that was not there, red blotches whirling and running through space, as if not to be contained within a man-made structure, as if about to consume the columns, the girders, the bridges, of cranes overhead. But the liquid metal had no

aspect of violence. It was a long white curve with the texture of satin and the friendly radiance of a smile. (28)

The second passage recalls the first because of its striking similarities: like it, it conveys a strong impression of a morning brightness emerging from darkness, of violently explosive energy. On a higher level of abstraction, the impression in both cases is one of happiness and freedom, of an aspiration which has escaped confinement. Yet the similarities between the two passages also highlight the differences. The later passage is dominated by an image of downward motion, of the liquid metal pouring out of the furnace, while the earlier one is dominated by images of upward motion. More importantly, the later one is a description of an industrial and technological artifact and, as such, of something that is placed by the most familiar ontologies in the realm of the body, while the former is a description of a work of art, the sort of thing that is conventionally consigned to the realm of the spirit. This sense of paradox, or more exactly, of a surprising similarity between opposites, is underscored by the deliberate paradoxicality of that latter passage, with its depiction of smiling innocence at the heart of danger and violence. The reader is prepared for a point of view in which seeming opposites are deeply connected, in which identity and connection underlie apparent difference and conflict.

This point is underscored by repeated and prominent doubling of words and images in the early chapters of *Atlas*, and by the structure of the chapters themselves. The first chapter both begins and ends with two identical lines of dialogue, "Who is John Galt?" The first occurrence of this line is delivered by an anonymous bum who never reappears, and the second by Owen Kellog, a talented young worker who has inexplicably resigned. The very title of this chapter, "The Theme," has a double reference: it could refer to the musical theme described in the passage I quoted above or, we realize later, it could refer to the single line that begins and ends the chapter. The second chapter, "The Chain," begins with the metal-pouring scene from which I have quoted, and we soon find out that the first thing made of the metal being poured is a small chain that Rearden gives to his wife. In the last line of the same chapter, his wife is describing the same chain, characterized at the beginning in terms of radiance and freedom, as "the chain by which [Rearden] holds us all in bondage" (43).

It is in the third chapter that this structural feature, the two ends united by similarity and yet contrasting, is the most pronounced and obvious. The title of the chapter is "The Top and the Bottom," and it begins in a dark, low-ceilinged, cellar-like room that is actually an expensive barroom on the top of a skyscraper. The bureaucrats and corporate executives who are secretly meeting there are at the top of their socio-political system in terms of power over it, though morally they are close to its bottom. The chapter ends with a scene in the employees' cafeteria in Taggart Transcontinental, a sparkling, high-ceilinged room with "a sense of space and light" (62), but which is in fact underground. Only two men are meeting there,

Dagny Taggart's unprepossessing assistant Eddie Willers and an anonymous worker in grease-stained clothes, who we find out hundreds of pages later is the John Galt referred to at the beginning and end of the first chapter. These two men are near the bottom of the system as far as political power and prestige are concerned, though morally they represent its highest and best.

This particular sort of formal organization does not persist beyond the early chapters of the book, and would become rather oppressive if it did.[2] However, as features of the early chapters, they are enough to cue the reader, from the outset, to be attentive to the dominant structural feature of the book: the "twinning" as I would call it, of meaning-bearing elements that are linked by salient similarities and at the same time opposed to one another in potentially significant ways. Once the reader's attention becomes open to it, this feature becomes omnipresent; never oppressive, but insistent enough to constantly influence the process of understanding.

The book contains, to begin with some of the less important examples, two marriages, both of which are oppressive and dysfunctional.[3] They contrast, though, in that each as it were reverses the sex roles of the other: in one, the woman (Lillian Rearden) is the oppressor, while in the other it is the man (James Taggart). There are two steel magnates: one (Rearden) is a self-made man who has contributed a fundamentally new product to the economy, and the other (Boyle) who got his start with lavish government grants and has swallowed many small enterprises. Two contrasting sub-plots deal with two lines of the Taggart railroad: one, the John Galt Line, serves the vibrant community around Wyatt Junction in Colorado, while the other serves the squalidly socialist People's State of Mexico. Two of the memorable action set-pieces of the book are train rides. In one, Dagny and Rearden ride with breathtaking speed up into the mountain heights of Wyatt Junction. The other, dominated by the juvenile, bullying bureaucrat Kip Chalmers, chugs laboriously down into the depths of the earth, toward death. The second ride is clearly cross-referenced to the first: the last thing the passengers see "on earth" as their train is swallowed by the Winston tunnel is the distant light of Wyatt's Torch. In a different way, the John Galt ride is twinned with another ride on the same line: in this one, Dagny rides alone and, instead of meeting a jubilant crowd at Wyatt Junction, finds a panicky mob and, in the distance, the burning ruins of the Wyatt oil fields. James Taggart's Hellish relationship with Cherryl Brooks is twinned with Dagny's affair with Rearden, which is consummated at the same time that James meets Cherryl (in both cases, in the wake of the triumphant John Galt ride).

The novel has two major characters with mixed premises, some sound and some unsound: Henry Rearden and Dr. Robert Stadler. These characters contrast in terms of the way in which they develop: Rearden develops in the direction of goodness and enlightenment, and Stadler in the direction of evil and confusion. There are also two physicists in the novel: Galt is a an individualist who refuses to work for the government and ultimately revolts against it, and Stadler cooperates with the government's attempt to nationalize and monopolize scientific inquiry in the hands of the State Science Institute. Both physicists are closely associated with a single invention, though the nature of invention as well as the nature of the character's association with it is sharply different in the two cases. Galt develops a new conception of energy as a means to creating his technological device. Stadler, who despises technology, develops his theory of cosmic rays—a subject that seems to have no technological implications—and ignores the workers at the State Science Institute who use his theory as a means to developing a new device for purposes of their own. The two inventions also have opposite characteristics. Galt's device is a generator, which converts static energy into kinetic, while the Stadler device is a destroyer, a weapon of mass destruction, which turns living beings and human artifacts into shapeless mush. One converts the static into the dynamic, and the other, so to speak, reverses the process. The book also has two utopian communities, both described in some detail. One is individualist and one is collectivist, one heavenly and one hellish. It also has two philosophers and two composers, each pair a study in very sharp contrasts. There are two institutions that are dedicated to the pursuit of knowledge. The name of one of them contains a reference to Patrick Henry, a symbol of freedom, and the name of the other contains a reference to the state.

Of course, these structural features of the book are not ends in themselves, nor are they inserted for the sake of some formalistic conception of beauty. In some cases, they serve to promote characterization or plot development. For instance, Dagny's second ride on the John Galt Line, and the fact that it repeats the first with a dramatic difference, serves to emphasize an important plot point: the triumph of the John Galt Line has come to nought. It thereby indirectly brings out a point that is thematically important as well: namely, the fact that the events dramatized by the first one, and in particular the fact that Dagny and Rearden lent their productive talents to the support of the increasingly corrupt system, have actually contributed to causing the disaster revealed in the second, the destruction of the Colorado industrial community.

However, most of these instances of mirroring-with-a-difference serve to lead the reader directly into the ideas that drive the narrative and everything in it. The two parallel descriptive passages I quoted at the outset implicitly make a theoretical claim that gradually becomes explicit as the novel unfolds: namely, the claim that there is a deep connection between the realm of art and that of industry and technology, and more fundamentally between those of the body and of the spirit. A related thematic claim is embodied in another pair of mirroring and contrasting passages. Francisco d'Anconia makes two philosophical speeches, both aimed at his "greatest conquest," the mind of Henry Rearden, and like the above two passages they also stand in sharp contrast, though in a different way. One is his speech on the nature of money (Part II, Chapter II), and the other is his speech on the nature of sex (Part II, Chapter IV). Here the contrast is in the subject matters of the passages: both money and sex are consigned by conventional ontologies to the realm of the body, but to radically different and sharply contrasting aspects of the physical side of existence. The two speeches are, however, closely related, in part by the fact that they share to a considerable extent the same logical structure: both explain their allegedly brute, physical subject-matter as rooted in the mind. Money is a consequence of the mind's capacity to produce, and sex is a consequence of our vision of our highest values and our conception of our relation to these values (that is, our self-esteem or the lack of it). Further, both speeches develop the thesis that people who in either case seek the effect without the cause, money without being productive or sex without having self-esteem, then the effect will only be to hasten their destruction.

These two examples of the twinning device suggest a somewhat broader thesis about how it functions in achieving the author's purposes. As most of her readers know, a few years after publishing *Atlas*, Rand worked out an epistemological theory which was based on the idea that some non-nominalist solution to the problem of universals must be true or knowledge itself would be impossible. Like any epistemology that is based on this idea, it places a peculiar sort of emphasis on consciousness of similarities: an indispensable component of knowledge is finding real similarities between things, common attributes that the things possess (though in different degree) that indicate that the things are of the same kind.[4] One of the results accomplished by Rand's twinning device is the directing of the attention of the book's readers in a way that invites them to make this sort of mental integration. Despite what you might think, a concerto and a new metal alloy are really instances of one kind of thing—the achievements of the human spirit. The fact that the two marriages in the book parallel one another encourages the reader to focus on what is essential to them: the similar techniques employed by the two oppressors involved (James and Lillian) and to abstract from what is inessential (the genders of the oppressors).

The real beauty of the twinning device, however, is that in addition to prompting the reader to note similarities it is equally well suited to provoking them to carry out a seemingly opposite sort of mental process, one that according to the same family of epistemological theories, is also indispensable for the creation of human knowledge. If it is true that the foundation of knowledge is the noting of similarities that aims at discerning real categories of things, then the mind must also distinguish each category from others.[5] The essential complement of noting real similarities is noting real differences. The fact that Rearden and Boyle, Galt and Stadler, are in certain salient respects similar throws a glaring light on their far more important differences. The fact that the two utopian communities have such different results compels the reader to consider the underlying differences that explain them. These distinctions that the reader makes in these cases are of course thematically central to *Atlas*.

Part of the power and the philosophical interest of Dostoevsky's *Brothers Karamazov* lie in the way its plot construction places the reader in a position that mimics the thought processes recommended by the author's epistemological views.

We know that Dimitri did not kill his father. But his behavior and the trail of evidence he leaves behind him say otherwise. The Prosecutor, using his brilliant human reason, shreds the arguments presented by the defense. The only characters who look at the evidence and reach the correct conclusion are the two who love Dimitri: Alyosha and Grushenka. We, the readers, find ourselves thinking that, as these two characters look at the evidence, they are seeing it in the right way. Though it is clearly possible to see the evidence as the Prosecutor sees it, their way really does seem better. Though they are going by "faith" rather than reason, they seem to know the truth. And we find ourselves hoping that the simple peasants on the jury will follow their hearts and ignore the beguiling sophistries of the prosecution. We find ourselves, in other words, thinking as Dostoevsky says we should think. In a similar way, Rand structures *Atlas* in a way the gets the reader's mind to mimic the sort of functioning that her epistemology treats as the best. Of course, this sort of mental functioning is one that is diametrically opposed to Dostoevsky's mysticism.[6] Her reader is immersed in a world in which rationality is possible and, indeed, is the best way to function. It is rewarded at every turn with new discoveries and new connections between them.

Notes

1   Citations to Atlas will be in parentheses, giving the page number in the first hardbound edition: *Atlas* Shrugged. New York: Random House, 1957.
2   To be more exact, it tapers off, rather than ending abruptly. Chapter IV, The Immovable Movers, begins and ends with sentences about what it is that moves the world, sentences that seem to give sharply different accounts of the matter.
3   Rather curiously, there is in all of Rand's works no full-length portrait of a successful marriage. In *The Fountainhead*, it is true, Dominique and Howard are married, but the book ends immediately afterward.
4   Ayn Rand. 1967. *Introduction to Objectivist Epistemology*. New York: The Objectivist: 16, 17 and Chapter 2, *passim*.
5   *Introduction to Objectivist Epistemology*. Pages. 40, 41 and Ch. 5 *passim*.
6   The relations between Dostoevsky and Rand deserve to be explored more fully than they have hitherto. To a considerable extent, the relation between them seems to be a beautiful example of negative influence: on crucial matters, her views look like inversions of his.

Chapter 6

Table of Contents for Ayn Rand's *Atlas Shrugged*[1]

Hans Gregory Schantz

Chapter V —The Climax of the d'Anconias

Chapter VI —The Non-Commercial

Chapter VII —The Exploiters and the Exploited

Chapter VIII —The John Galt Line

Chapter IX —The Sacred and the Profane

Chapter X —Wyatt's Torch

PART II: EITHER-OR

Chapter I —The Man Who Belonged On Earth

Chapter II —The Aristocracy of Pull

Chapter III —White Blackmail

Chapter IV —The Sanction of the Victim

Chapter V —Account Overdrawn

Chapter VI —Miracle Metal

Chapter VII —The Moritorium on Brains

Chapter VIII —By Our Love

Chapter IX —The Face Without Pain Or Fear Or Guilt

Chapter X —The Sign of the Dollar

PART III: A IS A

Chapter I —Atlantis

Chapter V —Their Brothers' Keepers

Chapter VI —The Concerto of Deliverance

Chapter VII —"This is John Galt Speaking"

Chapter VIII —The Egoist

Note

1   The page numbers were taken from the 26th printing of the paperback edition of *Atlas
     Shrugged*.

PART 2
Philosophy

Chapter 7

Atlas Shrugged's Moral Principle of the Sanction of the Victim

Tibor R. Machan

My Plan

Over the years that I have studied and found a good deal of truth in Ayn Rand's philosophic thought I have also witnessed the wrath of much of the academy hurled in her direction. Some of it has been outright vindictive, some merely disdainful in that supercilious fashion intellectuals tend to perfect as part of their verbal ammo, especially when they go by the merest of information concerning what they demean. Not only those whose views Rand has herself mercilessly attacked but many who should welcome her work have shown her the back of their hand.[1]

Rand's philosophical work has been mostly on the level of the architectural, instead of the mortar, engineering, or wiring work. Yet she did produce some fine nuanced philosophy, for instance in epistemology, or, more specifically, the theory of concept formation. Many of her broader philosophical insights and arguments have helped others develop the more detailed treatment of issues in the fashion that has been lauded as proper philosophy in the first two thirds of the 20th century.

It is in the spirit of helping along such development that I wish to explore here Ayn Rand's innovative idea, advanced first in *Atlas Shrugged*, of "the sanction of the victim." By this she meant, in her own words, "accepting as a sin the thing which [is one's] greatest virtue and the greatest of all human virtues: [one's] rationality, the desire to know and to understand."[2] A bit unusually, let me begin with a personal story involving the author of *Atlas Shrugged*, with whom I corresponded in 1962 on the topic of this essay. My plan here is to first examine the meaning of the idea, the sanction of the victim. Then I will indicate the scope of its application. Finally I will contribute somewhat to the development of one of the crucial assumptions underlying the idea, namely, free will and, in particular, the assumption that underlies free will, namely, agent causality.

The Sanction of the Victim: A Personal Story

I had a very fruitful exchange with Ayn Rand about the issue of the sanction of the victim when I sent her a letter I had written to a priest about having read and fretted about Thomas A. Kempis's *Imitation of Christ* (Baltimore: Penguin, 1952).

In late summer of 1962 I met Ayn Rand in her office in the Empire State Building. After a very cordial, even warm discussion with her, I promised to send her a particularly wrenching letter I had written to a priest during my struggles about a friend's divorce, struggles that perplexed me to no end, ultimately paving the way for me to become an atheist. When I got back to Washington I sent it. Here are the crucial excerpts from my letter to the priest and their relevance to my topic should become clear rather quickly:

> This letter is sort of confused. It didn't give me great problems; it only gives the problems of someone who thinks a bit. Thinking is driving him crazy. The only way he can keep away from sin is to think of rationalizing in sin or anything else. I have no problems but according to that book I have all the problems of the world. According to that book I have only read the beginning of it. I am bad from the day I was born to the day I die. Only Christ is good. But Christ was not human, he was God. Is there an answer?
>
> If you know it please try to tell it to me. Not in formal talk but in man to man talk, Father. I am scared of your priest[ly] advice because it makes me feel real bad. I look like a hypocrite or something of the sort. I am not a stupid guy. I can understand a bit of logic. The trouble is that I am always asking for the logic. And the more I will know the more I will want to know. What should I do, stop wanting to know?
>
> If you cannot write me a more logical explanation to the mixed up letter above than the books reveal (I do not believe that the writers of those books think it is possible to live the way they want us to live and still be 1% happy.), please do not bother to do any explaining. I promise I will never hold it against you or any one. I am not trying to find excuses for my sins. I am trying to find a way to avoid them, because I sure cannot do so now. I have my mind on things that I know as sin only. I want things that I know only as sin. Why? ...

Shortly after I sent the copy of this letter to her, when I was still in Washington, Rand wrote me a memorable letter commenting on how mine to the priest exemplified her principle of the sanction of the victim—which it did. The theme of Kempis's book, in essence, is that the human effort to know is an insult to God—it is a sign of pride and lack of proper humility. I read this work and wrote the letter above. The central portions of Rand's letter went as follows:

> Your letter to the priest projects, with startling accuracy, what an honest and intelligent young person would have to feel if he attempted to practice the altruist morality fully and conscientiously.
>
> The most terrifying indictment of religious morality is contained in the following lines of yours: "The trouble is that I am always asking for the logic. And the more I

will know the more I will want to know. What should I do to stop wanting to know?" I hope that you realize fully to what extent you were on the premise which I call "the sanction of the victim." You were accepting as a sin the thing which was your greatest virtue and the greatest of all human virtues: your rationality, the desire to know and to understand. I am sure that you will never make that mistake again, but I want to stress, as the most important advice I can give you, that no matter what intellectual errors you may make in the future, do not ever accept the idea that rationality is evil or that it can ever be proper to discard your mind. So long as you hold this as an absolute, you will be safe, no matter what errors you make. But if one doubts or rejects one's own mind, one commits an act of spiritual suicide and the greatest evil possible to man....

Ayn Rand (signed)

Rand's letter shows clearly how practically vital she believed is her idea of the sanction of the victim. What the letter does not show is just how wide the scope is of this practical vitality. That comes through in Galt's speech, when he discusses the idea and links it to "what was wrong with the world." But I will come to that presently.

The Scope of the Idea

What I wish now to suggest is that the scope of the idea of the sanction of the victim is much greater than it has been realized so far. First, it has implications for some of the difficulties experienced within the Objectivist movement, wherein quite a few persons have allowed themselves to be intellectually and emotionally bullied by others and who have, thus, sanctioned their own intellectual and emotional victimization. Second, it has implications for millions of other cases wherein someone submits to ill treatment by another—for example, in spousal or older child abuse. And, third, it has implications, most importantly, for how statism has managed and is managing to prevail throughout the globe.

First I wish to make clear that I take issue with a certain characterization of "the sanction of the victim," advanced by both Rand and Peikoff. Rand states that the thrust of the idea is that "it is the good, the able, the men of reason, who act as their own destroyers, who transfuse to evil the blood of their virtue and let evil transmit to them the poison of destruction" (Rand 1957, 972–3; 1961, 165). And it is Peikoff (1976) who states that "The 'sanction of the victim' is the willingness of the good to suffer at the hands of the evil, to accept the role of sacrificial victim for the 'sin' of creating values."[3]

Rand's statement in her letter to me is more precise: "[The sanction of the victim is] accepting as a sin the thing which [is one's] greatest virtue and the greatest of all human virtues: [one's] rationality, the desire to know and to understand." She does not suggest that those who do this are good, morally good, that is. The reason this is more accurate is that those who freely comply with evil done to them are not, at least in that respect, morally good. They are, of course, accurately characterized as victims, since wrongful treatment is perpetrated against them. It is a bit like this. Suppose you need to go to a neighborhood where car thefts are frequent and yours is a desirable model. Instead of locking up your vehicle good and hard, you leave the doors unlocked and the key in the ignition. It is, as most reasonably expected, stolen. Those who stole it aren't morally innocent, but neither are you. They perpetrated theft, you failed to be prudent.

Now consider all the millions of people who are victimized by statists throughout history and throughout the contemporary world. Many millions are willing victims of such statism, which, of course, also leads to strengthening the out and out statists as they victimize those who would rather not comply but are powerless to resist. Both those who sanction the statism and those who would resist it are victims since statism is wrong in and of itself, whatever the mental or psychological state of the victims. Abject compliance does not make the statism less statist, less coercive or less of a violence against human rights. But refusal to acknowledge that the statism is morally wrong is itself morally wrong, as is the refusal to take measures to fend it off.

The question as to why the principles of the free society aren't being fully accepted by people who are victims of statism arises often among those who advocate and work for the promotion of those principles. Many explanations are offered, too many of them self-defeating in that they assume a virtually mechanistic incentive structure that promotes statism. (Public choice theory is a bit like this, as are many explanations that point to the lure of power and how it drives the statists and their victims to fail to want to be free.)

Rand's idea of the sanction of the victim has not been well enough explored in this connection. Perhaps a reason for this is that so applying the idea suggests less than a utopian resolution to the problem. There is, in other words, not likely to be any time when those who exhibit the trait of sanctioning their own victimization will leave the human race and let only those who want to resist their own victimization, who do not want to sanction it, have front and center on the stage of politics. This is exactly why John Galt begins the passage where the sanction of the victim comes up with the words, "Then I saw what was wrong with the world ..." We must take Rand, via Galt, at her word: She means to be discussing here exactly what is wrong with the world, the central explanation of what is morally and politically amiss with it.

Indeed, this idea of the sanction of the victim promises, I contend, to be Ayn Rand's much better fundamental explanation than alternatives afoot for why morality and, especially, liberty do not prevail in the course of human events. To wit, men and women aren't consistently, persistently good enough human beings— or should I put it "good at being human"—so as to acknowledge the value of what is right, morally and politically, in their very own lives and their very own communities.

The Sanction of the Victim and Free Will

Of course, such an explanation assumes something that is very widely denied in our age, namely, the freedom of the human will. I think it is now going to be useful to spend some time on this because without a reasonably extensive discussion of the topic, why free will is so out of favor with most of the intellectual community and why this is wrongheaded, there is not going to be a full enough appreciation of the enormous significance of application of Ayn Rand's idea of the sanction of the victim.

The issue before us, then, is whether human beings are agents of their own conduct, whether they can initiate some of the crucial activities they undertake.

This then will be a brief discussion of some aspects of free will, at least the version that contends that human beings can cause and thus can be agents of their actions. They can initiate some of what they do or, alternatively, not initiate any action at all. Here "initiate" stands in for what others tend to label "choose" so as to distinguish between "choosing" and "selecting," the latter not requiring free will, which the former does.[4]

The point of this discussion is not to establish the existence of free will, although the conclusion I think sound will support this. Free will is established via different arguments, most especially by its undeniability in the context of seeking knowledge. If no free will exists, knowledge is not possible—all we do when we claim to know is manifest beliefs we have to take to be knowledge but we could never tell whether they are, in fact, knowledge. Knowledge requires an independent, free mind, one that isn't forced to believe in anything. That is what's assumed about the minds of jury members and research scientists, among others, who are implored to be objective, to focus on the facts and arguments and choose to avoid irrelevant matters as they reach their conclusions about matters before them. For our purposes here what stands in the way of the free will thesis, the thesis on which Ayn Rand's idea of the sanction of the victim most significantly rests, is the belief in the impossibility of agent causation, that some being can be the first cause of its actions. If this can be shown to be mistaken, then what remains to be shown is that free will actually exists, which will be less complicated without the impossibility of agent causality thesis standing in its way.

What, then, about the agency account of free will? When acting in the world, human beings tend to assume we, on our own, can cause things to happen. For one, we take our actions to be, well, our actions, not just movements or behaviors that we happen to have undergone. We often make or produce stuff, as I am doing when I write these thoughts down or you, when you compose a poem, organize a division of a company or arrange the flowers in your garden.

On the Possibility of Agent Causality

Indeed, human history is believed by many to consist of more or less significant things people have done, badly or well. Art, science, technology, politics, diplomacy, economics and the rest are all supposedly spheres of human conduct. Philosophy, too, fits here—so that, for example, we take it that philosophers have advanced their various positions of their own free will, not because they couldn't help it (although some have wished to have it both ways, such as Hegel and Marx). Critics of various human actions in the past, such as those who find racism, sexism, environmental mismanagement, the conduct of governments at home or abroad to have been wrong all assume that some other course of action could have been taken, so they assume this kind of causal agency and freedom of will on the part of most people.

People tend to distinguish actions from happenings. That earthquake in California and the one in Iran, those happened, as did yesterday's shower and the lightening that hit a neighbor's TV antenna. No one did these, they happened. The flood and the virus that has damaged us weren't our doing, nor the recent Southeast Asian tsunami. But the damage-control applied, not applied or misapplied to all were.

Now there are those who deny that there really is a difference between these two kinds of occurrences. They argue that both are happenings, with some, however, involving the rather complicated entity of a human being as an intermediary factor, while others lacking such involvement. But in the final analysis what persons do is no less a kind of happening in which we have a role, as a rather complex link in the chain of events that brings about the behavior we otherwise, misguidedly, consider acts we produce, than would be the happening of the wind slapping a person against a fence which then collapses as a result.

Indeed, the central issue in this dispute is whether when we do have such a part in the process that brings about the action, could we in any way be decisive, first causes, or must we be merely one of many steps in an event-to-event causal chain. And there are a great many rather influential thinkers who deny that we could be such first causes. We cannot originate or initiate anything—it would be "mysterious" if we could, as Dennett (2003, 100) puts it. As he states it, "How does an agent cause an effect without there being an event (in the agent, presumably) that is the cause of that effect (and is itself the effect of an earlier cause, and so forth)? Agent causation is a frankly mysterious doctrine, positing something unparalleled by anything we discover in the causal processes of chemical reactions, nuclear fission and fusion, magnetic attraction, hurricanes, volcanoes, or such biological processes as metabolism, growth, immune reactions, and photosynthesis."

Ayn Rand rejects Dennett's line when she states, "All actions are caused by entities. The nature of an action is caused and determined by the nature of the entities that act; a thing cannot act in contradiction to its nature. An action not caused by an entity would be caused by a zero, which would mean a zero controlling a thing, a non-entity controlling an entity, the non-existent ruling the existent. ... The Law of Identity does not permit you to have your cake and eat it, too. ..." (Rand 1957, 962–3). And Peikoff (1990, 147) states that "Choice ... is not chance. Volition is not an exception to the Law of Causality; it is a type of causation."

Rand, however, does not enter into an extended discussion of how it is possible for such causation to exist and how we could identify it in nature. She leaves it at identifying the fundamental act of human causation, namely, willing to think and at the failure to engage in such willing, which is to say "blanking out" or evading.

It is necessary, however, to address these matters in some more details so as to fend off Dennett & Co.'s claim of the mysterious nature of agent causation, of such alleged choice between willing to think or blanking out or evading.[5] And, furthermore, it is necessary to do so in order to make fully credible the Randian idea of the sanction of the victim and, especially, its broad application as an explanation for "what [is] wrong with the world."

Is Agent Causation Spooky?

So, then, why is it in fact not mysterious or spooky to be able for an entity to produce something on its own? On the one hand it seems to be, given that the event-to-event conception of causation is so widely accepted, taken to be axiomatic. On the other hand we certainly assume at times human beings can be the cause of some things, such as highway crashes or, to use a more elevated case, when Albert Einstein originated the theory of special relativity or Mozart his Requiem.

In fact, most persons think of themselves as engaging in original creations, as when they put together a funny expression or take an unusual picture. My own children often let on to their belief in having said something original, when after they said it they had a big grin on their faces, indicating that, yes, they know this is a novelty that they have produced.

OK, but perhaps we are just mistaken to think these self-aggrandizing thoughts about what we can do. The famous behaviorist psychologist B.F. Skinner, who taught at Harvard University, argued that these ideas are pre-scientific and prominent contemporary philosophers such as Dennett argue that the kind of freedom of the will, the kind that involves agent causation, is mysterious and, in any case, not worth having. This is the sort that would have us be capable of being original actors, creators, and producers. Dennett says we couldn't make any sense of such freedom of action, certainly not of any kind of responsibility for actions we take if it did exist. So let me explore the matter further and see why those like Dennett deny while those like Rand affirm the reality of agent causation.

First of all, despite Dennett's characterization of the agent causation theory as "a mysterious doctrine," it is no more mysterious than any arguments that rely on a dialectical and inferential reasoning.[6] If, as it turns out to be the case, free will is assumed even as one tries to deny it—in other words, the action of attempting to deny free will presupposes that the agent is capable of making original choices— that is sufficient to present a very strong case for free will (Machan 2000). And the kind of independent thinking involved in argumentation does exactly that, namely, presuppose free will, the capacity to make choices, to take the initiative as a conceptually conscious agent. For what worth would any argument be if it merely amounted to a computational or genetic process, as it were, going through the human organism? It would be no more compelling an argument as would be an "argument" advanced by a computer or parrot. The reason we can understand the reference to these as arguments it that we, human agents, can take them as such. But as products of computers or parrots they aren't arguments, only a bunch of sounds strung together.[7]

Second, there is that aspect of the case for free will that relies on introspection. We often know about things this way, as when we answer our doctors very confidently about where we feel a pain in our bodies, or remember an event for which there is no evidence any longer apart from our memory. These are completely reliable kinds of knowledge and part of what gives us knowledge of our free will is that we are well aware of the fact that we often choose, initiate action, produce or create what we didn't have to produce or create. As I am writing the next few words in this discussion, I know at every moment I could stop, get up and get a soda from the fridge or continue with my project, as indeed I am choosing to do. Indeed, without this capacity the ideas of commitment to a project, tenacity, perseverance, ambition and such would be vacuous. And whatever one were to say on a subject, it would all be the results of various impersonal forces, never one's own initiative and self-determined close attention, good judgment or the like.

Finally, is Dennett's distinction between determinism and inevitability (or fatalism) sound? Let's look again at what he says: "Inevitability means unavoidability, and if you think about what avoiding means, then you realize that in a deterministic world there's lots of avoidance. The capacity to avoid has been evolving for billions of years. There are very good avoiders now."

Now suppose that I am typing along here and someone maintains that I am fully determined to do this. I, however, in order to try to show that I am not, stop. Have I avoided something now? No, not according to determinism. Some factor, such as the presentation of the idea that I am determined, along with my responsiveness to such a presentation, have necessarily come into play to redirect the flow of events, so that I am no longer typing along but stopping, reacting to the factors or forces that unavoidably produced my "avoidance" behavior. Could I have done otherwise? Not according to Dennett's determinist view. Was it inevitable what happened? Surely, the presentation of the determinist's idea couldn't be avoided; my reaction couldn't either, and so on and so forth.[8]

So, pace Dennett, if we know what avoidance means, we know that, paraphrasing him, "in a fatalistic world there's lots of avoidance." Why? Because what is called "avoidance" is a form of behavior that is determined to occur, just as any other form of behavior is determined to occur by way of the daisy chain of efficient causal links that connect the primordial past with the endless future (as per the picture determinists' offer of reality).

Agent Causality isn't Yet Free Will but it is Causality

What the agent causation position does not show, of course, is the detailed correct or true full account of free will, only that free will exists. Indeed, its existence is undeniable for us who are the acting agents. A detailed theory of agent causality would serve as an account of free will, not as its proof.[9]

If such an account fails, however, perhaps the idea that we have free will is going to turn out to be false. Or perhaps a deterministic account of the phenomenon of free will shall succeed where the agent causality account will have failed.

So, it does matter whether the agent causality account of free will is sound. The first obstacle to this is the claim, made by Dennett and others, that the very idea of agent causation is mysterious, spooky. But why is Dennett so confident that agent causation would have to be mysterious? Well, to answer we need to consider a famous argument about the nature of causality that occurred back in the 18th century.

It was David Hume who reasoned that if we depended for knowing the world entirely and solely on our sensory information, then causality itself must not be thought of as any kind of production or power. The billiard ball that strikes another and is taken, thus, to have made the other move has no (empirically) demonstrable productive powers at all. Instead, if we depend on our senses for knowledge, all we can justifiably claim is that the first billiard ball's motion was followed by that of the second, and the oft-repeated instances of this result in our coming to gain the idea of causality. (This is an odd move, by the way, since Hume is depending on a productive notion of causality to explain our belief in causality.) Regular or constant sequences like that are, for Hume, all that causes are, involving no evident causal powers.

Now the assumption that all of what we know comes from our senses is a pretty radical one and although Hume's idea of causality was very influential, most scientists and nearly all the rest of us did not fully accept his claim about causality because it rested on his radical empiricism. But many did accept a good deal of it, so the idea that there can be something productive in a causal relationship has been dropped by most of those who think about causal connections in the world. It is this idea that is deemed to be spooky or mysterious by many because the productivity of a causal factor assumes something that is not directly evident—it isn't perceived by the senses. Instead it is inferred from the entire context of the causal situation.

So, for example, that the billiard ball has something about it—say, its solidity, its mass and density—that would produce an impact on another billiard ball so this other ball would be moved by it, is something that we do not see but infer. And although much of science welcomes direct evidence, first and foremost, as it considers convincing explanatory stories, science also makes room for inferred powers. For instance, black holes could not be detected by way of direct evidence for a long time, since by their very nature they didn't release any sensory information since their immense gravitational force did not allow such information, involving as it has to the emission of light, to escape for us to perceive it. So, the existence and nature of black holes were both discovered by inference, by noticing facts that could best be explained by the postulation of the black hole. (This is, of course, how the reality of many other beings are routinely established—for example, intentions, motives, wants, wishes, expectations, and so forth.)

In response to those like Dennett, then, who deny the possibility of agent causality because they regard productive powers of causal factors as something mysterious or spooky, such powers are not directly perceived but they can be inferred from other facts that can be. So, if the best explanation of what makes the second billiard ball move is that the first has certain properties—lacking in, say, a tennis ball—which can produce the typical movement in an entity such as the second ball, then that is a conclusion that is certain beyond a reasonable doubt (although not certain in the incorrigible, absolute sense of Descartes' idea of knowledge, which Hume deployed for sensory impressions, would have required). Similarly, the power of human agents to be first causes can also be inferred along these lines. Given a certain composition of their brains, given the properties of them, and given the mental capacities—of, say, concept formation and self-reflection—they could well be the kind of beings capable of making original choices, of taking the initiative, just as we ordinarily believe they are.

This isn't the place where the full story of this capacity can be told but it is the place where it can be noted that the requisite evidence for such a capacity could involve inferred powers without which what we do observe could not be explained, understood or given an account of.[10] These, in turn, need by no means be mysterious or spooky things, any more than the immense gravitational powers of black holes had to be deemed spooky or mysterious simply because no one could, until recently, directly perceive them, or one's intention to work hard for the next year or motivation to feed one's children need be mysterious or spooky things because these aren't directly perceived.

Limits of Empiricism

There is more to reality than just what the senses can record, even if what that is needs to be fully squared with what the senses can record. As Eyal Mozes has pointed out,

> On the view of causality as a relation of an entity to its actions, all causation—including all the processes Dennett lists ["nuclear fission and fusion, magnetic attraction, hurricanes, volcanoes, or such biological processes as metabolism, growth, immune reactions, and photosynthesis"]—involves as cause the entity rather than some earlier event. And all biological processes—including all the ones Dennett lists—are cases of self-generated action. Agent causation, therefore, far from being "'mysterious' and unparalleled by anything," is ubiquitous in nature; it is only Dennett's unquestioning acceptance of the event-event view of causality that makes him blind to this.

Dennett's effort to couple determinism with self-responsibility founders because by "responsible" he means no more than being a part of the process that brings it about that something happens. So human beings are no more responsible for their conduct than is a tree for its growth or a hurricane for the disasters in its wake. There is no room for moral responsibility here, a responsibility that requires that the agent could have done otherwise than he or she did, all things remaining equal. And, indeed, Dennett himself cannot quite escape invoking that kind of responsibility as he, for example, chides others for getting the matter about free will and determinism wrong—he implicitly holds that they ought to have gotten it right, even as they didn't.

Rand's Idea is Worth Reconsideration

If the above analysis of causality is sound and agent causation cannot be ruled out as some would wish to rule it out as part of nature, then the doctrine of free will that underlies Ayn Rand's idea of the sanction of the victim becomes quite credible. I have elsewhere defended free will, so I will not repeat this here. All I am interested in arguing is that the explanation Rand has John Galt give, for "what is wrong with the world," depending as it does on free will, and free will depending as it does on agent causation, has considerable credibility. It should be considered seriously, in preference to the umpteen deterministic explanations offered, especially, by classical liberal economists who are captive of the social scientific framework wherein only mechanistic, efficient causation finds a place in nature.

What to make of Galt's point then? When we wish to understand why things are not going well in the world—in the human world, that is, apart from "acts of God or Nature"—it needs to be taken seriously that the fundamental cause is bad human choices made by individuals who fail at realizing their full humanity. Thus contrary to perhaps the ill chosen language of Ayn Rand and her epigone Leonard Peikoff, the people who sanction their victimization aren't plainly good people. Nor was I good in so far as I let the Roman Catholic clergy intimidate me about using my mind to its fullest powers when I sanctioned the sophistry that suggested that life is supposed to be some kind of sacrificial ceremony and that seeking knowledge is a sin of pride. I happened to have improved by discontinuing the sanctioning of my victimization. Sadly not enough people around the globe do so, which then contributes in a decisive way to what is wrong with the world.

Which is to say, the things wrong in the world are due to what people do and do not do of their own initiative. To quote Shakespeare's *Julius Caesar*, "The fault, dear Brutus, is not in our stars; but in ourselves. ..."

Notes

1   For some of this, see the Chapter Six, "Ayn Rand and I," in Tibor R. Machan, *The Man Without a Hobby, Adventures of a Gregarious Egoist*. Lanham, Maryland: Hamilton Books, 2004, as well as other portions of that memoir.

2   Letter from Ayn Rand to Tibor R. Machan, 4 August 1962. The idea of the sanction of the victim makes its first public appearance in Galt's speech. See Ayn Rand, *Atlas Shrugged*. New York: New American Library, 1957. Reprinted in Ayn Rand, *For the New Intellectual*. New York: New American Library, 1961.

3   Leonard Peikoff, "The Philosophy of Objectivism," Lecture Series (1976), Lecture 8. Both Rand's and Peikoff's statements are quoted in *The Ayn Rand Lexicon, Objectivism from A to Z*. Edited by Harry Binswanger. New York: A Meridian Book, 1988, 433–44.

4   For a more detailed discussion of free will, see Tibor R. Machan, *Initiative—Human Agency and Society*. Hoover Institution Press, 2000. For a detailed discussion of agent causation, see Timothy O'Connor, *Persons and Causes*. Oxford University Press, 2002. See, also, Edward Pols, "Rational Action and the Complexity of Causality." *Journal of Theoretical and Philosophical Psychology* 22 (1) (Spring 2002).

5   I have myself characterized this blanking out as "being out to lunch," and I have heard others who find Rand's analysis sound identify the contemporary locution deployed by some, to the effect of saying "whatever," as symptomatic of the choice to blank out. But to render this philosophically palatable, the possibility of agent causation needs to be demonstrated. See, for more, Tibor R. Machan, *Classical Individualism*. London: Routledge, 1998, especially Chapter 3, "Human Action and the Nature of Moral Evil."

6   The argumentative approach here is akin to Aristotle's negative demonstration, not a proof resting on premises, since any premises, in the case of refuting the skeptic, would already require one's knowing something. In other words, that there are things, that there is existence, isn't something one can prove but neither is it meaningful to question it since the question itself, for example, exists and thus is an admitted instance of existence. Proving free will is like that—the proving activity itself presupposes that one is free to choose to prove or not to prove something.

7   For a very detailed and tight discussion of this, see Edward Pols, *Acts of Our Being, A Reflection on Agency and Responsibility*. Amherst, Masschusetts: University of Massachusetts Press, 1982 and "Rational Action and the Complexity of Causality," *Journal of Theoretical and Philosophical Psychology* 22, no. 1 (Spring 2002). (When I sent notice of this work to Dennett, he dismissed it all and noted that my credibility has suffered by showing it to him.)

8   What Dennett takes to be a serious difference between determinism and fatalism is only a difference in how detailed a story one is going to tell. Sure, there is no fatalism of the sort where merely large movements proceed, unstoppably; but there is a fatalism of the sort where zillions of micro-movements interact in ways that even a humongous and vastly complex computer could not predict exactly. Still, a sophisticated fatalist would rightly hold that whatever is going to happen, is fated to have happened, given that all the details that make up the evolution of the university had to happen just as they did happen.

9   For a start on such an account, see Roger W. Sperry, "Changing Concepts of Consciousness and Free Will," *Perspectives in Biology and Medicine* 9, August 1976, 9–19. For Sperry's broader discussion of the agency causation topic, see his *Science and Moral Priority*. New York: Columbia University Press, 1983.

10   This argumentative approach is dubbed "argument to the best explanation." Such arguments are deployed for various purposes—for example, Robert Nozick used it, in *Anarchy, State, and Utopia* (Basic Books, 1974) to defend his entitlement theory of justice based on the assumption that people have basic rights. Black holes were once so defended, as was the atomic structure of matter and, in courts of law, have been the intentions (*mens rea*) of criminals.

References

Binswanger, Harry. ed.. 1988. *The Ayn Rand Lexicon: Objectivism from A to Z.* New York: A Meridian Book.

Dennett, David C. 2003. *Freedom Evolves*. New York: Viking Press.

Machan, Tibor R. 2004. *The Man Without a Hobby*. Lanham, Maryland: Hamilton Books.

————. 2000. *Initiative-Human Agency and Society*. Stanford, California: Hoover Institution Press.

Mozes, Eyal. Review of Dennett. Online at: http://www.objectivistcenter.org/navigator/articles/navtemozes_review-dennett.asp.

Nozick, Robert. 1974. *Anarchy, State, and Utopia*. New York: Basic Books.

O'Connor, Timothy. 2002. *Persons and Causes*. Oxford, U.K.: Oxford University Press.

Peikoff, Leonard. 1990. The Analytic-Synthetic Dichotomy in Ayn Rand. *Introduction to Objectivist Epistemology*. Edited by Harry Binswanger and Leonard Peikoff. New York: New American Library.

————. 1976. The Philosophy of Objectivism. Lecture Series.

Pols, Edward. 2002. Rational Action and the Complexity of Causality. *Journal of Theoretical and Philosophical Psychology* 22 (1) (Spring).

———. 1982. Acts of Our Being. *A Reflection on Agency and Responsibility.* Amherst, Massachusetts: University of Massachusetts Press.

Rand, Ayn. 1961. *For the New Intellectual.* New York: New American Library.

———. 1957. *Atlas Shrugged.* New York: New American Library.

Sperry, Roger W. 1983. *Science and Moral Priority.* New York: Columbia University Press.

———. 1976. Changing Concepts of Consciousness and Free Will. *Perspectives in Biology and Medicine* 9 (August): 9–19.

Chapter 8

Forced to Rule: *Atlas Shrugged* as a Response to Plato's *Republic*

Roderick T. Long

In *Atlas Shrugged* Ayn Rand offers us two brief glimpses of her protagonist, John Galt, as a young man. In both cases the youthful Galt is rising to address a crowded room. The first instance, narrated to Dagny Taggart by the hobo Jeff Allen, occurs at the mass meeting where the workers of the Twentieth Century Motor Company are voting to put into practice the Marxist slogan "From each according to his ability, to each according to his need." Allen tells Dagny: "When he stood up, we suddenly turned dead-still. ... He stood like a man who knew that he was right. I will put an end to this, once and for all, he said" (Rand 1996, 617).

The second instance (though chronologically earlier in Galt's career) appears in a recollection by philosophy professor Hugh Akston of his first meeting with Galt. As Akston explains to Dagny:

> At the end of that lecture, John got up to ask me a question. It was a question which, as a teacher, I would have been proud to hear from a student who'd taken six years of philosophy. It was a question pertaining to Plato's metaphysics, which Plato hadn't had the sense to ask of himself. (Rand 1996, 721)

Is it a coincidence that Rand pairs a passage in which Galt rises to challenge the collectivism of the Starnes plan with a passage in which Galt rises to challenge the philosophy of Plato? Or is Plato very much on Rand's mind throughout *Atlas Shrugged*?

While a number of Plato's works could be relevant here,[1] I shall focus on his most famous work, the *Republic*—which, like *Atlas Shrugged*, attempts to integrate metaphysical, epistemological, ethical, and political themes into a single unified vision. My suggestion is that *Atlas Shrugged* is intended by its author to offer a sustained critique of, and alternative to, some of the central ideas of *Plato's Republic*.[2]

The chief topic of the *Republic* is the nature of justice, both in the individual and in society. Plato's account of individual justice is in fact one that shares considerable affinity with Rand's egoistic ethical outlook (perhaps not so surprisingly, since Rand's ethics is a development of Aristotle's ethics, which in turn draws on these aspects of Plato's); indeed, the *Republic's* central ethical claim is that there is no conflict between justice and self-interest—that a life of moral integrity, properly understood, is the fulfillment of an individual's flourishing, not an obstacle to it. This of course is a theme that runs throughout Rand's work as well. The unjust man, Plato likewise tells us, measures his success by the extent to which he outdoes other men, whereas the just man pays no attention to such comparison with others and instead measures his success by how well he measures up to an objective standard (I. 349b–50c); this is precisely Rand's contrast between the second-hander and the creator, as dramatized in *The Fountainhead*. Moreover, Plato identifies the objective standard in question as the requirements of successful human life-functioning (I. 352d–4a), which is also the position endorsed in Galt's Speech (Rand 1996, 926–7).

But when we turn to Plato's account of social rather than individual justice, any parallels with Rand quickly disappear. Plato advocates a highly regimented and micromanaged class society; endorses eugenics and thought control; condemns private property and material wealth; and demands the sacrifice of individual welfare to the welfare of the community as a whole. The entire system is to be ruled by wise and just philosopher-kings, who are to derive no personal benefit from their rule; and if these philosopher-kings are reluctant to rule, they must be compelled to do so:

> The nature of the true ruler is to seek not his own advantage but that of the ruled. ... Any man of understanding would prefer to receive benefits from another rather than to benefit another. ... Good men will not be willing to rule for the sake of money or renown. ... Some compulsion or punishment must be imposed on them if they are to be willing to rule. (*Republic* I. 347b–d)[3]
>
> We must not permit [philosophers] what is now permitted them: ... to refuse to go down among the prisoners. ... When we compel them to care for the others we shall say ... we have arranged for you to be born ... as kings and leaders in the hive. ... You are better and more completely educated ... so you must each descend in turn to live in common with others. ... For the city whose rulers are least eager to rule must be best governed and freest from strife. (*Republic* VII. 519d–20d)

What explains the *Republic's* odd fusion of ethical individualism and political collectivism? In particular, how can Plato offer us an ethical theory in which morality requires no sacrifice of self-interest, and then append to this a political theory according to which the wisest people will be so reluctant to perform their duty that they may have to be compelled? Plato seems to tell us in a single breath both that accepting the job of philosopher-king involves a necessary sacrifice of one's personal happiness for the greater good, and that the philosopher-kings really will be supremely happy after all[4] (IV. 420b–d; V. 465e–6a; VII. 519e–20a; IX. 587b–8a).

Part of the solution to this enigma may lie in the fact of Plato's extreme pessimism about the prospects for the success of wisdom and virtue in the real world—a pessimism no doubt reinforced by the fate of his beloved teacher Socrates. The wisest pilot, Plato tells us, will be thrown overboard by his crew (VI. 488b–e); the man who tries to free his fellow-prisoners from the cave will be executed (VII. 516e–17a); ordinary people are so hopelessly corrupt that a just society can never be achieved unless everyone over ten years old is first expelled (VII. 541a), and even then such a society would be doomed to decay in the course of time (VIII. 545d–7c). Hence while Plato insists, rightly from Rand's point of view, that virtue is the path to happiness, he sees no prospect for the virtuous person to attain worldly success in ordinary life, and so is led to an otherworldly conception of happiness. True reality lies in the realm of theoretical abstractions, secure from the clutches of the rabble; the material world with its imperfections and disappointments is only a realm of shadows. As for the ideally just society, it "makes no difference whether it exists anywhere, or ever will exist," since it is "a paradigm established in heaven for anyone who wishes to contemplate it" (IX. 592b). The mind, frustrated in its efforts in the material realm, is unfettered and unimpeded only in the realm of spirit.

I don't claim that this is the only motivation for Plato's otherworldly metaphysics and epistemology;[5] there are purely philosophical reasons driving him as well. Indeed, Plato's pessimism may be partly the effect rather than the cause of his metaphysics. But whatever the etiology, Plato's dualistic worldview plausibly serves as the glue holding his ethical individualism and political collectivism together. Since real-life society is hopelessly enmired in materialistic corruption, only the edicts of people like him, ruthlessly enforced, could possibly bring order; the abolition of private property and personal affection is simply a corollary of the necessity of subjecting the distractions of appetite and material concerns to the higher ideals of reason and spirit.

In *Atlas Shrugged* the primary fictional embodiment of this Platonic ambivalence is the character of Robert Stadler, the brilliant physicist who in true Platonic fashion worships theoretical science but has only contempt for applied science. Stadler justifies his quest for political power in terms reminiscent of Plato's own pessimism about ordinary human beings and the rational man's prospects for success in an irrational world:[6]

They're mindless animals moved by irrational feelings—by their greedy, grasping, blind, unaccountable feelings! They seize whatever they want. ... The mind? Don't you know how futile it is, the mind, against those mindless hordes? Our weapons are so helplessly, laughably childish: truth, knowledge, reason, values, rights! ... You don't know how lonely I was, how starved for some spark of intelligence! ... Why should a mind like mine have to bargain with ignorant fools? They'd never contribute a penny to science! Why shouldn't they be forced? ... Don't you know how noble a purpose it was—my vision of the future of science? Human knowledge set free of material bonds! (Rand 1996, 1023–4)

Plato's insistence that intellectuals should rule, and his own failed efforts to implement his ideas by influencing the tyrant of Syracuse, are finally echoed in Stadler's futile attempt to "seize control of Project X and ... rule a part of the country as his private feudal domain" (1032).

From Rand's perspective, the nature of Stadler's mistake—and of Plato's—is to bifurcate the human identity into opposing material and spiritual aspects, "a struggle between a corpse and a ghost" (939), and to dismiss the material aspect as devoid of moral value. On the contrary, Rand has Galt insist, "an enormous investment of virtue—of intelligence, integrity, energy, skill—is required" to build the industrial civilization which mystics like Stadler dismiss as the concern of "vulgar realists" (948.) Stadler finds it "outrageous" that Galt, a man with "the genius of a great scientist," would choose to be a "commercial inventor"; like Plato, he sees such a choice as a subordination of spirit to matter, of reason to appetite. "Why," he wonders, "did he want to waste his mind on practical appliances?" Nor does he understand Dagny's answer: "Perhaps because he liked living on this earth" (337). For Stadler, to live on this earth is to surrender the mind.

Dagny, by contrast, represents an integrated, anti-Platonic view of spirit and matter. During the first run of the John Galt line she reflects on the spiritual meaning of the machinery surrounding her:

> These things and the capacity from which they came—was this the pursuit men regarded as evil? Was this what they called an ignoble concern with the physical world? ... Was this the surrender of man's spirit to his body? ... Every part of the motors was an embodied answer to "Why?" and "What for?"—like the steps of a life-course chosen by the sort of mind she worshipped. The motors were a moral code cast in steel. ... They are alive, she thought, because they are the physical shape of the action of a living power—of the mind that had been able to grasp the whole of this complexity, to set its purpose, to give it form (Rand 1996, 230–35).

But the productive workers, the craftsmen and laborers who wrestle directly with tainted physical reality, are relegated to the lowest and most mindless level of Plato's ideal society; yet for Rand they are the Atlases whose minds make that society's existence possible.

As Francisco d'Anconia tells Dagny:

> Dagny, we who've been called "materialists" by the killers of the human spirit, we're the only ones who know how little value or meaning there is in material objects as such, because we're the ones who create their value and meaning. ... Dagny, learn to understand the nature of your own power and you'll understand the paradox you now see around you. You do not have to depend on any material possessions, they depend on you, you create them, you own the one and only tool of production. Wherever you are, you will always be able to produce. But the looters—by their own stated theory—

are in desperate, permanent, congenital need and at the blind mercy of matter. ... Who gave them the means to enslave you? (571)

When Hank Rearden comes to a similar insight he thinks, significantly, of Plato: Rearden imagines himself speaking to "a long line of men stretched through the centuries from Plato onward," telling them that "if I had not made it my highest moral purpose to exercise the best of my effort and the fullest capacity of my mind ... you would have found nothing to loot from me ..." (Rand 1996, 517). It is material production, driven by embodied intelligence, that sustains the Platonists even as they fantasize about disembodied intelligence, cast aspersions on vulgar material concerns, and struggle to maintain their ideological control over the producers.

Rand's choice of Atlantis as a symbol for her utopia of liberated producers may also be directed in part against Plato. The first recorded reference to (and probably invention of) the legend of Atlantis occurs in Plato's dialogues *Timæus* and *Critias*, where Atlantis is explicitly introduced (Timæus 17c–27b; *Critias* 110c–114c) as the enemy of a city organized along the lines of Plato's *Republic*—thus making Atlantis the original anti-Platonic society[7] (it's also worth noting that "Atlantis" and "Atlas" are cognates, and that Plato identifies Atlas as the first ruler of Atlantis: *Critias* 114a).

It is appropriate that Rand pairs Galt's challenge to the Starnes plan with Galt's challenge to Plato; for the Starnes plan, though explicitly based on a Marxist slogan, owes much to the earlier communist ideal of the *Republic*. Plato argues that the abolition of private property would bring an end to conflict and envy in society, and promote civic harmony (V. 464a–5c); but in his critique of the *Republic*, Aristotle—the philosopher that Rand has Ragnar Danneskjöld call "our teacher's first teacher" (1059; cf. 1068)—replies that common ownership would on the contrary be likelier to increase social strife, since "recriminations are bound to arise between those who enjoy or receive much while working little and those who receive less but work more"[8] (*Politics* II. 2. 1263a12–15). Rand's account of the collapse of the Starnes plan reads like a commentary on this text of Aristotle's:

> When it's all one pot, you can't let any man decide what his own needs are, can you? If you did, he might claim that he needs a yacht. ... So it turned into a contest among six thousand panhandlers, each claiming that his need was worse than his brother's. ... We began to hide whatever ability we had, to slow down and watch like hawks that we never worked any faster or better than the next fellow. ... Love of our brothers? That's when we learned to hate our brothers for the first time in our lives. (608–12)

When the plan fails, Ivy Starnes, one of its chief instigators, takes predictable refuge in the Platonic complaint that "the plan was a noble ideal, but human nature was not good enough for it" (616), and embarks on a quest for "the release from bondage to flesh, the victory over physical nature, the triumph of spirit over matter" (301)—while renouncing as a "world enslaved by matter" the realm of "machines, manufacturers and money" that represents, for Rand, the only true locus of spirit's triumph over matter. Starnes, like Stadler (though not his equal in intellectual stature), is an embodiment of Platonism.

Atlas Shrugged does not represent Rand's first fictional engagement with the ideas of the *Republic*. The dystopian society depicted in her early novella Anthem—with its government assignment of professions, state regulation of breeding and reproduction, and abolition of the family—indeed seems more closely modeled on Plato's ideal society than anything in *Atlas Shrugged*; and the prohibition of the word "I" in favor of "we" is a natural development of the *Republic's* requirement (V. 462b–4d) that all citizens say "mine" and "not mine" about the same things.[9] But there is one crucial aspect of the *Republic* that is not taken up until *Atlas Shrugged*: the notion of the philosopher-king's being forced to rule. The hero of *Anthem* is not forced to rule; he is relegated to the Home of the Street-Sweepers. His intellectual prowess is rejected, not pressed into the service of the collective. But in *Atlas Shrugged* the villains first threaten Galt (1005–10) and then finally torture him (1042–9), all in an effort to get him to agree to become their ruler. "We want you to take full power over the economy of the country," Dr. Floyd Ferris tells Galt. "We want you to become a dictator. We want you to rule. Understand? We want you to give orders and to figure out the right orders to give" (1043). This central paradox of *Atlas Shrugged* is lifted straight out of Plato.

The villains' attempt to coerce Galt into becoming their dictator dramatizes Rand's thesis that the Platonic contempt for material production disguises an unacknowledged dependence on just such production—an insight Rand had not yet reached in Anthem. It is the willingness of the Atlases of production to be harnessed, their willingness to keep the system going, that maintains the "mystics of spirit" in power. Forcing Galt to "rule" means forcing him to use the power of his intellect to figure out "the exact measures you'll take to save our system" (1043), to "give the orders" and "issue the directives" that will "make things work" (1007–8).

The hollowness of the entire system is revealed when the Atlases "shrug," withdrawing their cooperation. As in Hegel's master-slave dialectic,[10] true power ultimately lies with the subjugated producer, not with his subjugator—since the subjugator depends on the producer but not vice versa. This dependence is most chillingly dramatized in the final torture scene, when Galt forces his parasitic captors to realize that their very ability to operate the torture device they are using on him depends on the cooperation of productive intellects like himself (1047).

Plato's work is torn by an unresolved ambiguity as to whether the soul's descent into the material realm is a regrettable calamity (e.g., *Phaedrus* 246b–9c) or a providential imposition of order on unruly matter (e.g., *Timœus* 41b–2c); as we've seen, there is an analogous ambiguity in the Republic as to whether the philosopher-king's acceptance of the responsibilities of political administration makes for a life of painful duty or joyous fulfillment. The source of Plato's ambivalence here, Rand shows us, is his contempt for involvement in material concerns combined with his reluctant half-recognition that the theoretical and spiritual activities he values depend for their continued existence on just such involvement. Hence the realm of worldly affairs appears to him both as a distraction to be shunned and as a necessity to be embraced; he cannot resolve the contradiction because it is based on a deeper unresolved contradiction, a matter/spirit dichotomy. Since life depends on material business, such business, Plato feels at one level, must be embraced as a value; yet life should, Plato feels at another level, be independent of such unreliable concerns, and so material business is simultaneously disvalued.

Plato's conflicting attitudes on this issue also shed light on the *Republic's* unstable union of ethical individualism and political collectivism. The moral life, Plato sees, must be one of joyous and successful self-interested flourishing. But since on Plato's view the everyday world is irremediably hostile to such flourishing, the realm of success must be a purely spiritual one. All involvement with material production, then, though admittedly necessary, acquires the flavor of a sacrifice of personal happiness, a departure from the realm wherein fulfillment is possible, a life lived for others rather than oneself—and so the individualist aspect gives way to the collectivist one. The logic of Plato's position thus sets his own fundamental values in conflict with one another.

Failing to recognize the spiritual aspect of material production, Plato distinguishes the intellectual class that must give the orders from the producers who must carry the orders out. But because, as Rand sees, the spiritual and material aspects of production cannot truly be so divided, the supposedly exalted philosopher-king inevitably ends up taking on the characteristics of just one more subjugated laborer. John Galt, at once an engineer and a philosopher, likewise combines the character of Plato's producers, compelled to labor, and the character of Plato's philosopher-kings, compelled to rule. And Galt's refusal either to rule or to obey—his vow neither to "live for the sake of another man, nor ask another man to live for mine" (Rand 1996, 670–72)—shatters the foundation of the Platonic system and brings it down in ruins.

Notes

1   For example, *Atlas Shrugged's* treatment of sex and romantic love, as dramatized in the inner conflicts of the character of Hank Rearden, might be read as in part a comment on Plato's rather different treatment of those subjects in his *Symposium* and *Phædrus*.

2   It is a matter of controversy whether Plato is properly regarded as endorsing the arguments he attributes to the Socrates character in his dialogues. I think the correct answer is a (qualified) yes, but I shall not defend that interpretation here, since what matters for present purposes is that Rand in any case thinks so.

3   All translations from Plato or Aristotle are mine.

4   One is reminded of Ellsworth Toohey's assurance to Catherine Halsey, in *The Fountainhead*, that one must "kill the most stubborn of roots, the ego," and "only when it is dead … will you know the kind of happiness I spoke about, and the gates of spiritual grandeur will fall open before you" (Rand 1993, 365).

5   Though this interpretation of Plato's motives does cohere well with Leonard Peikoff's analysis of the myth of the demiurge in Plato's *Timæus*:

> Matter, we are told, was originally unformed and chaotic; a godlike soul enters and tries to shape the chaos into a realm of perfect beauty. The demiurge, however, fails; matter proves to be recalcitrant; it takes the imprint of beauty only so far, and thereafter resists all efforts to perfect it. Hence, Plato concludes, matter is a principle of imperfection, inherently in conflict with the highest ideals of the spirit. In a perfect universe, matter should obey consciousness without reservation. Since it does not, the universe … is flawed; it is a perpetual battleground of the noble vs. the actual (Peikoff 1993, 29).

In fairness to Plato it should perhaps be added that the otherworldly character of his philosophy gets considerably moderated in later dialogues like the *Sophist* and *Philebus*, while the authoritarian and collectivist character of his politics likewise gets moderated (though admittedly not much) in later dialogues like the *Statesman* and Laws.

6   Rand also addresses this sort of pessimism in her play Ideal (Rand 1986, 205–90), as well as by means of the characters of Dominique Francon and Gail Wynand in *The Fountainhead*.

7   It's puzzling how often commentators describe Plato's Atlantis as his vision of utopia. Plato's utopia is clearly the ideal state described in the *Republic*, and transposed in the *Timæus* and *Critias* to prehistoric Athens. Atlantis by contrast is portrayed as a society corrupted by pride and ambition that wages war against this ideal state.

8   For a Rand-influenced study of Aristotle's criticisms of Plato's political philosophy see Mayhew 1997.

9   I would also hypothesize that Equality 7-2521's journey down into an abandoned subway tunnel to discover an artificial light source is a deliberate inversion of Plato's allegory of the cave in *Republic* VII, in which the wise man ascends from the cave of physical reality, lit by the artificial light of the senses, to discover the "real" world of abstract Forms, lit by a sun of pure ineffable intellect. Rand's anti-Platonic trope of enlightenment lying underground (the Taggart tunnels and cafeteria; cf. Minsaas 2005, 30–31; McCloskey 2005, 140) or underwater (the "Atlantis" theme: e.g., Rand 1996, 147) runs throughout Atlas Shrugged as well.

10   For the place of Hegel's master-slave dialectic in Rand's thought, see Sciabarra 1995, 300–310.

References

Mayhew, Robert. 1997. *Aristotle's Criticism of Plato's "Republic."* New York: Rowman & Littlefield.

McCloskey, Susan. 2005. Odysseus, Jesus, and Dagny: Ayn Rand's reconception of the hero. In Thomas 2005, 119–43.

Minsaas, Kirsti. 2005. Structural Integration in *The Fountainhead* and *Atlas Shrugged*. In Thomas 2005, 17–37.

Peikoff, Leonard. 1991. *Objectivism: The Philosophy of Ayn Rand*. New York: Dutton Plume.

Rand, Ayn. 1996. *Atlas Shrugged*. New York: Signet.

———. 1995. *Anthem*. New York: Signet.

———. 1993. *The Fountainhead*. New York: Signet.

———. 1986. *The Early Ayn Rand: A Selection from Her Unpublished Fiction*. New York: Signet.

Sciabarra, Chris Matthew. 1995. *Ayn Rand: The Russian Radical*. University Park: Pennsylvania State University Park.

Thomas, William, ed. 2005. *The Literary Art of Ayn Rand*. Poughkeepsie: Objectivist Center.

Chapter 9

The Role and Essence of John Galt's Speech in Ayn Rand's *Atlas Shrugged*

G. Stolyarov II

Throughout *Atlas Shrugged,* Ayn Rand successively builds upon her plot to furnish an explanation for the collapse of the society of looters she portrays. John Galt's speech (923–79) is the culmination of this development, furnishing the most complete and philosophically integrated explanation for Galt's strike and his continuing removal of great minds from service to the looters. Moreover, it presents Rand with an opportunity to employ the story of *Atlas Shrugged* as a means to convey not only an implicit worldview, which can be found in every description and dialogue in the book, but also a systematic, thorough, unambiguous philosophy. Indeed, Galt's speech is the backbone of Rand's Objectivism, and serves a purpose outside its necessity to *Atlas Shrugged* itself, namely, to create a foundation of interest in and understanding of Objectivism and thus encourage readers to explore Randian thought in greater depth.

Context and Content

The entirety of the plot of *Atlas Shrugged* relies on a mystery: Who is John Galt? What is his role in the world's collapse? Why would he wish to accelerate its coming? When Dagny Taggart crash-lands in Galt's Gulch, she meets Galt in person for the first time and learns of the mechanisms by which Galt's strike is undertaken and rational men are removed from the control of the parasites who seek to enslave them while demanding them to continue to work in chains. From then on, the mystery becomes successively unraveled, until, in Galt's speech, the entire country becomes informed of the full depth of Galt's reasoning behind the strike, and the nature of his grievances against the types of government and society which he has renounced. The fact that the speech is broadcast by radio in place of Mr. Thompson's planned report to the country furnishes an ideal setting for the content of Galt's words. The radio is a marvelous feat of engineering, requiring an immense degree of both theoretical and technical knowledge to create and operate.

John Galt, inventor extraordinaire, possesses the skills needed to gain control over an airwave, while Mr. Thompson, the archetypical parasite, does not. Thompson has only had access to radio in the first place due to the tacit consent of shackled creators like Galt. Galt has but to withdraw his moral approval from such exploitation, and Mr. Thompson remains incapable of effective retaliation. Galt is able to flawlessly present his message, in a calm, deliberate voice, showing thereby a key insight of Rand's: the looters, moochers, and thugs of this world—indeed, all things evil—are powerless in the face of an impeccably rational man who does not allow them to subsist off the fruits of his productive work.

The content of the speech, like its setting, develops Galt's core thesis: that the triumph of evil can be facilitated only by the moral sanction of evil on the part of the good. Galt begins by addressing the looters themselves and the vast multitudes of mediocrities who had embraced the anti-rational doctrines which made the looters possible, mediocrities who nevertheless gape in fear at the destruction and chaos that now prevails in the world. Galt's shocking revelation to them is that such devastation has occurred not in spite of the mystics' moral code, but because of it. Though the mystics make an obsession of claiming that the path to prosperity lies outside the mind and brand the men of the mind as useless, Galt penetrates into the mystics' psychology and reveals that they know otherwise, that the dominant emotion guiding anti-rational doctrinaires is fear of a world the sole means of survival in which they have rejected. To escape this terror, the mystics must enslave the men of the mind and ruthlessly denigrate them, so that their rationality can sustain the mystics who have tossed aside rationality themselves. But the mystics' rejection of reason also renders the continuation of their lifestyle and the simultaneous continuation of the work of the men of reason mutually incompatible. Since "in any compromise between food and poison, it is only death that can win" (965), the mystics assure their own eventual death by the very impossibility of using the tribal ideology prevalent in a primeval jungle to "take over" and successfully manage skyscrapers, factories, and railroads. Since the antithesis of a rational life is non-life, or "the reign of the zero," the mystics must receive it in full eventually, but the question is: how soon? Will the rational man allow himself to be gradually worn down through the dictates of his overlords so as to sustain them for some time longer, or will he deny them outright and hasten their collapse?

Galt's speech is the beginning of Rand's colossal intellectual effort to debunk false dichotomies, including the split between mind and body which implies the fabricated antagonism between the "mystics of spirit" and the "mystics of muscle," one side advocating the view of the "virtuous" man as a ghost, the other—a corpse, both wishing, in reality, to co-opt his intellect and chain his body. The rational man is opposed to both sides of this dichotomy, since he understands that man's nature, in reality, is that of an integrated entity, whose mind and body must work in unison, or not at all. He will not be misled by visions of another life in a celestial realm where the soul is separate from the body, or of a utopian communistic paradise where the body exists in the absence of the mind and resources appear ...

somehow. Moreover, Galt's speech demolishes the dichotomies between theory and practice and between practice and morality by a clear exposition of the fact that a moral system which conflicts with the real-world requirements of human survival and prosperity brings a man closer to death the more he adheres to it, thus rendering complete fidelity to the system impossible. The refusal to relate the conclusions of a theory to man's material condition in the real world, as exemplified by Dr. Robert Stadler, is tantamount to asserting that reason and science have no value to man's life, and demanding, at the same time, that the government pour lavish funds into public laboratories to isolate scientific research from the free market and its dynamic of furthering life. Since the mystics' moral code can never be practiced with full consistency so long as the practitioners live, it is not a valid system, and John Galt is justified in stating that the collapsing society has never truly known morality and that, if it is ever to rise again, its members must discover it.

Foundations of Morality

If the old dichotomies and perceived antagonisms have been exploded, what is the foundation of the true morality? Galt's speech identifies it to lie at the very core of logic itself. It is the Aristotelian proposition, never quite grasped by the majority of the collapsing society, that A equals A, i.e., that a thing is itself and cannot be something else at the same time and in the same respect. From this principle, Galt draws three axiomatic, self-verifying corollaries: existence, identity, and consciousness. Something exists, it has a specific nature, and we must exist and be conscious of it, else we would not have grasped the former two truths. Galt's speech formulates the core of Objectivist metaphysics, the branch of philosophy which deals with the most fundamental concepts and generalizations pertaining to the whole of reality. Rand understands reality as strictly absolute, the nature of its existents remaining independent of anyone's wishes, whims, or feelings, and the essence of virtue characterized by a consistent recognition of and adherence to such absolutism in one's life and dealings with others. The primary offense of the mystic, states Galt, is the attempt to evade this fact:

> The extreme you have always struggled to avoid is the recognition that reality is final, that A is A and the truth is true. A moral code impossible to practice, a code that demands imperfection or death, has taught you to dissolve all ideas in a fog, to permit no firm definitions, to regard any concept as approximate and any rule of conduct as elastic, to hedge on any principle, to compromise on any value, to take the middle of the road. (965)

The result of accepting Rand's objective metaphysics, on the contrary, is an emphasis on the need for absolute perfection, not in one's factual knowledge or physical skill (since no man is omnipotent or omniscient), but in one's integrity in recognizing things for what they are and not seeking to escape the truth which appears before one's senses and reasoning mind. In discussing this, Galt's speech introduces Rand's innovations in the second branch of philosophy: epistemology, the study of knowledge and how humans can validly interact with reality. Galt states that the sole gateway to understanding is logic, defined as "the art of non-contradictory identification" (930), whose accurate practice requires that the individual allow no mutually incompatible statements, ideas, or data to pervade his thinking, once the incompatibility has been identified and confirmed. The application of logic to the data of reality is called reason, and it is indispensable to the individual. Galt emphasizes repeatedly that, even if an individual were to deliberately leave only a single island of irrationality in his life, this would mean automatically subverting all truth, all reality, and all his understanding thereof to this sacred realm beyond all question, to be accepted blindly on faith, the antithesis of reason. Thus, the tactic of compromising between the mystics and the men of thought, the act of rationality and irrationality striking a pact in the "middle of the road" can only lead to the greatest ruin possible for reason, since unreason can only thrive under such conditions (as pure, unmitigated unreason dooms its practitioners instantly).

Values, Virtues, and Rights

Having explained the absolutism of reality and the necessity of reason, Galt's speech develops Rand's insights in the third branch of philosophy, ethics, dealing with the nature of man's desired behavior and goals. In a streamlined and rigorously constructed passage (932–4) Rand lays out the three primary values of her egoist/individualist morality: Reason, Purpose, and Self-Esteem, and the seven virtues, habits of the body and mind, which are essential to obtaining those values: rationality, independence, integrity, honesty, justice, productiveness, and pride. It is instructive to note that these virtues encompass the entire scope of activity needed for a man to survive and prosper, and can direct him in establishing a proper conception of his treatment of himself, his relationship to others, and his study and transformation of the inanimate world—and they are quite possible to practice.

Under the egoist framework, Galt is able to recognize as heinously flawed the doctrine of Original Sin, which condemns man as evil and morally unworthy beyond any possibility for complete redemption. Rand's morality is not a tool for human suffering and self-loathing, but rather for the pursuit of individual happiness, from the desirability of which Galt's speech removes all qualms. Galt advises his audience to re-visit the state when, as children yet uncontaminated by the chronic guilt permeating a society built on the mystics' value-premises, they were able to wake each morning and face each day with the inviolate certainty of living in a rational universe. In a remarkable insight into human motivations, Rand traces the roots of the various myths of lost paradises in early history (from one of which comes the idea of Original Sin) not to actual events in mankind's distant past but to the past of the minds of the majority of people living in a society of contradictory premises, a past in which they had been able to enjoy the limitless potential rendered available by the exercise of reason, but a past that they had renounced. Perhaps the true Original Sin can be attributed not to all men, but only to those who have volitionally accepted a permutation of the mystics' code, and have thereby fallen from the state of complete grace and happiness which is only possible through a consistent application of reason and focus on this world.

The fourth branch of philosophy, politics, the study of the proper structure of human society, features prominently in Galt's speech, whose very broadcast is symbolic of the triumph of the power of individual innovation and rationality in rendering resistance by a totalitarian regime futile. The foundation of Objectivist politics is the idea of individual rights, derived, not from God or from society, but rather from the nature or identity of man as a rational being. Man is an individual organism, and nobody else can think in his place and suit the needs of his mind, just as nobody else can eat in his place and suit the needs of his stomach. In accordance with this inextricable fact, "Rights are conditions of existence required by man's nature for his proper survival. If man is to live on earth, it is right for him to use his mind, it is right to act on his own free judgment, it is right to work for his values and to keep the product of his work" (972). Because reason is an individual faculty and the objects of morality are individual goals, no external entity should coercively intervene with an individual's attempts to discover his own objective needs by a rational process. The greatest evil, and the most grievous political wrong, is the initiation of force by one party against another, be the offender a private criminal or a government. Initiating force against an individual is the equivalent of placing him in a double bind of death; he will either follow the requirements of reality, but be met by the barrel of a gun, or he will bow down to the gun, at the expense of his link to reality, his autonomous mind. Only retaliatory force is acceptable, and only because the retaliator seeks no positive gain from his use of force. He does not wish to loot the products of others' reason, but merely to "destroy destruction." To use force in response to criminals and tyrants has only the potential of preserving an individual's present values, but not of augmenting them. Thereby John Galt presents a defense of his friend turned pirate, Ragnar Danneskjold, who attacks only the convoys of goods that the looters had stolen from the producers, and always with the purpose of returning the wealth to its creators.

Furthermore, Galt's speech conveys Rand's firm conviction that property rights are indispensable to a consistent understanding of individual freedom. There can be no true liberty of thought without the liberty to implement one's thought in the material world, and to own the results of one's thought and work, i.e., one's property. Rand masterfully refutes the false dichotomy between "human rights" and property rights, stating that whoever perceives this split believes that some men have an automatic claim on the produce of others. Since those who are incompetent to produce themselves have nothing to trade with the producers, they resort, under such a false dichotomy, to expropriate the producers to fulfill their "basic human rights." But, states John Galt, "Whoever regards this as human and right, has no right to the title of 'human'" (973). Indeed, men ought to treat one another not as masters, slaves, rulers, dependents, or pack animals, but rather as traders who are free to exchange value for value on mutually agreeable terms. The entire story of *Atlas Shrugged* exhibits a marked contrast between the harmony in the relations of those who recognize the trader principle and the chaos, deceit, and violence among those who reject it as "vulgar" or "base," who, despite the tremendous improvement that the enterprise of the best minds among men has brought to the lives of even the least skilled janitor, have refused to grant the men of the mind a simple request: to be allowed to think, act, trade, and create as they see fit, and to enjoy the wealth they earned as profit, a payment which, according to Rand, can never suffice to reward the most productive among men, since the sum of the values they bring into existence far exceeds their compensation. Pure, unmitigated economic laissez-faire is indeed quite a reasonable reward to ask for the tremendous gifts that the best of men bestow upon everyone by the sheer fact of their activity, yet the mystics' mentality of sacrifice and coercion prevents the collapsing society from granting even this request. That the mystics and looters refuse to consent to laissez-faire further underscores the sheer malice of their true intentions. The anti-rational doctrinaires seek not to prosper themselves, but rather to diminish, suppress, and destroy the quality of life for others, and then to have their theories be called upon to justify the existence of the resulting misery.

Consequences and Extensions

In the aftermath of Galt's speech, the looters in the government, academia, and politicized industry are unable to respond or even formulate a coherent plan of approach toward Galt and his message. Chaos reigns in the studio where the key looter officials are gathered. Their reactions are precisely what Galt's speech foretold: evasion of facts, reliance on inter-subjective rather than objective views of reality, fear of "extremes," and a blatant rejection of reason. Finally, through a devious plan by Mr. Thompson to "try to meet Galt halfway," Galt is captured by the looters and given a choice to either accept an offer to rebuild their society or to face torture. However, Galt resists them stoically; he lives up to his statement in the speech that he has nothing to gain from the looters, and that they cannot harm him in any way if he withdraws his consent. In the end, Galt is saved by the efforts of his fellow rational thinkers and creators, while the looters' society destroys itself, thus showing that no amount of physical force, intimidation, and desperate last-minute efforts on the part of the enemies of reason to save themselves can have any effect against the man of the mind who does not allow his mind to be compromised in any way.

In the fifth branch of philosophy, esthetics, it may be asked how Galt's speech can be consistent with Rand's literary style of Romantic Realism, which emphasizes the conveyance of abstractions not by means of direct philosophical exposition, but rather through the actions and dialogue of characters, as well as through careful selection and description of scenery and details. However, Rand has already presented the entirety of the evidence needed for the reader to infer the conclusions made by Galt's speech in the story which has led up to it. Thus, Rand has already shown the reader the interplay of the concepts that Galt will speak about. But, since the depth, breadth, originality, and precision of Rand's insights are unprecedented, it would have been unwise to expect readers to piece the intellectual puzzle together themselves and then be left without a solution key to it, which Galt's speech provides. Since *Atlas Shrugged* is a sweeping philosophical mystery story, the nature of the crime being committed in it is not a mere isolated theft or murder, but a massive war against man's mind, explaining whose circumstances and essence could be reasonably expected to take sixty-six pages. Galt is the philosophical detective, presenting his brilliant solution to the case which has perplexed the world for twelve years, a solution not only in terms of "who did it," but also in terms of "how to correct it." Moreover, Galt's speech never departs from the storyline of *Atlas Shrugged*, often taking the form of Galt's address to his friends and nemeses alike, presenting to Francisco and Ragnar a vindication of their lifestyles during the collapse, offering a defense of Hank Rearden against the brutal abuses dealt him by the looters, accusing Dr. Stadler of the greatest possible intellectual treason against reality, and urging Dagny to give up on the looters' world, lest her titanic efforts serve to prolong the parasites' existence. However abstract, intricate, and lengthy it may be, Galt's speech remains, unambiguously, an event in *Atlas Shrugged*, maintaining the story's dynamic and captivating pace by means of the presentation of the philosophy of Objectivism using the same brisk, colorful language that characterizes the succession of prior and succeeding events in the novel. However, in the true spirit of Romantic Realism, the speech's implications extend far beyond the story itself, furnishing a timeless commentary on the human condition: on the state of man who is enslaved, man who is the enslaver, and man who is neither and prospers as a result of his own mind. Moreover, though Galt's speech presents the core of Objectivist philosophy, there is much more to be said about each of its five branches, a task pursuing which would take Rand many more years, non-fiction books, and magazine articles. The further development of Objectivism is an endeavor which still yields intellectual discoveries decades after Rand's death.

By giving readers the basics of Objectivism in Galt's speech, both as part of a dynamic story and as a systematic exposition worthy of the highest standards of intellectual scholarship, Rand gives them the interest and tools to become Objectivist philosophers in their own right, to explore further Objectivist books and treatises already in existence, and to develop the philosophy using the only genuine means of understanding reality: their own minds. Rand exhorts her readers to enter into a process of continual thought and continual refinement of their ideas; she recognizes that any man of reason, be he a scientist, philosopher, or businessman, will make errors of knowledge, since no man is omnipotent or omniscient. But, as Galt would say, an error made on one's own is superior to ten truths accepted on faith, since the former still leaves open the means to correct the mistake, while the latter annihilates the individual's very link to reality and ability to further refine his understanding thereof. While Rand considers the entirety of Galt's speech to be the irrefutable truth, she does not wish readers to acquiesce to it on blind faith, due to their "trust" of Rand as a philosophical authority. Rather, she asks nothing less than a complete understanding and integration of the contents of the speech into each individual's mind—that each man may know exactly why Rand wrote what she did and decide in his own capacity as a thinker if he agrees with her, and why. Objectivism, ultimately, is a tool for each man to live his own life and discover purposes consistent with his own nature as an individual, and Rand does readers a tremendous service through Galt's speech by not only presenting the fundamental concepts of the philosophy, but also the core methodology which each man should use when interacting with any data or ideas whatsoever.

PART 3
Literary Aspects

Chapter 10

Ayn Rand's Cinematic Eye

Mimi Reisel Gladstein

A young girl with large, dark, soulful eyes sits in the darkened movie theater, her gaze intent on the screen. Nothing on the screen escapes her keen examination— the angle of the shot—the perspective of the camera eye. Outside the theater is the drab and dreary world of the Soviet Republics, but on the screen is a vision of a world Alisa Rosenbaum could aspire to, a world she was to create, destroy, and rebuild in her own artistic vision. Writing for the screen became her goal.

By the time that young girl had become Ayn Rand, world famous novelist, Alisa Rosenbaum had achieved her goal. We are all familiar with the story of how the inexperienced young woman, armed only with a Remington Rand typewriter, and speaking the language inexpertly, landed a job with a titan of the film world, Cecil B. De Mille. Her first job in the film industry was, ironically for this atheist, as an extra in the religious film *King of Kings*. Subsequently, she was to work in the movie industry in a variety of capacities. Rand wrote synopses and suggestions for how to adapt properties to screen; she then worked in the wardrobe department of RKO before becoming a screenwriter. Her first income from writing in Hollywood came from selling her original screenplay *Red Pawn*. For many years Rand labored as a reader for both Paramount and MGM. At one point, she was under contract to Hal Wallis for whom she wrote the screenplays for *Love Letters* and *You Came Along*. Unlike a number of the big name fiction writers who first made their names by publishing short stories and novels and then reluctantly went to Hollywood, Ayn Rand's initial destination, once she got to this country, was American's movie capital. And, whereas writers such as F. Scott Fitzgerald and William Faulkner are on record as having "despised the collaborative hack-work" of movies (Mandal 13), Rand's concept of film was affirmative. For her Hollywood was the incarnation and culmination of the American Dream.

The role of the celluloid world in Ayn Rand's life cannot be overemphasized. Speaking of the importance of movies in her life, Ayn Rand remembers that as a young woman she "began to see movies every night. That was one of my happiest periods in Russia, in that it was almost as if I had a private avenue of seeing the world outside." One image from that period that remained engraved on her inner artistic eye is a shot of "the New York skyline, usually long shots, and I would sit through two shows just to catch it. It was just a glimpse but seemed completely incredible. I can't tell you how glamorous it was at that distance. My enthusiasm for America was formed then" (1999, 9). Not only did Rand's goal of going to the United States form then, but writing for the screen served as her elementary school as a creative artist. Though her greatest successes as an author came first from writing for the theatre and then as a novelist, evidence of her basic film training are sprinkled through her works, nowhere more tellingly than in her magnum opus *Atlas Shrugged*. From beginning to end, in what was to become her final novel, there is evidence of Ayn Rand's cinematic eye.

Substantiation of the influence of Rand's movie training appears in smaller and larger measure throughout *Atlas Shrugged*. For illustration, let us begin with how Dagny Taggart, the novel's protagonist and heroine, is introduced. It is decidedly cinematic, using Classical Hollywood cinema conventions. As yet not identified to the reader, Dagny is presented in what film texts refer to as an "establishing shot." She is framed at a train window. Rand directs the staging of the scene with her description of Dagny's position, "head thrown back, one leg stretched across to the empty seat before her" (12). A bleak tone is set as the camera eye focuses on the train window that frames "empty darkness" with only occasional flashes of light, thus establishing both the dreariness outside and Dagny's comfort within her own train space. Then, with a typical screen convention of the period, our eye is directed, not at the thrown back head, but at that stretched out leg. Laura Mulvey has identified it as the masculine gaze of the camera eye, what other feminist film critics describe as the "to-be-looked-at" presentation of women in film.[1] Marlene Dietrich, one of Rand's favorite actresses, was often presented in just this way as erotic object for both the audience and the male characters in the narrative of the film through a close-up of her famous legs. Thus, we readers, through Rand's direction of the narrative eye, which is analogous with the camera eye, move from a long shot to a close-up, not of Dagny, but of her leg. "Her leg, sculptured by the tight sheen of the stocking, its long line running straight over an arched instep, to the tip of a foot in a high-heeled pump, had a feminine elegance ..." (12). In this time of short shorts, mini-skirts, and film nudity, the sight of a leg does not have the same erotic impact that it did in the period of Rand's film training. But, when *Atlas Shrugged* was written Rand employed that film shorthand for female sexuality to introduce her heroine.

Rand's focus on Dagny's legs is but one instance of how her Hollywood training of seeing women through the masculine perspective of the camera eye affected her text. Throughout the novel, Dagny is described from the viewpoint of the male gaze, often with the emphasis on her legs. When Dagny and Francisco climb a cliff as teenagers, "he stood looking at her" and what he sees, besides "her shoulder showing through the torn shirt" is "her long, scratched, sunburned legs" (97). A beautiful woman, with her clothes partially torn off, is an iconic image for a movie poster. Even when the point of view is female, the emphasis is on what a man would see and find appealing. Dagny's mother focuses on her "long show girl legs" (102). The text is quite explicit, as it describes Dagny from Mrs. Taggart's perspective, that what is being presented is the girl/woman as she would be on display for male delectation. The scene is her debut, shorthand for being put "on the marriage market." Seeing Dagny all dressed up for her first ball, her mother stares at her with "shocked admiration." She thinks that "Dagny's bearing seemed almost indecent, because this was the way a woman would have faced a ballroom centuries ago, when the act of displaying one's half-naked body for the admiration of men was an act of daring ..." (103).

Dagny's entrance at the Rearden anniversary party is presented from a decidedly male camera eye.

> It was a black dress with a bodice that fell as a cape over one arm and shoulder, leaving the other bare; the naked shoulder was the gown's only ornament. ... The black dress seemed excessively revealing—because it was astonishing to discover that the lines of her shoulder were fragile and beautiful, and that the diamond band on the wrist of her naked arm gave her the most feminine of all aspects: the look of being chained. (136)

What but the male gaze would find the look of being chained the most attractive feminine aspect?

The masculine gaze of the camera eye is also evident in the scene of Dagny and Hank's first coupling. "He stood looking down at her naked body" the narrative explains (252). But then, "She knew that what she felt with the skin of her arms was the cloth of his shirt" (252). A standard of the masculine perspective is that female is nude, but the male isn't. Why does he have a shirt on while she is naked? The next morning, her nude body is meticulously described. "She looked at the glowing bands on the skin of her arm, spaced like bracelets from her wrist to her shoulder. They were strips of sunlight from the Venetian blinds on the window of an unfamiliar room" (253). The narration makes us aware of "the curve of her naked shoulder," but when the camera eye turns to Hank, it is on his eyes and his face. He dresses, and again, there is no description of his naked body—but instead what we view is his buttoning his shirt, and buckling the belt of his slacks. After he, fully dressed, gives her his "what I feel is contempt" and "it's depravity" speech, "She threw the blanket off with a stressed, deliberate sweep of her arm. She stood up. She saw her clothes on the floor and kicked them aside. She stood facing him, naked" (255). The influence of the celluloid world's traditional presentation of sexuality is blatant. The man is dressed; the woman is naked. It was not till after Rand's death that male nudity became a staple of world cinema.[2] Also at work in this scene is a classical cinematic technique called the shot/reverse shot formation. This formation is the cinematic equivalent of what Rand achieves by the changing points-of-view in her narrative. We are moved from the female to the male perspective and back. First we see Dagny from Hank's perspective; then we see her and then him through her eyes, though priority is given to identification with the male gaze. The camera accomplishes this by shooting first over the shoulder of one character and thus showing what that person would be seeing and then moving to the opposite direction so that the viewing subject becomes the viewed, thus we have a shot and then the reverse of that shot.[3] Rand's narrator presents these scenes in that manner.

Once, when Nathaniel Branden asked Rand why there was only one heroic woman, and variations on the heroic male in *Atlas Shrugged*, she responded that the novel was her fantasy, indicating that it was a woman's and not a man's wish fulfillment.[4] Still, her many years in Hollywood seem to have affected even her dramatization of a woman's fantasy, and though Dagny is the protagonist of *Atlas Shrugged*, the narrative, or as I argue, cinematic focus is on Dagny's body and not on the objects of her desire. In a love scene between her and Hank, Dagny looks down at herself and a strap of her slip had broken, the slip hanging diagonally from her one shoulder. Hank is "looking at her breast under the transparent film of the blouse. She raised her hand to adjust the strap. He slapped her hand down" (278). She again smiles mockingly and walks across the room. Then we are thrust into his perspective as he looks at her, at a "contrast he liked—the severity of her clothes, and the half-naked body, the railroad executive who was a woman he owned" (279). Again, the narrative cries for a shot/reverse shot formation, although the camera eye is not on Hank's body except for as it appears in his clothing. A fantasy, written from the perspective of woman, but for the strong influence of how Hollywood visualized sexuality, would have presented a more vivid portrayal of male physicality.

Lest I be accused of anachronistic critiquing, in not understanding the conventions of the presentation of male and female nudity of the times, let me argue that Rand breaks many of the contemporary conventions of sexuality. Rand's revolutionary and egalitarian presentation of female sexuality and the interconnection of mind and body are vital to what is so groundbreaking about this novel. Conventional morality would have categorized Dagny, who had pre-marital sexual relations starting as a teenager, then becomes the mistress of a married man, and while in that relationship begins another sexual relationship, as a villainess or fallen woman. Since Rand defied all such conformist thinking to make Dagny heroic and admirable, and since this was, after all a female fantasy, why is it that the men are not presented as the objects of her gaze in the same manner as she is presented? My supposition, in the context of this essay, is that she was so influenced by the traditional male gaze of the camera eye, that this is how she saw the love scenes. Woman as she appears to men is the perspective of the movie camera and thus the narrational perspective of Rand's presentation.

That Rand saw the narrative perspective of the writer as analogous to the camera eye is validated by what she taught about fiction writing. Erika Holzer remembers Rand telling her that in writing she had to be like a camera, not trying to describe everything in a scene, but being selective, and picking out specific things to focus on.[5] This awareness of the correlation of the eye of the author and the lens of the camera also evidences itself in how Rand depicts many of the scenes of the novel. Possible camera angles and focus suggest themselves throughout *Atlas Shrugged*. For example: the long shot is obviously called for when the narrator explains: "Rearden stood at the other end of the long room, looking at her." Then the camera switches to his perspective: "He watched her as she approached, but he did not step forward to meet her" (137). Another character who is introduced in long shot is Francisco. "In the lighted doorway, the length of the room between them, he saw the tall, arrogant figure of a man who had paused for a moment before entering" (140). In this case, it is Rearden whose extended eye defines the camera shot. Often a scene is ended in a long shot. After Dagny and Hank find the discarded motor at the ruins of the Twentieth Century Motor Company, Dagny looks down at the motor and then out to the country. The chapter ends as Hank looked out "Far below, in the valley, in the gathering night, there trembled a few pale smears which were the light of tallow candles" (291).

Earlier in this essay, Rand's comment about the long shot of the New York skyline as a key image in her young life is cited. In *Atlas Shrugged*, that iconographic cinematic image appears and reappears throughout. The lights of New York City are both synecdoche and metonymy for the city, the country, and civilization. When those lights go out, Atlas has shrugged and the building can begin again. One of the final long or panoramic shots in the novel is when, viewed from the airplane over New York City, there is that moment when the occupants of the plane realize "that the lights of New York had gone out" (1158).

On the other hand, Rand's narrative is often quite specific about when a close-up is called for. In the scene when Dagny encounters Hugh Akston in a diner in the wilds of Wyoming, Rand seems to be directing an extreme close-up of the cigarette he offers Dagny. First a medium shot is indicated: "She held the small remnant to the light of the dashboard, looking for the name of the brand." In this scene the camera eye includes Dagny as she looks at the cigarette. But then the camera zooms in tight to the cigarette. Only an extreme close-up would be appropriate to show that "Stamped in gold on the thin, white paper stood the sign of the dollar." (332)

Perhaps, the most important close-up in *Atlas Shrugged* happens at the beginning of Part III, A is A. This is a climactic moment in the novel when Dagny finally has an answer to the question, "Who is John Galt?" Dagny opens her eyes and sees, "sunlight, green leaves and a man's face." (701) The narration clearly directs the focus to Galt's face in close-up. It is a "face that bore no mark of pain or fear or guilt" and the text describes explicitly, mouth, cheekbones, eyes, but mostly the look. To portray such a look would be a tall order for an actor, but Rand makes it clear that the camera eye should remain on the face for some time before it moves back for a medium shot as Dagny becomes aware of Galt's body also.[6]

Camera is the perfect tool through which to present the scene of the inauguration of the John Galt line (238). "The long line of boxcars stretched off into the distance, in spaced rectangular links, like a spinal cord." This could be accomplished through a long shot, using a crane and interposing those views with close-ups and medium shots of the crowd and Dagny and Hank and Eddie. After Eddie cuts the ribbon "Then the engine was gone, and he stood looking across the crowded platform that kept appearing and vanishing as the freight cars clicked past him" (239). The narration continues describing the movement:

> Things streaked past—a water tank, a tree, a shanty, a grain silo. They had a windshield-wiper motion: they were rising, describing a curve and dropping back. The telegraph wires ran a race with the train, rising and falling from pole to pole, in an even rhythm, like the cardiograph record of a stead heartbeat written across the sky (240).

That Rand had film in mind is manifest in the text. Dagny describes the people that they pass as the Galt line hurtles 100 miles an hour. "But they went by so fast that she could not grasp their meaning until, like the squares of a movie film, brief flashes blended into a whole and she understood it" (242).

The visual, a series of those "squares of movie film" that Rand alludes to, is what the trip is made of. For example: "The cliffs ahead were a bright liquid gold. Strips of shadow were lengthening in the valleys below. The sun was descending to the peaks in the west. They were going west and up, toward the sun" (246). If it weren't a movie still, it could be a picture postcard. Another such instance is at the end of the ride, when Dagny has shaken hands with all the stockholders of the John Galt Line: "Above her head, above the heads of the crowd, the letters TT on a silver shield were hit by the last ray of a sinking sun" (248), a perfect fade out frame before the business of the next scene. Color, speed, and scenic grandeur are all part of Rand's text, setting visual instructions for how these scenes should be photographed. Rand's description of this technique, the many squares of film blending together to achieve meaning, resembles montage. Obviously, she had thought about it. D.W. Griffith, whose work she admired, is a key figure in the Montage Movement. Perhaps she studied the technique at the State Institute for Cinematography in Leningrad. The Montage Movement was influential in Soviet filmmaking during the 1920s.

In her study of the effect of film on the writing of three American major writers, Hemingway, Faulkner, and Fitzgerald, Somdatta Mandal explains the differences between the traditional novelistic perspective and a more film-influenced way of writing. She notes that the novelist's eye is usually away from the object and towards the eye of the observer, a mode usually practiced by stream-of-consciousness novelists. "On the other hand, there are distinct occasions when the novelist's focus is more on the object as something seen, and therefore closer to the cinematographic form" (138). This is the case with Rand in many sections of *Atlas Shrugged.* Often, characters are presented as something seen and she even gives instructions as to how they are to be seen. There are also some specific references to film in the text, such as the montage allusion above and in a scene where Francisco is described as "looking up as if he were watching the scenes of a movie farce unrolling on the ceiling" (122).

Another aspect of Rand's cinematic perspective may have been influenced by the time she spent working in the wardrobe department of RKO.[7] Her writing reflects a keen sense of costume, particularly how the costume is perceived by the onlooker. At the press conference before the John Galt line is inaugurated the text reads: "She [Dagny] wore a dark blue suit with a white blouse, beautifully tailored, suggesting an air of formal almost military elegance" (233). For the first run of the train Dagny wears "blue slacks and shirt" (237). Not just the women, but also the men's wardrobe is carefully depicted. When Hank and Dagny are riding together on the first trip on the John Galt line, his clothing is very precisely described:

> His tall figure in the single gray of slacks and shirt looked as if his body were stripped for action. The slacks stressed the long lines of his legs, the light firm posture of standing without effort or being ready to swing forward at an instant's notice; the short sleeves stressed the gaunt strength of his arms; the open shirt bared the tight skin of his chest. (243)

Not only is the costume depicted, but also the way it should fit him (274). The same is true for Dagny.

> She wore the tight gray skirt of an office suit and a blouse of transparent white cloth tailored like a man's shirt; the blouse flared out above her waistline, stressing the trim flatness of her hips; against the glow of a lamp behind her, she could see the slender silhouette of her body with the flaring circle of the blouse. (274)

These descriptions would make good instructions for the costume designer and wardrobe mistress.

When Lillian pays a surprise visit to Hank's bedroom, her garment is described in detail:

> She wore an Empire garment of pale chartreuse, its pleated skirt streaming gracefully from its high waistline; one could not tell at first glance whether it was an evening gown or a negligee; it was a negligee. She paused in the doorway, the lines of her body flowing into an attractive silhouette against the light. (304)

Though Hank has come into the room "undressing for bed," and putting on his pajamas, we do not learn anything about what he looks like or the color or style of his pajamas at that point. Later we find out that "the tall, straight, taut lines of his body [were] emphasized by the single color of the dark blue pajamas" (305).

Another aspect of her film training that may have influenced how Rand saw costuming, is the way dress would have been seen in a classical Hollywood movie because of the three-point lighting system. In this system a key light, fill light and then a backlight were used to illuminate and slowly reveal certain aspects of the star's costume and body. Thus the star is lit from three directions, creating a three dimensional sense of the body beneath the costume as is often the case in Rand's descriptions, whether they are of Dagny's "gray evening gown that seemed indecent, because it looked austerely modest, so modest that it vanished from one's awareness and left one too aware of the slender body it pretended to cover" (396) or the outline of Hank's legs in his gray slacks.

While Rand's narrative clearly relishes the beautiful dress of many of her characters, it is also mindful of how costume establishes character and how juxtaposition can serve for cinematic emphasis. In the text, Rand describes the "evening gown of bright green chiffon with a low neckline, a belt of yellow roses and a rhinestone buckle" (390) that Cherryl Brooks wears to a reception given by Mrs. Cornelius Pope. From the narrative, one can envision how the rest of the women at the party would be costumed in sleek satin gowns of black or navy or ivory. Costume establishes both literally and figuratively that Cherryl does not fit in.

The tenuous lines of influence from film to text even stretch to what traits Rand found appealing. Writing of Pola Negri, one of her favorite silent screen stars, when she was still Alisa Rosenbaum of Petrograd, Ayn Rand uses the language she would use over three decades later to describe some of her fiction heroes. Rand writes of Negri's "mysterious contemptuous smile" (1999, 31). The appeal of such a look is not restricted to her female characters. In her description of Francisco d'Anconia, Rand uses remarkably similar language. In one scene, Francisco gives Dagny a "glance of unmoving mockery" (104). Rand, trying to convey the allure of Negri, explains: "Her type is the proud woman-conqueror, often a tragic one, but powerful even in her suffering" (1999, 32). Francisco, also in the mode of conqueror, smiles down at Dagny, "confidently, derisively" (112). Here, Rand is translating what was appealing to her on film to the pages of her novel. Hank looks at Dagny with "the faint suggestion of a contemptuous smile in his face" (267). Dagny also gets her chance to be, if not contemptuous, at least mocking. When Hank throws her down to her knees, twists her body against his legs and then bends down to kiss her. Dagny laughs soundlessly, "her laughter mocking" (268). Furthermore, the description reads that "her mouth, distorted by pain, was the shape of a mocking smile" (269).

Music to accompany plot is a mainstay of Hollywood. It began with the silent film and continues to be of such importance that there are music categories in the Academy Awards for Film Score and Song. So, it might be argued that Rand's use of a musical theme to undergird and punctuate her plot is definitely cinema inspired. Though the novel reader cannot hear it, the notes of Richard Halley's concerto run through *Atlas Shrugged* like movie background music. The narration calls for the chords of Richard Halley's Fifth Concerto to be heard at the beginning of the story and at the end, and it appears at intervals in the plot, always connected to one of the heroes. Just as in *Jaws*, the audience always knew when the shark was coming by the sound of that theme music, so in *Atlas Shrugged* the Halley Concerto is sound foreshadowing, a piece of the puzzle that Dagny seeks to solve. Heroic movie themes often become popular and present instant association with the film. An example that comes to mind is the romantic Tara theme from *Gone With the Wind* or the heroic theme of the *Star Wars* trilogy. The association of character to a musical theme is made explicit in a scene between Dagny and Francisco. She sees him for the first time after a long separation. The text reads: "Unaccountably, by an association of feeling that astonished her, she remembered what had conveyed to her recently the same sense of consummate joy as his" (121). The allusion is to hearing the Halley Concerto. Association of character or event to theme music is a standard Hollywood convention and Rand employs it in the development of her very visual, but also aural text. In the final sprint of the John Galt line toward Wyatt Junction, Dagny is overwhelmed by the speed and emotion of the moment.

> They were flying down ... she felt as if the train were plunging downward head first. ... She heard the rising, accelerating sound of the wheels—and some theme of music, heard to the rhythm of wheels, kept tugging at her mind growing louder—it burst suddenly within the cab, but she knew that it was only in her mind: the Fifth Concerto by Richard Halley. (247)

Rand's cinematic eye is not always in focus. There are certain parts of this novel that are decidedly calibrated to be read, not seen. The most obvious is John Galt's 60 some odd page speech. Even audiences of the 16th century who were accustomed to sitting for long, sometime five hour plays, peppered with numerous monologues, would be hard put to remain attentive for the time required. The most famous monologue in Theater History, Hamlet's "To Be Or Not To Be," is only 35 poetic lines long, taking about 2 minutes to deliver dramatically. Read at an appropriate pace for comprehension John Galt's speech would take about three hours and thirty minutes.

Still, not all of the key philosophical monologues are quite so visually static and cinematically problematic. Some, in fact, are quite dramatic and Rand's narrative rather suggestive of how the scene would be shot and edited. One does not need much visual imagination to create the scene where Francisco delivers his "Money is the root of all good" speech at Jim Taggart and Cherryl Brooks" wedding. With a curtain-raising line, the scene begins with James Taggart mouthing his hypocritical bromide: "Money is the root of all evil." The rest of this scene is presented as if Rand were a choreographer, or as they say in theatre, as if she had "blocked" the scene. To emphasize his smallness and pettiness the point-

of-view or camera angle is from above, a crane shot. "He stood under the lights ..."
(392). He is in a circle of reporters. Then the camera pans to the opposite end of
the ballroom, which is peopled by Orren Boyle, Bertram Scudder, and their ilk. A
kind of choreographed dance of the moochers ensues as Boyle and Scudder move
about categorizing the guests into the "So!" or "Well, well!" group. The macabre
dance aspect, and the perspective of the overhead cam are emphasized by the
language that describes Jim with a "tail of figures" that "kept trailing and shifting
behind him" (393). Paul Larkin is blocked as "describing circles around Taggart"
(394). The scene builds dramatically with mini-conflicts, first Cherryl's
confrontation with Dagny, then Dagny's war of words with Lillian Rearden. Lillian
and Jim's encounter serves to foreshadow their later affair. A soft focus or blur
shot is called for as Hank walks among Lillian's friends; Rand's text reads: "He
listened like a foreigner who recognized some of the words, but could not connect
them to sentences" (397). He is in focus; they are not. Eventually, Francisco's
entrance is presented in a manner that is quintessential camera drama—we hear
him before we see him. And, rather than being on him, the camera eye is on Jim
Taggart as Francisco finishes his sentence about replacing the aristocracy of money
with "an aristocracy of pull." Rand's text then blocks the scene to underline
Francisco's entrance: "They whirled around and there is Francisco." Because his
"money is the root of all good" speech is given in a ballroom full of people, it does
not need to be static. The camera can cut to the shocked faces of most of the
guests, the frightened response of some and, on occasion, Hank's dawning
comprehension or Dagny's approval. Shooting Ragnar Danneskjold's anti-Robin
Hood speech to Hank Rearden is also replete with cinematic possibilities.

Why then, if Rand's life was so affected by and connected to the movies, has
her Magnum Opus, *Atlas Shrugged*, never made it to the screen? It certainly isn't
for lack of trying. In the decade before her death, Rand worked with Sterling
Silliphant on a script for a ten-hour television mini-series. Obviously, with the
length and complexity of the work, a mini-series would be a suitable format.
Silliphant explained that one of the problems was that Rand would not allow any
of the dialogue to be changed and that some of that "dialogue was dated."[8] I have
noted in my study of *Atlas Shrugged* that some of her lines read like B Hollywood
gangster movies, particularly the "The game is up" and the "Brother, you asked for
it" lines.[9] Other commentators have called the Galt rescue scene melodramatic and
hokey Hollywood. The script, though finished, was never made. Every so often,
the rumor mills buzz with word of a forthcoming production. There is an
Unofficial Atlas Shrugged Movie homepage.

But, my purpose is not to engage in the seemingly endless speculation about
whether the film will or will not be made or who should be cast if it is made,
problematic since the stars Rand may have visualized in the major roles have all
become elderly. My thesis is that irrespective of production issues, because of her

base in film writing and long history with the movies, Rand writes her novels with a "cinematic eye." Hers is a cinematic mode of narration.

Notes

1   Laura Mulvey. Visual Pleasure and Narrative Cinema. *Feminist Film Theory: A Reader*. Edited by Sue Thornham. Edinburg: Edinburg University Press, 1999, 58–69. This foundational essay was first printed in *Screen* 16:3, 1975, 6–18.

2   Chris Sciabarra, who was kind enough to read this in draft and make suggestions for its improvement, pointed out that Howard Roark is naked in the first scene of *The Fountainhead*. True, but Rand's screenplay did not include that scene. The movie begins with Roark being expelled.

3   See Silverman's article for a fuller explanation of the relationship between suture in writing and shot/reverse shot formation in film.

4   Nathaniel Branden. Was Ayn Rand a Feminist? *Feminist Interpretations of Ayn Rand*. Edited by Mimi Reisel Gladstein and Chris Matthew Sciabarra, University Park: The Pennsylvania University Press, 1999, 224.

5   In conversation, 8 January 2005.

6   Erika Holzer informs us that she and Rand had some "lighthearted casting conversations" in the mid 1960s. At that time Robert Redford (40 years younger) was Rand's choice. See "Passing the Torch."

7   In her *Hollywood: American City of Movies* Rand notes that costume designers are more famous than other kinds of designers in Hollywood. She mentions Erté, whose art deco designs earned him fame, and Howard Greer. Adrian, also an award-winning costumer, and his wife became good friends with Rand when she lived in Hollywood.

8   Silliphant is quoted in Barbara Branden's *The Passion of Ayn Rand*, 390.

9   *Atlas Shrugged: Manifesto of the Mind*, 43.

References

Branden, Barbara. 1986. *The Passion of Ayn Rand*. Garden City, New York: Doubleday & Company.

Branden, Nathaniel. 1999. Was Ayn Rand a Feminist? *Feminist Interpretations of Ayn Rand*. Edited by Mimi Reisel Gladstein and Chris Matthew Sciabarra. University Park: The Pennsylvania University Press, 223–30.

Gladstein, Mimi. 2000. *Atlas Shrugged: Manifesto of the Mind*. New York: Twayne Publishers.

Holzer, Erika. 2004. Passing the Torch. *The Journal of Ayn Rand Studies* 6, no. 1 (Fall): 21–65.

Mandal, Somdatta. 2004. *Reflections, Refractions, and Rejections: Three American Writers and the Celluloid World*. England & India: Wisdom House.

Mulvey, Laura. 1999. Visual Pleasure and Narrative Cinema. *Feminist Film Theory: A Reader*. Edited by Sue Thornham. Edinburg: Edinburg University Press, 58–69.

Rand, Ayn. 1957. *Atlas Shrugged.* New York: Random House.

———. 1999. *Russian Writings on Hollywood.* Ayn Rand Institute Press.

Silverman, Kaja. 1999. On Suture. *Film Theory and Criticism.* Edited by Leo Braudy and Marshall Cohen. New York: Oxford University Press, 137–47.

Chapter 11

Atlas Shrugged as a
Science Fiction Novel

Jeff Riggenbach

It has been observed by more than a few commentators—Nat Hentoff, Grover Sales, Ken Burns, others—that "jazz is America's classical music." Similarly, it might well be argued that works of so-called "genre fiction"—detective stories, westerns, science fiction—are the true American literature. For, while the work American critics have been willing to regard as "serious fiction" has long imitated British and other European models, the genres of "popular fiction" just named were either invented here or brought to their highest level of development here.[1]

Ayn Rand was always a great admirer of American popular culture. Though she never became a jazz fan,[2] she was a lifelong fan of American movies and American popular fiction. As a teenager in Petrograd (the former St. Petersburg, which was to become Leningrad before she finally made good her escape), she was enchanted by films from America; they fueled her passionate desire to become a resident of that seemingly magical place. Once she got here, in 1926, she made a beeline for Hollywood and sought employment within the motion picture industry. As she worked on her English in the years before she began publishing, she became a devotee of American detective fiction: in later years her favorite novelist was Mickey Spillane. She loved almost everything American—American architecture, American political ideas, the list seemed endless. She wanted to be an American writer. (Unlike her fellow fugitive from St. Petersburg, Vladimir Nabokov—who had written and spoken English since childhood—she didn't go on writing in Russian for years after leaving Russia; she immediately learned English and used it professionally from the beginning of her career.) But there was always a special place in Ayn Rand's affections for American popular culture.

And when she began publishing, a decade after her arrival as a wide-eyed girl of twenty-one, it was immediately evident how deep those affections ran. Her first professional success, her play *The Night of January 16th*, which enjoyed a respectable run on Broadway during 1935, is a murder mystery. Her first novel, *We the Living*, is strikingly similar to Margaret Mitchell's *Gone with the Wind*, published at almost exactly the same time (in May of 1936 to *We the Living*'s March), a book which Leslie Fiedler calls "a chief glory" of American popular fiction (212).[3] Her second novel, *Anthem* (1938), is a work of science fiction. And so, of course, is her magnum opus, *Atlas Shrugged.*

Though these last two statements are still not universally accepted in the world of Objectivism and its students and adherents, in the world of science fiction they are regarded as obvious—and utterly non-controversial. Open the latest edition of Neil Barron's *Anatomy of Wonder: Science Fiction*, for thirty years the standard bibliography in the field; you'll find both *Anthem* and *Atlas Shrugged* listed, each with a descriptive paragraph. Open the latest edition of Clute and Nicholls' *Encyclopedia of Science Fiction*, and you'll read of Ayn Rand that

> [h]er first and better sf novel, *Anthem* […] is a dystopia set after a devastating war. Individualism has been eliminated, along with the concept of the person, but the protagonist discovers his identity while escaping with a beautiful woman to the forest, where he christens himself Prometheus. *The Fountainhead* (1943) is a mainstream novel advancing AR's vision of things. In *Atlas Shrugged* (1957), which is sf, John Galt (AR's mouthpiece) and his Objectivist colleagues abandon an increasingly socialistic USA and retreat to the mountains as civilization crumbles, prepared to return only when they will be able to rebuild along the lines of Objectivist philosophy. (990)

To be sure, this is not a particularly accurate account of *Atlas Shrugged* (it treats the novel as a mere tract devoid of artistic interest or importance, which it most emphatically is not); nor is it a particularly charitable one. It is clear that Messrs. Clute and Nicholls would really rather not have a writer like Ayn Rand in their reference work at all, and that they regard her writings as largely worthless and contemptible. But they feel they must include her, since two of her novels, both quite widely known and quite widely read, are science fiction.

In light of this point, it is worth noting that the short, rather snippy summary of *Atlas Shrugged* which Clute and Nicholls do grudgingly provide doesn't even make clear why Rand's novel should be regarded as a work of science fiction. That issue, they seem to feel, is too obvious to require any comment. Nonetheless, let us devote a few paragraphs to "unpacking," as Rand might say, the concept of "science fiction."

On 8 February 1957, only a few months before *Atlas Shrugged* was published, Robert A. Heinlein, a novelist with whom Ayn Rand has often been both compared and contrasted and with whom she has long shared a substantial readership, delivered a lecture at the University of Chicago under the title "Science Fiction: Its Nature, Faults and Virtues." Heinlein began by noting that

> [t]he field now known as science fiction had no agreed name until about twenty-five years ago [i.e., ca. 1932]. The field has existed throughout the history of literature, but it used to be called by several names: speculative romance, pseudo-scientific romance (a term that sets a science fiction writer's teeth on edge), utopian literature, fantasy— or, more frequently, given no name, simply lumped in with all other fiction. (14–15)

Science fiction, Heinlein proposed, is

> Fiction [...] in which the author shows awareness of the nature and importance of the human activity known as the scientific method, shows equal awareness of the great body of human knowledge already collected through that activity, and takes into account in his stories the effects and possible future effects on human beings of scientific method and scientific fact. (16)

The author of *Atlas Shrugged* certainly shows "awareness of the nature and importance of the human activity known as the scientific method." Indeed, science, and its role in human life, is one of the more important sub themes of Rand's big novel. Rand (1969) wrote that "the theme of *Atlas Shrugged* is: "The role of the mind in man's existence" (58). But, of course, like any complex work of art, the novel also features a number of sub-themes, each of which contributes to the ultimate realization of the overarching theme Rand rightly identifies as lying at *Atlas Shrugged*'s core.[4] One of these sub-themes—the one that accounts, I think, for the lion's share of the novel's enduring popular success—is the role of the State in human life. Another is the psychology of achievement. Still another is the nature of science and its proper role in human affairs.

It may be helpful, in understanding the novel's treatment of science, to tell the story of *Atlas Shrugged* in a somewhat different order from the one Rand employs. Once upon a time, then, three young men—teenagers, really, since they were all of sixteen years old at the time (786)—enrolled at the Patrick Henry University of Cleveland, Ohio, at that time perhaps the preeminent American institution of higher learning. The three—John Galt, Francisco d'Anconia, and Ragnar Danneskjöld—pursued a double major in physics and philosophy (787), studying under the legendary philosopher Hugh Akston, who later retired and disappeared, and the brilliant physicist Robert Stadler, who later left the university to head the new State Science Institute. Upon graduation, the three went their separate ways: d'Anconia to work in his family's multi-billion-dollar international business, Danneskjöld to graduate school to prepare for a career as an academic philosopher, Galt to a career as an inventor, beginning with a post in the research laboratory of a commercial business enterprise, the Twentieth Century Motor Company of Starnesville, Wisconsin (789, 661).

While at the Twentieth Century Motor Company, Galt invents a new type of motor. As his former teacher, Dr. Robert Stadler, puts it years later, "[h]e wanted a motor, and he quietly performed a major revolution in the science of energy, just as a means to an end, and he didn't bother to publish his findings, but went right on making his motor" (356). What Stadler sees as a "major revolution in the science of energy," Dagny Taggart, the Vice President in Charge of Operation of Taggart Transcontinental, the nation's largest railroad, sees as "the greatest revolution in power motors since the internal-combustion engine—greater than that!" Looking, years later, at the wreckage of a no-longer-operational model of Galt's breakthrough, "a motor that would draw static electricity from the atmosphere, convert it and create its own power as it went along," she muses to her friend and associate, steel magnate Hank Rearden,

> Who'll want to look at a Diesel? Who'll want to worry about oil, coal or refueling stations? Do you see what I see? A brand-new locomotive half the size of a single Diesel unit, and with ten times the power. A self-generator, working on a few drops of fuel, with no limits to its energy. The cleanest, swiftest, cheapest means of motion ever devised. Do you see what this will do to our transportation systems and to the country—in about one year? (289)

All this presupposes, of course, that the motor can be repaired—which presupposes in turn that someone can reconstruct Galt's theoretical breakthrough, his new concept of energy, which is sketched only in part in a fragmentary manuscript found by Dagny and Rearden on the same scrap heap from which they rescued the motor itself.

Galt's motor is one of three inventions that propel the action of *Atlas Shrugged*. The second is Rearden Metal, invented by Hank Rearden, "an alloy that will render steel and aluminum obsolete" (Snider). Defending her decision to order rails of Rearden Metal for their railroad's decaying Rio Norte Line, Dagny Taggart tells her brother James, "it's tougher than steel, cheaper than steel and will outlast any hunk of metal in existence" (21). Rearden himself, looking back on his long struggle to perfect the new alloy, recalls that his goal was "a metal alloy that would do more than steel had ever done, a metal that would be to steel what steel had been to iron" (30). In conversation with Dagny Taggart, he envisions Rearden Metal rail cars, "which will be half the weight of steel and twice as safe," being pulled over Rearden Metal track by Diesel engines made of Rearden Metal. Those trains, he tells her, will be able to run safely at two hundred and fifty miles per hour. Still, she'll "have to look out for the air lines. We're working on a plane of Rearden Metal. It will weigh practically nothing and lift anything. You'll see the day of long-haul, heavy-freight air traffic." Nor do trains and planes exhaust Rearden's examples of the ways in which his metal can transform society. "Have you thought," he asks Dagny,

> of what it will do for chicken wire? Just plain chicken-wire fences, made of Rearden Metal, that will cost a few pennies a mile and last two hundred years. And kitchenware that will be bought at the dime store and passed on from generation to generation. And ocean liners that one won't be able to dent with a torpedo.

And, he wonders, "Did I tell you that I'm having tests made of communications wire of Rearden Metal?" (86–7).

The third of the three major inventions that propel the plot of *Atlas Shrugged* is the xylophone, which Dr. Floyd Ferris of the State Science Institute describes as "a scientific achievement of such tremendous importance, such staggering scope, such epoch-making possibilities that up to this moment it has been known only to a very few" (821). The xylophone is a weapon, based on the discovery that "there are certain frequencies of sound vibration which no structure, organic or inorganic, can withstand" (824). Dr. Robert Stadler observes an exhibition of the xylophone's power; before an audience of invited dignitaries, it reduces a farmhouse (with equipment and water tower) and a herd of goats to an inchoate pile of fur and rubble. Dr. Stadler

> turned away and saw that Dr. Ferris was still watching him. Dr. Stadler leaned back a little, his face austere and scornful, the face of the nation's greatest scientist, and asked, "Who invented that ghastly thing?"
>
> "You did."
>
> Dr. Stadler looked at him, not moving.
>
> "It is merely a practical appliance," said Dr. Ferris pleasantly, "based upon your theoretical discoveries. It was derived from your invaluable research into the nature of cosmic rays and of the spatial transmission of energy."

And finding the money necessary to turn Dr. Stadler's research into a monstrous weapon had been almost effortlessly easy, as it turned out. As Dr. Ferris tells Dr. Stadler,

> the State Science Institute had no trouble in obtaining funds for the Project. You have not heard of the Institute having any financial difficulties in the past two years, have you? And it used to be such a problem—getting them to vote the funds necessary for the advancement of science. They always demanded gadgets for their cash, as you used to say. Well, here was a gadget which some people in power could fully appreciate. They got the others to vote for it. It wasn't difficult. In fact a great many of those others felt safe in voting money for a project that was secret—they felt certain it was important, since they were not considered important enough to be let in on it. There were, of course, a few skeptics and doubters. But they gave in when they were reminded that the head of the State Science Institute was Dr. Robert Stadler—whose judgment and integrity they could not doubt. (825–6)

The potential impact of Galt's and Rearden's inventions is severely dampened or even cut off by government interference and "regulation." Galt's motor is, as it were, withdrawn from the market before it is ever put into practical use, a casualty of potential governmental interference.[5] Rearden's metal helps briefly to revitalize an important branch line of the Taggart Transcontinental system, and with it the entire region made up of Colorado, New Mexico, and Arizona; then, under the market-distorting provisions of the government's latest directives, Rearden's production is diverted from rail, bridges, ocean liners, and planes to golf clubs, "coffee pots, garden tools, and bathroom faucets" (361). Its potential to transform the economy, which had aroused such enthusiasm in Rearden and Dagny, is virtually lost. Similarly, another private-sector inventor, Ellis Wyatt, who, early in the novel, "had discovered some way to revive exhausted oil wells," announces a couple of hundred pages later a "process I've developed" to "get oil from shale—the cheapest oil ever to splash in their faces, and an unlimited supply of it, an untapped supply that will make the biggest oil pool look like a mud puddle" (10, 249). Wyatt's technological breakthroughs help fuel the brief boom in Colorado, New Mexico, and Arizona that is destroyed, along with Wyatt's business enterprise, by the directives of the Bureau of Economic Planning and National Resources.

Dr. Robert Stadler's unwitting invention, the xylophone, by contrast, has the sort of major, direct impact on society that Galt, Rearden, and Wyatt had only hoped to see from their own inventions. It not only places the State Science Institute in an enviable position with regard to funding, as Dr. Ferris reported to Dr. Stadler at the xylophone's unveiling; it also manages, in the novel's closing pages, to wipe out the Taggart Bridge over the Mississippi River, thereby severing the country and plunging it further into social and economic chaos. In the sort of world the United States has become in *Atlas Shrugged*, the inventions unleashed by market forces will tend to have minimal impact, while those subsidized by government and capable only of destruction will do far better.

In fact, the State Science Institute that is strengthened and empowered by Dr. Stadler's unwitting but fearsome invention is inevitably responsible for undermining science and reducing its genuine contributions to human happiness. Dr. Stadler, who had once told a student, "Free scientific inquiry? The first adjective is redundant," helps to sell the proposed institute to a wary American public by urging his countrymen to "[s]et science free of the rule of the dollar" (185). Yet it is in pursuit of just such dollars that the institute develops the xylophone. And it is in pursuit of the "popularity" that will make such dollars easier to obtain that the institute, much to Dr. Stadler's rage and embarrassment, publishes a trashy popular book by Dr. Floyd Ferris called *Why Do You Think You Think?*—a book that, Dr. Ferris candidly admits to Dr. Stadler, does provide logical support for the proposition that "science is a futile fraud which ought to be abolished" (346–7).

Rand's overall message with regard to science seems clear: the role of science in human life and human society is to provide the knowledge on the basis of which technological advancement and related improvements in the quality of human life can be realized. But science can fulfill this role only in a society in which human beings are left free to conduct their business as they see fit. Thus, for Rand, how science affects humans will depend in large measure on political, not scientific, developments. In his famous radio speech, John Galt refers to

those mystics of science who profess a devotion to some sort of "pure knowledge"—the purity consisting of their claim that such knowledge has no practical purpose on this earth—who reserve their logic for inanimate matter, but believe that the subject of dealing with men requires and deserves no rationality, who scorn money and sell their souls in exchange for a laboratory supplied by loot. And since there is no such thing as "non-practical knowledge" or any sort of "disinterested" action, since they scorn the use of their science for the purpose and profit of life, they deliver their science to the service of death, to the only practical purpose it can ever have for looters: to inventing weapons of coercion and destruction. (1066)

One further point remains to be made. In most bookstores, science fiction is displayed in the same section with another literary genre, assumed by most people to be a close relation of science fiction—namely, fantasy. And such thinking is far from confined to bookstore personnel. The Libertarian Futurist Society, which presents the annual Prometheus Award for the best science fiction novel with a libertarian theme, also presents one or more Hall of Fame Awards for classic libertarian science fiction and fantasy each year—lumping the two genres together as though they were pretty much the same thing. (*Atlas Shrugged* won the society's Hall of Fame Award in 1983; *Anthem* was the winner in 1987.) Rand herself spoke of science fiction in her posthumously published *Art of Fiction* as one of the "forms of literature that can be classified as fantasy." She distinguished it from other kinds of fantasy by noting that "science fiction [...] projects future inventions" (169).

This is in sharp contrast to the approach Robert A. Heinlein took to the subject in "Science Fiction: Its Nature, Faults and Virtues." For Heinlein, all events in all fiction are imaginary; fantasy is fiction in which at least some of the events depicted are both "imaginary-and-not-possible"; realistic fiction is fiction in which all the events depicted are "imaginary-but-possible [...] i.e., imaginary but could be real so far as we know the real universe." As far as Heinlein is concerned, "[s]cience fiction is in the latter class. It is not fantasy."

Heinlein acknowledges that "there is never full agreement as to the established facts nor as to what constitutes the real world," but he proposes that, for literary purposes, it would be sufficient to think of "the factual universe of our experience" in terms of how "one would expect such words to be used by educated and enlightened members of western culture" at the time we are living. He also notes that "[t]he science fiction author is not limited by currently accepted theory nor by popular opinion; he need only respect established fact" (19).

This is precisely how Ayn Rand proceeds in *Atlas Shrugged*. She freely disregards the fact that currently accepted theory regards such a motor as John Galt built or such processes as Ellis Wyatt perfected as impossible. But she is scrupulous in depicting nothing in her big novel that contradicts established fact. As Rand always insisted, she was a realist—to be more exact, a "Romantic Realist" (*Manifesto*, 168).

"Romantic"—Nathaniel Branden explained, "because her work is concerned with values, with the essential, the abstract, the universal in human life, and with the projection of man as a heroic being. Realist—because the values she selects pertain to this earth and to man's actual nature, and because the issues with which she deals are the crucial and fundamental ones of our age." (88)

This is correct, as far as it goes. Rand was a romantic realist. But she was also a science fiction writer. If that seems like a contradiction to you, remember what Francisco told Dagny when she came to him for money to finance the John Galt Line: "Contradictions do not exist. Whenever you think that you are facing a contradiction, check your premises. You will find that one of them is wrong" (199).

Notes

1   On jazz as America's classical music, see Nat Hentoff, *Jazz Is* (New York: Random House, 1976) and Grover Sales, *Jazz: America's Classical Music* (Englewood Cliffs, New Jersey: Prentice-Hall, 1984). Ken Burns's *Jazz* debuted on PBS in January 2001 and is now widely available for purchase as a set of ten DVDs. For a first stab at an argument that genre fiction is the true American literature see Jeff Riggenbach, "The National Letters," in *The Libertarian Review* (March 1980): 14–29. The western is, of course, uniquely and indisputably American. And it is generally acknowledged by historians of the mystery genre that it was Edgar Allan Poe who invented the detective story. A solid case may also be made for the claim that Poe invented science fiction— see Thomas M. Disch, *The Dreams Our Stuff Is Made Of: How Science Fiction Conquered the World* (New York: Free Press, 1998)—though a perhaps equally solid case has been made for the claim that Mary Shelley actually did the deed with the publication in 1818 of her novel *Frankenstein*—see Brian Aldiss, *Billion Year Spree: The True History of Science Fiction* (New York: Doubleday, 1973). In any case, it is evident that the main action in both these genres has always been on this side of the Atlantic and that, however brilliant some of their individual contributions to both detective fiction and science fiction have been, the British have been followers, not leaders, in the process of their development.

2   Rand wrote, in her foreword to the revised 1959 edition of *We the Living* (first published in 1936)*,* that "*We the Living* is as near to an autobiography as I will ever write. [...] The specific events of Kira's life were not mine; her ideas, her convictions, her values were and are" (xviii–xix). Early in the novel, Kira and Leo, her lover, make their first, abortive try at escaping the newly minted and already disastrously failing Soviet Union. To keep up each other's spirits as they prepare to stow away aboard an outbound ship, they remind each other of what they will find if only they have the courage to stay the course and discover a way over to the other side.

> Leo whispered: "Over there ... there are automobiles ... and boulevards ... and lights ...".
> An old man stood in a doorway, snow gathering in the brim of his frayed hat, his head hanging down on his breast, asleep over a tray of homemade cookies.
> Kira whispered: " ... lipstick and silk stockings ..."

A stray dog sniffed at a barrel of refuse under the dark window of a co-operative. Leo whispered: " … champagne … radios … jazz bands." (100)

Yet, according to Barbara Branden, it would be a mistake to infer from this passage that Rand herself was fond of jazz. "No, not especially," Branden told an interviewer in 1992, when asked, "Did Ayn Rand like jazz?" "On the other hand," Branden continued, "jazz had a kind of symbolic significance for Rand, and it was this—the 'larger meaning' of jazz—that led her to use it as she did in *We the Living*". According to Branden, "Rand said once […] that what she would love more than anything is not ever to have to think about politics, because it wouldn't be necessary. She loved what she saw as the frivolous in America, that this was a country where you didn't have to be concerned whether you were going to starve to death before tomorrow, or freeze to death, or to be put in prison, or sent to Siberia. You could be concerned with things like lipstick and silk stockings. And jazz. So […] even if she didn't care for jazz specifically, [it] was symbolic to her of everything that Russia didn't have and that America did." (See http://www.barbarabranden.com/interview4.html.) If anything, Branden may have understated the case when she said that Rand didn't "especially" like jazz. In May 1936, only a few weeks after the first publication of *We the Living,* Rand wrote to the radio announcer "Ev Suffens" (air name of Raymond Nelson), who had solicited input from his listeners as to the future of his late night program *Midnight Jamboree,* that "[a]s to the music, my vote is: more classics, particularly light concert classics such as you have been playing lately. Personally, I would say: all classics, but I don't mind suffering through a jazz number once in a while if it's necessary and if your audience demands it" (*Letters* 30).

3   For an extended discussion of the similarities between *We the Living* and *Gone with the Wind*, as well as of the relation of Rand's writing to so-called "popular fiction," see Jeff Riggenbach, "Ayn Rand's Influence on American Popular Fiction," *Journal of Ayn Rand Studies* 6 (2004): 91–144.

4   One is reminded of James Whistler's response when an art critic faulted his painting *Symphony in White No. III* on the grounds that "it is not precisely a symphony in white. One lady has a yellowish dress and brown hair and a bit of blue ribbon, the other has a red fan, and there are flowers and green leaves. There is a girl in white on a white sofa, but even this girl has reddish hair; and of course there is the flesh colour of the complexions." "*Bon Dieu!,*" Whistler replied, "did this wise person expect white hair and chalked faces? And does he then, in his astounding consequence, believe that a symphony in F contains no other note, but shall be a continued repetition of F, F, F?" (44–45).

5   More exactly, Galt withdrew the motor because the company for whom he designed and built it had adopted a new operating philosophy: "from each according to his ability, to each according to his need" (661).

References

Barron, Neil. [1976] 2004. *Anatomy of Wonder: Science Fiction*. Westport, Connecticut: Libraries Unlimited.

Branden, Nathaniel, and Barbara Branden. 1962. *Who Is Ayn Rand?* (New York: Random House.

Clute, John, and Peter Nicholls. 1995. *The Encylopedia of Science Fiction*. New York: St. Martin's.

Heinlein, Robert A. [1959] 1969. Science fiction: Its nature, faults and virtues. Edited by Basil Davenport. *The Science Fiction Novel: Imagination and Social Criticism*. Chicago: Advent.

Rand, Ayn. [1936] 1995. *We the Living*. New York: Dutton.

———. 1957. *Atlas Shrugged*. New York: Random House.

———. 1969. *The Romantic Manifesto: A Philosophy of Literature*. New York: World.

———. 1995. *Letters of Ayn Rand*. Edited by Michael S. Berliner. New York: Dutton.

———. 2000. *The Art of Fiction*. New York: Plume.

Snider, John C. 2000.But is it science fiction? *Ayn Rand's Atlas Shrugged*. Online at: http://www.scifidimensions.com/May00/books_ayn_rand.htm.

Whistler, James. [1890] 1916. *The Gentle Art of Making Enemies*. New York: Putnam.

Chapter 12

Ayn Rand's Recasting of Ancient Myths in *Atlas Shrugged*

Kirsti Minsaas

Introduction

Atlas Shrugged is a twentieth-century novel of epic range. Although it presents modern people in a modern world, it has an imaginative sweep that in its concern with grand heroes and large-scale events recalls the epic-heroic literature of earlier times. Contributing to this epic dimension is Rand's use of ancient Greek myths in forging her story. While in some of her earlier works, especially *Anthem* and *The Fountainhead*, Rand occasionally makes use of mythical allusions, in *Atlas Shrugged* she gives us a novel that in its basic conception and overall structure involves a deliberate recasting of mythical material.

This use of myth originates in Rand's desire to write a novel that would, as she herself stated, present "a new morality" (Rand [1958] 1986, Lecture III). Since myths, in their early forms, are stories about deities and supernatural beings that serve to explain the nature of the cosmos and to set down rules about human conduct, they sometimes come to be seen as transmitters of timeless truths that transcend the particular cultural context in which they arose. If an author wishes to challenge these truths, an effective way of doing so is therefore to give the myths in which they are embodied a new cast, suggestive of a new and radical vision of the world. This is what Rand does in *Atlas Shrugged*.

The Title: The Myth of Atlas

The most immediate manifestation of this is the title. Throughout most of the time Rand was working on the novel her working title had been *The Strike*, but in 1956 her husband suggested that she use "Atlas Shrugged," at that time only a chapter title, as her main title instead (Rand 1997, 390). Atlas—in Greek mythology the Titan who is condemned to carry the world on his shoulders—here symbolizes what Rand referred to as the creators: the best and most able minds among industrialists, thinkers, scientists, artists, and inventors. Clearly elitist in her thinking, Rand saw these creators, or the prime movers as she also called them, as society's Atlases. Like the Greek Titan, they are giants who carry the world on their shoulders by ensuring, through their exceptional creative and productive skills, the well-being and progress of society. In her novel, Rand demonstrates this point by showing what happens to the world when these giants go on strike, when they no longer want to carry the world on their shoulders but choose to "shrug." In so doing, she also demonstrates the novel's main theme: the importance of the creative mind in human existence.

Underlying and driving Rand's development of this plot-idea is her notion of the creator as a martyred victim, historically seen. Instead of being rewarded, Rand believed, the men of the mind have usually been exploited and maligned. In an early journal note on Atlas Shrugged, she thus describes the "genius" as a "martyr" who throughout most of history has had "to pay for his discovery and for his greatness, pay in suffering, poverty, obscurity, insults" (Rand 1997, 393). In her novel, she seeks to redress this injustice by having the creators go on strike, in protest against the many pains inflicted upon them by an envious and ungrateful society. Politically, the protest is directed at the exploitation Rand saw as an inherent aspect of the altruist-collectivist system; but psychologically it is directed at the tremendous cost in suffering this system imposes on its most productive individuals. All too often, Rand's criticism of altruism-collectivism in *Atlas Shrugged* is interpreted too one-sidedly in politico-economic terms, as if her main point is to show society's dependence on its best minds materially and financially. But Rand wanted to dig deeper than this. In her journal notes on the novel, she repeatedly stresses the importance of making clear the motivation for the strike, namely, the martyrdom of the strikers. It is rebellion against this martyrdom that drives them to lay down their work, to stop carrying the world on their shoulders. The shrugging Atlas indicated in the title is thus a suffering Atlas—in tune with the meaning of his name: "he who dares or suffers." This is a point made explicit in the novel itself when Francisco d'Anconia asks Hank Rearden what he would tell Atlas to do if he saw him standing with "blood running down his chest, his knees buckling, his arms trembling but still trying to hold the world aloft with the last of his strength, and the greater his effort, the heavier the world bore down on his shoulders." When Rearden, at a loss for an answer, asks Francisco what he would tell him, Francisco answers, "To shrug" (Rand 1957, 429). What incites the novel's Atlases to go on strike is consequently not just the desire to show the world how desperately it needs them but, more deeply, the desire to shake off a burden which is getting too heavy to carry. As Rand (1997) points out, her aim is not only to show "what happens to the world without the strikers—but also, what happens to the strikers" (397). Read with this in mind, *Atlas Shrugged* becomes a novel about the creators' quest for deliverance from tragic suffering, from the torture to which they have for so long been subjected.

What this implies is something Rand explores through her reworking of another Greek myth, that of Prometheus.

The Myth of Prometheus

In Greek mythology the myth of Atlas and the myth of Prometheus are closely interconnected. Not only are Prometheus and Atlas brothers, and so both Titans, but their stories are thematically related in that they both dramatize the never-ending sufferings inflicted upon a rebellious spirit for daring to defy divine authority. While Atlas is condemned to carry the heavens on his shoulders because he tried to rebel against the tyranny of Zeus, the king of the Olympian gods, Prometheus is chained by an angered Zeus to a rock in the Caucasian Mountains in punishment for the disobedient act of stealing fire from the gods and giving it to men. Here a huge vulture keeps tearing at his liver, and because his liver every night grows whole again, he is in fact condemned to endure eternal torments.

This myth had a special appeal to many Romanticists, who made Prometheus—whose name means "forethought"—a symbolic vehicle for many of their preoccupations. First of all, they saw Prometheus as a symbol of the creator, especially the artist, but also (sometimes more ominously, as in Mary Shelley's *Frankenstein*) the scientist and the inventor. But in addition, they saw him as the archetypal rebel, epitomizing the individual's struggle against all forms of oppressive authority, whether political, moral, or aesthetic. Thus, Percy B. Shelley, in his lyrical drama *Prometheus Unbound* (1820), presented Prometheus as a rebellious figure who, both morally and politically, stands up against a tyrannical god. It was, however, above all as the epitome of the rebellious artist that the Romanticists exalted Prometheus. This was especially the case in Germany, where, as M.H. Abrams informs us,

> The rebels of the genieperiode exploited the element of Promethean defiance against vested authority, in order to attack the authority of poetic rules .... Later Goethe developed Prometheus into a symbol for the poet's painful but necessary isolation, in his creativity, from both men and the gods. (Abrams 1953, 281)

Still later, Nietzsche extends this Prometheanism to the moral realm by conceiving of Prometheus as a "titanically striving individual" who, through a sacrilegious act of defiance against divine authority, makes "the sublime idea of active sin ... the truly Promethean virtue" (Nietzsche [1872] 1993, 50).

There can be little doubt that Rand was strongly influenced by this Romantic cult of the Prometheus figure. Although this is something she never discusses in her theoretical writings, we find ample evidence of the depth and extent of her indebtedness to the Promethean tradition in her fiction-writing, especially in her conception of the hero. In *Anthem*, this is made quite explicit when the hero, after having escaped from the darkness of a totally collectivized society, gives himself the name of Prometheus, in honor of the Titan's role as a bearer of light (Rand 1946, 115). But also the heroes of her later novels, most prominently Howard Roark in *The Fountainhead* and John Galt in *Atlas Shrugged*, can be seen as variants of a Promethean archetype—in both instances by virtue of a creative genius that clashes with the entrenched codes of society.

Distinctive to Rand's Prometheanism, however, is her growing resistance to the tragic implications of the Prometheus myth. While the Romanticists tended to see Promethean aspiration as a form of exalted but doomed striving for ideals set beyond the limits of what is practically possible, Rand envisioned a Prometheanism that emphasized the importance of struggling for attainable goals. Her position here is expressed in her rejection of what she referred to as the "Byronic view of existence," which, she argued, holds that "man must lead a heroic life and fight for his values even though he is doomed to defeat by a malevolent fate over which he has no control" (Rand 1975, 109). In opposition to this existential fatalism, Rand maintained a benevolent view of the heroic, one that gives the hero the chance to succeed in his aspirational efforts, both spiritually and existentially. Even if she recognized that human aspiration may meet with tragic failure, such failure, she held, is to be seen as abnormal, as an accident rather than as the normal way of things. As Rand lets Ragnar Danneskjöld formulate her view in Atlas Shrugged:

> We do not think that tragedy is our natural fate and we do not live in chronic dread of disaster. We do not expect disaster until we have specific reason to expect it—and when we encounter it, we are free to fight it. It is not happiness, but suffering that we consider unnatural. It is not success but calamity that we regard as the abnormal exception in human life. (Rand 1957, 706)

It is this anti-tragic stance towards heroic aspiration that informs Rand's recasting of the Prometheus myth in *Atlas Shrugged*. In mythical terms, therefore, the novel can be read as a powerful tale about how Prometheus, symbolizing man the creator, is liberated from his tragic enchainment. Of central importance here is Rand's notion of the "sanction of the victim," or the view that the creator to some extent is responsible for his victimization through his sanction of the moral code, the code of altruism, that condemns him for his productive abilities. Thus, in a journal note on Atlas Shrugged, Rand writes that the case of the genius often is "the tragedy of [an internal] civil war." Although Rand believed that the creator is made to suffer because he is tortured by the world, "that torture," she reflects,

> would have been easy to bear if the genius had not brought upon himself the torture within. It is he who does the world's dirty work against himself. Otherwise the pain would go only down to a certain point—and the genius would triumph, essentially, even if locked in a jail cell. The world is responsible for the [external] torture of the genius—and as a cause or source of the much greater torture which he imposes on himself by his wrong conception of the world. (Rand 1997, 404)

Armed with this insight, Rand sets out in her novel to deliver the genius from his suffering, showing how he is able to free himself from his torturers by discovering and withdrawing the sanction of the code which throughout history had made possible his victimization. In so doing, she transfigures the tragic Prometheus, turning him into a triumphant Prometheus who, finally released from his chains, is set free to create and produce.

This process of deliverance is presented on two levels, on an external plot level and on an inner psychological level. On the plot level, it is presented through the story of the strike and the strikers' decision to withhold the products of their creative work from society until they are left free to work in accordance with their own code, as free agents and not as tortured slaves. On the psychological level, it is presented through the spiritual journey of Hank Rearden as he, representing all the strikers, gradually wakes up to the recognition that the only weapon the exploiters have against him is his own co-operation with their altruistic code. According to Rand, it is this psychological dimension of the strike that made her want to write the story and that she thought would give it interest. "Without that point," she writes in a journal note, "the story would become merely the recital of the physical aspects of the strike, just plot events of a struggle that would not interest us very much because we are not let in on its essential purpose and motive" (Rand 1997, 397).

That Rand's "presentation of the strikers" deliverance from suffering in *Atlas Shrugged* involves a deliberate attempt to give the Prometheus myth an anti-tragic cast is clearly indicated in the novel itself by means of mythical allusion. Thus, at one point in the story we are told that John Galt is "Prometheus who changed his mind. After centuries of being torn by vultures in payment for having brought to men the fire of the gods, he broke his chains and he withdrew his fire—until the day when men withdraw their vultures" (Rand 1957, 486). It is here worth noting that the Promethean tradition itself offers attempts to liberate Prometheus from his tragic shackles. In a now lost play, entitled *The Unbinding of Prometheus*, the Greek playwright Aeschylus provides what is believed to be a resolution to the tragic dilemma of the hero which he presented in his earlier play Prometheus Bound. According to Walter Kaufmann ([1968] 1979, 179), this resolution is achieved when the Titan, in exchange for giving Zeus a valuable piece of information that prevents the god's undoing, obtains his own freedom. The tragic situation, that is, is brought to an end through an act of mutual accommodation. More than two thousand years later, Shelley, in his *Prometheus Unbound*, presented an alternative solution to Prometheus's dilemma. Seeing the hero's plight as the product of his hatred towards Zeus, a hatred that only fuels the power of his oppressor, Shelley lets him obtain his liberation by having him learn the benign feelings of love and pity, feelings that Zeus cannot endure and that consequently destroy him. Interestingly, Shelley here—in a striking parallel to Rand—makes Prometheus's enchainment the result of his own sanction, his willingness to be victimized by his oppressor, since it is only by virtue of the hero's hatred of Zeus that the god is enabled to exert his power over him. When Prometheus withdraws that hatred, Zeus loses his power. Since, however, in

Rand's version, the creator's sanction is not a matter of self-consuming hatred but of self-denying altruism, the withdrawal of the sanction takes on an entirely different cast, becoming an act not of forgiving love and pity, but—quite contrarily—of proud self-assertion. Ultimately, Rand's Prometheus emerges as a being not only of creative ambition but also of moral defiance, embodying an entirely new ethical vision which, informed by an ideal of rational egoism, aims to blast the whole tradition of altruism and its demands for tragic self-immolation.

Musical Analogues: The Halley Concerto and the Phaëthon Myth

To amplify her tragedy-defying recasting of the Prometheus and Atlas myths in *Atlas Shrugged*, Rand introduces some musical analogues. This she does by having the novel's composer, Richard Halley, compose works that assert the possibilities of triumphant heroic aspiration. This is most evident in Halley's operatic revision of the myth of Phaëthon, which Halley changes "to his own purpose and meaning" by giving the originally tragic story a happy resolution. Thus, in Halley's opera, we are told, "Phaëthon, the young son of Helios, who stole his father's chariot and, in ambitious audacity, attempted to drive the sun across the sky," does not perish, but is allowed to succeed (Rand 1957, 70).

This theme of defiant heroic triumph is further developed, but in a purely musical language, in Halley's Fifth Concerto, also entitled The Concerto of Deliverance. The dramatic and emotional movement of this Concerto is described as follows:

> It was a symphony of triumph. The notes flowed up, they spoke of rising and they were the rising itself, they were the essence and the form of upward motion, they seemed to embody every human act and thought that had ascent as its motive. It was a sunburst of sound, breaking out of hiding and spreading open. It had the freedom of release and the tension of purpose. It swept space clean, and left nothing but the joy of unobstructed effort. Only a faint echo within the sounds spoke of that from which the music had escaped, but spoke in laughing astonishment at the discovery that there was no ugliness or pain, and there never had had to be. It was the song of an immense deliverance. (Rand 1957, 20, 1083)

According to Rand, this description—which occurs both in the opening and towards the end of the novel—is a "philosophical-emotional summation of the ideas of the story" (Rand 2000, 50). What it conveys is the feeling of exalted freedom, of unimpeded effort, finally attained by the strikers in their quest to be liberated from their exploiters. It thus serves as an effective reinforcement of the theme of deliverance that informs Rand's reworking of the various ancient myths in the novel.

The Legend of Atlantis

A final manifestation of the anti-tragic slant of Rand's use of myth in *Atlas Shrugged* can be observed in her exploitation of the legend of Atlantis. According to Plato (the main source of the legend), Atlantis was a thriving and prosperous society, inhabited by a noble and partly divine race of men originally ruled by Atlas. Gradually, however, this noble race was corrupted, losing their divine nature, and in punishment the gods sent a deluge causing the island to sink into the sea and thus to vanish forever. Throughout her novel, Rand makes a number of allusions to this legend, utilizing it to convey the idea of a Utopian society where the men of the mind, the Atlases of the world, have their true home.

In Rand's version, the mythical Atlantis becomes above all a land of heroic beings, being described as "a place which only the spirits of heroes could enter" (Rand 1957, 149). The significance of this is subtly brought out in the scene where Dagny Taggart, at a point in the story when society as a result of the strike is being drained of its intellectual power, watches a "sinking" Manhattan from her window:

> Clouds had wrapped the sky and had descended as fog to wrap the streets below, as if the sky were engulfing the city. She could see the whole of Manhattan Island, a long, triangular shape cutting into an invisible ocean. It looked like the prow of a sinking ship; a few tall buildings still rose above it, like funnels, but the rest was disappearing under gray blue coils, going down slowly into vapor and space. This was how they had gone—she thought—Atlantis, the city that sank into the ocean, and all the other kingdoms that vanished, leaving the same legend in all the languages of men, and the same longing. (Rand 1957, 591–2)

This passage is a brilliant example of Rand's ability to give the events taking place in a modern world the haunting quality of timeless legend. The image of Manhattan, engulfed by clouds and appearing to sink into the ocean like a ship, vividly evokes the story of Atlantis vanishing in the sea, thus inviting the reader to contemplate the collapse of modern industrial civilization presented in the novel in analogous terms: as the destruction of a land of heroes. At the same time, this evocation of the Atlantis legend, invites us to see Dagny's wistful longing for the men of ability she sees disappearing from society in universal terms, as an expression of a general longing, shared by all humanity, for a perfect society left by the Atlantis legend and other legends telling of a paradise that once existed but was lost. The nature of this longing is elaborated upon in Galt's speech:

> Observe the persistence, in mankind's mythologies, of the legend about a paradise that men had once possessed, the city of Atlantis or the Garden of Eden or some kingdom of perfection, always behind us. The root of that legend exists, not in the past of the race, but in the past of every man. You still retain a sense—not as firm as a memory,

but diffused like the pain of hopeless longing—that somewhere in the starting years of your childhood .... you had known a radiant state of existence. (Rand 1957, 982)

Rand's use of the Atlantis legend is not, however, restricted to the sunken Atlantis. She also gives us a new Atlantis, letting it rise in the wilderness of the Rocky Mountains as a modern capitalist Utopia where the creators are free to produce, unhampered by the obstructions imposed by an altruist-collectivist society. Atlantis thus comes to represent more than a nostalgic longing for a perfect world that once was but is gone forever; it becomes a future possibility, the symbol of an ideal society to fight for and make real. This use of the Atlantis legend informs the chapter entitled "Atlantis," which, by giving us a brief glimpse of what society should be and ought to be, forms a shining contrast to the decaying society presented in the other chapters of the novel. But to gain entrance to this Utopia is not for everyone. The key of admission is that one has grasped the code of rational egoism, in its pure form, cleansed of all altruistic impurities. As Galt tells Dagny, after she has decided to leave the valley:

> If you fail, as men have failed in their quest for a vision that should have been possible, yet has remained forever beyond their reach—if, like them, you come to think that one's highest values are not to be attained and one's greatest vision is not to be made real—don't damn this earth, as they did, don't damn existence. You have seen the Atlantis they were seeking, it is here, it exists—but one must enter it naked and alone, with no rags from the falsehoods of centuries, with the purest clarity of mind—not an innocent heart, but that which is much rarer: an intransigent mind—as one's only possession and key. (Rand 1957, 755)

It is through the attainment of such an "intransigent mind" that the strikers achieve their spiritual deliverance and, as a reward, entrance to Atlantis—the society that only heroes can enter.

Moral and Metaphysical Implications

Through her recasting of ancient Greek myths in *Atlas Shrugged*, Rand challenges a central motif of much tragic literature: the danger of heroic aspiration. Common to the three myths she is dealing with in her novel is that they all present a hero coming to grief because of his overweening ambition. His primary sin, for which he must be punished, is what the Greeks called hubris, or insolent pride, the attempt to defy or oppose the gods. Thus Atlas and Prometheus are both made to suffer eternal torments because they dared stand up against Zeus, while Phaëthon is destroyed because he disregarded his father's advice. In all cases, the implied message is that one must not aspire beyond certain preset limits but must show some form of moderation or accommodation.

It is this tragic attitude towards heroic aspiration, the idea that to presume beyond one's natural limitations as a human being is to court disaster, that Rand seeks to demolish through her reworking of these myths. For her, they all reflect what she saw as a malevolent metaphysics, the belief that the universe is hostile to great achievement. In opposition to this belief, she insists upon the benevolent nature of the universe, arguing that metaphysically, i.e., essentially if not statistically, the world is open to happiness and success. This does not involve any simplistic claim to the effect that all aspiration is guaranteed a happy outcome; but it does involve the belief that great feats are possible, that daring ambition is not doomed to failure but may, when pursued rationally, lead a person to final triumph. What Rand wants to show in *Atlas Shrugged* is precisely the practical viability of such triumph, whatever its rarity in real life. The precondition, however, is that the aspiring individual rids himself of every vestige of the altruistic code and instead adopts a rational code of egoism. For it is only, Rand believes, that by withdrawing his sanction of altruism, by refusing to co-operate with his torturers, that the creator is set free and thus enabled to emerge as a triumphant hero.

In conducting this liberation of the creator, Rand holds up an exalted and inspiring image of human possibilities, giving us heroes who in forceful ways show us what is possible to man at his best and highest. Yet, powerful as this image is, it also raises some questions about the moral and metaphysical viability of Rand's benevolent conception of the heroic. For in her attempt to provide her heroes with a moral code that delivers them from their tragic affliction, Rand in effect ends up adopting a deified vision of man and with it what many will see as a naïve metaphysical optimism. This is especially evident in her portrayal of John Galt, who, with his apparent imperviousness to pain and suffering, is lifted above ordinary human frailties and turned into an invulnerable god. In my view, Rand here reveals an excessive trust in the practical efficacy of her moral code, investing it with a power to undo tragic suffering that far exceeds what seems both existentially and psychologically realistic. Even though there is much to support her view that the creator throughout history has been martyred by his sanction of the altruistic code, it does not follow that once the creator is liberated from the burden of altruism, he shall also be liberated from tragedy. As so much tragic literature demonstrates, including the myths Rand seeks to recast in *Atlas Shrugged*, human tragedy is not necessarily the product of altruistic self-sacrifice but arises rather from the tragic potential that will always reside in heroic aspiration. Since a hero, by definition, is someone who takes risks, who stretches limits, who defies authority, who soars above the ordinary and the common, he will always walk on the edge of tragedy—a fact duly recognized by the tragic tradition but perilously ignored, even defied, by Rand.

Notwithstanding this reservation, I believe that Rand's recasting of ancient myths in *Atlas Shrugged* opens up new and interesting perspectives on the role of heroic aspiration in human life. Even if one may question, as I do, the viability of her anti-tragic conception of the heroic, her presentation of an entirely new type of hero, informed by a new moral code, provides in its daring innovation and imaginative scope a thought-provoking image of man's heroic potential. Precisely because of her engagement with ancient myths in creating this hero, Rand has given us a novel that invites us to reflect upon the place and legitimacy of human heroism, challenging us to reconsider our thoughts on its deeper moral and metaphysical implications.

References

Abrams, M.H. 1953. *The Mirror and the Lamp: Romantic Theory and the Critical Tradition*. Oxford: Oxford University Press.

Kaufmann, Walter. [1968] 1979. *Tragedy and Philosophy*. Princeton: Princeton University Press.

Nietzsche, Friedrich. [1872] 1993. *The Birth of Tragedy*. Edited by Michael Tanner and translated by Shaun Whiteside. Harmondsworth: Penguin.

Rand, Ayn. 1946. *Anthem*. New York: New American Library.

———. 1957. *Atlas Shrugged*. New York: New American Library.

———. [1958] 1986. Lectures on Fiction-Writing. 12 lectures. Oceanside, California: Lectures on Objectivism.

———. 1975. *The Romantic Manifesto: A Philosophy of Literature*. Second revised edition. New York: New American Library.

———. 1997. *Journals of Ayn Rand*. Edited by David Harriman. New York: Dutton.

———. 2000. *The Art of Fiction: A Guide for Writers and Readers*. Edited by Tore Boeckman. New York: Plume.

PART 4
Aesthetics

Chapter 13

Atlas and Art

Ronald F. Lipp

For Ayn Rand, fiction came first and philosophy second—first historically, since most of her stories were written before most of her philosophical essays, and first in the conception of her mission, since she clearly conceived of literature as the primary modality in which to present her unique vision of existence and of man's place in it. Indeed, it may be said (in fact, has been[1]) that she developed her philosophy in order to provide a foundation and context for her fiction. If, for her, philosophy was art's handmaiden, it should be no surprise that she gave esthetics[2] an important place in her conceptual pantheon—including it along with metaphysics, epistemology, ethics, and politics as one of the principal branches of philosophy—or that she included among her numerous philosophical writings a volume, *The Romantic Manifesto*,[3] which attempted to set forth in one place her theory of art.

What is surprising is the scant attention she paid to her esthetic theory in her other writings and the degree to which her views on that subject were, until recently, virtually ignored by her legions of acolytes, students, and critics.

Atlas Shrugged is the fullest expression of Rand's vision, the artistic triumph of her mature years. Following the pseudo-autobiographical *We The Living*, the dystopic nightmare, *Anthem*, and the portrayal of the ideal man and of Rand's conception of ethical egoism in *The Fountainhead*, *Atlas* gives us Rand's explication of the motive force of the world and presents the contours of an ideal world that might be created from the moral wreckage of the existing one. At 1168 pages, it is far and away her longest book. And it is relentlessly didactic. Her ideas about metaphysics, epistemology, ethics, and politics are repeatedly and forcefully presented, culminating in John Galt's celebrated speech, articulating Rand's philosophy of Objectivism that goes on—some would say on and on—for more than sixty pages. But despite this, *Atlas* is largely silent when it comes to art. Among a large and diverse cast of characters, few are engaged with art. Balph Eubank and Gilbert Keith-Worthing are minor figures who caricature the sort of literati that Rand despised. The only artistic figure of note, the composer Richard Halley, is a hero, but a minor one. His chief contribution is a conversation with Dagny Taggart, the book's heroine, in which he serves as a mouthpiece for Rand's views on art.[4] Speaking of Taggart's enjoyment of his composition, Halley says,

> [Y]our enjoyment was of the same nature as mine, ... it came from the same source: from your intelligence, from the conscious judgment of a mind able to judge my work by the standard of the same values that went to write it .... Whether it's a symphony or a coal mine, all work is an act of creativity and comes from the same source: from an inviolate capacity to see through one's own eyes—which means: the capacity to see, to connect and to make what had not been seen, connected and made before.

This passage and other portions of the speech are wonderful as far as they go, elevating coal mining and other productive activities to the status of noble endeavors and forcefully presenting the shocking notion that great art is the product of the disciplined exercise of the same rational faculty and not, as Rand characteristically put it in the same speech, some spontaneous outpouring of feeling "like vomit out of a drunkard." But Rand's colorful metaphors hardly constitute a statement of a comprehensible theory of art and, as we shall see, her choice of a musical composer to speak her words and her focus on conscious activity are problematic for the esthetic theory which she did develop.[5]

For more than 30 years after Rand's art-related essays began to be published in the early 1960s, Objectivist esthetic theory suffered a benign neglect amounting to a sort of amnesia among her students and critics. Despite the occasional book review of *The Romantic Manifesto* or critical essay on related topics, her ideas on art largely languished unexamined by even her most ardent admirers.[6] Popular excitement over Rand's ideas tended to focus on her ethical and political concepts and her fulminations against contemporary culture; scholarly criticism added metaphysics and epistemology. As to art, to the extent that anyone thought about it at all, it was understood that Rand was a Romantic, loved Hugo, Dostoevsky, Rachmaninoff, and Vermeer, disliked Beethoven, Balzac, and Shakespeare, and loathed Tolstoy.[7] In time, whole books were written about her life and her philosophy; but with few exceptions, they had little or nothing whatsoever to say about her esthetics.[8] One prominent philosopher, whose life's work has been heavily influenced by Rand's ideas, has acknowledged having given little attention to her esthetics.[9]

This is a pity, because Rand has a great deal to say, some of it original, much of it important, and, as a totality, a unique formulation which is a crucial aspect of her philosophy. For her admirers, this neglect also amounts to a sort of betrayal because to Rand art is the primary means by which the abstractions of metaphysics, epistemology, and ethics can be made real and the indispensable transmission device to bring Objectivism to people in their actual lives on earth. To care about the rest of her philosophy, but not her conception of the role of art, risks treating the manifestation and realization of Objectivism as though it is an intellectual game, not a real quest with actual, practical consequences. As though ideas don't matter, or more strictly, as though they are the only thing that does.

The disregard of Rand's art theory may be partly the consequence of the considerable hurdles which she placed in the way of thoughtful analysis. *The Romantic Manifesto*, the principal written record of Rand's esthetic ideas, is not a single, integrated presentation but a compilation of essays written at various times on particular topics. Befitting Rand's engagement as a writer, it weighs in heavily on literary theory. Indeed, her concept of Romantic Realism seems more congenial to literature and the other narrative arts (e.g., story telling and the movies) than to painting or music. In fact, the subtitle of the book is *A Philosophy of Literature.* Nonetheless, it does purport to present a general theory of esthetics in its sometimes haphazard, truncated and contradictory fashion. The Romantic Manifesto also suffers from Rand's tendency to mix careful analysis with statements of personal preference, to engage in over-the-top polemics, and to confidently present opinions which serve more to expose her ignorance than to inform the reader. The last range from purely technical comments ("There is no art that uses glue as a medium" [RM 76]) to scathing character assassinations, as when she includes Zen Buddhists in a list of persons who "Have not achieved a free, joyous triumphant sense of life, but a sense of doom, nausea, and screaming cosmic terror" (RM 128). She apparently was unfamiliar with tempera and gesso and was seriously misinformed about Zen Buddhism.[10] But these difficulties afflict nearly all of Rand's work, and she has such important things to say that they should not have impeded serious study.

Whatever the past neglect, the drought ended with the publication in 2000 of the first book devoted entirely to Rand's esthetics: Louis Torres and Michelle Marder Kamhi's *What Art Is: The Esthetic Theory of Ayn Rand.*[11] It is thorough and scholarly. Its 315 pages of text are followed by 153 pages of endnotes and a 25-page bibliography which are themselves a treasure-trove for further study. It subjects Rand's ideas to careful analysis, challenges perceived errors, and suggests useful amendments. Taken together with two lengthy supplementary essays by these authors,[12] the work of Torres and Kamhi is a great achievement.

It also in some ways emulates Rand's shortcomings. While never engaging in her extreme vitriol, it is sometimes crabby, contentious, and arbitrary. It finds no criticism of others' work too trivial or hypertechnical to voice and relentlessly casts as defects and errors what might reasonably be seen as differences in viewpoint or expression. One comes away, after reading some of it, feeling that he has been through a session with the school disciplinarian intent on protecting his turf by giving a class of miscreants a thorough tongue-lashing for their innumerable offenses and deficiencies. Nonetheless, it has rescued Rand's theory of art from obscurity and placed it very much in the arena of public discourse. The immediate instance of that discourse was a symposium in the Spring 2001 issue of *The Journal of Ayn Rand Studies* of such eloquence and insight that more could hardly be asked for.[13] The work of Torres and Kamhi together with that of these interlocutors is the gold standard from which all future dialogue must proceed.

The issues surrounding Rand's esthetics are too numerous and complex to be treated properly in this brief space. It must suffice to summarize the core of Rand's theory, to identify some of the chief issues in dispute, and to suggest some avenues that might merit further inquiry.

Rand defined art as "a selective re-creation of reality according to an artist's metaphysical value-judgments" and said that it "brings man's concepts to the perceptual level of his consciousness and allows him to grasp them directly, as if they were percepts." " .... Art is the indispensable medium for the communication of a moral ideal" (RM, 19–21). The exact sense in which "recreation" is used is not clear, nor why it should not be "creation" since art creates a "reality" that has never been. And even if "recreation" one may wonder whether it should not be "aspects" of or "objects from" reality since every art work, no matter how ambitious, creates a slice of life in accordance with its purpose and cannot do more. Nonetheless, Rand provides a succinct and valuable foundational definition which integrates esthetics with metaphysics, epistemology, and ethics. It is also important for what it does not say. Notably absent from all of Rand's writings is any discussion of beauty, a traditional core focus of esthetics.[14] Since Rand distinguishes personal preference from greatness in art, one might conjecture that beauty in art might be the degree to which the artist succeeds in creating an integrated expression of a creative objective through mastery of his medium. But it's difficult to image that Rand (or perhaps most of us), would find beauty in the perfect portrayal of a determinist nightmare.[15]

For Rand, the crucial force in both the creation of art and the observer's response to it is the individual's "sense of life" for this is the essence that actuates the work of art. Rand says, "A sense of life is a pre-conceptual equivalent of metaphysics, an emotional, subconsciously integrated appraisal of man and of existence" (RM 25). An implicit sense of life is, she says, acquired at a young age, long before the individual is old enough to grasp such a concept of metaphysics. It acquires "the compelling motivational power of a constant, base emotion ... which is part of all his other emotions and underlies all of his experiences" (RM 25–6). In keeping with her rationalist view of man, she says that this early sense of life has a "fluid, plastic" nature which is easily corrected in youth, with more difficulty later, as the thinking individual amends his implicit judgment with an explicit, conscious metaphysics (RM, 29–31).

But the truth of that assertion is not self-evident. What we are speaking of is not a process of rational introspection, but of a transformation of one's personality. Rand says, "Since it is an emotional sum, it cannot be changed by a direct act of will. It changes automatically, but only after a long process of psychological retraining" (RM 31). As if to underscore the impotence of volitional activity to achieve this goal, Rand also says, "Introspectively, one's own sense of life is experienced as an absolute and an irreducible primary—as that which one never questions, because "the thought of questioning it never arises" (RM 31–2). Although Rand's notion of retraining is consistent with her concept of the sub-conscious as a sort of inner-computer,[16] constantly recalculating its view of life on the basis of additional input, the truth of her assertions depends on complex questions about human psychology, neurobiology, and the functioning of the subconscious (including, e.g., the role of innate drives, imprints, genetically predisposed neurological patterns, free will, and other subconscious content and processes of the sort that have been written about since ancient times and continue to be the subject of intense modern investigation).[17] There seems good reason— based on our individual life experiences and our observations of others—to wonder whether the pre-conceptual metaphysics of infancy and early childhood are indeed entirely malleable or open to modification by more mature and reasoned input. Does even a Howard Roark or John Galt fully extricate the mark forever hidden of his infantile subconscious, emotional sense of himself and the world? Until such questions are adequately addressed, it may be necessary provisionally to reformulate Rand's theory to its minimally justified form: "art is a selective re-creation of reality according to an artist's pre-conceptual, emotional, subconsciously integrated appraisal of man and of existence, as that may potentially be modified by his conscious metaphysics."

Rand says not only that the artist's sense of life underlies his creation, but that the observer's sense of life informs his experience of it (and also of love, the other arena in which sense of life is crucial). Insofar as the experience of art turns out to be the voice of the child in the artist speaking to a child-observer, the role for art and its impact on man would potentially be quite different than Rand believes. The point is not to say it is so, but that it may be and this may account for the deep-seated emotional pull of some artistic experiences.

This is of no small moment given the crucial role of art in man's life that Rand repeatedly emphasizes:[18] "Art is a concretization of metaphysics. Art brings man's concepts to the perceptual level of his consciousness and allows him to grasp them directly, as if they were percepts" (RM 19).

"Art is the indispensable medium for the communication of a moral ideal" (RM 21).

[Man] needs a moment, an hour or some period of time in which he can experience ... the sense of living in a universe where his values have been successfully achieved. It is like a moment of rest, a moment to gain fuel to move farther. Art gives him that fuel. (RM 38)

Man's profound need of art lies in the fact that his cognitive faculty is conceptual, i.e., that he acquires knowledge by means of abstractions, and needs the power to bring his widest metaphysical abstractions into his immediate, perceptual awareness. Art fulfills this need ... it concretizes man's fundamental view of himself and of existence ... In this sense, art teaches man how to use his consciousness. It conditions or stylizes man's consciousness by conveying to him a certain way of looking at existence. (RM 45)

The existence of Objectivist esthetics raises the question whether an objective standard might be applied to individual works of art. One standard might judge a work's success from a purely technical point of view and by the extent to which its creator has successfully projected his sense of life into it (although, given the subconscious character of that sense, this task might be quite difficult). But is it possible to do more—to judge whether Vermeer's *Astronomer* really is better than Renoir's *Balançoire* or *Claire de Lune* preferable to *It Ain't Necessarily So*, not simply from the perspective of craftsmanship, but because of the objective superiority of the sense of life each radiates? Rand recognized a distinction between objective value and taste: that a creation might be a great work of art, yet one might not like it. Yet Rand's expressions of preference seemed clearly to go beyond statements of personal taste to some more absolute judgment of quality. We hesitate to make absolutist statements, no doubt in part because of the daunting task involved, but also because the implicit elitism entailed in telling someone else what he should like. Yet within some broad parameters, most people seem to be able with some confidence to distinguish masterpieces from trash. Could it be said that a great work is that creation which a person with a perfect sense of life—a fully integrated, error free metaphysics—would prefer, so that what I dislike may be more a commentary on the fact that I am not Howard Roark than on the quality of the art? If Objectivist esthetics is not up to that task, can it be said, given Rand's statement of the clear relationship between esthetics and the rest of Objectivism, that it constitutes a full and robust philosophical system? Or should we respond that philosophical principles alone do not suffice to fill in the rich fabric of life, whether in metaphysics, art, or anything else?

Rand's theory of art also raises a host of questions—now the subject of a vigorous debate—as to just which forms of expression qualify as art under her criteria or some modification of them. Her notion of a selective recreation of reality in accordance with metaphysical value-judgments fits well with her own sense of herself as a Romantic Realist and with her theory of literature, indeed with the narrative arts in general. But some find it less suitable for the static forms, such as painting and sculpture, which are limited by the carrying capacity of single scenes. Particularly troublesome is the case of music. Music doesn't, strictly speaking, recreate anything and, with the partial exception of some programmatic music or music accompanied by a narrative text (say, *Peter and the Wolf* or the final movement of Beethoven's Ninth Symphony) isn't about anything, at least in the sense or to the degree that we use that term in connection with the narrative arts or representational painting.[19] Commentators have gone to great lengths to analogize music's auditory tone, mathematical base, or some other feature to some aspect of our experienced reality. But perhaps there is another way to come at it. There is a widely held view that successful art doesn't merely recreate some aspect of reality, but in doing so, creates a microcosm, an alternative realty in miniature form.[20] With a really good book or engrossing film, we surrender ourselves to a world of the artist's creation. Our experience in that world evokes an emotional response—the better the work, the more deeply and intensely it is felt. Perhaps it may be said that because of our unique sensory-emotional relationship with sound

—and especially rhythmic, harmonic sound—music is able to short cut this process by directly producing a feeling in us which the narrative arts can evoke only through the intermediate step of the particular images of their story.[21] It may be said that music reverses the place of emotional response by inverting the creative process: music directly evokes an emotional response which provokes an accompanying scenario (in the mind of the individual listener) rather than the customary sequence in other arts in which a scenario (embedded in the art work) triggers the emotional reaction. And perhaps this short-cutting accounts for the strikingly disembodied and abstracted character of musically induced emotion. When I read a tragic tale or see it performed and I am overcome by grief or sadness, I can identify with some specificity the source of those emotions in the story. I know, subject to the limitations of knowing my own subconscious, in respect of what I feel them. When I listen to Tchaikovsky's *Pathétique*, those feelings may be just as intense and seem equally authentic as pure emotion, but they are unconnected with any cognitively related source. The direct yet abstract emotional effect of the music may also account for both the strength of its pull and, ironically, our capacity to evaluate that effect—to engage the meta-emotion of music. In this respect music may occupy a unique psycho-physiological space in its capacity to directly trigger emotional response and require a modification of the definition Rand applied to other arts, a necessity that Rand herself appeared to recognize (see, RM 50–53).[22]

A similar objection that the test of recreation of reality has not been met is made about certain other media. Rand thought (RM 74), many still do, that photography fails to qualify as an art because a photo, however beautiful or dramatic, isn't a selective recreation or reality so much as a snapshot of it. Just as a sunset, however gorgeous it may be, is not art, so neither is a pretty picture of it. The increasing ability of photographers to manipulative images with filters, lighting, dark room alterations, multiple exposures, photomontage, and other techniques, cast doubt on that distinction. The current revolution in digital photography seems to render it entirely untenable. The exclusion of photography is a reflexive bias that needs to be seriously reconsidered and likely abandoned.

So, too, the condescension of the "fine" arts toward the "decorative" ones. Rand asserted that the decoration of utilitarian objects cannot qualify as art in the Objectivist sense, indeed, that to constitute art, a work must not have a practical utilitarian function[23] (RM 74–5). Insofar as mere decoration, design, and craft work are concerned, that seems to be so. And it is also true that the physical limitations of the object may be too constraining to permit much more. But it is not at all clear that the embedding in a useful object of what would otherwise be considered art is ipso facto ground for its disqualification, not should it be the case that a work of art ceases to be such because it also serves some practical purpose. Does a painting cease to be art because it is embodied in a triptych to be used (to proselytize) on an alter or a likeness because it appears (in order to propagandize) in a poster rather than a painting, or an operatic extract because it is used as a wedding march, or

Rand's novels because she intended them to serve a didactic purpose? Why must a work of art be only an art object? This wholesale distinction, without regard for the quality of a particular work seems a relic of an earlier time when the fine arts were the province of patrons whose class mores included a disdain for vulgar commerce and its associated products.

The chief case in point in regard to the classification of useful works is architecture. Rand included it among the visual arts, wrote a whole book about a creator whom she surely regarded as an artist. Yet some critics disqualify architecture precisely because its product is at least as much a utilitarian object as a work of art. No doubt the majority of buildings, even those built by architects, are more anti-art than art. But has anyone, in the presence of a great building—the Parthenon, Sainte-Chapelle, Obecní Dům in Prague, Fallingwater (or name your personal favorite)—not experienced the same sense of liberation that he gains from great sculpture or painting? In fact doesn't the intensely practical art of architecture literally create a microcosm—a miniature recreation of reality in three-dimensional form—more fully than any other art?[24]

The abundant outpouring of analysis of Rand's esthetics beginning with Torres and Kamhi's treatise in 2000 has not only rescued her theory from obscurity but also provided a solid foundation for further development and expansion of Objectivist art theory. The need for this could not be greater or more urgent. We live in a time in which art theory has become so degenerate and vacuous that it is possible to say with a straight face that art is anything that anyone who calls himself an artist chooses to call by that name. Or more recently that art is whatever serves the latest political agenda of radical chic.[25] The "art" which fully honors this standard includes both meaningless trash and literal filth. Nearly ninety years ago, Marcel Duchamp famously expressed his contempt for the art world by exhibiting a ready-bought urinal.[26] This, together with its kind, are said to have "revolutionized the concept of art in this century."[27] Dadists proclaimed "Kunst ist Sheisse": "Art is shit." Apparently so: today human excrement, conveniently packaged for exhibition, is displayed as an art medium and sought after by museums.[28] This is what has become of the sense of life of modern art.

As Stephen Hicks concludes in his brilliant essay "Why Art Became Ugly," "The world of postmodern art is a run-down hall of mirrors reflecting tiredly some innovations introduced a century ago. It is time to move on."[29] With the new attention to Ayn Rand's esthetics, I think we are now ready.

Notes

1   Machan (1999, 80). The subordination of philosophy to fiction resonates with her stance, referencing Aristotle, that literature is more important that history in its capacity to show life as it can and ought to be, rather than as it is.

2   One happy, if incidental, aspect of Rand's writing about art is her adoption of the spelling "esthetics" in lieu of the older and, I think, stodgier "aesthetics." Those— probably still the majority—who retain a preference for the latter, ought to consider whether we should also be speaking of "aether," "aetiology," and "oesophagus."

3   Rand (1975). This work will hereinafter be cited as "RM." Another volume related to her views on art was produced posthumously by Tore Boeckmann. It purports to present edited versions of lectures on fiction given by Rand in 1958, together with an introduction by Leonard Peikoff.

4   Any doubt that Halley is speaking for Rand is dispelled by the inclusion of a substantial portion of the speech (which goes on for more than two pages in *Atlas* [781–4; pb 727–9]) in one of Rand's later works, *For The New Intellectual*, under the heading "The Nature of An Artist" (139–41; pb 114–17). (Rand, 1961) That book set forth major portions of her philosophy by excerpting her fiction. The Halley speech was the only portion of the book explicitly devoted to art or esthetics.

5   However limited Rand's commentary about art may be in Atlas, there is no doubt that the novel is a signal achievement as a work of art. As Ed Younkins has pointed out, it is—among other attributes—remarkable for its use of irony, double meanings, symbolism, and the reworking of Greek mythology (Ed Younkins, private communication, 16 June 2005). See, also, Minsaas (2000) and particularly her discussion of the central importance of the Promethean myth in *Atlas* (at 192–6).

6   Kamhi and Torres (2000) give an excellent account of the reception and reactions to Rand's ideas about art through 1999.

7   Riggenbach (2000, 265–7) provides a vivid recollection of the reactions of early collegiate Objectivists to Rand's esthetics. Barbara Branden (1986) mentions various of Rand's artistic preferences and prejudices among artists. See, also, Merrill (1991, 123).

8   Without seeking to be exhaustive, a brief recitation of major works of this period may help to make the point. Den Uyl and Rasmussen (1986) and Kelley (1986) contain nothing on Rand's esthetic ideas. Merrill (1990) provides a sympathetic and thoughtful overview in a section titled "Objectivist Esthetics," but it is less than four pages long (122–6). O'Neill (1971) also included a sympathetic, but brief evaluation (153–7). Barbara Branden (1986) and Nathaniel Branden (1989) only superficially touch on the subject. Machan (1999) makes several fleeting references. Chris Sciabarra's groundbreaking and important work (Sciabarra 1995) touches on this topic at several points (chiefly, 304–10), but mainly from an historical perspective. The most prominent exception to this litany of neglect may be Peikoff (1991), which includes an entire chapter on Rand's esthetics. This book has had little influence on the ensuing dialogue.

9   Machan (2004, 9).

10   In fairness, her commentary, while excessive, seems sometimes quite justified. One cringes when she describes the image of man that emerges from contemporary art as "an aborted embryo . . . who crawls through a bloody muck, red froth dripping from his jaws . . . [and] screams in abysmal terror at the universe at large" (pb 130). But anyone who is familiar with the more outré paintings of Balthus or Francis Bacon, or of such early modern Symbolists as Félicien Rops, can hardly say that she is wrong.

11   At nearly the same time, another book of some interest, *From the Fountainhead to the Future and Other Essays on Art and Excellence* by Alexandra York, appeared. Despite the seeming reference to Rand's celebrated novel and the prominent discussion by

York of "Romantic Realism," the philosophy of literature with which Rand explicitly identified herself at least as early as 1963 [see RM 167]), York's book contains only scant reference to Rand or her writing. York is a passionate advocate for beauty and the heroic and her taste seems at least partly congruent with Rand's.

12   Kamhi and Torres (2000) and Kamhi (2001).

13   Great credit is due to R.W. Bradford, Stephen Cox, and Chris Sciabarra, the editors of the *Journal*, for publishing the Symposium and to the contributors for its extraordinary quality. The contributions include Bell-Villada (2001), Bissell (2001), Dipert (2001), Enright (2001), Hospers (2001), Hunt (2001), Kelley (2001), Newberry (2001), Riggenbach (2001), and Vacker (2001).

14   Notwithstanding, commentators continue to speculate on Rand's concept of beauty. See, e.g. Machan (1999, 143).

15   Rand clearly distinguishes personal enjoyment of a work from esthetic judgment of it as a great work on art (RM 42), but she says nothing of the relationship of greatness to beauty.

16   The concept of subconscious as computer runs throughout her discussions of the artistic process. See, Rand (2000, 54) and Rand (2001, 59).

17   For a partial recognition of potential problems with Rand's thesis that fails to come to grips with their full implications, see Torres and Kamhi (2000, 121–3 and especially n. 65). For an overview of the current debate over free will and determinism, see, e.g., Schwartz (2002), Walter (2001), O'Connor (2000), and Block (1999).

18   One of the current controversies over Rand's work is the function of art. Some commentators go so far as to claim that she failed to account for its function (see, e.g., Merrill, 125) or sometimes view the question quite narrowly (Torres and Kamhi 2000, 105–6). But it should be abundantly clear from the material above that Rand was quite clear about art's role.

19   For a contrary view, see Bissell (2004, 335–55).

20   For a discussion of the origin and role of the concept of "microcosm" in connection with Rand's art theory, see Bissell (1999, 59 and n. 3 and Bissell (2004).

21   For a vigorous discussion of the relationship of music to concepts, percepts, and sensation, see Dipert (2000, esp. 390–93), Bissell (2004) and Torres and Kamhi (2000, 78–90).

22   An interesting application of this argument—that music is art which succeeds in directly evoking an emotional response without the necessity of the intermediate imagery normally found in the arts—might apply in the case of painting. Rand contended, and her commentators mostly agree, that art must be representational. How can abstract painting convey metaphysical value judgments? One might suppose, however, that one who is particularly sensitive to abstract images of line and color, might respond to abstract painting in the same way we mainly do with music. The response might be that those reactions must necessarily be ones of memory or sentimental association, which most certainly are not the kind which qualify in the Randian sense. Of course, in all art forms, we must distinguish these affective reactions from those that spring from our sense-of-life-value-judgments.

23   RM 50–53. See also, Bissell (2004, 331–5) and Torres and Kamhi (2000, 23–4).

24   For a concurring view see Bissell (2004, 323–31).

25   See discussions in Torrey and Kamhi (2000, 94ff) and Kimball (2004, 3–12).

26 DuChamp said, retrospectively, "that he threw the bottle rack and the urinal into their faces as a challenge, and now they admire them for their aesthetic beauty" Kimball (2003, 5).
27 Seltz (1981, 189).
28 See Hicks (2004, 2, 8–9) and Kimball (2004, 9–11). The extent to which art criticism has become infected with the charlatanry of radical cultural politics is laid out vividly in Kimball (2004).
29 Hicks (2004, 9). This insightful essay follows on from his lucid and indispensable analysis of postmodernism from a broader perspective in Hicks (2004,1).

References

Bell-Villada. 2001. Nordau's *Degeneration* and Tolstoy's *What Is Art?* Still Live. *The Journal of Ayn Rand Studies* 2, no 2 (Spring): 291–7.

Bissell, Roger E. 1999. Music and Perceptual Cognition. *The Journal of Ayn Rand Studies* 1, no 1 (Fall): 59–86.

———. 2001. Critical misinterpretations and missed opportunities: Errors and omissions by Kamhi and Torres. *The Journal of Ayn Rand Studies* 2, no 2 (Spring): 299–310.

———. 2004. Art as microcosm. *The Journal of Ayn Rand Studies* 5, no 2 (Spring): 307–63.

Block, Ned, et al., ed. 1999. *The Nature of Consciousness.* Cambridge, London: The MIT Press.

Boeckmann, Tore, ed. 2000. *The Art of Fiction.* New York: Penguin Putnam.

Branden, Barbara. 1986. *The Passion of Ayn Rand.* New York: Doubleday.

Branden, Nathaniel. 1989. *Judgment Day: My Years With Ayn Rand.* Boston: Houghton Mifflin.

Den Uyl, Douglas and Rasmussen, Douglas B. eds. 1986. *The Philosophic Thought of Ayn Rand.* Urbana: University of Illinois Press.

Dipert, Randall R. 2001. The puzzle of music and emotion in Rand's Aesthetics. *The Journal of Ayn Rand Studies* 2, no 2 (Spring): 387–94.

Enright, John. 2001. Art: What a concept. *The Journal of Ayn Rand Studies* 2, no 2 (Spring): 341–59.

Hicks, Stephen R.C. 2004-1. *Explaining Postmodernism: Skepticism and Socialism from Rousseau to Foucault.* Tempe, Arizona: Scholargy.

———. 2004. Why art became ugly. *Navagator: An Objectivist Review of Politics and Culture* 7, no 7 (September): 5–11.

Hospers, John. 2001. Rand's aesthetics: A personal view. *The Journal of Ayn Rand Studies* 2, no 2 (Spring): 311–34.

Hunt, Lester. 2001. What art does. *The Journal of Ayn Rand Studies* 2, no 2 (Spring): 253–63.

Kamhi, Michelle Marder. 2003. What Rand's Aesthetics is, and why it matters. *The Journal of Ayn Rand Studies* 4, no 2 (Spring): 413–90.

Kamhi, Michelle Marder and Torres, Louis. 2000. Critical neglect of Ayn Rand's Theory of Art. *The Journal of Ayn Rand Studies* 2, no 1 (Fall): 1–46.

Kelley, David. 1986. *The Evidence of the Senses: A Realist Theory of Perception.* Baton Rouge: Louisiana State University Press.

———. 2001. Reasoning about art. *The Journal of Ayn Rand Studies* 2, no 2 (Spring): 335–40.

Kimball, Roger. 2003. *Art's Prospect.* Chicago: Ivan R. Dee.

———. 2004. *The Rape of the Masters: How Political Correctness Sabotages Art.* San Francisco: Encounter.

Machan, Tibor R. 1999. *Ayn Rand.* New York: Peter Lang Publishing.

———. 2004. *Objectivity.* Aldershot, England: Ashgate.

Merrill, Ronald E. 1991. *The Ideas of Ayn Rand.* LaSalle, Illinois: Open Court.

Minsaas, Kirsti. 2000. The role of tragedy in Ayn Rand's fiction. *The Journal of Ayn Rand Studies* 1, no 2 (Spring): 171–209.

Newberry, Michael. 2001. On metaphysical value-judgments. *The Journal of Ayn Rand Studies* 2, no 2 (Spring): 383–6.

O'Connor, Timothy. 2000. *Persons and Causes.* New York: Oxford University Press.

O'Neill, William. 1971. *With Charity Toward None: An Analysis of Ayn Rand's Philosophy.* New York: Philosophical Library.

Peikoff, Leonard. 1991. *Objectivism: The Philosophy of Ayn Rand.* New York: Dutton.

Rand, Ayn. 1957. *Atlas Shrugged.* New York: Random House.

———. 1961. *For the New Intellectual: The Philosophy of Ayn Rand.* New York: New American Library.

———. 1975. *The Romantic Manifesto: A Philosophy of Literature.* Rev. ed. New York: New American Library.

———. 2000. *The Art of Fiction.* Edited by Tore Boeckmann. New York: Plume-Penguin.

———. 2001. *The Art of Nonfiction.* Edited by Robert Mayhew. New York: Plume-Penguin.

Riggenbach, Jeff. 2001. What art is: What's not to like? *The Journal of Ayn Rand Studies* 2, no 2 (Spring): 265–90.

Schwartz, Jerry M., and Begley, Sharon. 2002. *The Mind and the Brain.* New York: Regan Books.

Sciabarra, Chris Matthew. 1995. *Ayn Rand: The Russian Radical.* University Park: The Pennsylvania State University Press.

Seltz, Peter. 1981. *Art in Our Times.* New York: Harry N. Abrams.

Torres, Louis, and Kamhi, Michelle Marder. 2000. *What Art Is: The Esthetic Theory of Ayn Rand.* LaSalle, Illinois: Open Court.

Vacker, Barry. 2001. Guggenheims and Grand Canyons. *The Journal of Ayn Rand Studies* 2, no 2 (Spring): 361–82.

Walter, Henry. 2001. *Neurophilosophy of Free Will.* Cambridge, London; The MIT Press.

York, Alexandra. 2000. *From the Fountainhead to the Future.* New York: Silver Rose.

Chapter 14

My Music: Why It's Romantic, and Why I Write It That Way

Roger E. Bissell

A Hugh Akston Memorial lecture by Dr. Richard Halley, composer-in-residence and professor emeritus of music theory and aesthetics, Patrick Henry University, Cleveland, Ohio, 2 September 2000, as transcribed from the audio taped lecture.

Good evening, ladies and gentlemen. I want to welcome you all—students, colleagues, and distinguished guests—to this Hugh Akston Memorial lecture on the topic of Romanticism in music, specifically in my own compositions. As you all know, this year marks the 25th anniversary of the Great Strike, spearheaded by some of the late Dr. Akston's own pupils, and this series of lectures was conceived for the purpose of celebrating this great man's role in helping to turn our world back toward rationality and individualism. As some of you also know, when I joined the faculty here at Patrick Henry, I engaged Dr. Akston numerous times, prior to his second retirement, in personal discussions on the topic of aesthetics and how the rational principles of art might apply to music, and the topic of this lecture is really an outgrowth of those discussions.

One of Dr. Akston's most original and brilliant contributions, of which there are many, was his insight that has come to be known as the Grand Unified Theory of the Arts. He held the view, which I share, that in order to be separate species of art, the different forms of art must have their own distinguishing characteristics; but in order to all be members of the genus of art, they must also all possess the common denominator for works of art. And this common denominator is what the ancients called "imitation of nature" and what we nowadays call the "recreation of reality." In his landmark essay, "The Cognitive-Symbolic Function of Art," he wrote that "all art, must re-create reality in some form, but may do so in any form, consistent with the nature of the physical medium employed and the cognitive mode addressed by a particular type of art." Music, of course, recreates reality in the medium of musical tones, and it is directed to the human understanding via the sense of hearing.

In another of his major essays, "Emotional Abstraction in Art," Dr. Akston pointed out that the reality recreated in art is an imaginary world that embodies a view of this world. That view of the world, Akston wrote, "is the meaning of the artwork, and the subject and style are the carriers of that view of the world, so they are for that reason the carriers of the artwork's meaning, or theme. This theme originates in the artist, and resonates in the viewer, as an emotionally tinged view of the world and is what gives art its enormous psychological power. The various schools of art are defined, at least in part, by their view on whether the world is intelligible, whether man can live in harmony with the world, whether man is good, or whether man can pursue and achieve values."

Dr. Akston went beyond this to assert that the various schools of art applied across the board to the various forms of art, just as their practitioners claimed but were unable to explain. In particular, he championed Romanticism in the arts. In yet another of his most significant essays, "The Nature of Romanticism," he wrote that "since emotions are consequences of the values one has chosen and achieved or not, Romanticism is not properly speaking an emotionalist school of art, but instead more fundamentally a style of art based upon the human drive to choose and achieve values."

His best developed explication of this view was in the field of literature, his undergraduate major, and he wrote compellingly of the nature of plot, characterization, and goal-directed series of events leading to a climax. However, because of his near silence on the subject of music, it has often been said that Dr. Akston over-generalized from his Romanticist philosophy of literature and claimed things about the other arts that could not possibly be true. Thus, part of the purpose of this lecture is to provide a long-overdue refutation of this misconception on the part of Dr. Akston's critics by showing how his theory about Romantic art applies to music. And thus the title of my lecture. Why, then, is my music Romantic, and why have I written it that way?

The key to answering these questions is to recognize that music, like literature, is a temporal art, being built up from patterns that require time in order to develop and complete themselves; music, like literature, is not ready-made for perception as are painting, sculpture, and architecture. More specifically, dramatic music, like dramatic literature, is a temporal art that re-creates reality by portraying a world of entities and their actions. However, the entities in music, which are melodies and chords, do not appear as images of human beings, nor do their actions, musical phrases and harmonic-rhythmic progressions, appear as images of human action. Instead, they function as "virtual characters" and "virtual plot." That is, melody is a musical analog to a dramatic literary character, in which the musical motif or melodic idea is repeated and varied and developed as the music unfolds—and musical progressions are an analog to dramatic literary plot, in which the melody goes through a process of repetition, variation, and development, as the music unfolds. Thus, whereas dramatic literature creates an imaginary fictional world that presents an image of fictional people and their actions, dramatic music presents an imaginary tonal world of melody and harmony and rhythm that function as the subject of music, a "musical individual" that engages in certain kinds of musical motion and action.

We human beings have a natural propensity to interpret and respond sympathetically to even the bare semblance of physical motion in anthropomorphic terms, as if it were a real or fictional person. The behavior of musical tones in dramatic music is naturally, unavoidably experienced in this way, as a convincing and engaging analogy to a human being located in space and engaged in physical movements and gestures and goal-directed activities that unfold through the passage of time. The natural basis of this goal-directedness, which is the essential core of dramatic music, is the anticipation of melodic and harmonic goals that arise from the relationships between the tones and chords of the diatonic scale, in its major and minor forms. Nearly all music since the Renaissance has been built upon this scale and has allowed composers to present a musical world of value-seeking, goal-directed action; and the epitome and fullest culmination of this has been the music of the Romantic school.

Now, at this point, I must apologize to the lay members of my audience, and for those of you taking notes, you may label this section:

Technical Matters

A full demonstration of exactly how goal-directedness and the resulting large-scale emotionality function in music is something that requires the background provided by several semesters of study of music theory and analysis, as my students, past and present, well know. However, I can give you at least a decent glimpse into the world of musical meaning by taking a look not at the long-winded, large-scale forms of serious music, such as symphonies or sonatas, but at the relatively more bite-sized popular music melodies and main themes from serious works. And there is only one basic thing that is required to understand what follows: the difference between the minor and major scales, especially the numbers one-through-eight of the notes or "degrees" of the scale, as well as the melodies and harmonies that are based on them. I must assume that those of you interested enough to attend this lecture already possess this basic knowledge. Just so those of you without a technical background are not completely in the dark, however, here is a brief demonstration. [Halley plays the C major and C minor scales at the piano, highlighting the lowered scale tones in the minor scale in comparison to the major scale. Throughout the lecture, he uses the piano to demonstrate the motifs, melodies, and themes given as examples. For those who want to ponder the examples at more length, he has compiled into a handout a listening list of songs and themes keyed to recordings in the Patrick Henry University Music Library.]

All right, in order to set the stage for our consideration of melody, we must first briefly consider a few basic facts about emotion and the elements of music.

Because the emotions associated with the pursuit of values are experienced as tension and release, the basis of smaller-scale emotional expression by musical themes and melodies is the nature and progression of tensions that exist between musical tones. (We are, please remember, setting aside the patterns of tension and release that exist in progressions of harmonies, which are the basis of plot and larger-scale emotional expression in music. If someone wishes during the question period to ask me about harmonic progression and emotional expression, I will be happy to do my best to explain how this works, along with some examples.)

Now, the tensions between musical tones are set up along three dimensions of melody: pitch, rhythm, and volume. It's interesting to note that pitch, rhythm, and volume are analogous to space, time, and mass in physics, and this indeed seems to be the reason that melodies are experienced as being analogous to physical objects in motion and, in particular, to literary characters. This should be no surprise, however, because there is no such thing as a free-floating emotion. No emotional state exists in disembodiment from a person who experiences that emotional state; all emotions are emotions of human beings. Thus, there can be no recreation of an emotion that does not rest more basically upon a recreation of at least something that resembles a person, in the key respects that pertain to emotion, such as auditory tonal intensity and volume, musical gesture, progressions of musical tension and release, etc. So, if a given passage of music is being experienced as expressive of a particular emotion, we must seek to understand how it does so by focusing in on the musical entity, the melodic material, presented in that passage.

To further simplify this discussion, I am going set aside considerations of rhythm and volume—again, I can try to discuss some examples during the question period, if anyone is interested—and I am going to look here only at pitch, and specifically, at the tonal tensions that arise from the notes of the scale themselves, as well as the distance and the direction notes are from each other. The distance between notes is measured in terms of how many notes of the scale lie between them, and the direction between tones is measured in terms of whether the second tone is higher or lower in pitch than the first, and the tonal movement from one note to the next accordingly is experienced as and referred to as "upward" or "downward." Further, notes of the scale all have their own emotional implications, either painful if they are some of the notes belong to a minor scale, or pleasurable if they are some of the notes belonging to a major scale, or neutral as are some of the notes belonging to either scale. Upward melodic motion can be thought of as "asserting" or expressing an "outgoing emotion," while downward melodic motion can be thought of as "accepting" or expressing an "incoming emotion." I prefer to think of them in terms of "investing" and "cashing-in" (or out)—or, if you prefer an agricultural metaphor over a financial one, "sowing" and "reaping." Here are some examples, and, as mentioned earlier, the numbers stand for the notes, in sequence, of the diatonic scale; and please bear in mind that while these are just the leading motifs from longer themes or melodies, they "do a lot of the work," so to speak, in setting the emotional tone for those longer melodic passages.

Consider the song "Don't Take Your Love from Me," which begins in the major mode with an upward-downward motif of 5-6-5, which connotes a longing for happiness, and compare it with Schubert's lieder "Ständchen (Evening Song)," which begins in the minor mode with an upward-downward motif of 5-b6-5 [five, flat six, five]—the 6th scale note is here lowered by one-half step, making it closer to the 5th, which connotes a mournful feeling. Now, note that Grieg's piano concerto in A minor utilizes both of these motifs. In the first phrase of the Grieg, there is a rising and falling motif of 5-b6-b7-b6-5 on an A minor chord, and in the second phrase there is a rising and falling motif of 5-6-7-6-5 on a C major chord. These two phrases connote a burst of anguish and mournfulness (due to the lowered 6th and 7th scale notes), followed by a burst of violent longing for happiness. These two phrases also, by the way, were essential ingredients in the main theme to my 4th piano concerto and its attempt to convey tortured struggle and the rebellious refusal to accept pain and suffering.

Consider the song "One Love" from the movie "Snow White." It begins in the major mode with a downward motif of 5-3-2-1, which connotes an accepting or welcoming of blessing or fulfillment. This same motif appears in the main theme of the opening movement of Tchaikovsky's 1st piano concerto, which begins in the major mode with the same downward motif of 5-3-2-1. Interestingly, the introduction to the Tchaikovsky concerto is in the parallel minor with a similar downward motif of 5-b3-2-1, but which, because of the lowered 3rd scale note, connotes a very different emotion of painful finality, acceptance of or yielding to grief. The abrupt turnaround into the main theme occurs almost as a blinding burst of sunlight in switching quickly from a state of anguish to one of exultation.

One more example: Consider the popular song "The Shadow of Your Smile," which begins in the minor mode with an upward motif of 5-1-2-b3, which, because of the lowered 3rd scale note, connotes an outgoing emotion of wistful longing, pure and simple. (One of the lyrics set to this motif even says "our wistful little star was far too high.") Then consider the popular song "You Are My Sunshine," which begins in the major mode with an upward motif of 5-1-2-3, which connotes an outgoing emotion of joy, pure and simple. Shostakovich's "Festive Overture" employs the same motif in the second theme, but adds an enormous amount of further development with other positive-tinged motifs that convey exuberance and fulfillment. This motif, by the way, is one of the most crucial elements of the main theme of my 5th piano concerto, what we have called the "Concerto of Deliverance." The notes flow upward, they speak of rising and they are the rising itself, they are the essence and the form of upward motion. Judging from the introspective reports of discerning listeners, this theme seems to embody every human act and thought that has ascent as its motive, which is a good indication of the power of the intervals I selected in constructing the theme. True, there were faint traces in the theme, minor, transient motifs, of a pessimistic connotation that conveyed the depths of unhappiness from which the music had escaped, but in fact it would have been impossible to construct the complex melody of my concerto's main theme without incorporating such elements. Since the whole point of the theme was to suggest astonished laughter at the discovery that there is no ugliness and pain, and there never had to be, there still has to be some passing reference to the ugliness and pain that is rendered insignificant by one's having risen up from bondage.

Now, with these examples as a sort of preliminary guide, we can generalize by combining the minor-major tensions and the upward-downward tensions into a fourfold way of classifying melodies or parts of melodies in terms of their general emotional content. They can be further sub-classified into eight different kinds in terms of their degree of vigor. For those taking notes, call this section:

Categories of Emotion in Melody

The first category, a melody in major tonality with upward melodic motion, conveys an active striving process characterized by an optimistic outlook, and, more specifically, exultant pursuit or quiet confidence, depending upon the level of vigor of the melody. As mentioned earlier, this is the type of melody I used in the main theme to my 5th piano concerto and that Shostakovich used in the second theme of his Festive Overture. The second category, a melody in minor tonality with upward melodic motion, conveys an active striving process characterized by a pessimistic outlook, and, more specifically, vigorous defiance or grim determination. Also, for point of reference, this is the type of melody I used in the main theme to my 4th piano concerto and that Beethoven used in the main theme of his 5th symphony. The third category, a melody in major tonality with downward melodic motion, conveys an absence of striving tinged with an optimistic outlook, and, more specifically, joyous celebration or serene happiness. This is the type of melody used by Tchaikovsky in the main theme of his 1st piano concerto and by Rachmaninoff in the 18th variation of his Rhapsody on a Theme of Paganini. And finally, the fourth category, a melody in minor tonality with downward melodic motion, conveys an absence of striving tinged with a pessimistic outlook, and, more specifically, bitter anguish or wistful mourning. This is the type of melody used by Tchaikovsky in the famous anguished theme in his 6th or "Pathetique" Symphony.

This is not all there is to melodic analysis, by any means. An important factor that intensifies the emotion expressed in a melody is the device of momentary or secondary switchbacks in the direction of the melody's motion. These are less important than the changeover to another melodic type, but still significant enough to have a bearing on the emotional expression of a given passage. A melody which goes predominantly upward, but with some reversals of direction of melodic motion, will convey an intensified sense of exuberance or defiance, and a melody which goes predominantly downward, but with some upward reversals of direction of melodic motion, will convey an intensified sense of fulfillment or despair. These melodic switchbacks are a principal means of going beyond simple melodic structures and creating more complex forms that convey more nuanced emotional states. Just a few examples from the serious and popular literature will have to suffice here, and please do avail yourselves of the listening list and the opportunity to hear these pieces in their "natural settings," so to speak.

Examples of exuberant or confident striving include the Chopin Etude in E Major and the popular songs "Close to You," "My Heart Stood Still," "What Kind of Fool Am I?," "The Impossible Dream," "I've Gotta Be Me," "My Way," and "When I Fall in Love." For defiance or doubt or grimly determined striving, consider Rachmaninoff's Preludes in G minor and C# minor (the first sections), the third movement of Beethoven's Moonlight Sonata, and the Chopin's Scherzo in B minor. Examples of sweet reflection or jubilant celebration include Handel's "Joy to the World," "Ode to Joy" from Beethoven's 9th symphony, and the popular songs "Namely Me" and "Early Autumn." For bitter or anguished or wistful mourning, consider the popular songs "Autumn Leaves," "How Insensitive," "A Day in the Life of a Fool," and "Nature Boy," as well as the theme from the movie "The Godfather."

Yet another factor is the fact that most complex themes, mine included, are actually hybrids of the four above types, as are the melodies of numerous popular songs. In using combinations of the four melodic types, expression of emotion in music can be very nuanced and powerful. Fritz Kreisler's "Liebesleid" (Love's Sorrow) contains sections with wistful mourning and sections with sweet reflection. Jacques Brel's "Ne Me Quitte Pas" (If You Go Away) contains sections with anguished mourning and sections with defiant assertion. As already noted, Tchaikovsky's 1st piano concerto opens with three statements of a defiant motif, which is then transformed into a passionately exuberant statement of the same motif in a major key. Rachmaninoff's 18th variation on a theme of Paganini contains phrases with joyous celebration, followed by phrases with passionate assertion, as does Saint-Saens' "My Heart at Thy Sweet Voice." The popular song "My Funny Valentine" is quite ambivalent, due to the swinging back and forth between motifs expressing doubt and confidence. While the Rachmaninoff 18th variation is entirely positive and optimistic in the motifs used, Saint-Saens' "The Swan" (from Carnival of the Animals), by contrast, is largely (over 80 percent) optimistic, but tinged with some doubt, due to the presence of two upward striving sequences in the minor mode, which is very likely the source of the poignancy of this beautiful cello solo.

Conclusion

So, as a result of this brief excursion into music theory and appreciation, you perhaps can see, in large part at least, why my music is Romantic. It is not simply a matter of writing music that is colorful or imaginative or exciting or emotionally intense. My music is Romantic, first and foremost, because it presents a musical world of rebellious, triumphant, joyous, and anguished melodies that seek after and achieve challenging harmonic-rhythmic goals. My music presents images, in sound, of a world in which value-seeking and achievement is possible to man.

As for why I write Romantic music—from an aesthetic standpoint, Romantic music is the best means for me to embody and express my feeling about life, my personal, inner view of how the world and human life is or should be and can be at its best. I write my music this way because it is my way of creating, for myself, the kind of world I want—and my way of living in that world while I am creating, performing, or hearing others perform the music. It is the kind of aesthetic experience I want to have and to share with others.

From an ethical standpoint, my reasons for writing Romantic music are essentially the same. I do it for my own selfish pleasure. And because I know there are others like me, who yearn for the same kind of life and strive for the same kind of values, I know that in writing for my own pleasure, I will also be giving pleasure to others. But my pleasing others with my music is only a value to me because it is, primarily, pleasing to me, and that the others who respond in the same way to my music are, in that respect, extensions of me. My own sense of ego expands to include and encompass those who are like me in their feeling about life, so there is a great ego satisfaction and visibility in being able to engage their minds and touch their lives in this way.

In other words, I am not an altruist. I do not write my music for the sake of others. The prevailing attitude of those who assumed that I do or should is what eventually drove me to go on strike. The resurgence of healthier attitudes in the listening public and in the world at large is what brought me—and all of us—back to the world. I asked John [Galt] what kind of world we were going to have post-Strike, and he said to me, paraphrasing one of the Founding Fathers, "a world of rational individualism, if you can keep it." Let us endeavor to do so, in music and the other arts, as in our lives. Thank you. [Sustained, enthusiastic applause.] Thank you very much. We have time for a few questions from the floor …

Question-Answer Session

Audience member: What do you think about Mort Liddy's screen adaptation of your 4th concerto?

Dr. Halley: After all these years? I don't think about it. That is, I don't dwell on it, for it is truly not a concern to me any longer. This kind of parasitic perversion of the work of creative individuals in a society inevitably results when the philosophy of altruism is welcomed by the populace. Since the Strike, things have changed for the better in regard to altruism and, thus, the second-handed mangling of the genuine creativity of true artists has become an insignificant fringe phenomenon.

One personally gratifying consequence of this is that, since the Strike, writers like me have been the ones to receive commissions to compose for motion pictures and television. The result of this is that we are now able to hear genuine, unmangled Richard Halley compositions in the movies and the concert hall and on television, radio, and CD and MP3 recordings.

[More sustained applause. End of tape 1, side 1. Q-A session continues on tape 1, side 2.] [The discussion continued to 3 a.m., as Patrick Henry University discussions often do, with questions ranging from popular music styles to the emotional function of rhythm and harmonic progression.

References

Bissell, Roger. 2004. Art as microcosm. *Journal of Ayn Rand Studies* 5, no. 2. (Spring).
————. 2004. Serous schmaltz and passionate pop: are there objective indicators of emotion in music? Presented to Free Exchange, San Francisco, March 2004.
Blumenthal, Allan and Joan Mitchell Blumenthal. 1974. *Music: Theory, History, and Performance.* 12 audiotaped lectures. San Francisco: Laissez Faire Audio.
Cooke, Deryck. 1959. *The Language of Music.* London: Oxford University Press.
Objectivism Reference Center, *Atlas Shrugged Chronology.* Online at: http://www.noblesoul.com/orc/books/rand/atlas/chronology.html.
Peikoff, Leonard. 1991. *Objectivism, the Philosophy of Ayn Rand.* New York: Dutton.
Rand, Ayn. [1957] 1992. *Atlas Shrugged.* 35th anniversary edition. New York: Dutton.
Rand, Ayn. [1969] 1975. *The Romantic Manifesto: A Philosophy of Literature.* Second revised edition. New York: New American Library.

Chapter 15

Fuel for the Soul

Russell Madden

> Romantic art is the fuel and the spark plug of a man's soul; its task is to set a soul
> on fire and never let it go out.
>
> Ayn Rand, *The Romantic Manifesto*, 152

Despite the enduring popularity of *Atlas Shrugged* for nearly half a century, lots of people "still don't get it." The misunderstandings, misrepresentations, and misapplications of this classic novel continue unabated.

Four decades ago, in a passage echoing with defiant loneliness, Ayn Rand faced the stark reality of the critical response she and her highest literary achievement had received:

> It is a significant commentary on the present state of our culture that I have become the object of hatred, smears, denunciations, because I am famous as virtually the only novelist who has declared that her soul is not a sewer, and neither are the souls of her characters, and neither is the soul of man. (*The Romantic Manifesto* [RM], 172)

While some might dismiss this passage as an example of self-righteous sour grapes, Rand's centennial year continues to provide clear evidence of how negatively her opponents view her final novel. Even self-confessed libertarians declare that her writing is "clunky," "turgid," "drained" of "all life and beauty," that her ideas are "eccentric," "extremist," and "unrealistic."

One prominent libertarian expressed sympathy with a television cartoon character's statement that *Atlas Shrugged* is "garbage" and a "piece of shit." Another found parallels between the novel and "communist or fascist propaganda" and derided the central ideas as nothing more than "dogma" laced with "odder features" that falsely portray opposing viewpoints as straw men.

Given these "failings," one must wonder how *Atlas Shrugged* has managed to dupe so many millions of readers for so many decades.

A conservative television commentator demonstrated a similar—though more positive—tunnel vision when he informed us that *Atlas Shrugged* had "one good idea": that capitalism is "splendid." Had she lived to hear this less-than-insightful "analysis," Rand might well have sighed and shaken her head ... but she would have understood its cause, as well the source of the motivations that elicit such left-handed compliments.

Despite the misapprehensions of many, *Atlas Shrugged* is not about capitalism. It is not even about politics. Or statism. Or individualism versus collectivism. Or reason versus irrationality. Perhaps most shockingly and surprisingly, it is not even about philosophy or objectivism.

Any thoughtful observer of modern life is well aware that life can sometimes feel like an endurance contest. Each of us must wrestle with these difficulties. At work, we may have to face obstreperous customers or annoying coworkers. At home, rebellious children, distant or thoughtless spouses, or household calamities may try our patience. At leisure, crowded beaches and false promises of relaxation may require a vacation from our vacation.

Emotional ups and downs, bouts of sickness and disease, precarious financial concerns, periods of drudgery, mistakes and failures ... death ... all take their toll.

Beyond this common heritage of humanity, for that small minority of folks who still understand, appreciate, and hope for liberty, there are wider, even more insoluble cultural complications added to the already sometimes overwhelming burden each of us must, at times, carry. The constricting noose of government restrictions on our freedoms of expression and self-defense; increasing losses of privacy at the hands of the State; mounting taxes that steal our wealth directly and soaring inflation that does so via stealth; deteriorating educational and health care systems; burgeoning wars scattered across the globe; a State that claims a mandate to micromanage our lives ... such encroachments on the dignity and autonomy of the individual contribute to a depressing loss of personal control; a questioning of how much the system can endure before the whole unwieldy mass collapses under its own weight; a serious doubt about how much more we can bear before we lose the last shredded bits of our humanity.

It is at such a crossroads that hope can sour into despair, happiness warp into sadness, enthusiasm wilt into apathy.

At these dark crystalline moments in our lives, we cannot only benefit from an uplifting of our spirits, we need such a rejuvenation if we are to continue existing as fully functioning human beings. "Art does have a purpose and does serve a human need; ... a need of man's consciousness. Art is inextricably tied to man's survival ... to the preservation and survival of his consciousness" (RM, 17).

"The primary value [of art] is that it gives [a person] the experience of living in a world where things are as they ought to be. This experience is of crucial importance to him: it is his psychological life line" (RM, 170).

The proponents and supporters of statism and collectivism, of the irrational and the mystical, of altruistic sacrifice and abject self-denial have no shortage of venues that reflect their views of life and the world. We are immersed in a steaming bath of those ideals. In television and movies, in books and magazines, in politics and churches, messages reinforcing the essential evil of humanity, the impotence of the human mind, and the relativistic nature of reality abound.

Luckily for those who reject immolation from within and without, a few peaks manage to rise above the suffocating fog that has become the norm. Freedom-lovers cling to those isolated havens, knowing that to abandon them would lead to a depressing demise of unpleasant intensity.

But most such avenues of renewal are undependable fountains, at best. In *Atlas Shrugged*, Ayn Rand achieved a consistency of vision and depth of execution unparalleled in the freedom movement. Though some libertarians lambast Rand and *Atlas Shrugged* for its "totalism," that very coherence is, of course, one of the book's greatest strengths. The consonance between theme and plot, the congruity between character and action create a symmetry of structure and a unity of purpose and achievement that has rarely been duplicated:

> my life purpose is the creation of the kind of world (people and events) that I like—that is, that represents human perfection. In a book of fiction the purpose is to create, for myself, the kind of world I want and to live in it while I am creating it . . . (Rand, *The Journals of Ayn Rand*, 479)

As Ayn Rand made clear, the primary purpose of *Atlas Shrugged* was not to present the struggle between opposing political, economic, or philosophical systems. Unlike many of her readers, she clearly distinguished the goal that she sought to reach in her fiction writing and the means she used to accomplish that task.

Having grown up in a totalitarian regime in the U.S.S.R. and having witnessed the steady erosion of American liberty under FDR, Rand felt more keenly than most the slow, withering disappearance of a social milieu that touched her on a deeply emotional level.

For very personal reasons, then, Rand undertook the monumental task of creating the world of *Atlas Shrugged*. "The motive and purpose of my writing is the projection of an ideal man" (RM, 162).

What Rand could not readily experience in her daily struggles, she sought to distill in the framework of her novel. Who existed and how they acted in that projected universe formed the core of her task. As she said, ". . . I write—and read—for the sake of the story" (RM, 163). In making her decisions on how to proceed, she was guided by a fundamental principle: "My basic test for any story is: Would I want to meet these characters and observe these events in real life? Is this story an experience worth living through for its own sake? Is the pleasure of contemplating these characters an end in itself?" (RM 163).

Precisely because so few others had endeavored to reach this destination in a manner consistent with her view of the world, Rand took upon herself the mission of furnishing the "emotional fuel" she so desperately desired. Her gift to herself secondarily became a boon for any readers willing to embrace her grand perspective.

Despite momentary fits of despondency at the unmerciful demands of her work and the ocean of apathy and hostility in which she swam, Rand knew she could and would succeed in her primary design. Part and parcel of this certainty was her belief in the benevolent universe premise and how that meshed with her sense of life.

While Rand did not believe that the universe was literally "benevolent," she did accept that:

> injustice (or terror or falsehood or frustration or pain or agony) is the exception in life, not the rule.' One feels certain that somewhere on earth—even if not anywhere in one's surroundings or within one's reach—a proper, human way of life is possible to human beings, and justice matters. (Rand, *The New Left: The Anti-Industrial Revolution,* 118)

She knew that if one acted in accordance with reality, then success in achieving one's goals should be the expected rather than the unusual. When setbacks occur, one deals with them, not surrenders to them.

Rand defined a sense of life as ". . . an emotional, subconsciously integrated appraisal of man and of existence. It sets the nature of a man's emotional responses and the essence of his character" (RM, 25). It is "[t]he integrated sum of a man's basic values . . ." (RM, 29) and ". . . is experienced by him as a sense of his own identity" (RM, 31). For each individual, "The . . . subconscious criterion . . . is: 'That which is important to me' or: 'The kind of universe which is right for me, in which I would feel at home'" (RM, 28).

While a person's sense of life is experienced in and influences many areas of existence, one of the most important venues for its expression is in art. Art functions as a kind of ". . . metaphysical mirror; what a rational man seeks to see in that mirror is a salute; what an irrational man seeks to see is a justification . . ." (RM, 39)

These points help explain why even many libertarians virulently denigrate and demean Rand and *Atlas Shrugged*. To accept the sense of life infused throughout *Atlas Shrugged* would be for them to reject their own views that life requires "compromises"; that "principled action" is "impractical"; that a cohesive worldview is either impossible or undesirable; that mysticism and sacrifice aren't so bad.

These are the people who "seek . . . a justification," an excuse for their lapses in thought and their failure to achieve their dreams. For them, *Atlas Shrugged* provides a slap in the face, not an avenue for discovering an invaluable supply of emotional fuel. Better to be obtuse, evasive, and ignorant, they vaguely feel, than to change the fun house mirror that is their own sense of life. For them, the universe of *Atlas Shrugged* is not something to be coveted.

Rand's sense of life, however, led her in an entirely different direction: towards the rarest type of artistic endeavor to be found today. "Romantic art provides '. . . the emotional experience of admiration for man's highest potential, the experience of looking up to a hero—a view of life dominated by values, a life in which man's choices are practicable, effective and crucially important—that is, a moral sense of life.'" (RM, 147)

The greater the size and frequency of hardships one experiences, the more one will yearn for a sense that one is not alone; that one's efforts are not pointless; that life is not futile. Many readers return again and again to the well Rand constructed half-a-century ago. Luckily for them, *Atlas Shrugged* provides any number of opportunities for the receptive reader to find "fuel for the soul," to recharge his mental and emotional batteries. Indeed, the story traces an arc from gloom to glory, a rising pathway that mirrors the steps many of us have trodden on our journey to freedom.

In *Atlas Shrugged*, Hank Rearden expresses just how isolated and deserted a lover of liberty can feel and how draining that condition can become: "He felt a desolate loneliness . . . He wished he had a friend who could be permitted to see him suffer, without pretense or protection, on whom he could lean for a moment, just to say, 'I'm very tired,' and find a moment's rest" (AS, 206).

But regardless of the inroads into our rights that society makes, regardless of the pain that others inflict upon us through their acts of thoughtlessness and willful betrayal, we can find solace in Rand's benevolent universe premise and know—as Dagny Taggart understands—that eventually "this, too, must end":

> She was able to survive it, because she did not believe in suffering. She faced with astonished indignation the ugly fact of feeling pain, and refused to let it matter. Suffering was a senseless accident, it was not part of life as she saw it ... She knew these were the words, even in the moments when there was nothing left within her but screaming and she wished she could lose the faculty of consciousness so that it would not tell her that what could not be true was true . . . (AS, 114–15)

Many—if not most—people in our society would claim that they want to establish "freedom." Yet when presented with the steps actually necessary to achieve liberty, they shy from those suggestions with alarm and denial. Unlike Dagny, they have yet to grasp that their hollow words devoid of action condemn them out-of-hand:

> It was a strange foreshortening between sight and touch . . . between wish and fulfillment, between . . . spirit and body. First, the vision—then the physical shape to express it. First the thought—then the purposeful motion down the straight line of a

single track to a chosen goal. Could one have any meaning without the other? Wasn't it evil to wish without moving—or to move without aim? (AS, 229–30)

No matter how clearly a defender of freedom presents his case, no matter how many objections from his detractors he answers, no matter how fully he explains and expands and elucidates, he will inevitably face those who do not want to know, who implicitly demand that no one "confuse them with the facts." Allies in the defense of the individual are, sadly, a scarce commodity. As Dr. Robert Stadler tells Dagny about those who seek to destroy greatness in their aberrant attempts to preserve the status quo:

Miss Taggart, do you know the hallmark of the second-rater? It's resentment of another man's achievement . . . They bare their teeth at you from out of their rat holes . . . while you'd give a year of your life to see a flicker of talent anywhere among them. They . . . dream of greatness is a world where all men have become their acknowledged inferiors. They don't know that that dream is the infallible proof of mediocrity, because that sort of world is what the man of achievement would not be able to bear ... Have you ever felt the longing for someone you could admire? For something, not to look down at, but up to? (AS, 339)

Even many who declare their allegiance to liberty are more concerned with how the statists "feel" about them than they are in the fact that it is the enemies of freedom who should fear our condemnation, our judgment of their corrosive ideals and destructive actions. No one should feel guilty in identifying as immoral those who would prefer to hide behind a facade of respectability and compassion. Hank Rearden faces this brand of cowardice and appeasement from fellow businessmen who fear that his directness and honesty in declaring his own value and rights will somehow create difficulties for them:

"In my opinion, Mr. Rearden, it was extremely unwise of you ... We can't afford to arouse resentment."

"Whose resentment?" he asked ...

"Well, I don't know ... We've been trying hard not to give any grounds for all those accusations about selfish greed ..."

"Would you rather agree with the enemy that you have no right to your profits and your property?"

"Oh, no, no, certainly not—but why go to extremes? There's always a middle ground."

"A middle ground between you and your murderers?"

"Now why use such words?"

"What I said at the trial, was it true or not?'

'It's going to be misquoted and misunderstood."

"Was it true or not? ...

"It's no time to boast about being rich ... It's just goading them on to seize everything."

But telling them that you have no right to your wealth, while they have—is going to restrain them? (AS, 455)

The unique experience when we first realize that the ideas, the wishes, the opinions of those seeking our slavery are, on a fundamental level, unimportant and trivial is incredibly refreshing and liberating. Hank Rearden comes to such an awakening when he recognizes the true nature of his wife, Lillian:

> He stood motionless, held by a feeling he had never experienced before. He knew that he would have to think later, to think and understand, but for the moment he wanted nothing but to observe the wonder of what he felt.
> It was a sense of freedom, as if he stood alone in the midst of an endless sweep of clean air, with only the memory of some weight that had been torn off his shoulders. It was the feeling of an immense deliverance. It was the knowledge that it did not matter to him what Lillian felt, what she suffered or what became of her, and more: not only that it did not matter, but the shining, guiltless knowledge that it did not have to matter. (AS, 499)

As important as it is to reject the unwarranted negative judgments of people seeking to use us for their own ends, it is even more vital to reject our own baseless criticisms of ourselves arising from a misplaced trust in the ideas of those unworthy of any honest commitment. Hank Rearden at last breaks such self-imposed mental shackles:

> He thought: Guilty?—guiltier than I had known, far guiltier than I had thought, ... — guilty of the evil of damning as guilt that which was my best ...
> ... I accepted their code and believed ... that the values of one's spirit must remain as an impotent longing, unexpressed in action, untranslated into reality, while the life of one's body must be lived in misery ...
> I broke their code, but I fell into the trap they intended ... I did not damn them, I damned myself, I did not damn their code, I damned existence—and I hid my happiness as a shameful secret. I should have lived it openly ....
> ... I placed pity above my own conscience, and this is the core of my guilt. (AS, 528–9)

Freed from his intellectual and emotional fetters, Hank is ready to accept the core of any proper social relationship, the essence of what it means to live a fully human life: "I SWEAR BY MY LIVE AND MY LOVE OF IT THAT I WILL NEVER LIVE FOR THE SAKE OF ANOTHER MAN, NOR ASK ANOTHER MAN TO LIVE FOR MINE" (AS, 680).

The world that Rand created is one that defies traditional expectations, traditional thought, traditional morality. To understand and to live completely in a world that is truly free and based upon the best in humanity rather than the worst requires more effort, more challenge, more focus than most people are willing to expend. Yet as John Galt makes clear to Dagny, neither he nor she deserves anything less ... and that can be a hard lesson to learn:

> Did it ever occur to you, Miss Taggart, ... that there is no conflict of interests among men ... if they omit the irrational from their view of the possible and destruction from their view of the practical? ... A wish for the irrational is not to be achieved, whether the sacrificial victims are willing or not ...
>   ... No one's happiness but my own is in my power to achieve or to destroy ... (AS, 742)

In explaining this to Dagny, Galt makes it clear that the only thing holding us back from breaking from the calcified ideals of the past is ourselves:

> If you fail, ... if, like them, you come to think that one's highest values are not to be attained and one's greatest vision is not to be made real ... don't damn existence ... one must enter [Atlantis] naked and alone, with no rags from the falsehoods of centuries, ... an intransigent mind ... as one's only possession and key. You will not enter it until you learn that you do not need to convince or to conquer the world. When you learn it, you will see that ... nothing had barred you from Atlantis and there were no chains to hold you, except the chains you were willing to wear. (AS, 755–6)

Attempting to "fool" people into supporting liberty—trying to disguise the reality of what freedom is and what it entails—will not only not work but is, worse, a treason to the very things we cherish and seek to obtain:

> Honesty is the recognition of the fact that the unreal is unreal and can have no value ... that an attempt to gain a value by deceiving the mind of others is an act of raising your victims to a position higher than reality, where you become a pawn of their blindness, ... while their intelligence, their rationality, their perceptiveness become the enemies you have to dread and flee ... (AS, 945)

What is disheartening for those of us struggling to advance freedom is that the values many people exhibit in their private lives vanish when the context is switched to the "public" arena. The evil actions they would readily condemn in their neighbors or themselves are somehow transmuted to golden "virtues" via the simple act of voting. When the majority of those heroes-in-waiting hear—truly hear—and understand Galt's words, accept them, and transform that knowledge into action, then, perhaps, we will be far on the road to restoring better than ever the legacy of freedom, justice, and dignity that is our birthright:

> Your destroyers hold you by means of your endurance, your generosity, your innocence, ... your love of life, which makes you believe that they are men and that they love it, too. But the world of today is the world they wanted; life is the object of their hatred ... In the name of your magnificent devotion to this earth, leave them,

don't exhaust the greatness of your soul on achieving the triumph of the evil of theirs. (AS, 992–3)

We can leave no better legacy to those who come after us than to create within ourselves—and through our deeds, within the world itself—a society based on reason, purpose, and self-esteem; a nation that honors rationality, productivity, and earned pride; a country that demonstrates in reality as well as in words that independence, integrity, honesty, and profound respect for the individual, his values, and his goals are not merely empty sounds but the solid framework for a moral universe fit for a truly human existence.

> . . . since [a person's] pursuit and achievement of values is a lifelong process—and the higher the values, the harder the struggle—man needs a moment, an hour or some period of time in which he can experience the sense of his completed task, the sense of living in a universe where his values have been successfully achieved. It is like a moment of rest, a moment to gain fuel to move farther. Art gives him that fuel ...
>
> The importance of that experience is not in what he learns from it, but in that he experiences it. The fuel is not a theoretical principle, not a didactic message, but the life-giving fact of experiencing a moment of metaphysical joy—a moment of love for existence. (RM, 170)

In *Atlas Shrugged*, Ayn Rand succeeded with admirable skill and thoroughness in realizing her remarkable goal of creating people and a world that ought to be. Each of us needs a respite from the woes that beset and bedevil us as we wend our way through life. *Atlas Shrugged* provides us that indispensable breather we need to face our burdens as we work to craft our own values. For that gift alone, Rand deserves our thunderous applause.

In return, Rand figuratively asked for only one thing from those of us who have benefited so immeasurably from her achievement: "Don't work for my happiness . . . —show me yours—show me that it is possible—show me your achievement—and the knowledge will give me courage for mine" (*The Fountainhead*, quoted in RM, 171).

PART 5
Political Economy

Chapter 16

The Economics of *Atlas Shrugged*

Peter J. Boettke

As a matter of record, Rand's economic education was a function of common-sense and Ludwig von Mises.[1] She was a staunch anticommunist since her youth and a defender of individualism against collectivism. She developed in her own mind an individualist philosophy, which she dubbed Objectivism. In so doing, she claimed originality as a philosopher. But she did not claim originality in economics. She made it clear to her followers that her economics came from the leading free-market advocates of her age—Henry Hazlitt (1946) and Ludwig von Mises (e.g., 1949).[2] Hazlitt acknowledged Mises as the greatest economist of modern times, and Rand took that endorsement as her own as well. Rand, however, disagreed with Mises (and Hazlitt) on the moral defense of individualism. Both economists subscribed to a form of utilitarianism, whereas Rand built her moral case from an "objective" ethics. We need not go further into the disagreements between Rand and her economist friends for our present purposes.[3] Instead, I want to focus on the basic principles she learned from Hazlitt and Mises and how she then tried to communicate those ideas in narrative form through the story of *Atlas Shrugged*.

These are the basic principles of economics that one would find in Hazlitt and Mises:

1. Bad economics looks only at the immediate consequences of an action or policy, whereas good economics looks at both the immediate consequences and the longer term consequences of any action or policy.

2. Private property and the price system work to coordinate the economic activities of millions of individuals in a harmonious manner through the realization of mutually beneficial exchange.

3. Interference with the price system leads to distortions in the allocation of resources.

4. Taxation discourages production.

5. Inflation is socially destructive because it distorts the pattern of exchange and production and breaches trust in the monetary unit, which links all exchange activity.

Both Hazlitt and Mises thought the project of economic literacy was essential to establishing and maintaining a free and prosperous commonwealth.[4] This task was quite difficult for two reasons: (1) economics requires that the reader follow long chains of logical reasoning to sort out the consequences of any action and policy, and (2) special interest groups are constantly pleading their case. The difficulty of reasoning economically from first principles to logical conclusions combined with unmasking the sophisms of special interest groups led Hazlitt and Mises to devote their lives to economic education through the written and spoken word.

It is my contention that Rand picked up that challenge and attempted to provide economic enlightenment to her readers through the story of *Atlas Shrugged*. The book is no doubt one of the most philosophical novels of the twentieth century—whatever one's judgment is of that philosophy—but learning philosophy through Rand is not my topic. Instead, my concern is with learning economics through Rand and here I believe one would be hard pressed to find a more economically literate novel written by a noneconomist.[5]

I will make use of passages from *Atlas Shrugged* to demonstrate the principles Rand attempts to illuminate in her novel. Rand's message was that if the men of achievement stopped allowing themselves to be exploited by lesser men, then the social system of exchange and production would come to an abrupt stop. The reader is led to realize that the prime mover of progress is the bold individual living by his reason and pursuing his own self-interest. Collectivism in all aspects of life, Rand informs us, is a false ideal that must be eradicated from our minds and hearts. In the economy, the individuals of achievement are represented by industrialists and entrepreneurs. The government through policies of taxation and regulation attempt to live parasitically off these individuals of achievement and the masses are deluded by ideologies that justify the theft. Rand postulates that the system only continues to plod along because these men of achievement allow the parasitic system to continue to live off them. If they reject the parasite, the culture of parasitism and all who live by its code will wither and eventually die. Rand's protagonists are the men of achievement who persuade others of the parasitic nature of the culture of redistribution and government control of business, science, law, scholarship, and the arts. Her basic point is unassailable. What indeed would happen if the innovators and wealth creators in a country simply shrugged and stopped allowing themselves to be taxed, regulated and controlled against their will? A collapse of the economy would indeed ensue.[6]

Atlas Shrugged was first published in 1957. We have to remember the economic and social ideas that were dominant in the post-World War II period. First, this was the beginning of the Keynesian hegemony in economic theory and public policy. The main idea was that a market economy was not self-regulating and was prone to business cycles caused by irrational swings of pessimism and optimism on the part of business. It was for the government's macroeconomic policymakers to ensure full employment, utilizing monetary and fiscal policy tools to make sure that macroeconomic imbalances did not occur. Second, not only was the profession preoccupied with macroeconomic instability, and government's role in correcting it, but there was little faith left in the efficiency claims of a market economy in a microeconomic analysis. The market economy was said to suffer from problems of wasteful competition, monopolistic tendencies, and externalities—all of which required proactive government policies to correct for the failures of voluntary action to promote a harmony of interests. Finally, in the aftermath of the Great Depression and World War II, socialism was seen as not only a viable alternative economic system, but as a morally superior economic system. The classical economic idea of laissez faire was challenged on every conceivable front by the academic elite, among the decision makers in Washington D.C., and throughout popular culture. Paul Samuelson (1948, 152), in his popular principles of economics book, summed up the sentiments of the time:

> No longer is modern man able to believe "that government governs best which governs least." In a frontier society, when a man moved further west as soon as he could hear the bark of his neighbor's dog, there was some validity to the view "let every man paddle his own canoe." But today, in our vast interdependent society, the waters are too crowded to make unadulterated "rugged individualism" tolerable. The emphasis is increasingly on "we're all in the same boat," "don't rock the craft," "don't spit into the wind," and "don't disregard the traffic signals."

Perhaps nineteenth-century America came as close as any economy ever has to the state of laissez faire, which Carlyle called "anarchy plus the constable." The result was a century of rapid material progress and an environment of individual freedom. Also there resulted periodic business cycles, wasteful exhaustion of irreplaceable material resources, extremes of poverty and wealth, corruption of government by vested interest groups, and too often the supplanting of self-regulating competition in favor of all-consuming monopoly.

Samuelson argues that, coming out of the nineteenth-century experience, we learned to apply the methods of Alexander Hamilton to achieve the goals of Thomas Jefferson. In other words, we started to use the powers of the state to secure the public interest. Regulation of utilities and railroads were followed by regulation of commerce between the states and the establishment of antitrust laws. Banking regulations were instituted and a central banking system was established. Food and drug legislation was passed in order to ensure product safety and humanitarian legislation improved the plight of the working man. Theodore Roosevelt's "Square Deal" was replaced by Franklin Roosevelt's "New Deal" and, according to Samuelson, our democracy can never again allow itself to go backward to the nineteenth-century ideal of laissez faire. "Where the complex economic conditions of life necessitate social coordination and planning," Samuelson wrote in a thinly veiled critique of Hayek, "there can sensible men of good will be expected to invoke the authority and creative activity of government" (153). Samuelson even suggests that our failure to recognize the need to reject laissez faire and adapt to the changing economic conditions of modernity led to the breakdown of democracy in Germany, the rise of Nazism, and the need to fight the most expensive war to that point in human history (World War II).

Wow, talk about rhetorical flair being used in economics and the construction of a narrative in attempting to get across a point! Who could possibly argue against Samuelson? Only a handful of economists and intellectuals would resist this line of argument and in the world of the literati only Ayn Rand would stand tall. Buttressed by the economic writings of Hazlitt and Mises, Rand was able to challenge every one of the premises—theoretical, historical, and moral—contained in the line of argument summarized by Samuelson. No wonder one of Rand's favorite lines was "check your premises." *Atlas Shrugged* was her attempt in novel form to challenge each of the Samuelson era's premises and conventional wisdoms.

Consider the scene when Rearden meets with Dr. Potter of the State Science Institute about the introduction of Rearden metal (Rand 1957, 172–5). The economy is in a precarious position and the introduction of Rearden's superior product could disturb that already precarious position. The competition on the market would throw out of business the steel producers who cannot keep up and this could lead to serious "social damage." Rearden informs Dr. Potter that he does not worry about the fate of other companies, but only for the success of his endeavors as judged in the marketplace. Potter's response to this individualist outlook is to inform Rearden that cooperation between business and government is required in this day and age and that to fight this trend is to create enemies instead of friends in high places. He then offers to buy the rights to Rearden metal with government money. Rearden refuses. Potter ends their conversation by threatening Rearden with government action against his company unless he cooperates.

The scene illustrates important free-market economic principles. The first is that the social responsibility of business is to earn profits—nothing more, nothing less. Second, state involvement in the economy is justified on the nebulous grounds of "social damage." In this instance, the social damage is caused by a superior firm out-competing the less effective producers of steel in the marketplace. The claim is being made by Potter that the economy's balance requires cooperation not competition and that this cooperation will be best maintained via state involvement. But once the state is allowed to be involved in economic decision-making, Rand quickly stresses that those in positions of power will wield that power to the advantage of themselves and their friends.

The theme of political pull backed by the threat of violence versus voluntary persuasion on the market is repeated throughout *Atlas Shrugged*. Orren Boyle, a competitor to Rearden who has aligned himself with the state, is described as a man who fails to fulfill contracts, and spends his time pursuing pet projects for a social cause rather than improving his business (202). The mutually beneficial aspects of trade are spelled out by Francisco d'Anconia in perhaps the single most sustained discussion of economic principles in the work when he states:

> Money is a tool of exchange, which can't exist unless there are goods produced and men able to produce them. Money is the material shape of the principle that men who wish to deal with one another must deal by trade and give value for value. Money is not the tool of the moochers, who claim your products by tears, or of the looters, who take it from you by force. Money is made possible only by the men who produce. (387)

Money, as the medium of exchange, links individuals together within the economic system and in so doing guides production and exchange. But it does so because:

> every man is the owner of his mind and his effort. Money allows no power to prescribe the value of your effort except the voluntary choice of the man who is willing to trade you his effort in return. ... Money permits no deals except those to mutual benefit by the unforced judgment of the traders (388).

At the end of Francisco's discussion, he sums up the basic point by stating:

> Until and unless you discover that money is the root of all good, you ask for your own destruction. When money ceases to be the tool by which men deal with one another, then men become the tools of men. Blood, whips, and guns-or dollars. Take your choice—there is no other—and your time is running out. (391)

The culture of moochers and looters, not that of producers and traders, is what is evil and leads to economic ruin and political tyranny when followed to its ultimate conclusion. Rand uses as a particular target of derision the legend of Robin Hood:[7]

> He is remembered, not as a champion of property, but as a champion of need, not as a defender of the robbed, but as a provider of the poor. He is held to be the first man who assumed a halo of virtue by practicing charity with wealth which he did not own, by giving away goods which he had not produced, by making others pay for the luxury of his pity. He is the man who became the symbol of the idea that need, not achievement, is the source of rights, that we don't have to produce, only to want, that the earned does not belong to us, but the unearned does. ... Until men learn that of all human symbols, Robin Hood is the most immoral and the most contemptible, there will be no justice on earth and no way for mankind to survive. (540–41)

The first demonstration of the perverse consequences of pursuing the principle of need over the principle of productivity is the fate of the Twentieth Century Motor Company. Ivy Starnes, the daughter of an industrialist, regarded her father as evil because he cared for little else but business. When she and her brothers took over the factory, they set out to change that and institute a new order of business based on equity and communal spirit, not profit.

> We brought a great, new plan into the factory. It was eleven years ago. We were defeated by the greed, the selfishness and the base, animal nature of men. It was the

eternal conflict between spirit and matter, between soul and body. ... We put into practice that noble historical precept: From each according to his ability, to each according to his need. It was based on the principle of selflessness. It required men to .be motivated, not by personal gain, but by love for their brothers. (302)

The plan, we are told, failed miserably.[8] With the incentives for production and innovation absent, the company is led to bankruptcy within a few short years and in the context of Rand's story it is the beginning of the unraveling of the U.S. economy as the men of achievement begin to refuse to submit to the ideology and forceful rule of the looters and moochers. In the process, Rand's main heroic character John Galt moves from mythical to concrete status within the book—he was the first to walk out when confronted with the new plan. As Rand would have Galt say later on: "We are on strike against self-immolation. We are on strike against the creed of unearned rewards and unrewarded duties. We are on strike against the dogma that the pursuit of one's happiness is evil" (937).

Rand's story is one of the alliance of moochers and looters against the producers and traders. In her description of how the alliance between the moochers and looters formed, she explicates many of the basic principles of public choice economics—namely the concentration of benefits on the well-organized and well-informed and the dispersal of costs among the uninformed masses. The political tug and pull associated with government interventionism reaches its highest form in the discussion of Directive 10-289 written by Wesley Mouch. Economic freedom had been tried, according to Mouch, and failed. Now force must be introduced to coordinate economic activities and fix the ailing economy. Directive 10-289 would provide the necessary powers and policies to accomplish that goal according to Mouch. Mouch is a creature of the political world, neither a man of academic nor business accomplishment, but he is able to climb up the political ranks through connections and unscrupulous behavior. Now he drafts the directive to be put in place to plan the U.S. economy. In the room to discuss the directive with Mouch are Orren Boyle, James Taggart, Fred Kinnan, and Dr. Ferris. As point after point is introduced, it becomes clear to all who are thinking even a little bit that the plan is completely unworkable and in fact destructive to the economy.

As they jockey with one another to see who is more committed to the ideology of selflessness, labor leader Fred Kinnan finally speaks bluntly and cuts through the haze. "Are we here to talk business or are we here to kid one another?" And then he puts it plainly to all in the room: "All I've got to say is that you'd better staff that Unification Board with my men. ... Better make sure of it, brother—or I'll blast your Point One to hell" (507). The others in the room are uncomfortable with Kinnan's forthrightness, but only because he is unmasking the underlying realities. Eventually he gets what he wants. The others in the room are still squeamish about explicit statements of the consequences of their policies and Kinnan does not eliminate their squeamishness when he states: "Well, this, I guess, is the anti-industrial revolution." When Ferris counters that "Every expert has conceded long ago that a planned economy achieves the maximum of productive efficiency and that centralization leads to super-industrialization" and Boyle chimes in with "Centralization destroys the blight of monopoly," Kinnan mockingly says "How's that again?"—recognizing that centralizing is in fact the monopolizing of an economy in the hands of the state and its protected parties. As Kinnan points out when he is told that as long as business respects the rights of the workers, he will be expected to respect the rights of the industrialists, "Which rights of which industrialists?"

Directive 10-289 goes into effect with the approval of the men representing business, science, labor and government—each with their cut of the U.S. economy guaranteed (515).

By contrasting the conscious and deliberate planning of industrialists, such as Dagny Taggart or Hank Rearden, as they conduct business, with the proposed attempts at comprehensive central planning of the economy by government and a consortium of business, labor and government, Rand makes the very important point that the critique of socialism was never against rational planning per se. Rather the question was who was to do the planning and the scope and scale of the plan proposed. Individual- and firm-level planning is an essential part of the capitalist economy and the main driver in this planning process is the search for profit. Government planning of the economy centralizes the planning and attempts to shield decisions from the profit and loss calculus of the market economy. In such an environment, the planners will find themselves without the requisite information to rationally calculate the best use of resources and will lack incentives to be efficient in the attempt to produce. Consistent with economic principles and with Rand's story, the politics of pull will substitute for the lure of profits in guiding exchange and production under these circumstances. The slippery slope that Hayek, Hazlitt, and Mises warned about—where one failed intervention begets another failed intervention—is neatly illustrated in Rand's story. Moreover, as in the work of these economists, the reversal of public policy away from statism and toward freedom will not occur until a sea change in the underlying ideology takes place. So one can read in Rand's novel both the dynamics of intervention- ism and the mechanism of effective social change that a variety of classical liberal economists since Adam Smith have attempted to articulate in their articles and books.

Notes

This essay is an excerpt from "Teaching Economics Through Ayn Rand: How the Economy is Like a Novel and How the Novel Can Teach Us About Economics." *The Journal of Ayn Rand Studies* 6, no 2. (Spring 2005): 445–65.

1   It has been argued by Bernice Rosenthal (2004) that the first-hand experience of economic collapse that Rand acquired—during World War I, the revolutions, and under communist rule—is the source of Rand's understanding of economics.

2   In a letter to Martin Larson dated 15 July 1960, Rand (1995, 582) recommends the following works to dispel the myth that the market economy is depression-prone and to prove that depressions are caused instead by government intervention in the economy: "I refer you to such books as *Capitalism the Creator* by Carl Snyder, *Economics in One Lesson* by Henry Hazlitt, *How Can Europe Survive* by Hans Sennholz, and the works of the great economist Ludwig von Mises."

3   However, for an excellent discussion of ethics as social science and how the Hazlitt and Mises position need not be confined to moral relativism, as Rand thought it must, see Leland Yeager 2001. There is an exchange between Yeager and William Thomas on the subject of that work in the current volume.

4   A wonderful discussion of what Mises thought were the primary objectives in proper economic education can be found in his memorandum of 1948 to Leonard Read concerning the tasks of the newly founded Foundation for Economic Education, where Mises was an advisor to Read. See Mises 1948.

5   I make the qualification about noneconomist only because Breit and Elzinga have used the genre of detective novels (Jevons [1978] 1993; 1985; 1995) and Russell Roberts (2001a; 2001b) has also more recently used the novel form to explicitly teach the principles of economics to their readers.

6   In an irony of timing, the last time I taught from *Atlas Shrugged* we were going over Rearden's trial when Judge Jackson's ruling on Microsoft came down. It made for a great week or two of class. The havoc an antitrust policy can have when based on poor economic reasoning was perhaps best summed up by Judge Robert Bork (1978, 92) when he said: "A determined attempt to remake the American economy into a replica of the textbook model of competition would have roughly the same effect on national wealth as several dozen strategically placed nuclear explosions."

7   As Chris Matthew Sciabarra has pointed out to me, Rand actually saw Ragnar Danneskjöld as an inversion of the Robin Hood legend. Rand's intellectual style was one that often began with a conventional icon, appropriating it, and then inverting it. Ragnar, she writes in a 30 Octoaber 1948 journal entry, is a "Robin Hood who robs the [parasitic] humanitarians and gives to the [productive] rich" (Rand, 1997, 585).

8   A thorough discussion of the consequences of Ivy Starnes's plan at the Twentieth Century Motor Company is provided in *Atlas Shrugged* when Dagny meets a tramp who was a former employee at the company at the time of its introduction (Rand 1957, 616–27). In many ways, this discussion is actually the best discussion of economics in the novel and in particular provides a logical explanation of how the best of intentions are dashed by the inability of government planning to achieve its purpose because of incentives and the unworkability of state planning of the economy, and thus the cumbersomeness of the tasks is exploited by those who seek power to rule over others. "But when the people are six thousand howling voices, trying to decide without yardstick, rhyme, or reason, when there are no rules to the game and each can demand anything, but has a right to nothing, when everybody holds power over everybody's life except his own—then it turns out, as it did, that the voice of the people is Ivy Starnes. By the end of the second year, we dropped the pretense of the "family meetings"—in the name of "production efficiency and time economy," one meeting used to take ten days—and all the petitions of need were simply sent to Miss Starans' office (623). Hayek's thesis from *The Road to Serfdom* (1944) about both how the worst get on top and the limits of democratic agreement could not have been better illustrated than in

the treatment in Rand's book. The very unworkability of the ideology of the moochers and the aspirations of planners provides the opportunity for the looters to wield power to their favor for as long as the system lasts.

References

Bork, Robert. 1978. *The Anti-Trust Paradox*. New York: Basic Books.
Hayek, Friedrich A. [1941] 1975. *The Pure Theory of Capital*. Chicago: University of Chicago Press.
———. 1944. *The Road to Serfdom*. Chicago: University of Chicago Press.
Hazlitt, Henry. 1946. *Economics in One Lesson*. New York: Harper and Brothers.
Jevons, Marshall. [1978] 1993. *Murder on the Margin*. Princeton: Princeton University Press.
———. 1985. *The Fatal Equilibrium*. Cambridge, Massachusetts: MIT Press.
———. 1995. *A Deadly Indifference*. New York: Carroll and Graf.
Mises, Ludwig von. [1948] 1990. The objectives of economic education. Reprinted in *Economic Freedom and Interventionism*. New York: Foundation for Economic Education, 179–86.
———. 1949. *Human Action: A Treatise on Economics*. New Haven, Connecticut: Yale University Press.
Rand, Ayn. 1957. *Atlas Shrugged*. New York: New American Library.
———. 1995. *Letters of Ayn Rand*. Edited by Michael S. Berliner. New York: Dutton.
———. 1997. *Journals of Ayn Rand*. Edited by David Harriman. New York: Dutton.
Ricardo, David. [1821] 1951. *On the Principles of Political Economy and Taxation*. Cambridge, United Kingdom: Cambridge University Press.
Roberts, R. 2001a. *The Choice: A Fable of Free Trade and Protectionism*. New York: Prentice Hall.
———. 2001b. *The Invisible Heart: An Economic Romance*. Cambridge, Massachusetts: MIT Press.
Samuelson, Paul. 1948. *Economics*. New York: McGraw Hill.
Smith, Adam. [1776] 1976. *An Inquiry into the Nature and Causes of the Wealth of Nations*. Chicago: University of Chicago Press.
Yeager, Leland. 2001. *Ethics as Social Science*. Cheltenham, United Kingdom: Edward Elgar Publishing.

Chapter 17

Atlas, Ayn, and Anarchy: A is A is A

Larry J. Sechrest

Check Your Premises

Ayn Rand's ultimate professional achievement was the novel *Atlas Shrugged*. Of that there can be little doubt. She herself thought of it as her crowning glory, the thing toward which she had aimed all her life. Moreover, it remains, half a century after its publication, one of the most influential books on Earth. It is an adventure story, a philosophical tract, a love story, a dissertation on political economy, and trenchant social commentary, all wrapped up into one dense, inimitable package. It is, above all, a magnificent vision of what men and women can and should be: Bound by reality, but never bound by the envy, guilt, cowardice, and mysticism that afflict so many of their fellows.

It is indeed a work of genius. It is both a tale of high drama and a tightly integrated worldview which reveals the principles applicable to such seemingly disparate topics as romance, business, science, and politics. And yet, I believe that the genius who created it was blind to one of its more powerful messages. As one might guess from the title of this essay, I maintain that *Atlas Shrugged* offers a persuasive vindication of anarcho-capitalism. I am of course very aware of—and saddened by—the fact that Rand herself would be outraged by such an hypothesis. She frequently condemned libertarian anarchists such as Murray Rothbard and, by extension, the Libertarian Party for "harboring" such "disreputable" persons. She even went so far as to refer to them as her "enemies." But even geniuses can be wrong. Rand was certainly brilliant, but not infallible. In any case, even if my hypothesis proves to be insupportable, why should merely stating the proposition offend any person who seeks the truth, that is, who wants to apprehend reality?

Some anarchistically-inclined readers might focus exclusively on Galt's Gulch as Rand's unintentional exemplar of free-market anarchism at work. While I will certainly not ignore the features of that Colorado locale, my approach to the issue will be broader.

What I want to suggest is that woven throughout the tapestry of the story are elements which powerfully convey the spirit of anarchism. To me, the peculiar fact is that Rand never consciously came to grips with the deeply radical nature of her political philosophy. It is peculiar because, in other realms, she realized full well how far outside the mainstream of American culture she lay. She knew, for instance, that she would shock readers when she declared that selfishness—not altruism—was virtuous. Or when she defended businessmen as being "the most persecuted minority." Or when she declared that laissez-faire capitalism constituted the only moral social system. Yet, when it came to politics, she wrapped herself in the familiar patriotic colors of the Constitution and the Declaration of Independence.

Why should this be so? I most definitely do not want to engage in some Freudian psychoanalysis of Rand"s life, but I am nevertheless tempted to think that the Bolsheviks are to blame. She was, undoubtedly, deeply affected by the Russian Revolution and its rampant thuggery, as any rational person would be. In her case, however, instead of drawing the correct conclusion, that statism in any guise is the enemy of peace-loving, productive men, she seems to have concluded that all anti-statists must be nihilists at heart. And this visceral reaction by the adolescent Alissa Rosenbaum was later transformed into an eloquent rationalization by the adult Ayn Rand. It is tirelessly repeated, with limited appreciation of all the issues involved, by most of her admirers.

To the Fearless Mind

Rand is reputed to have believed that all her emotions were the products of her explicit philosophical convictions, and of only those convictions. That she had no subconscious, no emotional responses that were not fully integrated into her conscious thought. That Rand the artist and Rand the philosopher were co-extensive. We are fortunate that she was wrong in this, because otherwise *Atlas Shrugged* would be a different book in certain valuable particulars. This is not self-evident, so allow me to explain what I mean.

My favorite characters in the book, by far, are Hank Rearden and Ragnar Danneskjold, but for very different reasons. Through most of the book, the former struggles with his own irrational sense of guilt as well as a stubborn naivete. He has "flaws," but ultimately overcomes them. As a result, many readers have singled Rearden out as the most "human" of Rand"s heroes, and I do not disagree. Readers are more likely to see themselves reflected in Rearden's inner conflicts than in the cool self-possession of, say, John Galt. Clearly, however, Rand fully intended the reader to be privy to Rearden's struggle, for his evolution is an integral part of the saga. Danneskjold, on the other hand, appears on the stage fully formed and complete. Indeed, in the story Ragnar is, along with Galt and Francisco d'Anconia, part of the trinity who together first identified the evil of altruism and resolved to lead America back to a philosophy of reason (Rand [1957] 1996, 971).

Moreover, Ragnar is an outlaw, a man of peace who has been driven to a life of "crime" by the inverted morals of the day. He is explicitly called a "pirate," whose ship repeatedly—and successfully—attacks naval vessels and government supply ships.

First of all, one thing must be clarified. Ragnar is not a pirate, but a privateer. Privateers were men who outfitted private armed ships in order to engage in combat on the seas, a practice which was common among maritime nations from the thirteenth to the nineteenth century. Privateering originated as a method of obtaining restitution for violations of individuals' rights that occurred in the course of maritime commerce. Later, it evolved into an instrument of national defense. What is particularly surprising to many people today is the persuasive evidence that privateers, being motivated principally by the desire for profit, were often both more effective and more efficient than public naval vessels (Sechrest 2003).

Ragnar is the quintessential privateer, because he is a private crusader for justice. He forcibly repossesses from the agents of governments the wealth that has been stolen from productive, creative men by those governments and then returns it to its rightful owners.

Thus Rand the artist apparently understood the validity of private justice, but Rand the philosopher vehemently rejects it. I do not see how the classically anarchistic actions of Ragnar Danneskjold can possibly fit into her consciously-held political philosophy. In her nonfiction work, Rand consistently maintains that "[i]f a society left the retaliatory use of force in the hands of individual citizens, it would degenerate into mob rule, lynch law, and an endless series of bloody private feuds or vendettas" (1967, 331). Moreover, "even a society whose every member were fully rational and faultlessly moral, could not function in a state of anarchy; it is the need of objective laws and an arbiter for honest disagreements among men that necessitates the establishment of a government" (334).

And yet, here is Ragnar, a man of the highest moral principles who does not delegate to the existing government the exclusive use of retaliatory force. He takes retaliatory force into his own hands and wields it with electrifying efficiency—and against that very government (Rand [1957] 1996, 459, 462, 526). What permission, sanction, or popular vote does he require? Obviously none whatsoever. Only his own sovereign, fearless mind, identifying what is just and what is unjust, is needed for the task.

To the Inviolate Truth

No doubt, at this point Rand would remind me in no uncertain terms that I have taken Ragnar out of the proper context, and thus have misinterpreted his meaning. She would surely tell me that the governments portrayed in *Atlas Shrugged* have long since expanded their functions far beyond the sole legitimate one of protecting individuals' rights. These nation-states tax and regulate unmercifully. They set wages and prices, create monopolistic cartels, indulge in massive welfare programs, dictate the allocation of the factors of production, even nationalize whole industries. In short, they confiscate the products of the men of the mind. Therefore, Ragnar's vigilante sort of approach to the situation is justified, but only because these particular governments have themselves become aggressors. They no longer serve purely as protectors of rights; they have ceased to be proper governments.

But any such declarations by Rand would be woefully inaccurate historically. They would also fly in the face of many scholars' analyses of the incentives that motivate the agents of governments. First of all, no government has ever remained strictly limited to the sole function of protecting individuals' rights. Even if one restricts the discussion to the federal government of the United States, any unbiased observer would have to concede that the American government has in fact already committed most, if not all, of the kinds of transgressions against which Ragnar fights so valiantly. Nor should that be surprising. The reality is that government cannot be "limited." It is a utopian dream to think otherwise. Those granted a legal monopoly on the use of force will ever seek to expand the range of their activities.

And even if government somehow never expanded, there would still exist a potentially thorny economic problem that has received very little attention. Certainly, Rand herself shows no awareness of the issue. There are two horns of the dilemma. First, because of problems with "free riders" (persons who benefit from certain goods or services but do not bear their costs), it is nearly certain that truly voluntary funding of government would prove insufficient. Thus, compulsory taxation would be necessary. Second, all known methods of taxation produce "non-neutral" effects. That is, all taxation affects different taxpayers to different degrees, which means that all taxation constitutes a redistribution of income and/or wealth (Sechrest 1999). Since, presumably, all redistributions are violations of property rights, then one cannot but conclude that no government can avoid violating rights. If so, then no government can be moral, because no government can effectively be limited only to the protection of rights.

I must note that Rand's formal defense of limited government is in part an error of knowledge. That is, she regrettably exhibits no familiarity with the extensive history of privately-developed, or "customary," legal systems. Prominent examples include Anglo-Saxon common law, admiralty law (the law of the sea), merchant law (or *lex mercatoria*), and the legal system of medieval Ireland (Rothbard 1973, 235–43), to which must be added that of medieval Iceland (Sechrest 2000, 180–81). If government is a necessary pre-condition for the effective defense of individual rights, how does one explain the centuries of human experience with non-governmental legal systems?

Ragnar "the pirate" is not the only major element in *Atlas Shrugged* which seems blatantly anarchistic. For that matter, he is not the only "outlaw" who is willing to take the law in his own hands. Rather early in the tale one finds Dagny Taggart threatening to kill any politician who interferes with the progress of her branch railroad, the Rio Norte Line (Rand [1957] 1996, 186). When the first train is run on that line there spontaneously appear hundreds of men armed with everything from "costly rifles to ancient muskets," all determined to guard the train along its route (227). During a riot at the Rearden Metal mills, Francisco d'Anconia, looking "like a hero of Western legend," shoots rioters from his position on top of one of the roofs (912). In the climactic rescue of John Galt, effected by Dagny, Hank, Francisco, and Ragnar and backed up by "about half the male population" of Galt's Gulch, all are armed and willing to use deadly force (1049–59).

Let me make it clear that I do not, however, equate anarchism with vigilante action. Indeed, I would argue that the most likely form of purely private justice would involve business firms—such as insurance companies—whose effectiveness would give their clients little reason ever to take up arms (Rothbard [1970] 1977, 1–9; 1973, 219–47). Libertarian anarchism is not the social ideal that it is because it compels everyone personally to seek redress of grievances at the point of a gun. Nevertheless, in an anarcho-capitalist society, unlike Randian minarchy, no one would ever be required to renounce the use of retaliatory force.

No reader can forget that Galt's Gulch (also known as Mulligan's Valley) is, in an important sense, the focal point of the novel. Clearly, the Gulch is a paradigm of anarcho-capitalism. According to Galt himself, "[W]e have no laws in this valley, no rules, no formal organization of any kind. We come here because we want to rest. But we have certain customs, which we all observe, because they pertain to the things we need to rest from" (Rand [1957] 1996, 655). Later, the valley's original occupant, Midas Mulligan, declares that it is "not a state … just a voluntary association of men held together by nothing but every man's self-interest" (686).

It is difficult to imagine a better succinct description of the motivation behind or the essential method of libertarian anarchism than these words of Mulligan's. To be fair, Mulligan does issue a disclaimer of sorts when he also says that Galt's Gulch is "not a society of any kind" (686). In what sense he means this escapes me. Admittedly, those residing in the valley are a small, very select group, but surely it is a society in the important sense that it involves a variety of biologically unrelated persons pursuing many different vocations and interacting both commercially and socially. It is not an extended family, a tribe, or a clan. One might think that Rand was merely inattentive when she put such words in Mulligan's mouth. But that is highly unlikely given the well known fact that Rand was an extremely meticulous writer. After all, she spent thirteen years crafting *Atlas Shrugged.*

Could it be that Rand, through her creation Midas Mulligan, subscribed to a collectivistic notion of society as some manner of organism? That is not credible. There would seem to be only one plausible explanation. That is, Rand appears to have implicitly associated the concept "society" with the concept "nation." However, to do so is unjustified, because "nation" is usually taken to signify a nation-state. In other words, doing so presupposes the very conclusion which Rand wants to be able to draw, that no civilized society can exist without government. It is as if Rand the artist saw that Galt's Gulch was the antidote to the predatory State, but Rand the philosopher found some of the implications of that intolerable. Thus, she provided herself with an escape mechanism. The Gulch only appears to be anarchistic. It is not a stateless society, because it was not a society.

Allow me to put it in the following way. Rand herself, while functioning as a creative artist, seems to have realized at some level of her consciousness that the solution to the invasive State is a stateless society. Here is the genius at her radical best. When she later offers a more formal argument in her nonfiction works, the daring insights of the artist are buried under the conventionality of the philosopher.

Not only does Rand the novelist grasp the desirability of the stateless society and the validity of private justice, she also comprehends, however imprecisely, the superior effectiveness of private defensive agents. She has her characters describe Ragnar's ship as "a better ship than any in the People's State of England" and declare that "[n]obody can catch him ... the navy can't cope with him" (145–6). In a similar vein, she ridicules the ineptness of the State Science Institute, whose metallurgical department had failed to produce any useful products after thirteen years of effort (180). Later, she has a young engineer opine that governmental scientific inquiry is a "contradiction in terms" (353). Furthermore, she is acutely aware of the deep corruption that infects the "aristocrats of pull." Throughout the book Rand sprinkles examples of backroom deals, sleazy bureaucrats, and legislation driven only by a thirst for power (338–40, 403–4, 494–5, 835–6, 858).

Why could Rand not reason from such particulars to the correct generalization? How is it that she understood that governmental enterprises were riddled with waste, inefficiency, graft, and corruption and yet could not see that that must also apply to the "legitimate" functions of the armed forces, police, and law courts? Others have certainly recognized the inherent problems with all governmental activities. For example, Hans-Hermann Hoppe has pointed out that "[u]nder monopolistic auspices the price of justice and protection must rise and its quality must fall. A tax-funded protection agency is a contradiction in terms and will lead to ever more taxes and less protection" (1999, 33–4).

Ayn Rand prided herself, quite rightly, on being one who recognized that reality is the ultimate arbiter. Surely she would have said that she was dedicated to truth, wherever that truth might lead. And yet, perhaps due in part to her limited knowledge of economics, Rand the philosopher failed to grasp that limited government is a contradiction in terms. Minarchy is simply not part of that inviolate truth.

A is A is A

I have already offered reasons for interpreting Rand, the explicit minarchist, as an implicit anarchist. I would like also to explain why the issue is of such importance to me personally. I have always been fascinated by the myths we humans create. In terms of their value as an instrument of edification, myths seem to fall into one of two categories. The mythology of ancient Greece or Rome or the mythic sagas of Scandinavia I find insightful and inspiring. Their purpose is to reveal vital aspects of our humanity and, especially, to applaud the heroic. They cause us to reflect soberly and maturely on both our virtues and our vices. While not literally factual, they nevertheless convey something significant about the real world.

On the other hand, there are those myths whose net effect is not liberation or enlightenment, but imprisonment. The widespread conviction that there must be some supreme being, some God who created all that exists (except of course Himself) is of this kind. It entraps believers in a world of incomprehensible magic. It undermines their only guide to a meaningful existence. That is, it demeans a man's mind and discredits his use of reason. The assumption that there "must be" a God—despite its nearly universal acceptance—has done incalculable harm. The destructive nature of such mysticism was thoroughly understood by Rand. She wrote of it on numerous occasions.

But there is another, equally harmful myth. And it is, if anything, even more nearly universally believed. It is the assumption that if individuals' rights are to be protected, there "must be" a government. Some have stated the problem thusly: Church and State are the roots of all evil. That may be somewhat hyperbolic, but the core sentiment is on target. Men do not need God in order to apprehend reality or to identify proper ethical principles. Neither do men need government in order to build a world of peaceful co-existence.

There is even an element of mysticism involved in the latter assumption. Minarchists like Rand invariably presume that individuals—as either the consumers or suppliers of defensive and judicial services in anarcho-capitalism—are incapable of protecting rights. In Rand's case, this partially stems from the supposed absence of "objective laws." But then minarchists turn right around and further presume that those same individuals, as voters under a limited government, are fully capable of identifying which constitutional provisions, which policies, and which politicians will truly protect their rights. What magic is this? What is it about the presence of government that transforms the populace? In particular, how is it that "objective laws" can only be identified and implemented via a political process?

The truly radical thinker realizes that man qua man needs neither god nor government. Rand revealed the first of these two destructive myths as a tawdry lie foisted upon some men by others as a means to control and exploit them. Sadly, she defended the second. I would suggest that men will never truly be free until both are seen to be comfortable, but unjustified assumptions.

References

Hoppe, Hans-Hermann. 1999. The private production of defense. *Journal of Libertarian Studies* 14 (Winter): 27–52.

Rand, Ayn. [1957] 1996. *Atlas Shrugged*. New York: Signet Books.

———. 1967. *Capitalism: The Unknown Ideal*. New York: New American Library.

Rothbard, Murray N. [1970] 1977. *Power and Market: Government and the Economy*. Kansas City: Sheed Andrews and McMeel.

———. 1973. *For a New Liberty*. New York: Macmillan.

Sechrest, Larry J. 1999. Rand, anarchy, and taxes. *Journal of Ayn Rand Studies* 1, no. 1 (Fall): 87–105.

———. 2000. Taxation and government are still problematic. *Journal of Ayn Rand Studies* 2, no. 1 (Fall): 163–87.

———. 2003. Privateering and national defense: Naval warfare for private profit. Edited by Hans-Hermann Hoppe. *The Myth of National Defense: Essays on the Theory and History of Security Production*. Ludwig von Mises Institute.

Chapter 18

The Businessman and Ayn Rand: Galt's Gulch in Real Time
Eroding the Randian/Libertarian Divide

Spencer Heath MacCallum

Like many before and after him, the late Werner Stiefel (1921–2005) was inspired and awakened philosophically by reading *Atlas Shrugged*. He acknowledged that debt when asked, in the last year of his life, what he might say to Ayn Rand if he were magically given the opportunity to speak with her. He answered simply that he would say, "Thank you, Ayn Rand." He was too modest to mention his own contribution to her legacy.

Ayn Rand gave us a wonderfully overarching philosophy for living a meaningful personal life. She contributed little of a practical nature, however, toward showing how our public affairs could be conducted consistent with that philosophy. When it came to applying her principles in the mundane world, the pragmatic businessman Werner Stiefel went a full step beyond his mentor, calling to mind the Japanese adage that the mark of excellent teaching is the student who, not content with what he has learned, builds on and carries it further. While Stiefel did not expand upon Randian principles, he made a great stride in their practical application. In doing so, he banished an inconsistency in Rand's stance and showed her philosophy to be more potent than she herself had recognized.

Rand's inconsistency arises where she talks about the role of political government. None can presume to speak for Ayn Rand, but we must recall the temper of the times. Statism was in full ascendancy. While Rand was ahead of many of her contemporaries in advocating a limited government, she stopped there, perhaps fearful that to go further would be to add the proverbial straw, branding her thought as anarchistic and thereby consigning it to intellectual oblivion. But whatever Rand's reason, her inconsistency was more than merely academic. The collectivist cast of mind necessitated by state advocacy was to prove costly and tragic (Shaffer 2004).

Today, public choice economics has made clearer than it ever was in Rand's day how incompatible is political government with Objectivist philosophy.

Reduced to its simplest terms, men act in their own interest as they perceive it, and that is no problem when they are dealing with their own person and property. But when they acquire discretionary authority over persons and property not their own, problems arise, since their perceived interest and that of the owners must at some point diverge. The private individual then must resist, even to the forfeit of his life if he cannot prevail, or live for the sake of another. The oath taken by all in Galt's Gulch was: "I swear by my life and my love of it that I will never live for the sake of another man, nor ask another man to live for mine" (Rand 1956, 680).

Rand could only suggest limiting the problem, and she had no more success than anyone else, then or since, at showing how that might be done. Her best suggestion was to enact a constitutional separation of economy and state, while leaving the taxing power intact. How such an amendment could be accomplished or made to stick if it were is moot, and it does not address the root of the inconsistency, which is taxation. The answer to this ancient riddle of the Sphinx is, of course, not to attempt to keep the problem small, with the ever-present likelihood that it will grow large again, but to seek an alternative way of conducting community affairs that would be altogether consistent with private property. How might this be done without drawing the epithet of anarchism?

A Star to Steer By

In retrospect, Rand could have adopted the position of her contemporary, the late F.A. ("Baldy") Harper, founder of the Institute for Humane Studies, who believed we must entertain the ideal of no government at all if we are ever to realize a limited government. Without that guiding star, the notion of limited government is a chameleon, a slippery goal, because it is undefined. Limited with respect to what? Any government, however despotic, is limited by comparison with some other that we might experience or imagine. But if, as an ideal, we entertain the vision of no government at all (in the sense of overriding of property rights), then that gives us a reference point against which to make course corrections in our everyday decisions. Harper had no idea whether humankind might one day attain a stateless society, but he found that prospect no more necessary than for the mariner to reach the North Star. It is enough that steering by it brings him into Liverpool, which is where he wants to go.[1]

Not only would this insight have given Rand a star by which to navigate toward a freer society, it would have brought her into harmony with the then nascent libertarian movement. It would have given Objectivists and libertarians a common high ground. For it opens our mind to the search for new, nonpolitical ways of doing things. Especially in this age of onrushing technology, to conscientiously embrace the ideal of no government requires daily review of every area where government is active to ascertain the least intervention needed or if, indeed, any is needed at all. Yet such a position does not require rejection of the state forthwith. By no stretch is this anarchism.

Galt's Gulch and Mr. Stiefel

Had Rand, in her fictional writing, wished to pursue the question of reconciling public life with private life guided by Objectivist philosophy, she had at her disposal a powerful heuristic device, a perfect laboratory in which to conduct her experiments. That laboratory was Galt's Gulch. As a practical matter, how was Galt's Gulch administered? How were needed public services provided? Here she could have shown Harper's approach at work, the inhabitants looking for innovative ways of handling recurrent types of conflicted interests that away from the Gulch were dealt with routinely and unthinkingly by legislation.

However, Rand never touched upon how Galt's Gulch, a subdivision, was to be organized and administered. The question was left moot. All she suggested was that if any disharmony arose (in *Atlas Shrugged* none ever had), Judge Narragansett would arbitrate (Rand 1957, 695). She didn't address the conflicts of interest that Public Choice economics has so clearly illuminated. As a novelist, dealing in fiction, she was under no necessity of doing so.

Werner Stiefel, on the other hand, was not so privileged. He was not a novelist, much less a philosopher, but a pragmatic businessman. He had experienced Nazi Germany in the 1930s. Unable to rescue any assets from their family soap manufacturing business in Germany, he and his father and brother set up business in the United States, based only on what they carried in their heads. Today, Stiefel Laboratories is a small, family-owned multinational company producing dermatological soaps and related products in more than 40 countries.

After World War II, Werner read *Atlas Shrugged* and woke up to a thoroughly pragmatic question. When conditions for life had deteriorated in Germany in the 1930s, many people had fled to the United States. But in the United States, even then, Werner saw symptoms of the same thing happening that he had witnessed in Germany. When the time came, he asked, where could people flee to from the United States?

Taking his cue from Rand, Werner conceived of a "Galt's Gulch" (aka "Mulligan's Valley," aka "Atlantis") in the form of a floating settlement on the high seas outside the political jurisdiction of any nation. He adopted the name "Atlantis"[2] and, drawing entirely on his personal resources rather than those of the company, set about to make his dream a reality. His efforts to bring this about are a fit subject for a heroic novel.

Werner started by purchasing the Saugerties Motel, near the company's main plant in Saugerties, New York. The Motel became a kind of a think tank to which he invited libertarians to come and live while working in the surrounding area and, in their off-times, helping plan the Atlantis Project. He conceived of the project in three stages. Atlantis I was the Saugerties Motel. Atlantis II would be a ship at sea, and Atlantis III would be a community on floats or on dredged-up land on a coral atoll or submerged seamount. The ship would serve as a supply vessel and living quarters in the construction of Atlantis III.

At Saugerties, Atlantis I, Werner undertook to transform those who had joined him into a seasoned team that could work under any conditions by assigning them the daunting task of themselves building the ferrocement ship that would be Atlantis II. The team passed this first test and sailed the ship down the Hudson and south into the Caribbean—where a tropical storm destroyed it.

Undaunted, Werner obtained another vessel and found a spot in the Caribbean outside of any political jurisdiction where the depth was only four feet at low tide. He completed the arduous task of constructing four sea-walls and was at the point of dredging sand to create a dry foothold from which to extend the land of Atlantis III when one of Haitian dictator "Papa Doc" Duvalier's gunboats showed up and leveled its guns at his crew. Someone had found silver nuggets on the sea bottom nearby and had cut a deal with Papa Doc for protection from pirates. The gunboat captain had no idea who these people were or what they were doing in the area, but thought it best to run them off.

Werner then long-term leased a site for his base in a freeport operated by the Haitian government. But when a copy of his newsletter, *The Atlantis News,* fell into an official's hands and revealed his underlying philosophy, the government forthwith canceled his lease. From this experience, Werner learned the importance of keeping a low profile.

Next Werner set about to create land on Misteriosa Banks, a submerged seamount mid-way between Cuba and Honduras, the same location that self-styled Prince Lazarus Long would later publicize as the site for his ill-starred New Utopia. Werner bought and towed to the site an oil rig of the type that, once on location, could be inverted to stand on three legs. Before it could be put in place, a hurricane blew it out to sea and destroyed it.

Still undismayed, Werner purchased property on Grand Cayman and constructed an attractive building complex for his center of operations, one that would also serve as a retreat for the staff of Stiefel Laboratories. This garden setting, which still exists, became, among other things, the office of the Atlantis Trading and Commodity Purchasing Service (ATCOPS), which Werner founded as the forerunner of the Bank of Atlantis. Over the years, ATCOPS made profits for many clients, the present writer included, and minted an attractive silver coin, the Atlantis *Deca*, so-called because it contained a decagram of silver.

From his base at Grand Cayman, Werner bought an island off the coast of Belize and constructed improvements on it, his ultimate goal being to negotiate either an independent sovereignty or a grant of freeport status from the government of Belize. Plans did not work out as he had hoped, however. With age advancing on him, Werner finally put up the island for sale.

The Constitution of Atlantis

From all of this Herculean effort came, nevertheless, an intellectual construct that survived Atlantis and has found application in the plans of others who, in years since, have been similarly caught up in the idea of developing a non-political "free zone" on earth or on the new frontiers now seeming to beckon to us from outer space.

The need for this construct arose because Werner was treating his "Galt's Gulch" as much more than a literary device. He had set about to apply it in the real world. He could not ignore the question, therefore, of how it would be administered. There was no easy answer to the question. By 1969 or 1970, he had reached a low point and almost despaired of the project, agonizing over the question of how Atlantis could be administered as a community and yet its inhabitants remain free—not live for the sake of another man nor ask another to live for his. What form of government should he choose? Surveying the history of human society and politics, he found no form of government that was not prone to repeat the same tired, old round of tyranny the world has known for thousands of years.

At that point, Werner chanced upon the ideas of Spencer Heath and quickly saw their relevance. Heath had pointed out an advantage in keeping the title to the land component of a real-estate development intact and parceling the land into its various lots by land leasing rather than subdividing. This creates a concentrated entrepreneurial interest in the success of the development, enabling it to be administered as a long-term investment property for income. The incentive for those holding the ground title is to supply public services and amenities to the place, creating an environment that the market will find attractive. To the extent they do so, they can recover not only their costs but earn a profit to themselves and their investors. Heath forecast that in time whole settlements would be established on this nonpolitical basis. He thought this would become the future norm for communities—each competing in the market for clientele. He foresaw community services becoming a major new growth industry.

The modern hotel was Heath's inspiration and provided him a pilot demonstration. A hotel resembles a community in having private and public spaces. Its corridors are its streets, its landscaped lobby the town square. Its public transit happens to operate vertically rather than horizontally. In-house medical and security services assure round-the-clock safety of guests, visitors, and property. The hotel provides utilities and zones its space in an orderly manner for shopping, dining, entertainment, and other appropriate land uses. All it lacks that we customarily find in communities is a city hall exercising tax and other kinds of discretionary authority over the inhabitants and their property.

The growth of multi-tenant income properties in the United States, largely since Heath wrote, shows the working of this market principle in many land-use applications besides the hotel. In the order of their appearance, examples include apartment buildings and office buildings, luxury liners (hotels afloat), commercial airports, shopping centers, RV/camp grounds, mobile home parks (now becoming communities of homes each on a long-term ground lease that can be separately mortgaged), small-craft marinas, research parks, professional and business parks, medical clinics, theme parks and, increasingly, combinations of these and others to form mixed-use developments more complex and less specialized, approaching communities as we are accustomed to think of them.

The success of this organizational model led to explosive growth. Shopping centers, a community of landlord and merchant tenants, were experimental when World War II ended. There were fewer than a dozen, and even the name had yet to be coined. Today, they approach 50,000 in the United States alone and accommodate half of the retail trade of the nation. Hotels have grown in size and complexity to the point that many are virtually self-contained cities, easily exceeding in population (guests, service staff and visitors) the city of Boston at the time the United States gained its independence from England.

Werner already had just such a working community in Atlantis I—his Saugerties Motel. Here he administered all the community services contractually on an ordinary, business-like basis. Pragmatic businessman that he was, he now recognized that here was his desired form of government—a proprietary, free-market government in which there was no violation of property rights. All relations were contractual, negotiated among the parties. He needed only to preserve this form of organization and take it out to sea.

Why had no one thought of this before? Why wasn't it common wisdom? Doubtless the reason was that the dynamic, evolving market process, at least to the degree that we know it today, is a recent phenomenon in human history. Boston's Tremont House, regarded in the industry as the first modern hotel, was built only 175 years ago. All subsequent forms of modern, multi-tenant income properties have evolved since then. Only with the advent of modern technology and business practice, including all the various supportive institutions of banking and finance, insurance, communications, market price, modern accounting methods, and so forth, could a community fully take the form of a competitive business enterprise.

Werner saw that the master-lease form would be critical. It would be Atlantis's social software, capable of generating an elaborate but internally consistent web of relationships, all spelled out in the wording of the leases, subleases, and sub-subleases, etc. The sum of agreements actually in effect at any given point in time would be the written constitution of Atlantis. Agreements could be as specialized and distinct as circumstances might warrant, so long as they did not contradict the master lease form.

In the absence of any body of legislated law to fall back upon, the wording of the master-lease form would be key to the success of Atlantis. To carry out this writing assignment, Werner commissioned Spencer Heath's grandson, the present writer, who had already studied the question from the broad viewpoint of social anthropology and had recognized and written the first account of multi-tenant income properties as a special class of phenomena (MacCallum 1970). No mere theoretician, Werner assigned for this task of writing Atlantis's social software a generous two-percent equity in the venture.

The resulting master-lease form survived Atlantis and took on a life of its own as others over the years critiqued it and offered improvements. A kind of open-source social software, it was published in several iterations with Werner's permission, but not under the name of Atlantis. Werner had learned the value of keeping a low profile, especially in the developing stages of a project, and he wanted to avoid prematurely drawing the attention of governments to the notion of private interests settling the oceans. So the master-lease form was offered simply as a heuristic exercise in the private provision of community services. Instead of Atlantis, its fictional setting became "Orbis," one of a cluster of hypothetical settlements in outer space. Accordingly, it became known as the "constitution for Orbis."

Application in Somalia

In the late 1990s, the Orbis constitution was adopted and modified for a proposed freeport development in northwest Somalia. The development was to be on a tract of land that the Samaron Clan, the fifth largest in Somalia and traditionally a stateless society, was considering leasing long-term to a private consortium. The late Michael van Notten, a Dutch lawyer and author of *The Law of the Somalis: A Stable Foundation for Economic Development in the Horn of Africa* (Red Sea Press 2005) spearheaded the project. He had married into the Samaron Clan and lived with them the last twelve years of his life, promoting economic development and studying their traditional law and politics.

The goal of the Somali freeport venture was to develop a multi-tenant income property, writ large. Provisionally called "Newland," it was and is intended to be a purely private business undertaking with no flags, anthems, or any of the ritual panoplies and paraphernalia associated with a political nation. If successful, it will be something like a small, latter-day Hong Kong, offering a business and professional environment freed of all taxation and burdensome bureaucracy. For the Samaron, it will be a stepping-stone to full participation in the developed world, offering in their own back yard, as it were, sources of employment, training, investment, and educational opportunities. Many Samaron aspire to full world participation—economic, technological, scientific, and cultural—provided they can do so without coming under the domination of a political government, their own or any other.

In adapting "Orbis" to the Somali situation, Michael van Notten made an important contribution. A trained lawyer and student of law, he sketched out a set of natural-law principles together with supporting procedural rules that could be incorporated in the master-lease form. This would enable a system of law to be in place from the beginning of the development, from which point it would evolve of its own accord. It would be a law, moreover, to which everyone in the community had consented.

Natural-law scholar Roy Halliday (2002) writes of this innovation that it

> comes as close as anything I have seen to establishing the framework for a civil society consistent with liberty and natural rights. The idea of incorporating a description of natural rights into the master lease for a proprietary community is brilliant. It satisfies both the strong natural rights advocates ... and the skeptics who believe rights are created by contracts. The lease contract provides a way to specify how rights are to be enforced.

Conclusion

Thus did Werner Stiefel, in his "Galt's Gulch," aka Atlantis, aka Orbis, inaugurate a plan for a wholly proprietary and responsible, nonpolitical public authority—a form of government, moreover, for which broad empirical precedent already exists. Here was one Objectivist's answer to the question of how to have public administration and yet everyone be empowered over his own person and property.

In Atlantis, Somalia, or somewhere on the frontiers now beckoning in outer space, Werner believed humankind would outgrow government as we know it. But the resulting society would be far from anarchic, as that term is popularly understood. In that sense, indeed, the term more accurately describes our present condition of nations warring upon one another and upon their own populations. Werner Stiefel foresaw a universal life for humankind under the rule of law—not rules thought up and dictated by legislators but rather customary law, approximating as closely as fallible humans can come to what Michael van Notten calls the natural law. Suffice it to say, there is nothing mystical about Van Notten's concept of "natural law." He uses it, following Belgian scholar Frank van Dun, to denote the underlying principles of successful human association, where "successful" means association that can endure because it respects the integrity of all of the individuals comprising it.

This particular line of thought reconciling imperatives of public community administration with the Objectivist principles of the good life for individuals was a direct result of the stimulus of *Atlas Shrugged* on the mind and heart of Werner Stiefel. We can speculate that Galt's Gulch might have given rise to many such creative turns of thought, had the inquiring spirit existed there that Baldy Harper's guiding star analogy makes possible. It is unfortunate that Ayn Rand did not, like

Baldy Harper, discover a way out of her inconsistency that would not have branded her with the scarlet letter "A," for "anarchist." Nevertheless, Stiefel's and now Van Notten's saga are descended from her novel. I can only think that such a fall-out from her writing would have intrigued and delighted Ayn Rand.

Notes

1   I do not know whether Harper published this idea, but the North Star image came up frequently in discussion after we became acquainted in 1954.
2   Not to be confused with the Atlantis Project to promote a floating sea city, also on the ocean but not apolitical, led by Erik Klein in the years 1993–1994.

References

Halliday, Roy. 2002. Email communication to the writer. Quoted by permission. 17 December.

Harper, F.A. 1968. Personal communication.

Heath, Spencer. 1957. *Citadel, Market and Altar: Emerging Society*. Baltimore: The Science of Society Foundation.

MacCallum, Spencer. 1970. *The Art of Community*. Menlo Park, California: Institute for Humane Studies.

———. 2005. The Free-port Clan. In Chapter Five of *The Law of the Somalis: A Stable Foundation for Economic Development in the horn of Africa*, Michael van Notten. Trenton, New Jersey: Red Sea Press.

Rand, Ayn. 1957. *Atlas Shrugged*. New York: New American Library (A Signet Book).

Shaffer, Butler. 2004. The Libertarians' Albatross. 3 November. Online at: www.LewRockwell.com.

Van Notten, Michael. 2004. The Law of the Somalis: A Stable Foundation for Economic Development in the horn of Africa. Trenton, New Jersey: Red Sea Press.

Chapter 19

Ayn Rand's "Atlantis" as a Free Market Economy

Sam Bostaph

The Isles of the Blessed. That is what the Greeks called it, thousands of years ago. They said Atlantis was a place where hero-spirits lived in a happiness unknown to the rest of the earth. A place which only the spirits of heroes could enter, and they reached it without dying, because they carried the secret of life within them. Atlantis was lost to mankind, even then.

Introduction

This visualization of the lost city of Atlantis comes from a female guest at Henry and Lillian Rearden's wedding anniversary party early in *Atlas Shrugged*. She's telling Dagny Taggart that John Galt is not just a popular catch-phrase expressing despair—"Who is John Galt?" Instead, he's the man who discovered Atlantis. Francisco d'Anconia responds to Dagny's scornful disbelief by insolently affirming the truth of the story, thus revealing and concealing two central physical and metaphorical secrets of the novel at the same time. They are that John Galt and "Atlantis" exist in the fictional world of *Atlas Shrugged*, and both carry the secret of life.

Ayn Rand's fictional Atlantis is a free society concealed within a crumbling authoritarian one, bleeding out the hero-spirits who are all that stand between the remnants of social order and total chaos, between the interventionist economy and no economy. The contrast between the two societies is an argument that the order of the market, and the prosperity it generates, can exist only so long as the rule of law and the existence of property rights provide a context for creative and productive men. Interventionism and authoritarianism destroy that context and eventually destroy those men and their production by eliminating both the incentive and the ability to produce.

In the progression of events before Dagny's crash-landing in Atlantis, creative men and the work of their minds increasingly disappear, and their possessions and tools deteriorate in the hands of others, until there are so few diesel engines and competent men to direct their use that it is a coal-burning locomotive driven by a drunken engineer that takes the Taggart Comet into the Taggart Tunnel and disaster. The collapse of the Taggart Tunnel occurs only a few days before Dagny enters the valley refuge of those on strike against a system of ideas that made the tunnel's destruction its logical product.

Prelude to Atlantis

Dagny's month within the valley provides readers of *Atlas Shrugged* with Rand's vision of a free society with a free market economy. It follows 600 pages of a sketch of the reasons for, and reality of, the decline of an authoritarian and interventionist United States of America.

The reality of the decline is pictured in three ways. First, and most obvious, is the physical decline within the United States. The deterioration of the infrastructure of the country—streets, roads, bridges, buildings and public services—is an early part of the description of the novel's setting. In the first few pages of the first chapter, Eddie Willers walks along streets lined with damaged or abandoned buildings, seeing broken windows, structural cracks and grime. His acceptance of their prevalence and the general gloominess of the scene underscore the perceived permanence of the decline. As the narrative progresses, it is clear that the country's existing buildings, machinery, vehicles of all kinds and transportation networks are all deteriorating and there is no net increase in their amount or extent.

Second, there is the decline in the business sector. Again, at the beginning of the novel one out of every four small businesses passed by Eddie Willers in his walk is closed. Bankruptcies are increasing, industrial production is declining and there is a rising black market in raw materials as legal sources diminish. To compound the problem, competent and productive businessmen and employees are disappearing at an increasing rate, the quality of workmanship and product are both declining and increasing business regulation in the Eastern states is driving businesses to Colorado. Once there, they soon succumb to the restrictions placed on them by politically-driven directives of the federal government's Bureau of Economic Planning and Natural Resources.

Third, is the accelerating decline in the standard of living. At first, rising unemployment and increasing poverty afflict only the lower and middle-income segments of the population. As the decline in the business sector spreads, even members of the upper-income segment and the politically powerful begin to experience the low quality and uncertain availability of everyday products and conveniences. Throughout the country, isolated areas regress to pre-industrial revolution conditions as the industries that fed their prosperity shrink, collapse and disappear. Starnesville, the former home of the Twentieth Century Motor Company, is the prototype for the eventual fate of the country as a whole. The destruction of the Twentieth Century Motor Company by the Starnes family's socialist experiment presents in miniature the story of the destruction of the economy of the United States of the novel. The intellectual roots of both disasters are the same.

The ultimate reasons for the decline of the Twentieth Century Motor Company and the interventionist economy are, of course, philosophical. Identifying the metaphysical, epistemological and ethical premises that are destroying all firms and all societies, and showing the reality of their consequences, is the main purpose of *Atlas Shrugged*. The more immediate reasons for the decline of the U.S. economy in the novel are institutional and political. The driving force of value creation within the business sector, the profit motive, is considered to be morally bankrupt by the collectivist intellectual and cultural leaders of the country. They work to replace it with the doctrine of the "social responsibilities" of business, an ambiguous term with its content dictated by every arrogant "humanitarian" and scheming plunderer in Rand's gallery of villains. The "social responsibilities" of business becomes a cover term for thievery. Consequently, as the novel progresses business firms become the milk cows of "social reform," or they fall victim to business rivals with political "pull," until their owners, managers and employees either abandon them or they collapse under the weight of taxation and regulation.

Far from existing as a protection of the rights of the population and the foundation of the market process, law becomes purely a tool of control. A revealing moment in a conversation between Henry Rearden and Dr. Floyd Ferris shows how far the abuse of the principle of the rule of law has gone. Ferris attempts to use blackmail to force Rearden to supply Rearden Metal to the State Science Institute. Knowing that Rearden has illegally supplied the metal to coal magnate Ken Danagger, Ferris offers to overlook the illegal sale if Rearden will supply the metal to his institute. Rearden counters, "But, after all, I did break one of your laws." Ferris replies, "Well, what do you think they're for?" A law that exists to be broken, and thus to invent criminals, relegates law to the status of being a tool in the expansion of government power and the rule of law to a historical footnote.

The final blow to the rule of law and the elimination of freedom in the United States of the novel is Directive 10-289 of the Bureau of Economic Planning and Natural Resources. It eliminates all property rights and relegates the population to the status of government slaves. In the face of a rapidly collapsing economy and disintegrating social order, the purpose of the directive is to force an artificial "stationary state" or general equilibrium in the economy by freezing the status quo. Its realization would be a slave state, the completely planned economy. The free economy and society of the hidden valley of Atlantis stands in stark contrast to the outside world of Directive 10-289.

The Economy of Atlantis

Unlike physical orders, social orders are held together by human decisions, by the minds of men. Physical orders exist because of the laws of nature, social orders because of the laws, customs, institutions and practices of men. Physical laws are constants set by the physical natures of the things whose orders they describe; social laws, customs, institutions and practices come into existence and persist by the consent of those who adopt and follow them. Only the decisions of men can make the laws—whether legislated, common or unwritten—that together will constitute the rule of law in any particular society; and, only the decisions of individual men will determine whether or not each conforms his actions to those laws. The particular order of a society depends vitally on its laws, the manner of their application and whether or how they are observed. Because man is a living being with a specific nature, it follows that there is a structure of laws that is suited to that nature and will best further his existence and create a social context within which he will thrive. There is no certainty that those are the laws he will adopt. He must discover them and choose to adopt them. Because he is an animal possessing volitional consciousness and the capacity to reason, he has the free will to choose to ignore that structure of law and to reject that social context. Ultimately, the choices he makes will determine his individual and social existence. A society ruled by the whims and dictates of only one or a few persons will be far different from one ruled by the dictate that all relations between adults must be consensual and no one may initiate the use of physical coercion against another.

The primary requirement for the existence of the free society and free economy is the rule of law in the form last mentioned. The laws must protect everyone in the same way and all must obey the law that forbids the initiation of coercion by any one member of society against another. This is what makes all legitimate relations among men consensual, and law the protection of their rights.

Foremost among these rights are those of private property and of contractual relations. In a free society, property law, contract law, the law of torts and criminal law all exist to preserve a peaceful social order of consensual relations and to penalize those who act to disturb or contravene that order. The result is a liberation of the creative and productive powers of all members of the society.

In Atlantis, Ayn Rand presents in microcosm a sketch of the free society and free economy. She assumes no government and replaces the word "law" with the word "custom" to indicate a less formal agreement. As John Galt explains to Dagny during her first breakfast in the valley, "We have no laws in this valley, no rules, no formal organization of any kind … But we have certain customs, which we all observe …" Later, banker Midas Mulligan informs Dagny that the residents of the valley are a voluntary association held together by each individual's self-interest. If disputes occur, they are to be arbitrated by Judge Narragansett. As the original owner of the valley, Mulligan presumably has stipulated the conditions of use of the property he owns, as well as of that he has sold. The question of enforcement is not addressed.

The residents of the valley are all refugees from the world outside, productive men and women who have gone on strike against the prevailing ethos of that outside world and removed their minds and capabilities from it. In Atlantis, they are free to produce and trade what they wish and as they wish so long as they observe the valley's customs, which presumably include the stipulation that all social relations are consensual. All are ends in themselves rather than being wholly or partially the means to the ends of others, as they were in the world outside. Some practice the trade or profession they formerly practiced in the outside world, or a simpler version of it. Some engage in different productive endeavors or are employees of others. Some have more than one occupation. Compared to their outside level of existence, most live in reduced circumstances but consider themselves better off existentially because of their freedom and the prospects for physical improvement. As Ellis Wyatt tells Dagny Taggart, "I'm richer now than I was in the world (outside). What's wealth but the means of expanding one's life?"

Whatever their jobs or professions, all in the valley trade the fruits of their labor for those of the labor of others. There are no taxes, welfare transfers or free services. Despite John Galt's words to the contrary, there are gifts. Galt pays Midas Mulligan for the rent of his car, rejecting Dagny's view that it should have been given "as a courtesy" with the statement that the word "give" is forbidden in the valley. Yet, only a few pages before, Galt had explained that the solid gold dollar sign sitting on a granite column on a ledge above the valley had been given to Midas Mulligan by Francisco d'Anconia as a joke present. Even before entering the valley, Dagny had received gifts of cigarettes from Hugh Akston and Owen Kellogg.

So far as the actual trading activity is concerned, the population of the valley uses gold and silver coins minted by Midas Mulligan. It is said that immigrants into the valley brought in what gold they had and that Ragnar Danneskjoeld has almost completed his task of adding to the gold balances in accounts in the Mulligan Bank. This would make the amount of gold in the valley a given. There is no explanation of how it is determined what quantity of gold to mint into currency, which then circulates within the valley, nor is there an indication of the relative value of gold itself. A reasonable hypothesis for the minting process would be that those creating accounts in the Mulligan bank, including Mulligan himself, would withdraw gold in the form of coins when needed for payments and personal cash holdings, and it would be redeposited as a matter of course. Or, the currency would be transferred from one account to another to settle a debt. This would make the Mulligan Bank a bank with 100 percent reserves. Loans made by Mulligan either would be made in currency or by the creation of an account, transferring gold from Mulligan's own account to that of the borrower. Withdrawals or transfers would follow the same procedure and have the same result as previously mentioned. The monetary system itself would be a 100 percent reserve gold standard system. So far as the question of the value of gold as compared to other commodities goes, and the related question of the creation and operation of the relative price system of the entire valley, those are more difficult questions to answer from Rand's text.

When John Galt is showing Dagny Taggart the building housing the Mulligan Mint, he stipulates that only gold and silver coins minted by Mulligan are the currency of the valley and says, "We accept nothing but objective values." This is similar to the statement made earlier in the novel at James Taggart's wedding by Franciso d'Anconia that, "Money is the material shape of the principle that men who wish to deal with one another must deal by trade and give value for value." He goes on to praise gold as "an objective value, an equivalent of wealth produced." And yet, on the same occasion, Francisco also says that money allows people to obtain for their goods and labor only "that which they are worth to the men who buy them." He later tells Dagny in Atlantis that he is richer there than he was in the outside world because the small amount of copper he produces is totally his property. Richard Halley reinforces the implied subjectivity of wealth and value by telling Dagny that her subjective appreciation for his music is what he seeks in playing it for her. Obviously, trade in Atlantis need not involve either money or tangible goods and services.

Rand's theory of price is less ambiguous than her theory of value. In a conversation between Ellis Wyatt and Dagny Taggart, Wyatt explains that he is improving his process of extracting oil from shale and states that as the effort to produce oil decreases (and, presumably, the amount of production increases), "I ask less of the men to whom I trade it for the things I need." Given these brief words, it is difficult to avoid the conjecture that Rand is assuming a real-cost theory of pricing rather than a demand theory. She would have to be assuming some connection between the amount of resources expended to produce a given quantity of something of value and the amount of currency for which it would exchange for Wyatt's words to make sense. There is no indication in the various commodity prices mentioned of how the prices in the valley came to be established in the first place. The prices themselves are stated in gold dollars and are significantly lower than prices outside the valley. If one assumes a demand theory of pricing, a reasonable hypothesis would be that the initial structure of relative prices for the various commodities would be patterned after that in the outside world and then adjusted to changes in commodity mix and relative production amounts and demand within the valley. To assume otherwise would be to assume that a relative price system in a new currency could be designed without reference to the past—something impossible to conceive of doing unless one assumes a real-cost theory of pricing, such as a labor theory. Rand appears to make this error.

Given the fixed amount of gold in the valley and the productive growth Dagny sees all around her, prices in general would tend to decline as the valley's economy expands—making the value of gold and silver rise, and stimulating their own production as a profit-making enterprise. This would occur even without Rand's erroneous—and perhaps rhetorical—assumption that prices could be real-cost determined. Also, the economy of the valley would expand; it has all the requisites for economic growth and development—the rule of law, individual rights of property and contract, peace, a plethora of natural resources, a skilled and dedicated workforce, money, aggressive competition and the moral basis for non-exploitative exchange relationships in the character and personal ethics of the inhabitants.

The role of competition in the economy of Atlantis is especially pronounced and productive of economic growth. When Dagny Taggart visits the Stockton Foundry, Andrew Stockton reveals that his ruined competitor is now one of his employees. Stockton's superior productivity attracted all his former competitor's customers, and then Stockton hired that former competitor because he knew he could use him productively within Stockton's own firm. Working together increases their joint efficiency and both are better off as a result. The principle at work here is that of specialization according to comparative advantage—although the term is not used and the principle only implied by the example. Further, one of Stockton's other employees is former coal magnate Ken Dannager. Dannager has the potential to become Stockton's competitor, but Stockton employs him because he's the best employee he can find at present to do the job he's doing. Both gain from the arrangement—as all would gain if Dannager did become Stockton's "most dangerous competitor." Competition, in conjunction with production according to the principle of comparative advantage, drives economic growth and development for the benefit of all within Atlantis as it does within any single economy or in the economy of the world.

Atlas Shrugged is a novel, and Atlantis only a sketch of a free society and free economy. Yet, the basic conditions for economic development and growth are clearly and compellingly presented. The complexity possible to a free economy and the virtually unimaginable wealth that can be created within it belie the simplicity of its foundational principles—principles well known at least since the time of Adam Smith. But, that is not the strongest argument for it. Ayn Rand has Ellis Wyatt summarize that argument succinctly: above a certain minimal level of nutrition and comfort an economy is nothing more than a medium for the expansion of human life. If human life is the moral gold standard, the free society is the social context within which individual purposive actions produce the greatest individual and social prosperity, in all senses of the word.

Conclusion

Although written and published half a century ago, *Atlas Shrugged* is a forewarning of mankind's future if present trends in ethics and politics continue.

Ideas do have consequences in both personal and social life, as Ayn Rand strove to illustrate in the novel. The fictional world of *Atlas Shrugged* is not the reality of today's United States of America, but it may be that of tomorrow's. The technological context of the novel certainly is outdated; however, the moral and political principles are timeless. Someday it may be physically possible to make bread out of stones; it will never be possible to create wealth by thievery, nor for the planned economy to be a free and prosperous one.

Interventionism is more pervasive now in the U.S. economy and it is growing with the general growth in government. Each year property rights become more closely circumscribed, both by legislation and by judicial decisions at all levels. The assault on the morality of business and businessmen in cultural and journalistic forums grows ever more intense, while the moral corruption in government and popular culture worsens. Thievery and deception in business earns prison terms; in government it advances careers.

There are some positive signs to set against the negative ones. The failure of the Soviet Union's planned economy, among others, has dimmed the influence of socialist economists. Fifty years ago, few economists argued the superiority of the market order over that of government planning. Now, few openly argue for the planned economy, while most argue the superiority of the market process. In addition, libertarian think tanks—such as The Ludwig von Mises Institute, the Foundation for Economic Education and the Future of Freedom Foundation—are growing in resources and influence. Public perception of government as either benign or benevolent also has eroded significantly over this same time period. Opinion polls consistently reveal a deep skepticism of public officials and their proposals. It is no longer unusual to see voters revolt and recall obviously incompetent or dishonest officials from office. These are heartening signs to those who believe in the ultimate supremacy of ideas. Historically, the policies of the future are the children of the ideas of the present.

Will the Atlantis of *Atlas Shrugged* ever become our world? It is our responsibility to create it if we wish to live as free men and women.

Chapter 20

Atlas Shrugged and Public Choice:
The Obvious Parallels

Bryan Caplan

'We are at the dawn of a new age,' said James Taggart, from above the rim of his
champagne glass ... 'We will set men free of the rule of the dollar ... We will build
a society dedicated to higher ideals, and we will replace the aristocracy of money
by –'
    '– the aristocracy of pull,' said a voice beyond the group. (381–2)

Ayn Rand's Sausage Factory

According to an old saying, "If you like sausages or legislation, you should never
watch either being made."[1] It is no wonder, then, that Ayn Rand puts the political
process under a microscope. Regulation does not just "happen" in *Atlas Shrugged*.
The reader goes behind the scenes to witness Jim Taggart help Wesley Mouch
blackmail Hank Rearden in exchange for raising railroad rates over the objection
of Orren Boyle. All for the "general welfare," of course!

When Rand published *Atlas Shrugged* in 1957, most social scientists were still
naive enough to take politicians' speeches about "the general welfare" at face
value. But that was soon to change. In the 1960s and 1970s, economists began to
use their standard tools to understand how democracy works. "We would never
believe a businessman who claimed to work for the public good," they reasoned.
"Why should we believe a politician?" Instead, they assumed that politicians
maximize votes, just as firms maximize profits. The result was public choice
theory, and eventually won James Buchanan a Nobel Prize (Buchanan 2001).

Though there is little evidence of mutual influence,[2] Ayn Rand and public
choice converge on a strikingly similar vision of the political process. Both
emphasize the contradiction between the propaganda of government intervention
and the reality. Government supposedly intervenes to advance the interests of the
majority. In reality, however, its goal to advance the interests of political insiders
at the expense of everyone else (Tullock 1967; Krueger 1974).

One of public choicers' favorite examples is airline regulation. The Civil Aeronautics Board claimed to protect travelers from rapacious airlines. In fact, the mission of the CAB was to keep airfares up by restricting competition. To say that "regulation did not work" is rather misleading. It failed in its official goal of helping consumers, but it succeeded in its actual goal of shielding the regulated industry from competition (Friedman and Friedman 1979).

This is the story of virtually every act of government in *Atlas Shrugged*. In each case, the altruistic rhetoric is a smokescreen. Laissez-faire would make most people better off, but financially endanger or even bankrupt the politically connected forces behind the expansion of government power.

The Anatomy of Legislation

The fictional politics in *Atlas Shrugged* is pure public choice. Each piece of legislation has the following components:

1. A public-interest rationale.
2. Supportive interest groups with a hidden financial agenda.
3. Negative consequences for the general public.

Consider the following case studies.

The Anti-dog-eat-dog Rule

The National Railroad Alliance, "the better to enforce" the laws long since passed by the country's Legislature, imposes a ban on "destructive competition" known as the Anti-dog-eat-dog Rule. In concrete terms:

> [I]n regions declared to be restricted, no more than one railroad would be permitted to operate; that in such regions, seniority belonged to the oldest railroad now operating there, and that newcomers, who had encroached unfairly upon its territory, would suspend operations within nine months after being so ordered; that the Executive Board of the National Alliance of Railroads was empowered to decide, at its sole discretion, which regions were to be restricted. (77)

The altruistic rationale for the Rule is to prevent a shortage of transportation. Railroads have to stop destroying each other by competing in markets with room for only a single line.

But we should not be misled by the fact that "No railroad was mentioned by name in the speeches that preceded the voting" (76). The real story is that Jim Taggart wants to put a successful new entrant—Dan Conway of the Phoenix-Durango—out of business. So he works out a deal with steel magnate Orren Boyle.

Boyle agrees to deliver the necessary votes from his friends in the National Alliance of Railroads. In exchange, Taggart uses his Washington influence to help Boyle pass the Equalization of Opportunity Bill. (50–51)

Since the real goal of the Anti-dog-eat-dog Rule is to help Taggart, not the public, it is not surprising that its purported benefits are the reverse of the truth. Assure transportation? Before the Rule passed, the worst-case scenario was that *one* of the two competing lines would eventually go out of business. After the Rule passes, Dagny has to move mountains to prevent an interruption of service.

The Equalization of Opportunity Bill

The Equalization of Opportunity Bill forbids any person or corporation to own more than one business concern. The public-interest rationales overflow:

> The editorial said that at a time of dwindling production, shrinking markets and vanishing opportunities to make a living, it was unfair to let one man hoard several business enterprises, while others had none; it was destructive to let a few corner all the resources, leaving others no chance; competition was essential to society, and it was society's duty to see that no competitor ever rose beyond the range of anybody who wanted to compete with him. (127)

The Bill's hidden intent, however, is to help Orren Boyle compete with Rearden Steel. Rearden produces his own iron ore, and Boyle has trouble finding a reliable supplier. Forcing Rearden to divest makes it easier for Boyle—or at least harder for Rearden—to get the ore. To secure the Bill's passage, Boyle calls in a favor from Jim Taggart; after all, Boyle helped Taggart get the Anti-dog-eat-dog Rule. Taggart persuades Rearden's Washington man, Wesley Mouch, to double-cross him. Mouch's reward is the assistant's job in the Bureau of National Planning[3] (373).

Needless to say, the Equalization of Opportunity Bill does not revive the economy. To some extent, businessmen get around the law by setting up dummy corporations, but this charade is the least of the damage. The main problem is that production falls drastically when owners who won their position in a competitive marketplace have to sell their companies to people who—almost by definition— have never successfully run a business.

The Colorado Directives

The success of the John Galt line sparks an economic boom in Colorado. Forbidden to own more than one business, many ambitious businessmen actually sell their existing companies in order to start fresh in Colorado (257–60).[4] In response to the Colorado boom, Wesley Mouch imposes a surprise package of new directives, most notably:

- Maximum speed and car lengths on railroads
- Requiring railroads "to run the same number of trains in every state of a zone composed of five neighboring states" (317)
- Limits on steel production
- Forbidding manufacturers to move from their present location without regulators" permission
- A five-year moratorium on railroad bonds
- A five percent tax on Colorado's gross sales to pay for administrative costs

The official reason for the directives is to deal with the "national emergency." Colorado is booming while the rest of the country spirals downwards, and it is only fair to make Colorado share the pain.

In reality, however, these Directives are a bold power play by none other than Jim Taggart.[5] Dagny realizes too late that "[T]he John Galt Line had been only a drainpipe that permitted Jim Taggart to make a deal and to drain [the bondholders"] wealth, unearned, into his pocket, in exchange for letting others drain his railroad ..." (318). The plan works:

> Jim boasted that this had been the most prosperous six months in Taggart history. Listed as profit, on the glossy pages of his report to the stockholders, was the money he had not earned—the subsidies for empty trains; and the money he did not own—the sums that should have gone to pay the interest and the retirement of Taggart bonds, the debt which, by the will of Wesley Mouch, he had been permitted not to pay ... "You have always considered money-making as such an important virtue," Jim had said to [Dagny] with an odd half-smile. "Well, it seems to me that I'm better at it than you are." (333)

For the large majority of the nation, however, the directives are disaster. They kill the Colorado boom, even leading Ellis Wyatt to torch his own oil fields and vanish. Production plummets, along with hope for a more prosperous future—a Second Renaissance.

Directive Number 10-289

As the economy disintegrates, Wesley Mouch calls a secret summit of the nation's interest groups. As Mouch explains to his fellow luminaries:

> The economic condition of the country was better the year before last than it was last year, and last year it was better than it is at present. It's obvious that we would not be able to survive another year of the same progression. Therefore, our sole objective must now be to hold the line ... Freedom has been given a chance and has failed. Therefore, more stringent controls are necessary. (503)

After some deliberation, they all assent to a package of eight radical policy changes known as Directive Number 10-289 (505–6). Point One makes it illegal for workers to quit or be fired. Point Two forbids business closings. Point Three abolishes patents and copyrights. Point Four prohibits the introduction of "new devices, inventions, products, or goods of any nature whatsoever" (505). Point Five makes it illegal for firms to expand or contract production relative to the Basic Year. Point Six enjoins everyone to spend the same amount of money as they spent in the Basic Year. Point Seven imposes universal price controls. Point Eight makes the Unification Board the final arbiter and interpreter of the directive.

The putative motive of 10-289 is "to protect the people's security, to achieve full equality and total stability" (505). In the words of Eugene Lawson, the resident idealist:

> We must not let vulgar difficulties obstruct our feeling that it's a noble plan motivated solely by the public welfare. It's for the good of the people. The people need it. Need comes first, so we don't have to consider anything else. (499)

Mr. Thompson, the Head of the State, seconds Lawson's message but wants prettier packaging: "That's the line, Wesley. Tone it down and dress it up and get your press boys to chant it—and you won't have to worry" (499).

In fact, however, the "good of the people" is a very low priority. Several of the participants are openly contemptuous of altruistic rhetoric. Floyd Ferris smugly announces "[T]here's a certain old-fashioned quotation which we may safely forget: the one counting on the wise and the honest. We don't have to consider them. They're out of date"[6] (501). At one point, Taggart even snaps "If we are to perish, let's make sure that we all perish together. Let's make sure that we leave them no chance to survive!"[7] (506). Labor leader Fred Kinnan, who doubles as comic relief ("Are we here to talk business or are we here to kid each other?") (507) even admits: " … I'm not going to say that I'm working for the welfare of my public, because I know I'm not. I know that I'm delivering the poor bastards into slavery, and that's all there is to it" (508).

The overarching aim of Directive Number 10-289 is to allow the members of the summit to retain power. Most if not all of them realize that their policies have had disastrous consequences for the nation, but they refuse to admit their errors and resign. So they impose new policies to cement their grip on the economy, whatever the damage. As the nation's elite, they figure that they can prosper even if the average standard of living plummets. In Jim Taggart's words: "We'll be safe for the first time in centuries. Everybody will know his place and his job, and everyone else's place and job—and we won't be at the mercy of every stray crank with a new idea. Nobody will push us out of business or steal our markets or undersell us or make us obsolete" (510).

Within the framework of 10-289's radical changes, the summit is politics as usual, as the usual suspects squabble over the details. Union leader Fred Kinnan gets the upper hand with a blunt ultimatum: "[Y]ou'd better staff that Unification Board with my men ... or I'll blast your Point One to hell" (507). Given the strength of his bargaining position, he refuses to share power: "Who is the public? If you go by quality—then it ain't you, Jim, and it ain't Orrie Boyle. If you go by quantity—then it sure is *me*, because quantity is what I've got behind me" (508).

Eugene Lawson briefly stands up for freedom of the press. Directive Four, he notes, prevents the publishing of any new books.[8] Mouch argues against making exceptions, but Ferris wins the summit over by explaining that 10-289's tacit censorship is one of its benefits:

> You don't want some recalcitrant hacks to come out with treatises that will wreck our entire program, do you? If you breathe the word "censorship" now, they'll all scream bloody murder ... But if you leave the matter alone and make it a simple material issue—not a matter of ideas, but just a matter of paper, ink and printing presses ... [y]ou'll make sure make sure that nothing dangerous gets printed or heard—and nobody is going to fight over a material issue. (512)

Lingering resistance can be defused, Ferris notes, by giving friendly intellectuals "moderately comfortable salaries and extremely loud titles" (513).

The least expected political maneuver comes, however, from Taggart. Taggart wants to raise railroad rates before the price controls kick in. Boyle is opposed, and at first, so is Mouch. But Taggart wins out by offering Mouch the information he needs to blackmail Rearden into signing over the patent for Rearden Metal.

The actual effect of 10-289 is disastrous for the overwhelming majority of Americans. The economy falls to pieces. Riots and famine erupt. Competent people quit their jobs and vanish more rapidly than they did when it was legal to do so. Still, it prolongs the reign of those in power, and for the members of the summit, that is what counts.

The End Game

Once Directive 10-289 takes effect, special interests lose their enthusiasm for passing new laws. Instead, they focus on beating the system. The elite's public-interest rhetoric gets more and more hysterical as its time horizon gets shorter and shorter. Gangsters like Cuffy Meigs, anxious only to make a quick buck before the economy collapses, spread like a virus through both government and business:

> These were the men whom official speeches described as "the progressive businessmen of our dynamic age," but whom people called "the pull peddlers"—the species included many breeds, those of "transportation pull," and of "steel pull" and "oil pull" and "wage-raise pull" and "suspended sentence pull"—men who were dynamic, who kept darting all over the country while no one else could move ... (847)

There are a few last gasps of legal wrangling, most notably the Railroad Unification Plan and the Steel Unification Plan. But we catch an interesting glimpse of the ruling elite's last resort when Head of State Thompson confesses to Dagny:

> There's one clique—the Ferris-Lawson-Meigs factions—that's been after me for over a year to adopt stronger measures ... Frankly, what they mean is: to resort to terror. Introduce the death penalty for civilian crimes, for critics, dissenters, and the like ... Nothing will make our system work, they say, but terror. And they may be right, from the look of things nowadays (1008).

As expected, Dagny's alternative—start decontrolling—falls on deaf ears. The ruling elite prefers mass murder to personal defeat. Yet they preach the public welfare to the bitter end. Thompson tells the world that Galt "has heard your pleas and has answered the call of our common human duty! Every man is his brother's keeper! No man is an island unto himself!" (1045)

From Fiction to Social Science

The men in Ayn Rand's sausage factory come to a bad end. Their careful machinations work for a while, but eventually blow up in their faces. In part, the reason is specific to Rand's narrative. John Galt has secretly organized history's first strike of the "men of the mind." The interest groups who control national policy therefore repeatedly over-estimate how much wealth they can squeeze out of the economy.

The effectiveness of Galt's strike is probably the most economically implausible feature of *Atlas Shrugged*. It only works because of a miraculous correlation between productive ability and adherence to Randian philosophy.[9] In the real world, Dagny and Rearden would not be the only "scabs." Plenty of business and scientific geniuses sincerely embrace statist philosophy and/or pragmatically prefer to work with the system, despite its flaws.

But Galt's strike is not the only reason the system collapses. Rand also argues that pressure group warfare leads to disaster when it gets out of hand. Francisco explains the logic in his speech on money:

> Such looters believe it is safe to rob defenseless men, once they've passed a law to disarm them. But their loot becomes the magnet for other looters, who get it from them as they got it. Then the race goes, not to the ablest at production, but to those most ruthless at brutality. When force is the standard, the murderer wins over the pickpocket. And then society vanishes, in a spread of ruins and slaughter. (390)

Galt's speech elaborates on this theme:

> You did not care to compete in terms of intelligence—you are now competing in terms of brutality ... Your system is a legal civil war, where men gang up on one another and struggle for possession of the law, which they use as a club over rivals, till another gang wrests it from their clutch and clubs them with it in their turn ... (989–90)

Public choice has a special name for Rand's scenario: "full rent dissipation." The idea is simple. If the government has $1,000,000 to hand out, lobbyists will spend up to $1,000,000 to sway the legal process to get their hands on it. So begins a legal "arms race"; the more the government distributes, the harder interest groups fight to get their cut.

Furthermore, lobbying cannot remain unusually profitable for long, because high rewards attract new entry—like the ruthless Cuffy Meigs. The long-run effect is not to enrich the special interests, but to destroy wealth. This is a common explanation for the failures of India's economy (Krueger 1974). Everything is politicized, so vast resources that could have been used for production instead chase after government privileges. So public choicers can basically buy Rand's saga of economic collapse. They expect production to unravel once the whole economy is up for grabs.

But why does democracy put the economy up for grabs, if it is such a bad idea? Public choicers' standard answer blames voters' rational ignorance. Paying attention to politics has virtually no payoff for the average voter, so it is rational to not pay attention. The result: Few see through the smokescreen of public interest rhetoric to the sordid reality of the sausage factory. Even fewer realize that government intervention is the fuel of pressure group warfare.

The appeal to rational ignorance has its critics (Wittman 1995). Big problem: There is a difference between ignorant and gullible. If voters were really "rational ignorant" about politics, they would greet altruistic rhetoric with skepticism: "Wesley Mouch says Directive 10-289 will help the public, but I don't have time to verify his claims, so I remain unconvinced." If rational ignorance were the central weakness of democracy, voters could protect themselves with a simple slogan: "When in doubt, vote No." If the voting public in *Atlas Shrugged* had followed this rule of thumb, none of the destructive legislation Rand chronicles would have come to pass!

Like public choicers, Rand ultimately blames the failures of democracy on voters. But she targets their irrationality, not their ignorance (Caplan 2001). Voters favor destructive policies not out of lack of information, but intellectual dishonesty:

> [T]hat nameless act which all of you practice ... the act of blanking out, the willful suspension of one's consciousness, the refusal to think—not blindness, but the refusal to see; not ignorance, but the refusal to know. It is the act of unfocusing your mind and inducing an inner fog to escape the responsibility of judgment ... .(944)

Listen to how Galt ridicules the typical voter's view of the world:

> You propose to establish a social order based on the following tenets: that you're
> incompetent to run your own life, but competent to run the lives of others—that you're
> unfit to exist in freedom, but fit to become an omnipotent ruler—that you're unable to
> earn your living by use of your own intelligence, but able to judge politicians and to
> vote them into jobs of total power over arts you have never seen, over sciences you
> have never studied, over achievements of which you have no knowledge, over the
> gigantic industries where you, by your own definition of your capacity, would be
> unable successfully to fill the job of assistant greaser. (974)

If voters were plain ignorant, they would have the modesty to leave other people in
peace. They would not eagerly support Wesley Mouch's latest witch-hunt. In
practice, however, the man in the street combines ignorance with self-righteous
dogmatism—and votes for politicians who pander to his folly. The ultimate source
of destructive policy, for Rand, is grassroots neglect of the virtue of rationality:
"This dismal wreckage, which is now your world, is the physical form of the
treason you committed to your values, to your friends, to your defenders, to your
future, to your country, to yourself" (984).

At times, admittedly, Rand seems to accuse intellectuals—the "mystics of
spirit" and the "mystics of muscle"—of ideologically seducing the public. Yet the
intellectuals' contradictions are too blatant to make this a credible excuse. All it
takes to see through their rhetoric is the common sense of a Fred Kinnan: "Save it
for Jim Taggart, Doc ... I know what I'm talking about. That's because I never
went to college" (507). If intellectuals brainwash the public, they brainwash it by
engraved invitation.

Rand and public choice agree that interest groups are the proximate cause of a
lot of wealth-destroying legislation. But in my judgment, she is one step ahead of
the standard public choice story. *Atlas Shrugged* makes an important contribution
to social science. Yes, lobbyists enrich themselves at the expense of the majority,
but only after the majority paves the way for the lobbyists by electing statist
politicians. Jim Taggart hides behind altruistic rhetoric while he does his dirty
work. But he succeeds only because much of the public refuses to give his flowery
words the respect they deserve. Instead, like the woman at Taggart's wedding, they
say: "I feel it. I don't go by my head, but by my heart. You might be good at logic,
but you're heartless" (392). The sausage factory is right in front of the voters, but
they refuse to see it—or even think about what goes on inside.

Notes

1   Some versions of this quote are usually attributed to Otto von Bismarck. Online at:
    http://www.worldofquotes.com/author/Otto-von-Bismarck/1/.

2   However, Rand and public choice probably share some common ancestors—most notably Ludwig von Mises.

3   As if these machinations were not complex enough, we later learn that Jim Taggart knew that the Bill would hobble the domestic copper industry, leading to a large increase in imports. He took advantage of his insider knowledge by buying a large stake in Chile's d'Anconia Copper (384–5).

4   This appears to be a genuinely unintended consequence of the Equalization of Opportunity Bill. Forbidden to own more than one business, many ambitious entrepreneurs sell out in order to start new firms in the economic boom in Colorado.

5   This does not mean that Taggart is the only lobbyist behind the directives, of course. We eventually learn that Taggart fought against limits on steel production after learning that Boyle opposed his bond moratorium (372).

6   Ferris is even more blunt in his conversation with Hank Rearden: "You'd better get it straight that it's not a bunch of boy scouts you're up against—then you'll know that this is not an age for beautiful gestures. We're after power and we mean it" (411).

7   Soon afterwards, Taggart has an even more revealing outburst against Eddie Willers: "You're going to learn a lesson—all of you!—all of you spoiled, self-indulgent, undisciplined little two-bit clerks, who strut around as if that crap about your rights was serious!" (585)

8   It does not, Mouch points out, prevent printing more copies of old books. Hardly surprising, given that Mouch recently lunched with the low-sales literary figure Balph Eubank (512).

9   Robert Stadler is the only obvious exception, though perhaps Dan Conway also qualifies.

References

Buchanan, James. 2001. A conversation with James Buchanan. *Frontiere Centre for Public Policy.* Online at:
   http://fcpp.org/publication_detail.php?PubID=236.
Caplan, Bryan. 2001. Rational ignorance versus rational irrationality. 2001. *Kyklos* 54, 3–26.
Friedman, Milton, and Rose Friedman. 1979. *Free to Choose: A Personal Statement.* New York: Avon.
Krueger, Anne. 1974. The political economy of the rent-seeking society. *American Economic Review* 64, 291–303.
Rand, Ayn. 1957. *Atlas Shrugged.* New York: Signet.
Tullock, Gordon. 1967. The welfare costs of tariffs, monopolies and theft. *Western Economic Journal* 5, 224–32.
Wittman, Donald. 1995. *The Myth of Democratic Failure.* Chicago: University of Chicago Press.

Chapter 21

Francisco d'Anconia on Money: A Socio-Economic Analysis

Steven Horwitz

Introduction

The fiction of Ayn Rand has, perhaps, more economic content to it per page than that of any other novelist. This is not surprising given that her uncompromising belief in both the efficacy and morality of markets and capitalism is the driving force behind her work, especially *Atlas Shrugged* (1957). There are a variety of topics in political economy that one could explore using the novel, and several other essays in this volume tackle some of them. Perhaps the most direct statement on economic matters in the novel is Francisco d'Anconia's speech denouncing the view that money is the root of all evil. In a few short pages, Rand, through her character, raises a whole number of issues about money's roles both in the marketplace and in the social order more broadly. The speech takes place about a third of the way through the book, and d'Anconia is a fairly typical Randian protagonist. The setting is a dinner party the night before the value of d'Anconia's company will be wiped out by his own actions as a way to bankrupt the various villains of the novel who have invested in his firm. In classic Rand fashion, d'Anconia's speech is a long reply to an off-the-cuff remark by another character about money being the root of evil, made under the assumption that everyone in the room would agree and that no one who disagreed would have the temerity to respond with equal or greater vigor. By refusing to acquiesce in the face of a claim to the moral high ground, d'Anconia exemplifies Rand's notion of refusing to provide the sanction of a moral code's victim.

Although the overriding theme of that speech is the morality of money, both as a social institution and as an object of human acquisition, it also elucidates, in a very concise way, several fundamental aspects of the economics and sociology of money. For the most part, Rand is right on target with these observations, and in this essay, I hope to expand on some of her insights and tie them to scholarly work in economics and beyond.

Money as a Medium of Exchange

Any attempt to understand the socio-economic significance of money must begin by recognizing that money is, most fundamentally, nothing more or less than a generally accepted medium of exchange. The formulation "generally accepted medium of exchange" contains two elements: the social notion of being "generally accepted" and the individual intention captured by being a "medium of exchange." That is, money relies both on individuals wanting to exchange and on using something in exchange that other individuals are willing to accept. It is a social convention resting on mutual trust. As Rand (1957, 387) says through Francisco: "Money is made possible only by the men who produce. ... When you accept money in payment for your effort, you do so only on the conviction that you will exchange it for the product of the effort of others." In this way, money is the epitome of a society based on mutual exchange, whether of goods and services more specifically, or "value" more generally.

Rand's ethical code is centered around the trader as the symbol of ethical behavior and justice (Rand 1971). For her, all human interaction can be understood in terms of trade and exchange, whether it is an economic relationship or a romantic one. This leads naturally to seeing money in moral terms, as it is through the use of money that exchange not only becomes genuinely possible, but is also able to spread across human societies and become the dominant mode of economic discourse. Money gives to each individual no more or less than they deserve: "Money permits you to obtain for your goods and your labor that which they are worth to the men who buy them, but no more. Money permits no deals except those to mutual benefit by the unforced judgment of the traders" (1957, 388). The result of this process of exchange is that those who produce the most value will see their goods and services sold more and will accumulate more wealth as a result. That accumulation of wealth by producers will correspond to consumers seeing the best products emerge from the process of competition:

> And when men live by trade—with reason, not force, as their final arbiter—it is the best product that wins, the best performance, the man of best judgment and highest ability—and the degree of a man's productiveness is the degree of his reward. This is the code of existence whose tool and symbol is money (1957, 388).

Money both symbolizes and facilitates the behavior that exemplified Rand's moral code.

A further element of Rand's view of the interplay between money's socio-economic functions and its moral standing is her discussion of money as a "tool" (1957, 388). This is an aspect of its role as a medium of exchange. Money cannot determine which exchanges to make; it can only facilitate those one wishes to make. For Rand, even though money epitomizes the ideal world of her moral code, it also makes possible the sorts of immoral behavior that she deplored.[1] Just after

Francisco's speech concludes, he makes it known to those at the party that his company's stock is about to collapse, and a near-panic ensues as the array of Randian villains in attendance scramble to save the fortunes they have accumulated while simultaneously denouncing money as evil (1957, 397–8). The moral of that story for Rand is that those who attempt to acquire wealth by immoral means (e.g., working for monopolistic favors from the government or more directly shaking down those who produce) ultimately do not understand what it means to "make" money, and thus do not really understand money. As she says through Francisco, "money will not give [man] a code of values, if he's evaded the knowledge of what to value" (388). Had they really understood what Francisco is saying about money, they would have long ago realized that there was no way he was going to continue to allow the immoral to profit from his productivity.[2] In this sense, money cannot be the root of all evil. As a tool it will further the values of those who use it, and it is only humans who can be good or evil.

Though Rand correctly understands money's role as a medium of exchange, and, by implication, the idea that it is essentially a tool for achieving whatever values we might have, Francisco's speech does blur one important distinction in places. Throughout the speech, Rand has Francisco moving back and forth between money considered as a social institution and money as a synonym for wealth. In both cases her arguments are largely right, but the speech does move back and forth between the two notions of money without indicating the difference. The arguments for why the social institution of money is not the root of all evil and for why possessing a great deal of money/wealth is not the root of all evil may well be related, but they are distinct.

More generally, it is important to distinguish between "money" and "wealth." Rand never does so explicitly, so she moves from the argument that Americans "created the phrase 'to make money,'" to saying "Americans were the first to understand that wealth has to be created" (1957, 391). It is clear that Rand is treating those two statements as equivalent, even though she never makes the explicit point that when we say "make money" we really mean "create wealth."[3] Understanding money's role as a medium of exchange should also make it clear that when we trade money for goods, we are simply changing the form in which we hold wealth. Buying something does not reduce our wealth because we part with money; in fact it increases our wealth, at least subjectively, as we are presumed to value the good or service more than the money we gave up. That Rand understands these issues is clear from the context, but a more explicit discussion of these distinctions can help shed new light on her already powerful insights.

Money and Say's Law of Markets

Implicit in Francisco's speech is an understanding of one of the most important principles in economics: Say's Law of Markets.[4] The colloquial interpretation of Say's Law is that "supply creates its own demand." However, if taken literally, that version of the Law simply cannot be true. Is this version to be understood as saying that the mere act of supplying a good creates a demand for it? If so, then it is clearly false, because were it true, firms would never go out of business. Say's Law must refer to something else in order to be meaningful in any sense.

Another understanding of Say's Law has to do with the aggregate supply and demand for goods and services. In the hands of critics such as Keynes, the Law was understood to be saying that the aggregate demand and aggregate supply of goods and services could never be in disequilibrium. That is, under any and all circumstances, a capitalist economy would demand, in the aggregate, exactly what it had produced, in the aggregate. This version too seems implausible, as hundreds of years of periodic recessions and depressions in largely capitalist economies would attest to.

Neither of these versions of Say's Law gets at the meaning in the original text, however. What concerned Say was explaining how demand, in general, was determined. Working from where Adam Smith's insight that "the division of labor is limited by the extent of the market" left off, Say tried to explain what would determine just how large a market there would be for products in general. His insight is worth quoting directly:

> A man who applies his labor to the investing of objects with value by the creation of utility of some sort, can not expect such a value to be appreciated and paid for, unless where other men have the means of purchasing it. Now, of what do these means consist? Of other values of other products, likewise the fruits of industry, capital, and land. Which leads us to a conclusion that may at first sight appear paradoxical, namely, that it is production which opens a demand for products (Say 1971 [1821], 133).

Say's last line, "that it is production which opens a demand for products," captures the essence of his Law of Markets: production is the source of demand. What creates a great market for sellers is that there are many other sellers in the same market. At one point in his discussion Say asks whether it is better to be a monopolist in a small town or one of many sellers in a large city. His answer is the latter, precisely because it is in the large market where there are enough other sellers who have the resources to purchase your wares, even if you are in competition with numerous other sellers. Put differently, one can only afford to demand products from other sellers if one has already successfully sold one's own products. Income comes before expenditure; production is the source of demand.

Say's Law has some implications for money that resonates with points Rand makes through Francisco's speech. Given that in an economy based on monetary exchange buying and selling do not happen simultaneously (i.e., we sell our labor services or products, acquire money, then at some later point purchase what we want), there is a period of time during which those who have already sold their products are in possession of money awaiting the opportunity to purchase from another. In this way, holdings of money represent production that has already taken place and been deemed valuable by others. Rand understands this point when she says, "Those pieces of paper ... are a token of honor—your claim upon the energy of the men who produce" (1957, 387). She later adds that "Money is made—before it can be looted or mooched—by the effort of every honest man, each to the extent of his ability. An honest man is one who knows that he can't consume more than he has produced" (1957, 387–8).

The notion that money is a "claim upon the energy of the men who produce" resonates with the "production is the source of demand" understanding of Say's Law of Markets. When one is holding a stock of money, that money represents value that has been created for others with the implicit understanding that the holder will soon enough come calling for values created in return. In a properly functioning capitalist economy, money represents claims to future wealth.[5] Money holders have created value already and hold "claims upon" the value created by other producers. The temporal separation of ultimate purchase and sale that money makes possible not only permits the kinds of advanced, complex exchanges that drive economic growth, but also embues the holding of money with the status of a claim to the "energy of the men who produce." However, as economies move away from voluntary exchange as the basis of human interaction and toward what Rand calls "looting" and "mooching," this description of money's role becomes progressively less accurate.

The Debasement of Money

One prominent example of how money's role gets undermined is inflation. There are two steps in the process of moral and economic destruction that inflation engenders from a Randian perspective. First, inflation undermines the role of money as an "objective" standard by which human actors can determine market values. In doing so, it also undermines rationality and the efficacy of human choice. Second, with money's role as an arbiter of market value weakened, human interaction becomes less and less a matter of voluntary exchange and increasingly subject to regulation and other forms of coercion. It shifts the social power base from those who produce and trade, to those who have a comparative advantage in the direct or indirect use of force. For Rand, this shift represents the undoing of human morality.

In Francisco's speech he recognizes the role of money as a "barometer of a society's virtue" (1957, 390). Rand has Francisco make the two step argument from above in the reverse order presented there. He begins this section of the speech with a somewhat apocalyptic vision of the collapse of civilization, and then suggests that we "watch money" for the signs of that collapse. Specifically, "when you see that trading is done, not by consent, but by compulsion—when you see that in order to produce, you need to obtain permission from men who produce nothing ... you may know that your society is doomed" (1957, 390). Rand identifies the shift from monetary exchange to political exchange as being the evidence of the collapse of the moral code that makes civilization possible. When Francisco says "when you see that money is flowing to those who deal, not in goods, but in favors—when you see that men get richer by graft and pull than by work," he is identifying the sort of political or "crony" capitalism that characterizes economies in which monetary exchange has been undermined for one reason or another.

He then argues that the debasement of money is one path to that destruction: "Whenever destroyers appear among men, they start by destroying money, for money is men's protection and the base of a moral existence" (1957, 390). Specifically, money can be destroyed by inflation and similar forms of devaluation. Francisco's speech notes only one, which is the substitution of paper for gold. The passage (1957, 390) in full reads:

> Destroyers seize gold and leave to its owners a counterfeit pile of paper. This kills all objective standards and delivers men into the arbitrary power of an arbitrary settler of values. Gold was an objective value, an equivalent of wealth produced. Paper is a mortgage on wealth that does not exist, backed by a gun aimed at those who are expected to produce it.

Although the general thrust of this argument is right, it is worth spending some time on the details to get a better sense of the dangers of inflation.

The premises that gold is an "objective value" and that the substitution of paper for gold is, in and of itself, a significant problem are both open to criticism on more careful consideration. The "objectivity" of gold is nothing inherent in gold, but rather a statement about the need for any monetary system to have an anchor in something of value outside of that system itself. Historically, gold (and other precious metals like silver) have played this role as an anchor. That role for gold reflects a convergence of cultural selection processes (but not a unanimity, as things other than gold have served this role in other societies) on that particular precious metal as being both subjectively valued by actors and being sufficiently scarce to function as a medium of exchange. As the economist Carl Menger (1892) argued over 100 years ago, a medium of exchange must emerge from the actual exchange activities of economic actors, so that any good serving as money must have a value of its own before it became used as money. In this sense, Rand's observation that gold had "objective value" is accurate. One cannot start a monetary system literally from scratch; the value of the money commodity must be linked up with the value the money commodity had as a commodity.[6]

The transition from gold to paper need not be problematic in and of itself. The use of paper currency and checks was, historically, a matter of convenience so as to avoid the costs of physically exchanging gold every time trades occurred. The key was that the paper instruments were still redeemable in gold if the holder so desired. When Rand has Francisco talk about the gold being "seized," presumably this refers to removing any role for gold in the monetary system. If so, then the claim that what is left is just a "counterfeit pile of paper" is somewhat closer to the truth. However, even in that case, the paper is not literally worthless. As long as people continue to believe that the paper can be used as a medium of exchange, it will retain some value. The issue that is more important than the move from gold to paper is the degree of discretion to change money's quantity without regard to the demand for its services that any change in the monetary regime gives the producers of money.

What the "seizing" of gold does is dramatically weaken, if not eliminate, the penalty to money producers who inflate the money supply. With commodity-backed money, excess supplies of money will eventually be returned to the producer in exchange for the underlying commodity (e.g. gold). In this case, the money producers face constraints on how much money they can produce. Without the commodity backing it, there are only political costs to inflating the money supply, and the political benefits of inflation often outweigh them. It is here where the economy is, in Francisco's words, delivered into "the arbitrary power of an arbitrary setter of values" (1957, 390). When the money producer only faces political, as opposed to economic, costs, inflation is a likely result. As inflation permeates the economy, it undermines the signaling function of prices, thus weakening their ability to serve as "objective" measures of value. Rather than prices reflecting the best judgments and knowledge of traders, individual prices are distorted by the degree to which they are affected by the injection of the excess money supplies. This causes prices to change from reasonably reliable indicators of mutually agreed upon value too much more arbitrary and less reliable social signals.

As prices lose their ability to provide knowledge to economic actors, the very rationality of markets begins to fall apart. From this Hayekian (1945) perspective on the role of prices, the rationality that capitalism makes possible is not something that is a psychological or even ethical feature of individual humans, but is rather a pattern of behavior that is made possible and induced by the structure of market prices. The link between money and reason is to be found here—it is money, and commodity-backed money at that, that makes possible exchange and therefore money prices. With money prices, humans are able to engage in calculative/rational behavior in the economic realm. Prices allow for the calculation of possible future benefits and costs as well as figuring the costs and benefits of past actions as a way of informing future ones. More generally, a well-functioning price system (i.e., one that does not suffer from inflation or deflation) makes possible levels of human rationality that would otherwise not be possible.

With the demise of the market as an arena for rational planning and action, and exchange at the basis of human interaction, thanks to inflation destroying the signaling function of prices, humans look to other forms of interaction, such as "favors, graft, and pull." On the margin, even the most well-intentioned producers will find turning to the political process to be more productive as inflation scrambles prices. And those with a comparative advantage in dealing in "favors, graft, and pull" will quickly move in to take advantage. Inflation's destruction of the price system increases their ability to command resources and direct them in ways they value, rather than by the consumer/producer rationality of the market. It is not coincidental that the chapter containing Francisco's speech is titled "The Aristocracy of Pull," as that is a result that is made possible when money is debased through inflation or other means. In an otherwise unhampered market with a well-functioning money, there is no "aristocracy" as only those who serve the needs of consumers gain power and influence, and for only as long as they produce what others want. When the means for determining which actions are rational are taken away—when those who are producers are blinded—it will be those with a comparative advantage at gaining and keeping power who benefit. That group can maintain its hold on power in ways that the producers cannot. However, as the main theme of *Atlas Shrugged* points out, their power ultimately rests on the sanction of the victim, namely the willingness of the producers to continue to produce wealth that the aristocracy of pull can "loot or mooch." Through Francisco, Rand shows a keen understanding of how the debasement of money will undermine the rationality and morality of the marketplace, replacing the creators and producers with, in her words, the looters and moochers, and lead to the eventual demise of the market and impoverishment of all.

Blood, Whips and Guns—or Dollars

One of the most provocative sections of Francisco's speech is the final paragraph, particularly the last three sentences: "When money ceases to be the tool by which men deal with one another, then men become the tools of men. Blood, whips and guns—or dollars. Take your choice—there is no other—and your time is running out" (1957: 391).

The imagery is powerful here (critics would say "hyperbolic"), but the underlying argument is a sound one. Unpacking the argument we can note that there are, at bottom, three ways in which individuals can interact with each other: coercion, verbal persuasion, and exchange. Although the lines that divide each from the other are sometimes hazy, it seems unarguable that these are three distinct modes of human action.[7] If we want others to act in particular ways, we can either attempt to force them to do so, attempt to persuade them (verbally) to do so, or we can attempt to offer them something in exchange for them undertaking the action. If we wish to obtain a book from the person who possesses it, we can either club her over the head and steal it, try to talk her into giving it to us, or offer her money or some other good or service in exchange for it. The same would be true of actions that did not involve the movement of physical goods. Other options for human interaction in such situations seem non-existent.

To see Rand's point, we need to understand why Francisco's conclusion excludes (verbal) persuasion as one of the options. As early as *The Wealth of Nations*, Adam Smith (1976 [1776]) understood the reasons why exchange would come to dominate persuasion. In the beginning of the book, he notes that humans, like other animals, generally try to "fawn upon" others in order to get them to do what we wish. Through various forms of persuasion or sycophancy, we might try to get others to do what we would like them to. In addition, sometimes we might attempt to get to know a person well enough to be able to determine what he or she wants and provide it in an act of pure altruism. Conversely, we might try to let others know us well enough so that they will act with accurate altruism toward us. What Smith notes is that all of these strategies are limited when we move into the world beyond our close friends and family.

The world of what Hayek (1973) called "The Great Society" is a world of anonymity. The vast majority of the people we interact with, and in some sense must interact with, are people we know very little about. Smith (1976 [1776], 18) understood this over 200 years ago when he wrote:

> In civilized society [man] stands at all times in need of the co-operation and assistance of great multitudes, while his whole life is scarce sufficient to gain the friendship of a few persons. ... But man has almost constant occasion for the help of his brethren, and it is in vain for him to expect it from their benevolence only. He will be more likely to prevail if he can interest their self-love in his favor, and show them that it is for their own advantage to do for him what he requires of them. ... It is not from the benevolence of the butcher, the brewer, or the baker, that we expect our dinner, but from their regard to their own interest. We address ourselves, not to their humanity but to their self-love, and never talk them of our own necessities but of their advantage.

In the anonymous order of modernity, we cannot know most of the "others" with whom we must interact well enough to act altruistically toward them, nor do we have the opportunities to engage in the face-to-face contact necessary for the sorts of verbal persuasion that is the only other non-coercive alternative to exchange. Within the realms of face-to-face contact, such as the family or a workplace or other intimate social groups, persuasion of this sort remains a viable option, as does altruism, but in the anonymous world of the Great Society, the choice is between coercion and exchange.[8]

As I have argued above, for exchange to coordinate behavior beyond a very small group, it will have to make use of money. In any society that has reached even a minimal level of economic well-being, monetary exchange will be the dominant way through which humans move goods and services. If that society rejects money because it is "the root of all evil," it is implicitly rejecting monetary exchange as this crucial form of human interaction. Without monetary exchange, Rand is arguing through Francisco, there is no alternative but coercion as a way to coordinate human action. One of the central themes of *Atlas Shrugged* is that all of the machinations of the "aristocracy of pull" and the exchange of favors it involves are but a thin veneer over the acts of coercion that ultimately back them up. Those who moralize against money can argue for whatever alternative way of solving the problems money solves that they wish, but Rand's point is that all such alternatives eventually boil down to coercion: "Blood, whips, and guns—or dollars."

When money is weakened as a social institution, the whole basis of the anonymous order of the Great Society is undermined. If money is declared to be morally evil, or debased through inflation, it will be less frequently used and the various ancillary institutions that rely on it will be weakened as well. Contracts will be difficult to write and execute, the calculation of profit and loss will be difficult to impossible, and consumers will find it challenging to create budgets and track expenditures. Most important, the undermining of money will cause the destruction of the whole price system, depriving actors of the knowledge necessary for economic coordination. In short, as money is weakened, so is the market and voluntary exchange more generally. With markets less appealing as processes for wealth accumulation, actors will, on the margin, be more likely to use political means or other forms of coercion to acquire it.[9] These forms of wealth acquisition are not, as the market is, mutually beneficial, rather they are zero-sum at best. The use of "blood, whips and guns" rather than dollars is not only morally problematic but also destructive of economic well-being. Of course we normally do not equate "political means" with "blood, whips, and guns" in democracies, but Rand's point was that even in democracies, political power ultimately rests on coercion.

Conclusion

The enduring popularity of *Atlas Shrugged* is as much a result of Rand's shrewd insights on politics and culture as anything else. Her ability to understand human motivation and behavior has made it into a moral guide along the lines of something like a "secular Bible." But beyond those observations about human behavior and the moral context in which they sit, Rand had a solid understanding of the operation of social and economic institutions. In numerous places in the novel, the plot turns on interpretations of events that demonstrate Rand's knowledge of political and economic theory and history. Francisco d'Anconia's speech on money as the root of all evil is an excellent example of this point. As I have argued above, Rand packed a large number of important insights about money into a few short pages of prose. Unpacking those insights reveals the depth and breadth of Rand's insights. *Atlas Shrugged* remains not just a great philosophical novel, but a great social-scientific one as well.

Notes

1 In this way, money is much like language and other similar social institutions. On the parallels between money and language, see Horwitz (1992).
2 This is one of several examples in the book of "Atlas shrugging."
3 After all, counterfeiters could also be described, literally, as "making money," as could the U.S. Treasury. Again, Rand's meaning here is clear, but for some purposes of more technical economic analysis, it is vitally important to distinguish between money and wealth, and to recognize that one can be quite wealthy without having a large holding of money.
4 Complementary scholarly discussions of this issue can be found in Horwitz (2003a), Sechrest (1993), and Hutt (1974).
5 The next section will explain the need for modifying "capitalist economy" with "properly functioning" in this context.
6 This is the result that is known as the "regression theorem" and was first and most clearly articulated by Ludwig von Mises in his 1912 book *The Theory of Money and Credit* (1980 [1912]). The argument is really an extension, though a crucial one, of Menger's insight that a medium of exchange must start as an object of exchange itself.
7 Even so, there is a line of argument that dates back to Adam Smith that sees exchange as a form of persuasion. More on this argument will follow.
8 For a discussion of the relationship between Rand and Hayek on these issues of the differences between intimate groups and the anonymous Great Society, see Horwitz (2005).
9 See Horwitz (2003b) for a more thorough discussion of this point in the context of the costs of inflation.

References

Hayek, F.A. 1945. The use of knowledge in society. *Individualism and Economic Order*. Chicago: The University of Chicago Press.
———. 1973. *Law, Legislation, and Liberty* 1. Chicago: The University of Chicago Press.
Horwitz, Steven. 1992. Monetary exchange as an extra-linguistic social communication process. *Review of Social Economy* 50, 2 (Summer).
———. 2003a. Say's Law of Markets: An Austrian appreciation. *Two Hundred Years of Say's Law: Essays on Economic Theory's Most Controversial Principle*. Edited by Steven Kates. Northampton, Massachusetts: Edward Elgar, 82–98.
———. 2003b. The costs of inflation revisited. *Review of Austrian Economics* 16, (March): 77–95.
———. 2005. Two worlds at once: Rand, Hayek, and the ethics of the micro and macro-cosmos. *Journal of Ayn Rand Studies* 6 (Spring) forthcoming.
Hutt, W.H. 1974. *A Rehabilitation of Say's Law*. Athens: Ohio University Press.
Menger, Carl. 1892. On the origin of money. *Economic Journal*, 2.

Mises, Ludwig von. 1980 [1912]. *The Theory of Money and Credit*. Indianapolis, Indiana: Liberty Press.

Rand, Ayn. 1957. *Atlas Shrugged*, New York: New American Library.

———. 1971. *The Virtue of Selfishness*. New York: New American Library.

Say, Jean Baptiste. 1971 [1821]. *A Treatise on Political Economy*. New York: Augustus M. Kelley.

Sechrest, Larry J. 1993. *Free Banking: Theory, History, and a Laissez-faire Model*. Westport, Connecticut: Quorum.

Chapter 22

Human Productivity in *Atlas Shrugged*

Jack Criss

With the publication of *Atlas Shrugged* in 1957, novelist Ayn Rand provided a heretofore unprecedented explanation, defense and thorough breakdown of the workings of the free market system. By doing so in a work of fiction, Rand was able to demonstrate—through the actions of various characters—the tangible results of a given person's moral code, character, commitment to principle (or lack thereof) as well as how these individual traits affect the work habits of the character.

The latter is of special importance for the study of economics and remains one of the great contributions of Rand in *Atlas Shrugged*. In providing an integrated view of her characters, Rand took the dry and overly analytic subject of economics and made it real, flesh and blood with demonstrable results, both for good and ill. The "organization man" became, in *Atlas Shrugged*, the integrated man: those characters who practiced a commitment to reality and concomitant love of and passion for work generally succeeded; those that denied responsibility and relied on evasive excuses, failed. This is made clear in the book due to Rand's presentation of the respective characters' own personal thinking habits, or philosophy.

Production and creative ability in Atlas is shown time and time again to be as "human" as romantic love. The emotions for both, in fact, are quite similar and equally intense. Thus, instead of the blood, sweat and tears of Marxist mythology (read: struggle), *Atlas Shrugged* dramatically presents the thoughtfulness, planning and creativity (read: love) of a true capitalist.

Human Productivity Requires Freedom

Economics requires careful and diligent human thought. Production is the result of a mind envisioning potential and then reasoning to produce tangibility. In order to think to engage in such production, man first must be free to do so. Productivity is not possible when commanded by force. Directive after directive is issued by the government in *Atlas Shrugged* to stop the economic hemorrhaging caused by the exodus of the producers, yet such commands can no more foster growth than wishing or hoping. Whereas, historically, relative freedom produced the greatest economic boom in world history (the late 19th and early 20th centuries), government-mandated aggression stifles and outright eliminates creativity and production. When all the producers strike, the cause of wealth is removed and the effect is shown by the disaster the country's economic system becomes.

Atlas Shrugged paints a world in which the United States government has taken significant, almost total, control of the nation's economy. In the novel, Rand shows the government breaking up productive, successful companies and compelling them to share their market and ideas with less efficient competitors. The result is the minds of the innovators and leaders of these companies become shackled under the threat of government coercion; what innovations they can create become expropriated by the state.

Examples of such government intervention abound in Atlas, the most ominous being Directive 10-289, a freeze issued on all economic production. A directive stopping production—banning the use of the mind—is the most anti-life attempt at force the fictional government in Atlas takes and is shown to be disastrous. Equally offensive (and ridiculous) is the suggestion late in the book that protagonist John Galt be forced to assume the role of dictator of the United States. Rand shows, through the ignorance of Atlas's villains, how statists will try to use coercion to jumpstart production and that it cannot be done, that it flies in the face of reality to even try. Looters eventually seize much of the nation's factories and industries in the novel yet cannot get them to produce. Rand shows that it takes intelligence to maintain wealth as well as create it. The attempts at force fail time after time.

A fundamental economic issue made clear in Atlas is that what matters is not what kind, how many, or on whose behalf a government control is issued: the essential conflict is between a controlled economy versus an uncontrolled one. Laissez-faire is the total separation of state and economics not, as the villains in Atlas or modern media maintain, government control of economics for the benefit of businessmen. In *Atlas Shrugged*, this idea is made explicit for the first time and is shown to be a defining principle of capitalism.

Rand demonstrates in *Atlas Shrugged* that all of human progress and prosperity depend on rational, independent thinking. Government force disrupts, hampers and, ultimately, destroys that thinking. "Human" productivity means the use and application of reason, as reason is the key definer of what it is to be human: The application of a thinking, conceptual mind to practical questions of survival and sustenance resulting in new products, inventions and ideas.

Human Productivity as Expressive and Central

As in no other novel before or since, *Atlas Shrugged* demonstrates eloquently that industrial production is as creative—and as exciting and glamorous—as writing a symphony or writing a novel. Creation, on whatever scale, is production. Contrast this view with the modern one of industrialists' work as lowly, callous, non-exciting ... dirty. Productivity—as embodied by the characters of John Galt, Dagny Taggart, Hank Rearden ... and symphony composer Richard Halley— represents more than the use of pure intellect; their emotional life and passion for work is evident throughout the novel and is the centerpiece of their existence, from which all other values spring. Atlas demonstrates the respective characters' admiration, attraction and love for the great producers responsible for mankind's progress, such as through Dagny Taggart's love of John Galt.

Productivity as both practical and spiritual is established in Atlas, thus fusing a long-held dichotomy in Western thought. This is seen most explicitly in the character of Hank Rearden, who is shown early on in the novel as being torn between what he knows is a love of work and what he thinks is a responsibility to family and others. His ultimate resolution of this conflict is a demonstration of Rand's extraordinarily original insight that work and personal life/love, i.e., practical and spiritual, feed off and flow from the other.

Whereas historically artists have been venerated as the only men of spiritual stature, Rand shows throughout Atlas how mistaken this idea truly is. Far from being the dreaded "materialist," the productive capitalist is an artist is his own right: the process, joy, and result of creation is the same. Yet the spiritual artist archetype has been presented through the ages as noble and heroic. In Atlas, for the first time in world literature, producers—businessmen—are portrayed as the heroes.

"Whether it's a symphony or a coal mine," Richard Halley tells Dagny Taggart in Atlas, "all work is an act of creating and comes from the same source— from an inviolate capacity to see through one's own eyes; which means the capacity to form a rational identification; which means the capacity to see, to connect, to make what had not been seem connected and made before."

Human productive purpose supplies control of one's life. Rand has maintained that people without purpose are "depraved." As a central focal point, productive work provides the fulcrum for all of a man's life, Atlas dramatizes. To reverse this order, Rand maintains, is a result of many individual and societal ills. Productivity is a supremely moral value: A course of virtue is required to gain and keep this value. Purpose, effort and a commitment to focus and independent judgment are virtues necessary for a businessperson to succeed. Productive work incorporates into the daily life of a businessman the values and virtues of a proper human existence; it is an essential use of his reasoning mind which should properly carry over to all of his other decisions and choices.

Human Productivity as Moral

In Atlas, again in unprecedented fashion, Rand shows productivity as key to man's happiness. Productivity is a supreme moral value. Consequently, means and ends are tied together: to produce, to create, equates into using one's mind to its fullest extent, to be happy with the doing and with the results. Reshaping the material world for pleasure and progress brings with it happiness, a sense of satisfaction and the joy of accomplishment, i.e., it is moral—it benefits man's life, both the individual producer's and those who benefit from his work.

Human intelligence is the prime source of wealth. This is explicit in Atlas Shrugged. Intelligence is the volitional power of an individual mind to form broad abstractions with a long-range perspective. The mind, therefore, directs the organization of production. Raw material represents only potential, not actual, wealth. It takes the independent, free mind to produce goods from such raw material. Then, men can trade the products of their thinking, but not the thinking as such. Capitalism is the only social system that protects the right of an individual to act on his own judgment which is why it is the only wealth-creating economic system. All other systems survive only insofar as they expropriate wealth or to the extent they allow any modicum of free thought. Production is the link of thought to emotions to creativity. These lessons are brought home in dramatic fashion in Atlas Shrugged.

Human productivity in *Atlas Shrugged*: in her masterpiece, Ayn Rand demonstrates forcefully and beautifully that, indeed, there is no other form of productivity but human.

References

Binswanger, Harry, ed. 1986. The Ayn Rand Lexicon: Objectivism From A to Z. New York: New American Library.

Branden, Nathaniel. 1962. Who Is Ayn Rand? New York: Random House.

Peikoff, Leonard. 1991. Objectivism: The Philosophy of Ayn Rand. New York, Dutton.

Rand, Ayn. 1957. Atlas Shrugged. New York: Random House.

Salsman, Richard. 1998. The 'Invisible Hand' Comes to Life: Economics in Atlas Shrugged. Audio cassette. Second Renaissance Books, Inc.

PART 6
Human Relationships

Chapter 23

Dagny and Me

Karen Michalson

April. Morning. Massachusetts. Sunday. And so even the blessed sunlight goes dull. Something in a Massachusetts Sunday makes the light go weird and slightly opaque, thickens the world with enforced uselessness, distorts even the most industrious individual into a freakishly slothful version of herself.

It was on a Massachusetts Sunday, in a dark April, that I first decided to meet Dagny Taggart. But before I discuss that meeting, I must explain what a Massachusetts Sunday is. Because context matters. In my experience, context destroys. And so even though I long to take inspiration from Dagny's glorious self-actualization, from her creator Ayn Rand's vision of the individual transcending all else, I can't. I have never met anyone who was more powerful than her context. Context trumps us all. That is my working definition of tragedy.

Context. Sundays in Massachusetts are a weekly dose of cloying lassitude. I used to think that this was a result of the damned blue laws, but the commonwealth finally gutted those ugly things in 1994, permitting retailers to open any time on Sundays, and so presumably to change the soul-deadening tone of this day into something more conducive to getting something—anything—done. And yet, the sluggishness remains. You may now do business on Sunday, but don't expect to feel like business is getting done, or to feel anything that definable, because the day itself still deadens your sensibilities. Trains run slower, merchandise grows mysteriously sparse. Even the weather never produces what it promises to, and the finest Sunday dinner is always spiced with the taste of famine. The weekly Sunday drain is a Massachusetts tradition that nobody really likes, but that nobody can summon the energy to change.

Much as I've tried, I have never been able to confuse this weekly torpor with a "day of rest." For one thing you can't rest. Curl up in a quiet room with a good book? Forget it—the words on the page go thin, the author's voice reads like it's drowning, the light weirds out and gets wrong for reading, even if the light would be right for reading on any other day. You end up pacing the room and just wishing the damn day would pass. Take a nature walk? Nature will—how can I describe this—pack up its things and leave. You'll see trees and rocks, maybe some animals, but you'll also get the feeling that the trees and rocks are trussed up in

Sunday lassitude, that even the animals aren't being themselves, and that you'll need to come back on Monday to really see them.

It's generally understood in Massachusetts that whatever happens on Sunday never really happens, or never really happens in any way that will affect the rest of your life. See churchgoers.

On Massachusetts Sundays humanity repels—groups of people give off the desultory energy of a yard sale of unidentifiable items that have been in somebody's attic too long. Individuals lose the most interesting edges of their personality and become blurs of themselves. Meet someone during the other six days and, and if you and the stranger are so inclined, a business or personal relationship may ensue. Meet someone on Sunday, and, even if you continue to meet that person on every Sunday for the rest of your life, neither of you will ever think you have any dealings with the other, ever.

Enough context.

It was on a Massachusetts Sunday, in April, that I first decided I needed to meet Dagny Taggart. And it was at some kind of afternoon party with no clear purpose, in a dreary, slightly unkept apartment, that I made this decision. The woman who rented the apartment, and who piqued my sluggish Sunday interest in Dagny, was trying her level best to become a fictional character, but I did not recognize her ambition at the time. To me she only succeeded in conveying a kind of cryptic arrogance. I instantly disliked her enough to promptly forget her name, but I haven't forgotten her strikingly inchoate pretentiousness. But it was Sunday, and so of course I expected anybody I happened to deal with to seem less than she would on any other day. However, nobody completely destroys her need for admiration, and this woman's need was stronger than the ennervating Sunday energies. I'll give her that.

She chain smoked, and managed to work great hand flourishes in between every puff. This elicited low-pitched sounds of admiration from her associates, because, as I later learned, Randian heroes smoke with more ferocity than European fashonistas. She proclaimed, at least 29 times, in a voice like cracked concrete, that she was "an architect" for "a large company." After the third or fourth repetition of her job title, I half-expected to hear someone play a minor chord to underscore the word "architect."

Being clueless as to how she expected me to respond to her constant announcing of her profession, I chose not to remark on it. She then grew visibly annoyed at my lack of response, increased her intake of cigarettes, and informed me, gravely, that Ayn Rand had much to say about the architecture profession. Which was cool, I guess, although I hadn't yet read any of Rand's work, and so I had no way of knowing whether Rand's assessment of architects was flattering. I presumed, however, from my hostess's antics, that Rand must have considered architects to be very special, and that I was expected to treat my Sunday companion accordingly. I also remember remarking on the ultra-drab, boxy design of the apartment, which reminded me of nothing so much as an ambitious state college dorm room, complete with cheap copies of bad art. I wondered if this architect was distressed by her remarkably uninspiring environment, but I decided that she wasn't when she blithely informed me that the buildings she designed were all mass produced.

So why was she so bloody proud of herself for being, near as I could figure, an assembly-line architect? Why did she need me to worship her for that? Because Ayn Rand had some hero or other who was an architect, and so this woman wanted everyone to see her, to admire her, in the same way that she admired the Rand character. At least, that was my impression. And her mass-produced designs meant that she presided over an implied hierarchy in which she created company buildings and "other people' did the less heady work of building them. And this context allowed her to shake her hair around in a sort of helplessly dramatic gesture, take hard puffs on her cigarettes, and quietly enjoy the chorus of approval that came from her friends. The only impediment to her complete enjoyment on that day was yours truly, because I wasn't yet Rand-literate and so couldn't catch the literary hairpins she kept desperately dropping.

"My hair now has a reddish tint," she said archly. Puff, puff, shake the head. Long exhale of smoky breath, as if she'd just accomplished a difficult feat. "That's what happens."

"That's what happens when?" I asked, feeling like I was expected to know and comment on some agenda concerning her hair color, while her friends clucked some kind of weird approval. "Is it Clairol?"

She screwed up her face into an expression of quiet frustration at me obviously not getting it, and stared intensely at the tip of her cigarette. "No," she said patronizingly, in a tone that implied that the simplicity of her answer was a rebuke to my obvious ignorance.

"Have you read Ayn Rand's *The Fountainhead*?" asked one of her friends, only her voice sounded more like an accusation than a question.

"No." I answered as simply as my hostess did, and perhaps as snobbily.

OK, whatever. This was all annoying enough, but tolerable. You don't spend the number of years that I have in publishing, music, or academia without encountering much worse displays of unearned ego on a daily basis. What made my hostess's behavior so special was her implied assumption that I would now care enough to go home, suss out her particular weirdness by reading *The Fountainhead*, and then have a thunderous epiphany and get quietly impressed with her august self. When I finally did get around to reading *The Fountainhead*, I did remark that Rand's protagonist, Howard Roark, was an architect with red, or rather, orange-rind colored, hair. I did not confuse him in any way with the oddball woman I survived a Massachusetts Sunday afternoon with, although I did recognize that was probably her agenda.

"You don't know *The Fountainhead*?" someone else demanded.

My simple "no" had unwittingly become an engraved invitation that said, "Please feel free to berate me with your unhealthy obsessions. After all, this is a party." Because the entire henhouse started screeching and cawing at once about Rand, Objectivism, conspiracies among educational institutions to suppress Rand's books, reason, people they had 20-year grudge matches with, and "real literature." It was ghastly. All the more so because I was writing my dissertation for a doctorate in English, thought I knew a little about "real literature," and wasn't afforded the courtesy of being allowed to speak. There is nothing more annoying than being lectured to by cretins about an area that you've put years of serious study into. It is especially annoying when that area is a subjective discipline like English, because then everyone passionately believes that "it's all opinion anyway" and that everybody's opinion is as valuable as everybody else's, years of scholarship be damned. I later discovered that Objectivists are among the worst in this regard, despite the lip service they sometimes pay to hard work and excellence. They develop this sense of life which demands that their opinions, no matter how ill-informed, must eclipse everyone else's at all times. Evaluating the conclusions of an informed expert gets viewed as a regrettable sort of mysticism. Perhaps that is because once you get taken up in a Rand novel and start confusing yourself with Howard Roark, admitting that you aren't an expert in everything becomes viewed as a moral failing. But the oddest part of this gang-lecture was, being Sunday, even the sudden cawing sounded fuzzy and not quite in earnest.

My self-important hostess waved the chatter away with her cigarette and imperiously claimed the position of front woman for her little posse. "My theory of real literature," the architect grandly intoned, "is ... science fiction." I tried to tell her that science fiction is a genre, not a theory, but she was too Objectivist to get caught up in facts. "A lot of people aren't capable of understanding science fiction." Another smoky exhale, as if she had the only brilliant mind in the world who could understand this genre, and I was lucky to be the recipient of her literary insights. "But I'll tell you what science fiction is. It's—" she took another long annoying pause while she blew more smoke, and basked in the exhibitionist attention of her associates. "It's all ... ideas." I guess that was supposed to show me, because after all, I couldn't possibly understand that science fiction was a literature of ideas without her help. Especially since my dissertation dealt with the historical reasons for the exclusion of fantasy, a related genre, from the canon. But neither she nor her breathless myrmidons cared to hear my opinions, which they had clearly decided were less valuable than theirs. "Heinlein wrote real literature, in my opinion. So did Rand, but nobody acknowledges that. Read *Atlas Shrugged*. If you haven't read it, you haven't really read anything."

So Chaucer, Shakespeare, Spenser, Milton, Pope, Byron, Dickens, Joyce and all the other great writers I'd spent my life in the company of weren't "really anything" because I'd somehow missed Rand.

I started to leave, feeling like my life's work had gotten its share of disrespect for the day. And that's when my new party friends started chattering self importantly, "Dagny. Dagny Taggart. I'm going to study engineering. When I read *Atlas Shrugged*, it clarified my call to make things work like Dagny does. Rand had much to say about engineers, too." If this had been a coven of witches instead of a cadre of pseudo-intellectuals at a boring Sunday afternoon party, Dagny Taggart would have been their version of the Great Goddess. Despite everything, I was now intrigued.

Why? Because years of reading texts, and studying people's reactions to texts, have taught me that when a group of people get religion about a character, something in that character is worth studying. The women in front of me were as irritating as a week of Sundays, but their quasi-mystical enthusiasm for Dagny Taggart was worth seeing. Dagny, whoever she was, had co-opted their lives, their choice of profession, their self-image, their sense of worth. And Dagny had called forth a truly impressive ego, a ravenously insistent self-importance, in all of them. My hostess couldn't tell the difference between herself and Howard Roark, but the rest of the room had clearly commingled their hearts and minds with Dagny.

And so I longed to meet Dagny. Dagny clearly had power. And I wanted some. In a half-hearted, Sunday sort of way.

Remember context? Any decision suffered or experience endured on a Massachusetts Sunday fails to achieve viability on the other six days. Not because Sunday is an island unto itself with its own rules, because the day isn't definable enough to carry the necessary strain of romanticism for that sort of splendid isolation. And not because Sunday is evil. Sunday isn't sharp and definable enough to be evil. Sunday is blanked-out and blotchy and has no power except as a parasite, as a second-hander to the rest of the week.

I truly believe that is why, when I read *Atlas Shrugged* and made Miss Taggart's acquaintance, that I could see, but not really feel, how beautiful and heroic she is. I took her many places—into my home, my heart, the grove in the woods I sometimes read in, my backpack. I invited her into my dreams. I would be friends with you, Dagny, and have your love. Teach me how to live, how to be strong, how to make the trains run against impossible odds. Show me what it means to honor one's self without apology or shame. Help me transcend the limited context of my life. We can even start with a silly prank like outlawing Sundays. Let there be self-actualization seven days a week!

But there wasn't. Any self-actualization, I mean. And that is where my relationship with Dagny Taggart got interesting. I admired Dagny's ability to take charge of her life, to obliterate every obstacle, to be as sure of herself as a First Principle. I wanted wanted wanted to develop those traits in myself. But I also noticed that her hero status was not entirely earned. She had inherited her prominent position at Taggart Transcontinental, and it was that position that provided a necessary frame for her extraordinary feats. When Dagny gives orders to the crew on the Taggart Comet to proceed through a red light, the first reaction of the engineer is to ask, "Yeah? Who says so?" (23) From his perspective, this strange woman had no right to assume an air of authority with him and his crew and issue orders. When he recognizes her face, and realizes that she is Taggart Transcontinental Vice-President in Charge of Operations, he follows her orders with more speed than a working Taggart train. Dagny's reputation for supreme competence is a factor in the engineer's respect. "That's who runs Taggart Transcontinental," he says to a young brakeman. (24) However, I couldn't help thinking that if Dagny really had been a stranger, and just as supremely competent, "Who says so?" would have ended the exchange, and Dagny would not have been able to right the Comet.

The thing to be wished, I thought, is to have both brilliance and the clout to get that brilliance noticed. In my experience, the latter is much more difficult to achieve. Dagny was most fortunate to have it given to her. Nobody was going to give me a major company to run, I was going to have to earn a stage for my talents through hard work, if at all.

Also, the obstacles Dagny had to destroy were more clearly defined and therefore much easier to strategize about than anything I had ever encountered in my own life. The Rio Norte runs or it doesn't, and there isn't much room for argument as to whether the former or the latter is true. I was facing an academic job market in the humanities, where every mark of achievement, from teaching to publication to committee effectiveness, was fuzzy and subjective. It wasn't clear to me whether I'd even get work in my field. Dagny had inherited permanent employment. Even though we both had to navigate heart-crushing politics in our respective fields, Dagny had the advantage over me of inarguably concrete skills. If she saved a railroad line, well, then, the trains would run. You could see that. Maybe her rivals could steal credit, but no one could argue with the raw reality of her achievement. When a scholar writes a paper interpreting a work of literature, it's never clear to anyone, including the scholar, to what degree that interpretation has achieved anything.

When Dagny's brother James informs her that the "consensus of the best metallurgical authorities" is "highly skeptical about Rearden Metal" (27), Dagny confidently dismisses this consensus without the need for conducting her own independent quality tests. James asks her,

> "Well, whose opinion did you take?"
> "I don"t ask for opinions."
> "What do you go by?"
> "Judgment."
> "Well, whose judgment did you take?"
> "Mine."
> "But whom did you consult about it?"
> "Nobody." (27–8)

When Dagny finally informs James that Reardon's own tests convinced her of the worth of Reardon Metal, I was divided between three reactions: admiration for Dagny's self-assurance, irritation with her smug dismissal of premises she never bothered to check, and dismay that she was capable of claiming the sanctity of her own judgment while actually relying on the judgment of somebody else. The last two traits were also particularly strong among the women at that strange and annoying Sunday party. They were in love with Dagny's self-assurance, but had only managed to pick up her habit of dismissing other opinions and of parroting the collective judgment of their clique.

So I can't describe how I felt about Dagny. I felt passion, certainly, but it was a passion ennervated by indignation. I wanted very much to be the glorious hero she was, but I lacked her cleanly cut context for action. I reluctantly decided that humanities scholars cannot be Randian heroes. Context matters. I loved the concept of a Randian hero, but at the same time I realized it would always be just out of reach. My reaction was a blotch, a kind of emotional Sunday.

And yet, my reaction to Dagny remains. Most characters are forgettable, but the tension she produces between unattainable longing to be like her, and the knowledge that we do not transcend our contexts, has informed my life. Rand never said that excellence was available to everyone, and yet, Rand's novels show us a world where anyone can choose to be excellent. Some people might consider this a philosophical inconsistency. In my world, many choose to be excellent, to carve their scholarship and writings out of their very blood and bones, to become human emblems of their work in the way that Dagny considers John Galt to be a human emblem of her railroad line (660). But although many choose the Randian values of hard work and purposeful devotion to a goal, few are chosen. Just ask any recent Ph.D.s in the humanities field of your choice. In the real world, A often equals anything but A.

So here's where it is with me and Dagny. It's always Sunday between us. I admit she is a beautiful ideal, a model of what the best kind of life is like. But I also understand that context makes the hero, and that context is almost always owned by the crowd. That is why what happens between me and Dagny always resembles a Sunday afternoon that never really effects anything else in my rest of my life. Dagny inspires me without motivating me, provides thoughtful contemplation without the expectations of any intellectual breakthroughs, provides fodder for romantic fantasies without ever inducing me to indulge in them. She is the only character in my personal canon that I both intensely admire and feel absolutely no passion for, for whom I carry a lukewarm flame. She is like a Massachusetts Sunday, unconvincing and undefeatable. For me she is a type of all unattainable ideals.

Reference

Rand, Ayn. 1957. *Atlas Shrugged*. New York: Penguin.

Chapter 24

Atlas Shrugged: The Dream of Every Woman

Joy Bushnell

Attractive Single White Female in search of attractive, fit, philosophically secure, single or married male who can stop the motor of the world. I'm a hopeless Romantic who enjoys trains, planes and business cartels. Financially secure, enjoy classical music, candlelit dinners, and working against impossible odds. Partner must be omniscient, omnipresent, and omnivorous and must demonstrate actual proof of such. Potential men need not apply.

Dagny Taggart, the heroine of *Atlas Shrugged*, could have described her search for the perfect partner with such an ad; it sums up the romantic element woven through Rand's sweeping saga, *Atlas Shrugged*. Dagny is a unique woman in search of a unique man. Her quest to find the destroyer who is draining the world of men of ability, ultimately leads her to the man of her dreams.

Early in the novel, Dagny expresses her contempt for most men: "What men? There wasn't a man there I couldn't squash ten of" (AS 101).

Fifty years after Rand wrote *Atlas Shrugged*, those words describe most men of today. It is the dream of any rational woman to find the man who can love and appreciate her strengths while being able to challenge her—a man that can claim what he knows to be his in the most intimate and profound way. What does it take to be such a man? Dagny's relationships with Francisco, Rearden and Galt each illustrate important principles of Objectivism as they apply to romantic relationships and demonstrate just what it is a woman searches for in relationships.

The world of *Atlas Shrugged* is one in which it is the norm for women to tend to their families in the home rather than pursue careers outside the home—as it was during the 1950s in the real world. It is a woman's duty to tend to home and children and those who choose a corporate life, such as Dagny, are held to blame for the decline of culture and family values. Nearly fifty years later, in the real world, women have made it the norm to scale the corporate ladders and have exercised their choice to raise their children in daycare centers rather than at home. Some argue that such women are responsible for the decline of social culture and that they emasculate men, while many regard it as a huge step forward for women and families, empowering women.

The women in *Atlas Shrugged*, except for Dagny, are portrayed as befuddled and helpless creatures such as Dagny's mother or evil shrews like Rearden's wife, Lillian. Cherryl Taggart is a notable exception, a young woman who is shown to learn the nature of her mistake in idolizing James, but dies as soon as she realizes her mistaken premise. Cherryl, like the Wet Nurse both demonstrate potential, but never achieve the actual in terms of being allowed to live with their newly discovered premises.

Actual versus potential is a theme throughout *Atlas Shrugged* and the romantic relationship between Dagny and Francisco demonstrates one aspect of it. Potential in terms of one's ultimate character—whether or not there exists some spark in an individual to survive the irrational world and potential in terms of becoming a fully rational being as an adult. Rand illustrates this with two sets of siblings: Dagny and James Taggart and Hank and Phillip Rearden. The same parents raised each, but ultimately they choose opposing values to live by. The young runaway, John Galt, never accepts the concept of original sin, fully understands the nature of what he is facing and ends up stopping the motor of the world, despite his lack of parenting. What did Dagny, Rearden and John possess that is lacking in James, Phillip, and all the other looters? Dagny, Rearden and John possess an internal and inextinguishable spark that survives the irrationality of the world—they remain human.

Dagny's first lover, Francisco d'Anconia, orbits around Dagny in much the same way that Halley's comet orbits earth. Their childhood years are golden memories for Dagny, the most remembered highlights of her childhood and teen years. Francisco seems to be everything that Dagny has dreamed of as a child, and like a child, her unbridled innocence acknowledges that such a relationship knows no bounds—nothing is too mundane, or too powerful to experience. Dagny gives freely of herself in response to her love and respect of Francisco, so much so, that it rouses the ire of her brother, James, who is driven to comment:

> "All those airs you put on, pretending that you're an iron woman with a mind of her own! You're a spineless dishrag, that's all you are. It's disgusting, the way you let that conceited punk order you about. He can twist you around his little finger. You haven't any pride at all. The way you run when he whistles and wait on him! Why don't you shine his shoes?" "Because he hasn't told me to," she answered. (AS 93)

On another occasion during her childhood visits with Francisco, she jokingly suggests that perhaps she should play dumb in order to be popular at school:

> Francisco stopped, looked at her and slapped her face. What she felt was contained in a single instant, while the ground rocked under her feet, in a single blast of emotion within her. She knew that she would have killed any other person who struck her; she felt the violent fury which would have given her the strength for it—and as violent a

pleasure that Francisco had done it. She felt pleasure from the dull, hot pain in her cheek and from the taste of blood in the corner of her mouth. She felt pleasure in what she suddenly grasped about him, about herself and about his motive.

She braced her feet to stop the dizziness, she held her head straight and stood facing him in the consciousness of a new power, feeling herself his equal for the first time, looking at him with a mocking smile of triumph.

"Did I hurt you as much as that?" she asked.

He looked astonished; the question and the smile were not those of a child. He answered, "Yes—it if pleases you." (AS 99)

Why then does Dagny choose to believe the public persona that Francisco adopts, despite their previous history together? Why does she consciously choose to believe that this man, whom she has known and loved so well, would inexplicably become a debauched playboy?

Francisco certainly provides clues that he is embarking on some plan of action with forethought and with reason, some quite blatant:

Next time we meet, you will not want to see me. I will have a reason for the things I'll do. But I can't tell you the reason and you will be right to damn me. I am not committing the contemptible act of asking you to take me on faith. You have to live by your own knowledge and judgment. You will damn me. You will be hurt. Try not to let it hurt you too much. Remember that I told you this and that it was all I could tell you. (AS 112)

For ten years she wrestles with this contradiction, never once considering any other answer than that he has succumbed to corruption.

Dagny's solution to this contradiction in her life is to force it all from her mind as some incomprehensible cosmic error rather than discover the truth or take a leap of faith. Dagny goes as far as to ask a noted philosopher, whom she considers to be one of the finest minds left in the world, about Francisco, if he is proud of what he has become—he replies, "More proud than I had ever hoped to be." Despite his answer, she cannot allow herself any other explanation for Francisco's behavior and continues to believe he has become a philandering playboy.

Their every meeting in subsequent years underscores the contradiction:

That's not true, not if he laughed like that, not if he looked as he did. The capacity for unclouded enjoyment, she thought, does not belong to irresponsible fools; an inviolate peace of spirit is not the achievement of a drifter; to be able to laugh like that is the end result of the most profound, most solemn thinking.

Dagny continues to suffer, despite claiming to abhor such an act and the other side of the mind and body dichotomy surfaces at one of their last meetings together:

He did not follow her to the door. She had put her hand on the doorknob when she turned—and stopped. He stood across the room, looking at her; it was a glance directed at her whole person, she knew its meaning and it held her motionless.

"I still want to sleep with you," he said. "But I am not a man who is happy enough to do it." ... "You want it, too, don"t you?"

She was about to answer "No." but realized that the truth was worse than that. "Yes." She answered coldly, "But it doesn't matter to me that I want it." (AS 122)

Dagny consciously dismisses the demands of her body, which still responds to Francisco; her conscious mind refuses to ignore the available facts that remind her of Francisco's betrayal.

The lesson of Dagny's relationship with Francisco illustrates the key element of Objectivism—accepting the facts of reality as they are rather than on how one would wish them to be, or how one remembers what might have been in the past. The past and the future are not to be considered in establishing the reality of now. The actual facts of reality, as they exist in the here and now are the only correct means of judging one's actions.

Rand's idea is the antithesis of modern Western culture where romantic relationships are built on future plans and dreams, where couples embark on the grand adventure of marriage filled with hope and expectations. Many such relationships do indeed fail, ending in divorce because those expectations are not met. A long-term relationship cannot exist on illusions and evasions.

After the destruction of the John Galt Line, Francisco comes to see Dagny and attempts to explain his actions. Even then, she cannot accept that Francisco's actions have a rational explanation. She continues to view him with deepest suspicion:

This was the bond between them, she thought: that she would never be astonished if he came when she needed him most, and that he would always know when to come. This was the danger: that she would trust him, even while knowing that it could be nothing but some new kind of trap, even while remembering that he would always betray those who trusted him. (AS 479)

Dagny cannot accept Francisco based on her own observation of his actions, her own judgment of what his actions mean. Dagny would not and could not accept Francisco on faith, despite his explanations that reveal his purpose and despite his actions that reveal his love for her. She simply cannot love a man that appears to be a hopeless playboy. She would not allow herself to hope that he could or would change. She struggles with her rejection of him for ten years, despite her abhorrence for suffering, despite her attempting to believe it was all some horrible cosmic joke.

Francisco eventually confesses to her the reasons for his actions, but by then, it is much too late:

"It was for the way you looked that night, for the way you talked about your railroad—for the way you had looked when we tried to see the skyline of New York from the top of a rock over the Hudson—I had to save you, to clear the way for you, to let you find your city—not to let you stumble the years of your life away, struggling on through a poisoned fog, with your eyes still held straight ahead, still looking as they had looked in the sunlight, struggling on to find, at the end of your road, not the towers of a city, but a fat, soggy, mindless cripple performing his enjoyment of life by means of swallowing the gin your life had gone to pay for! [...]" (AS 707)

His arm swept out to point at the valley. "There it is—it's your earth, your kingdom, your kind of world—Dagny, I've always loved you and that I deserted you, that was my love." (AS 706)

Francisco, like Galahad the heroic knight, with full knowledge that he could lose the woman he loves, does not sway from his chosen quest. It is his quest, for his own ends, for his love of a woman. A woman he understands might not be there at the end, but with the secret hope that she would be waiting for him, as his grandmother had waited for his grandfather so long ago.

Dagny chooses not to wait.

By the time of Francisco's admission, Dagny has already become Hank Rearden's lover. Rearden—a successful industrial, producer, and competent businessman, the antithesis of what Francisco has become. Through Hank and Dagny's relationship, Rand explores the theme of the mind and body dichotomy. Rand contrasts Hank's personal and business beliefs to his beliefs about his own sexuality to illustrate that the same principles are involved. This is the most significant element of the relationship between Dagny and Rearden.

They have been aware of each other in a professional capacity and as the business climate worsens, they come to depend on each other as the only competent business people holding the world together. During an emergency conference, Dagny becomes intrigued by his aloof manner:

She thought suddenly that she was wrong about his lack of emotion: the hidden undertone of his manner was enjoyment. She realized that she had always felt a sense of light-hearted relaxation in his presence and known that he shared it. He was the only man she knew to whom she could speak without strain or effort. This, she thought, was a mind she respected, an adversary worth matching. Yet there had always been an odd sense of distance between them, the sense of a closed door; there was an impersonal quality in his manner, something within him that could not be reached. (AS 86)

Rearden represents the intellectual adversary Dagny has been searching for as well as an interesting personal challenge—to find the real man beneath the austere exterior. To pay a tribute to both herself and to him, saluting their achievements. Dagny's desire to see Rearden again, prompts her to attend an event she otherwise would never have considered—Rearden and Lillian's anniversary party. Her presence and her appearance are startling to many:

> Seeing her in the suits she wore, one never thought of Dagny Taggart's body. The black dress seemed excessively revealing—because it was astonishing to discover that the lines of her shoulder were fragile and beautiful, and that the diamond band on the wrist of her naked arm gave her the most feminine look of all aspects: the look of being chained. (AS 131)

The look of being chained. It is likely that many women of today would be outraged by such a description, while a minority would hold that statement as a symbol of pride.

Dagny's bold move in exchanging her own diamond bracelet for Lillian's bracelet made of Rearden metal sets the stage for the entire relationship between Dagny and Rearden. Dagny openly expresses her interest in sleeping with Rearden proudly while Rearden retreats to the role of dutiful if completely disinterested husband, in shame and guilt:

> He was crossing the room, carrying a tray of drinks requested by someone in Lillian's group—an unbecoming act of informality which nobody had ever seen him perform—when Dagny approached him. She stopped and looked up at him, as if they were alone in the office. She stood like an executive, her head lifted. He looked down at her. In the line of his glance, from the fingertips of her one hand to her face, her body was naked but for his metal bracelet.
>
> "I'm sorry, Hank," she said, "but I had to do it."
>
> His eyes remained expressionless. Yet she was suddenly certain that she knew what he felt: He wanted to slap her face.
>
> "It was not necessary," he answered coldly, and walked on. (AS 150)

An ordinary woman would never have made the exchange, nor would she understand the significance of Rearden's reaction. Dagny is no ordinary woman and continues to pursue him, compelled by desire. At their next meeting, the issue of the bracelet is put aside while they embark on a game of lustful teasing:

> "You'd give me a job?"
>
> "Any time."
>
> She looked at him a moment. "You're only half-kidding, Hank. I think you'd like it—having me ask you for a job. Having me for an employee instead of a customer. Giving me orders to obey."
>
> "Yes. I would."
>
> She said, her face hard, "Don't quit the steel business. I won't promise you a job on the railroad."
>
> He laughed. "Don't try it."
>
> "What?"
>
> "To win any battle when I set the terms."

> She did not answer. She was struck by what the words made her feel; it was not an emotion, but a physical sensation of pleasure, which she could not name or understand. (AS 159)

They continue to see each other in a professional capacity. Rearden however is tortured by his own desire for her:

> Don't you suppose I know how much I've betrayed? The only bright encounter of my life—the only person I respected—the best businessman I know—my ally—my partner in a desperate battle ... The lowest of all desires—as my answer to the highest I've met ... Do you know what I am? I thought of it, because it should have been unthinkable. For that degrading need, which should never touch you, I have never wanted anyone but you ... I hadn't known what it was like, to want it, until I saw you for the first time. I had thought: Not I, I couldn't be broken by it ... Since then ... for two years ... with not a moment's respite ... Do you know what it's like, to want it? Would you wish to hear what I thought when I looked at you ... when I lay awake at night ... when I heard your voice over a telephone wire ... when I worked, but could not drive it away? To bring you down to things you can't conceive—and to know that it's I who have done it. To reduce you to a body, to teach you an animal's pleasure, to see you need it, to see you asking me for it, to see your wonderful spirit dependent upon the obscenity of your need. To watch you as you are, as you face the world with your clean, proud strength—then to see you, in my bed, submitting to any infamous whim I may devise, to any act which I'll perform for the sole purpose of watching your dishonor and to which you'll submit for the sake of an unspeakable sensation ... I want you—and may I be damned for it! ... (AS 193)

When Rearden and Dagny finally consummate their relationship at Wyatt's house, Rearden reveals his disgust for their act of passion quite deliberately, with the greatest contempt. Dagny however only laughs once she understands the nature of his ranting:

> Did you call it depravity? I am much more depraved than you are: you hold it as your guilt, and I—as my pride. I'm more proud of it than of anything I've done, more proud than of building the line. If I'm asked to name my proudest attainment, I will say: I have slept with Hank Rearden. I had earned it. (AS 240)

Rearden is slow to understand the nature of sexual need and desire. Again and again, he finds himself at odds with his attraction to Dagny and his duty as a husband to Lillian. He struggles with himself though Dagny is patient, secure in the knowledge that his actions demonstrate his true beliefs and she accepts that he will work out the knowledge in the end because he is already living by those values in his work, in his personal dealings and needs only to extend his understanding to his sexuality.

As the world around them descends into darkness and chaos, the only joy open to Dagny and Hank is their relationship with each other. Their often violent release is tempered by Hank's sentimental gift giving, the one point of romance he does seem to understand though it is tainted by his acceptance of what others think of it:

> "I like giving things to you," he said, "because you don't need them."
> "No?"
> "And it's not that I want you to have them. I want you to have them from me."
> "That is the way I do need them, Hank. From you."
> "Do you understand that it's nothing but vicious self-indulgence on my part? I'm not doing it for your pleasure, but for mine."
> "Hank!" The cry was involuntary; it held amusement, despair, indignation and pity. "If you'd given me those things just for my pleasure, not yours, I would have thrown them in your face."
> "Yes … Yes, then you would—and should."
> "Did you call it your vicious self-indulgence?" "That's what they call it."
> "Oh, yes! That's what they call it. What do you call it, Hank?"
> "I don't know," he said indifferently, and went on intently. "I know only that if it's vicious, then let me be damned for it, but that's what I want to do more than anything else on earth." (AS 346)

Their relationship continues in a whirl of confusion on Rearden's part, but Dagny is patient in teaching him the proper values when it comes to sexuality. Ironically, Francisco helps Rearden understand the nature of sexuality more fully. Rearden's errors in that realm are understandable to Dagny and despite the fact that Rearden feels he's hurt her on several occasions by improper responses to their various adventures, Dagny is not hurt by his actions. Rearden eventually learns, but by then, Dagny has moved on once more.

The difference between Francisco and Rearden is that Francisco portrays himself as a worthless playboy—a man without purpose while Rearden is clearly a man with incredible purpose. Rearden's only flaws are excusable and correctable errors of judgment.

Both Francisco and Rearden ultimately fail to capture her mind in the profound way she desires. While Dagny is still Hank's lover, she has a poignant revelation:

> She felt—as she had felt it one spring night, slumped across her desk in the crumbling office of the John Galt Line, by a window facing a dark alley—the sense and vision of her own world, which she would never reach … You—she thought—whoever you are, whom I have always loved and never found, you whom I expected to see at the end of the rails beyond the horizon, you whose presence I had always felt in the streets of the city and whose world I had wanted to build, it is my love for you that had kept me moving, my love and my hope to reach you and my wish to be worthy of you on the day when I would stand before you face to face. Now I know that I shall never find you— that it is not to be reached or lived—but what is left of my life is still yours, and I will go on in your name, even though it is a name I'll never learn, I will go on serving you, even though I'm never to win, I will go on, to be worthy of you on the day when I would have

met you, even though I won't ... She had never accepted hopelessness, but she stood at the window and, addressed to the shape of a fogbound city, it was her self-dedication to unrequited love. (AS 585)

Dagny, after all this time and two different lovers, knows she has not yet met the man of her dreams. Neither Francisco nor Rearden have touched that internal ideal she holds for herself.

Dagny's quest for the man she has envisioned is intertwined with her desperate race to catch "the destroyer", the man she vows to kill on sight should they ever meet. In the moments after she crash lands in Galt's Gulch, she wakes to suddenly find herself in the world she had imagined at sixteen.

And face to face with the man she thought of as "the destroyer":

> She was looking up at the face of a man who knelt by her side, and she knew that in all the years behind her, THIS was what she would have given her life to see: a face that bore no mark of pain or fear or guilt.
> "What is your name?"
> "John Galt."
> She looked at him, not moving.
> "Why are you frightened?" he asked.
> "Because I believe it."
> He smiled, as if grasping a full confession of meaning she attached to his name; the smile held an adversary's acceptance of a challenge—and an adult's amusement at the self-deception of a child. (AS 648)

Above all, Galt's appeal to Dagny, is that he reawakens that innocent, dreaming child within the professional businesswoman; the child hidden away, protected from the irrationality of the world at large; the child who has sought the company of men of action, production, clarity, truth, and most of all rationality. Dagny's entire experience at Galt's Gulch mirrors this first introduction—every man there treats her with the indulgence one would give to a respectful but precocious child or an impudent sibling. Even Dr. Hugh Akston comes to acknowledge her as a daughter, along with his other three "sons." It is a very special homecoming, though Dagny remains a stranger there, of her own choice and conviction, unconvinced that their actions are the solution to the problem of evil in the world.

It is however, a place where she feels she can take a rest from her battle, though she is among the very people who are determined to destroy her.

> She lay still, her arms around him, her head on his shoulder, and she thought: For just a few moments—while this lasts—it is all right to surrender completely—to forget everything and just permit yourself to feel ... When had she experienced it before? — she wondered; there had been a moment when these had been the words in her mind, but she could not remember it now. She had known it, once—this feeling of certainty, of the final, the reached, the not-to-be questioned. But it was new to feel protected, and to feel that it was right to accept the protection, to surrender—right, because this

peculiar sense of safety was not protection against the future, but against the past, not the protection of being spared from battle, but of having won it, not a protection granted to her weakness, but to her strength ... (AS 649)

Dagny's strength, her conviction, her heroic efforts are all finally acknowledged in her time with Galt and all the other men at the valley—all her former business associates as well as those who used to work for her. Their treatment of her is respectful admiration, indulgence and goodwill. A salute to all she has done, despite literally being the enemy at this point in time. She remains unconvinced that their path is the correct one, but as adversaries, the respect and affection remain between them.

Dagny's conversations with Galt reveal his obsession with her:

"I remember your plane circling to land. But that was the one and only time when I didn't think of you. I thought you were coming by train."
She asked, looking straight at him, "How do you want me to understand that?"
"What?"
"The one and only time when you didn't think of me."
He held her glance; she saw the faint movement she had noted as typical of him: the movement of his proudly intractable mouth curving into the hint of a smile. "In any way you wish," he answered. (AS 657)

Galt tells her that he has been watching her for ten years, the ultimate stalker. He tells her of the many personal details he knows of her life, including how she looks when she sleeps and her favorite music. It becomes clear that he has been a major, if unnoticed presence for ten long years. The omnipresent man of her dreams, always in the background of her life, working for the destruction of everything she loves.

Galt takes Dagny to see Francisco's house in the valley, the silver crest of the d'Anconia family glinting in the sunlight:

When she was seated beside him once more, he said, "That was the first man I took away from you."
She asked her face stern, open and quietly defiant, "How much do you know about that?"
"Nothing that he told me in words. Everything that the tone of his voice told me whenever he spoke of you."
She inclined her head. She had caught the sound of suffering in the faintest exaggeration of the evenness in his voice. (AS 673)

Galt spares Dagny nothing in his listing of conquests he had wrested from her—each man, each action performed for the purpose of his goal to stop the motor of the world and Dagny's railroad:

As they drove on along the edge of the lake, she asked, "You've mapped this route deliberately, haven't you? You're showing me all the men whom"—she stopped, feeling inexplicably reluctant to say it, and said, instead—"whom I have lost?"

"I'm showing you all the men whom I have taken away from you," he answered firmly.

This was the root, she thought, of the guiltlessness of his face: he had guessed and named the words she had wanted to spare him, he had rejected a good will that was not based on his values—and in proud certainty of being right, he had made a boast of that which she had intended as an accusation. (AS 664)

John is a man sure of his knowledge and confident in his response to that knowledge. A man of informed action and fearless courage in achieving the most impossible of goals—demonstrating that nothing is impossible for a human being.

Dr. Akston sums up the essence of the special nature of his three "sons" [Francisco, John and Ragnor]:

and don't make the mistake of thinking that these three pupils of mine are some sort of superhuman creatures. They're something much greater and more astounding than that: they're normal men—a thing the world has never seen—and their feat is that they managed to survive as such. It does take an exceptional mind and a still more exceptional integrity to remain untouched by the brain-destroying influences of the world's doctrines, the accumulated evil of centuries—to remain human. ... (AS 725)

John is the man that discovered the answer to the world's problem and the man that had the strength and courage to implement the strike. The rest of the men followed his lead, of their own volition—only Dagny opposes him to the very end.

He [John] raised his eyes slowly to hold hers across the room, and the submerged intensity that pulled his voice down, blurring its tone to softness, gave it a sound of self-mockery that was desperate and almost gentle: "Then I knew that abandoning my motor was not the hardest price I would have to pay for this strike." (AS 719)

Like Francisco, John has a vision of how he believes the world should be, and unlike Francisco, John knows the question and formulates the solution—being both omnipresent and omniscient, the great conductor of the world's liberation from the looters. This was the peerless man for the peerless woman.

Such is the dream of every woman, though not always realized either in today's world or in the world of *Atlas Shrugged*.

On Dagny's tour of Galt's Gulch they come upon a woman who has been relaxing in the warm sun on a pier, surrounded by fishing poles. She jumps up at the sound of John's car and races to meet John, asking when he had gotten in. As John drives on:

Dagny jerked her head to look back and saw the glance with which the young woman stood looking after Galt. And even though hopelessness, serenely accepted, was part of the worship in her glance, she experienced a feeling she had never known before: a stab of jealousy.

"Who is that?" she asked.

"Our best fishwife. She provides the fish for Hammond's grocery market."

"What else is she?"

"You've noticed that there's a what else for every one of us here? She's a writer. The kind of writer who wouldn't be published outside. She believes that when one deals with words, one deals with the mind." (AS 664)

Chapter 25

Friendship in *Atlas Shrugged*

Peter Saint-Andre

Friendships are more valuable than gold.

James Taggart

Love is the expression of one's values, the greatest reward you can earn for the moral qualities you have achieved in your character and person, the emotional price paid by one man for the joy he receives from the virtues of another.

John Galt

Although the novels of Ayn Rand are usually considered to be thinly-veiled philosophical or even political treatises, softer themes often figure prominently therein. Indeed, from one angle *Atlas Shrugged* (Rand 1957) can be seen as something of a meditation on love and friendship. In this brief essay, I investigate both Rand's philosophical insights into the nature of friendship and the extent to which the relationships between the four main characters in *Atlas Shrugged* (Dagny, Francisco, Rearden, and Galt) live up to Rand's ideal.

Dagny and Francisco

Dagny and Francisco are childhood friends (94) long before they become lovers. Yet after they become romantically involved, theirs is a strange friendship. While in college, Francisco "did not come to visit her in New York that winter, even though he was only a night's journey away. They did not write to each other, they had never done it" (97); Dagny "knew nothing about the events of his life, had never known and would never need to know" (98); she "did not question him about the university" or even about his two friends there (ibid.), who it turns out later are Galt and Ragnar; "She knew little about Francisco's life. It was his last year of college; he seldom spoke of it, and she never questioned him" (108); "She did not see him often in the next two years. She never knew where he was, in what city or on what continent, the day after she had seen him" (109–10); He said, "There's something wrong in the world. There's always been. Something no one has ever named or explained." He would not tell her what it was (110); "He was twenty-three when his father died and he went to Buenos Aires to take over the d'Anconia estate, now his. She did not see him again for two years" (110); he began to write to her "at random intervals" but "he wrote about d'Anconia Copper, about the world market, about issues affecting the interests of Taggart Transcontinental" and never, it seems, about their relationship (110); he does not tell her that he loves her until more than ten years after their relationship has ended (111, 463, 463, 576, 711, 712); and before breaking off their relationship to go on strike he refuses to tell her why he is doing so or to share his thoughts and feelings with her (113), preferring to leave her frightened (113) and doubtful (191) even though he acknowledges that his course of action is cruel (113) and hurtful (114).

Much is missing from the relationship between Dagny and Francisco. Most basically, they hardly ever spend time together, which effectively prevents their relationship from blossoming (cf. Aristotle 1984, 1156b26–7). Although they share an interest in productive work, they do not engage in shared pursuits of the kind that might define a common life between them (Aristotle 1984, 1167a22, 1172a5, 1241a16–18, 1245b3; Lewis 1960, 43; Sherman 1989), perhaps because such pursuits would require the kind of time, energy, and commitment that would be difficult for highly productive individuals to devote (Telfer 1970, 267) and that therefore would be at odds with what I call "the ethics of the great task" (Saint-Andre 2006). Furthermore, whereas intimacy and reciprocal self-disclosure are important aspects of friendship (Thomas 1990, 49), the lack of communication between Dagny and Francisco is of epic proportions. This is critical to the suspense of the story (it would not do to have Dagny visit Francisco at college and thus meet Galt early in the novel), but the result is a relationship that borders on the dysfunctional. While Dagny and Francisco evidently have strong feelings for each other, feelings are not enough for a thriving relationship. Thus we must look to other relationships in *Atlas Shrugged* for a paradigm of friendship.

Galt and Francisco

During Francisco's college years, he becomes inseparable friends with two fellow students: Ragnar Danneskjöld and John Galt. Very little interaction between Francisco and Ragnar is presented in the novel, but two telling passages elucidate Francisco's attitude towards Galt. The first is the scene in which Rearden discovers that Francisco was Dagny's former lover (598):

[Francisco] was looking at Rearden, but it was not Rearden he was seeing. He looked as if he were facing another presence in the room and as if his glance were saying: If this is what you demand of me, then even this is yours, yours to accept and mine to endure, there is no more than this in me to offer you, but let me be proud to know that I can offer so much.

The second is a passage in which Dagny realizes who that other presence was (736):

'Hell, no, John!' he said, laughing, in answer to a question—but she caught suddenly the particular quality of his glance whenever it rested on Galt: it was the quality she had seen in his eyes when he had stood in her room, clutching the edge of a table to outlive an unlivable moment; he had looked as if he were seeing someone before him; it was Galt, she thought; it was Galt's image that had carried him through.

Consider: historically, when most people have visualized an unseen presence to whom they freely offer up whatever is demanded of them, that presence has been a god. Although Rand is a secularist, she did seek to bring religious concepts down to earth (Rand 1968), and the quality that Dagny saw in Francisco's eyes was worship. Indeed, Francisco comes perilously close to imputing godhood to Galt during a conversation with Dagny (594):

'You know, Dagny, we were taught that some things belong to God and others to Caesar. Perhaps their God would permit it. But the man you say we're serving—he does not permit it. He permits no divided allegiance, no war between your mind and your body, no gulf between your values and your actions, no tributes to Caesar. He permits no Caesars.'
    'Galt permits no Caesars. Is that because he is a jealous god?'

Even if Galt is not literally a god, he is, significantly, described as a godlike person who "had come into the world like Minerva, goddess of wisdom" (731). And, as Aristotle points out, "the friendship of ... men to gods is a relation to them as to something good and superior" (Aristotle 1984, 1162a4–5), a relationship in which "it is perhaps enough ... to give them what one can" (Aristotle 1984, 1164b4–5) since "they surpass us most decisively in all good things"(Aristotle 1984, 1158b35); the result is that friendship with them can never attain the equal trade that is characteristic of healthy human friendships (Aristotle 1984, 1158b26 ff., 1162b27 ff.).

In his relationship with Galt, Francisco "gives what he can"—his inheritance, his career, his reputation, his woman—and he even does so joyfully. Because Galt is far superior even to Francisco, their friendship, too, does not provide a model for normal human relationships.

Dagny and Galt

The relationship between Dagny and Galt is even more strikingly colored by Galt's godlike qualities. Although Francisco acts in service to Galt after having befriended him, Galt is portrayed as the motive power of Dagny's existence even before she has met him: "his presence somewhere in the world had been her motor through the years before she ever heard his name" (930). Even quite early in the novel she realizes that despite all her achievements "there was still one response, the greatest, that she had missed. She thought: To find a feeling that would hold, as their sum, as their final expression, the purpose of all the things she loved on earth ... To find a consciousness like her own, who would be the meaning of her world ..." (210). Dagny realizes that Francisco and Rearden always represented a future potential to her, whereas Galt represents the "final form of the promise that had kept her moving" (718). As Dagny explains it to Rearden, Galt "is the love I had wanted to reach long before I knew that he existed, and I think he will remain beyond my reach, but that I love him will be enough to keep me living" (800). Thus Dagny is quite willing to renounce a love that she can achieve in real life (with, say, Francisco or Rearden) for the sake of a one-way, unrequited love that would forever remain beyond her reach (so much for "a philosophy for living on earth"!). It is clear at the end of the novel that Dagny and Galt will probably marry, but it is less clear that their romantic relationship is based on friendship rather than the superiority of one of the parties (see Shanley 1981, 276–8). Further, given the fact that Dagny sees Galt as "the meaning of her world", one can doubt whether she has retained a healthy measure of distance from him (see Cicero 1967, xxii.82; Paton 1956, 140; Emerson 1841, 231; Rand 1936, 96). Thus here again we see that Galt's godlike qualities lead even strong characters to "give what they can" with little thought of an equal trade.

Indeed, given Galt's overwhelming superiority as a person, it is difficult to see why he would want or need friends. Consider a relevant passage from *The Fountainhead* (Rand 1943, 136):

> Heller, the fighter against compulsion, was baffled by Roark, a man so impervious to compulsion that he became a kind of compulsion himself, an ultimatum against things Heller could not define. Within a week, Heller knew that he had found the best friend he would ever have; and he knew that the friendship came from Roark's fundamental indifference. In the deeper reality of Roark's existence there was no consciousness of Heller, no need for Heller, no appeal, no demand.

Just like Roark, Galt seems fundamentally to have no need, awareness, or feeling for other people. Why should he, since he is at root self-sufficient? One might argue with the Stoics that friendship is not truly needed for someone of Galt's caliber but that it is nevertheless desired because it presents opportunities for noble action (Seneca 1917, 121; cf. Cicero 1967, ix, 29–30), but that does not seem to be a promising foundation for an Objectivist approach to friendship.

Francisco and Rearden

Perhaps a friendship between two mere mortals will provide a better model. The friendship between Francisco and Rearden is portrayed as "irresistably right" (926): they are described as like childhood friends (392, 926) and their relationship is referred to as a kind of love (431, 599). Francisco inspires in Rearden "a feeling of expectation that held curiosity, amusement, and hope" (386), "a smiling, light-hearted feeling, the feeling of being certain that it was right" (386), "a joyous feeling that seemed like a flow of energy added to his own" (431), a feeling of "an incredulous wonder" (926). Rearden thinks to himself that he needs Francisco because "I need the knowledge of one single man whom I can trust, respect and admire" (459), a man who could be his "spokesman" (386) and "sole ammunition" (459) in his struggles. Yet the relationship is not a one-way transfusion of energy, for Francisco too loves Rearden (599) and finds the same effortless joy in their relationship.

This is far from the indifference and self-sufficiency of Roark toward Heller or of Galt toward others: Rearden and Francisco need each other and have deep feelings for each other. In large measure this is because Rearden and Francisco are equals: the godlike Galt is not involved and their love is not romantic love between the sexes, which for Rand always seems to have involved some superiority on the man's part.

Here we may finally have a relationship in which each is to the other truly "another self" (Aristotle 1984, 1166a30, etc.). In general, that would seem to imply several things. First, that friendship is a source of self-knowledge (Sherman 1989, 106; Cooper 1980, 317–34; Branden 1980); Rearden experiences this most deeply, since he learns a great deal about himself and his values through his many conversations with Francisco. Second, that the other-regard of friendship mutates into self-regard (Aristotle 1984, 1168a35 ff.; Aquinas 1947, 172) and that friendship thus may be a path toward overcoming the opposition of egoism vs. altruism (Aquinas 1947, 167, 178, 182; Kant 1930, 211; Emerson 1841, 230); this appears to be true of both characters: consider the scenes at Rearden's mills in which

Rearden saves Francisco's life during the furnace break out (429–33) and in which Francisco returns the favor during the staged worker uprising (924–7). Third, that love of other relies on love of self—that in order to love another as I love myself, I must first love myself (a position not original to Rand and expressed even by medieval Christian philosopher Aelred of Rievaulx in the 12th century A.D.; see Aelred 1974, I.35 and also Lewis 1960, 43); here again this is especially true of Rearden, who struggles with accepting his love of Francisco until late in the novel when he has learned to appreciate and love his core characteristics and values.

More than any other relationship in the novel, the friendship between Francisco and Rearden is dynamic. Far from gazing into each other's eyes, worshipping each other, or otherwise treating each other as the literal mirrors of the ancient image of friendship, their relationship is characterized by both tension and dynamic interaction, not static reflection (cf. Emerson 1841, 230). Their relationship has its ups and downs, which makes it far more interesting and instructive than other friendships in *Atlas Shrugged*.

Randian Theory

How consistent are the foregoing friendships (or, indeed, normal human friendships) with Rand's theoretical discussions? In his radio speech, John Galt says (959): "Love is ... the emotional price paid by one man for the joy he receives from the virtues of another." What does it mean for love to be a price that buys joy? The basic thought seems to be that much as money buys things, so love and friendship buy joy. This may appear to be a crassly transactional approach to personal relationships: "I'll give you some love if you'll give me some pleasure." Yet there is classical precedent for a view something like Rand's "trader principle" in the ethics of Aristotle, who writes that in complete or perfect friendship "each gets from each in all respects the same as, or something like what, he gives; which is what ought to happen between friends" (Aristotle 1984, 1156b34–35) and that "each, then, both loves what is good for himself, and makes an equal return in goodwill and in pleasantness; for friendship is said to be equality, and both of these are found most in the friendship of the good" (Aristotle 1984, 1157b34–1158a1). Thus Rand updates Aristotle's idea of equality or similarity of result with her principle of trade in healthy human relationships. This viewpoint also seems to be consistent with what the evolutionary psychologists call "reciprocal altruism" (Trivers 1971), which in its more sophisticated forms (Tooby and Cosmides 1996) might better be described as a kind of reciprocal benevolence.

But questions arise. Is love or friendship truly an "emotional price"? If so, then love would seem to be primarily a feeling or emotion rather than primarily a form of action and commitment; yet we have seen that feelings are not enough for successful relationships. And what could it mean to pay for joy with love? The language of payment would seem to imply that friendships are not more valuable than gold, they literally are spiritual gold: love is the objective currency one uses to pay for the pleasure of interacting with a person one values or esteems. Yet is this what people are actually doing in friendship? Money can be divided into interchangeable units of measurement, each of which is just as good and useful at the other. But love and friendship are more central to and expressive of one's being than that—they are constitutive in a way that a currency is not. Particular instances of love and friendship cannot be substituted one for the other, since a relationship is a form of personal commitment and investment. Whereas a mere unit has all of its measurements omitted, the hallmark of close personal relationships is the feeling "don't omit my measurements, appreciate and admire me for my individuality!"

Granted, all of this is overly literal; most likely Rand used the language of trade and currency to draw an analogy between the economic realm and the spiritual realm rather than to equate them. There is a connection here to Rand's *Introduction to Objectivist Epistemology*, wherein she writes that the spiritual currency of one's life consists of thought, interest, and action (Rand 1990, 34; cf. Saint-Andre 1993, 149–58). Because love and friendship involve all three of these, the more productive question is: how are thought, interest, and action involved in love and friendship? We can unpack "thought" as meaning that friendship involves working to understand one's friend, oneself, and the relationship between the two individuals—thus connecting friendship with the pursuit of self-knowledge and the examined life. We can unpack "interest" as meaning that friendship involves attending to one's friend, valuing him or her, freely willing what is best for him or her, finding important what one's friend finds important—thus connecting friendship with empathy, goodwill, and the emotional life of individuals. We can unpack "action" as meaning that friendship involves not just thinking about and being interested in one's friend, but implementing those values through actions towards and with one's friend, achieving good things with one's friend, creatively building value together—thus connecting friendship with the ethics of the great task (where the great task is expanded to include not only the creation of physical or intellectual value but also the creation of a magnificent life).

In a way, such a richer approach to friendship echoes the expansion of economic relationships in recent human history. Agricultural economies were characterized by resource extraction and physical laborers; early capitalism was characterized by goods-trading and merchants; industrial capitalism was characterized by physical production and industrialists; post-industrial capitalism has been characterized by service industries and knowledge workers. Similarly, I think it is best to see Randian friendship at its highest not as the exploitative extraction of value, as the explicit trade of existing goods, or even as the "purchase" of joy with created values of character, but as a kind of ongoing, consultative relationship of reciprocal service between intelligent individuals. Not service in the sense of giving what one can or must to someone who is superior, but in the sense of mutual ministration, knowledge, discovery, empathy, interest, involvement, achievement, and enjoyment. (Interestingly, as work and play increasingly merge in the knowledge economy, so too relationships are becoming more equal and balanced, suggesting that increased integration of mind and body is occurring in both the economic and spiritual realms of human existence.)

Granted, Rand's philosophy of friendship is more of a promissory note than a lived reality for either her characters or, too often, her followers. She limits the value of close relationships to chosen relationships (64) and thus ignores entirely the realm of family life, which for Aristotle and the ancients was a core arena of *philia* (Cooper 1980, 301–302). She is overly enamored of the image of friends as mirrors for each other, rather than as individuals who are committed to joint action and mutual exploration. Her conception of the great task is too often limited to purely external projects (writing novels, running railroads, and the like) rather than also building one's character, one's personal relationships, and one's understand of self and of life in general. Thus, in large measure, discovering the value of friendship and integrating it into one's life are left by Rand as exercises for the reader. This is unfortunate, since the art of the novel can portray such vibrant examples of human interaction. While the relationship between Rearden and Francisco provides many tantalizing hints, in the end it is up to those who would lead a full and examined life to extrapolate from Rand's novels in order to translate the promise of close personal friendships from abstract theory into full-blooded reality.

References

Aelred. 1974. *Spiritual Friendship.* Excerpts in Pakulak 1991, 129–45.

Aquinas, T. 1947. *Summa Theologiae.* Excerpts in Pakulak 1991, 149–84.

Aristotle. 1984. *The Complete Works of Aristotle.* Princeton: Princeton University Press.

Badhwar, N.K. 1993. *Friendship: A Philosophical Reader.* Ithaca: Cornell University Press.

Branden, N. 1980. *The Psychology of Romantic Love.* Excerpts in Badhwar 1993, 65–72.

Cicero. [1967]. *On Friendship.* Excerpts in Pakulak 1991, 77–116.

Cooper, J. 1980. Aristotle on friendship. In Rorty 1980, 301–40.

Emerson, R.W. [1841]. Friendship. In Pakulak 1991, 218–32.

Kant, I. [1930.] *Lectures on Ethics.* Excerpts in Pakulak 1991, 208–17.

Lewis, C.S. 1960. Friendship—the least necessary love. In Badhwar 1993, 39–47.

Pakulak, M. 1991. *Other Selves: Philosophers on Friendship.* Indianapolis, Indiana: Hackett.

Paton, H.J. 1956. Kant on friendship. In Badhwar 1993, 133–54.

Rand, A. 1936. [1946.] *Anthem.* Caldwell, Idaho: The Caxton Printers.

———. 1943. *The Fountainhead.* New York: Bobbs-Merrill.

———. 1957. *Atlas Shrugged.* New York: Random House.

———. 1968. Introduction to the Fountainhead. *The Objectivist* (March 1968), 417–23.

———. 1990. *Introduction to Objectivist Epistemology.* Expanded second edition. New York: Meridian.

Rorty, A.O. 1980. *Essays on Aristotle's Ethics.* Berkeley: University of California Press.

Saint-Andre, P. 1993. A philosophy for living on earth. *Objectivity* 1:6, 137–73.

———. 2006. Nietzsche, Rand, and the ethics of the Great Task. *Journal of Ayn Rand Studies,* forthcoming.

Seneca. [1917]. *Epistulae Morales.* Excerpts in Pakulak 1991, 119–24.

Shanley, M.L. 1981. Marital slavery and friendship: John Stuart Mill's *The Subjection of Women.* In Badhwar 1993, 267–84.

Sherman, N. 1989. Aristotle on the Shared Life. In Badhwar 1993, 91–107.

Telfer, E. 1970. Friendship. In Pakulak 1991, 250–67.

Thomas, L. 1990. Friendship and other loves. In Badhwar 1993, 48–64.

Tooby, J. and L. Cosmides. 1996. Friendship and the Banker's Paradox: Other pathways to the evolution of adaptations for altruism. *Proceedings of the British Academy* 88, 119–43.

Trivers, R.L. 1971. The evolution of reciprocal altruism. *The Quarterly Review of Biology* 46:1, 35–57.

Chapter 26

Romantic Love in *Atlas Shrugged*

Jennifer L. Iannolo

Though all of Rand's fictional plots involve affairs of the heart, her reverence for the subject is most poignantly addressed in the novel *Atlas Shrugged*. It is, after all, a love story. One that also encompasses philosophy, politics, economics—and even swashbuckling—but above all, it is the story of a dynamic young woman who seeks total passion for the total height.

Rand most concisely expresses her thoughts on love via John Galt's speech: "Love is the expression of one's values, the greatest reward you can earn for the moral qualities you have achieved in your character and person, the emotional price paid by one man for the joy he receives from the virtues of another" (946).

Romantic love, however, is the ultimate expression of these values, and the recognition of their reflection in another human being; it is "one's final, irreplaceable choice" (788). There is no more profound way to feel recognized on this earth, and to celebrate the joy of one's existence. Lovemaking itself is the ultimate act of reverence, where one can offer a kind of worship that is not possible in any form of religion; man himself becomes the object of worship.

To give life to her views, and to fully illustrate the difference between this kind of love and all others, Rand delicately weaves a collection of contrasts, demonstrating love as it shouldn't be, might be—and ought to be.

In doing so, she allows the reader a glimpse of the ramifications of each, and how they affect the human spirit.

Love as it Shouldn't Be

In its lowest form, love is experienced as a type of penance, where duty and obligation are worn as a torturous, exhaustive weight. Alms are given out of pity, or even worse, out of hatred for the good.

Rand shows that this chain of false virtue can be worn either by those with truly blackened souls, or by those who are indeed virtuous, but have made an error in their thinking. The former is personified in James Taggart, and the latter in Hank Rearden.

Taggart, a man who cannot live but by the sanction of others around him, chooses a wife of the lowest means he can find, because in elevating her to the status of a socialite, he can forever exact a promissory note on her soul; she will forever be indebted to his kindness—not in a financial sense, but in a spiritual one. His wife Cheryl, however, is a woman of virtue, and in honor of the man she thinks her husband to be, she earns the right to her new position in society. She takes lessons in etiquette, becomes a proper hostess, and learns all of the niceties a woman of her social status is expected to know. She transforms herself to be worthy of the gift she has been given.

Rather than embrace and glorify her efforts, however, Taggart begins to hate her for daring to take flight from her lowly position. He preferred her "in the gutter," where she could constantly be reminded that if it weren't for him, she would still be a poor young waif living in a slum; the thought of it elevates his spirits, giving him a false sense of self-esteem and virtue. When Cheryl exposes his true character, the violence it does to his self-image physically manifests in a slap across her cheek; and when she realizes the truth about his soul, she is unable to withstand the agony of this knowledge—and ultimately takes her own life rather than live in his kind of world.

In the character of Hank Rearden, Rand exemplifies the concept of "sanction of the victim" (435), in which a person's virtue is used as a tool against him, to manipulate, control, and hold power over him—because he allows it.

Rearden is a hostage of his own making, and must follow a very difficult path toward self-discovery to uncover his errors. Successful, strong in spirit, and noble at heart, Rearden is chained to a thankless wife and a mooching family. He remains in the situation because of a strong sense of duty, and a refusal to forsake his promises.

His wife, Lillian, is a kindred spirit of James Taggart. She fully sees the virtue in her husband, and is determined to bring it to its proverbial knees. She seeks to hold his spirit in a vice, and does so by perpetuating the notion that his desire for sex is the result of his base, animalistic urges, reminding him that he may be a hero in the office, but in the bedroom he is no better than any other vile man. It is not until Francisco d'Anconia shows him the error of his premises that he is able to break free from the chains he has placed upon his own soul.

Of all the love relationships in *Atlas Shrugged*, it is Hank Rearden's that is most painful for the reader to experience. One is drawn in, outraged on his behalf, but helplessly wonders why he cannot see the mistake in his thinking, and why he does not walk away.

When the time comes for his epiphany, it is with bittersweet justice that he finally realizes what love truly is, and how it is to be properly expressed—but finds he has lost the love of his life to another who earned her first.

Love as it Might Be

Dagny Taggart, as the heroine of the novel, experiences a progression of relationships that are her path toward perfect romantic love. As she moves from one hero to the next, one can witness the growth in her understanding of what this value means, and how it is to be encompassed in another human being.

Francisco is her beginning; he is the first to offer her a glimpse of what the future might be. Their childhood and teen years are marked by the time they spend together, where each is fully recognized and treasured by the other. This beautiful sense of innocence and purity cannot be marred by the outside world, and offers a brilliant promise of the future for two achievers who will surely reach the kind of existence they desire.

His purported betrayal, however, is one that sends her mind and spirit reeling for many years. She cannot understand why he has chosen a path of destruction, and cannot come to answer a question whose premises are riddled with contradictions. Instead, she numbs herself to the pain, willing it away as unimportant; she refuses to accept suffering as a blemish on her existence. She also realizes, however, that for her, there will be no other love in her life such as the one she shared with Francisco.

When she later feels a desire for him, in spite of all she has experienced, she realizes "… what she felt for Francisco had always been a celebration of her future, like a moment of splendor gained in part payment of an unknown total, affirming some promise to come" (708).

In Hank Rearden, she finds a partial payment for the present; a kindred spirit and a fellow warrior in her battle against the looters. She and Hank admire one another's virtues of productivity and integrity; their companionship is an easy one, with a considerable passion at its core.

Given Hank's misunderstanding of the meaning of love and sex, however, he first assumes it is his vile nature—his animalistic urges—that draw him to Dagny. He enjoys reducing her to a helpless female, making her submit to his will. Until Francisco explains the roots of such pleasure to him, he does not realize that what he is offering Dagny is his highest expression of personal value. She does, however, and hopes he will one day reconcile this contradiction within himself.

Dagny knows that Hank is not her ultimate choice; instead, she enjoys her time as his mistress, admiring him fully, and accepting him on whatever terms he has to offer. She knows that he will stay with his wife—for however long—out of a false sense of duty, and asks no more of him.

Knowing this is not her appropriate end, or one worthy of her, Dagny makes a hopeless, solemn vow to an empty night sky:

> You … whoever you are, whom I have always loved and never found, you whom I expected to see at the end of the rails beyond the horizon, you whose presence I had always felt in the streets of the city and whose world I wanted to build, it is my love for

you that had kept me moving, my love and my hope to reach you and my wish to be worthy of you on the day when I would stand before you face to face. Now I know that I shall never find you—that it is not to be reached or lived—but what is left of my life is still yours, and I will go on in your name, even though it is a name I'll never learn, I will go on serving you, even though I'm never to win, I will go on, to be worthy of you on the day I would have met you, even though I won't ... (583)

This desire for the heroic poignantly captures the longing in Dagny's spirit for a reflection of herself; another human being who has traveled a sometimes arduous road of self-understanding, of virtue, toward an end that is just. Given what she has seen in the world around her, the hope that such a man exists has been extinguished, but still she knows that to forsake what he represents would be a violation of all she is. And though she will continue on with fervid determination to uphold her values, one knows she will do so with a void in her spirit, however small.

It is this longing that captures the essence of the importance of romantic love as Rand portrays it. There can be no other—but a person possessing the highest possible value—to whom one may grant that love, and the cost for Dagny to earn that reward is "price no object."

When Dagny discovers John Galt, she comes to fully realize the meaning of this: The man she wants does exist, but in order to have him, she must earn him, and that process entails the questioning of some of her core beliefs. It is with bittersweet recognition that she sees her dream before her, knowing she may never possess the right to reach out and seize it.

Her interaction with Galt thus becomes a test of will, determination, and certainty; it is a battle to the very end. There are times when Dagny revels in the thought of bringing this man to his knees, simply with the power of who she is, and what she means to him. She wants to both conquer him and be conquered by him.

Both Dagny and Galt believe themselves to be right, and Dagny is unable, at first, to fully grasp his reasons for abandoning the world. When at last she does, and is united with him, one can sense the feeling of victory, and the elation of spirit as captured in Rand's words. At last, Dagny has come home.

But the story's denouement is not without sadness—at least for some readers. One is left knowing that Francisco, Galt's best friend, has paid the ultimate price for his virtue, and must now reconcile himself to the fact that the friend he treasures most on earth has claimed the title Francisco wished to hold, but to which he is no longer entitled. Many readers have commented that this was not an appropriate end for Francisco (this particular reader still hasn't gotten over it), but that the ending is a just one, based on the groundwork Rand laid in all the action and philosophy preceding it. It is this one detail that best conveys why there are no conflicts of interest among rational men—in love or other matters.

The reader is not furnished with a great amount of information with regard to Dagny and Galt's happy times together, but one can assume that their existence is a peaceful one, with mutual admiration, adoration, and worship. Perhaps these details were thought by Rand to be self-evident, and thus unnecessary, but their absence does sometimes leave the reader wanting more.

Love as It Ought to Be

Though it is clear that Dagny Taggart and John Galt are intended to be the ultimate love duo in *Atlas Shrugged*, with just a few moments of vivid imagery and detail, Rand conveys a powerful vision of love as it ought to be: A sanctuary, where perfect understanding, admiration, and peace form the central tenets of togetherness.

Little is told of their story, but Ragnar Danneskjöld and his wife, Kay Ludlow, appear as if crafted from a perfect, complementary mold. When they are together, the outside world is but an afterthought, and what matters is the radiant, peaceful joy that each feels in the presence of the other.

While he is out fighting the evils of the world—sinking the looters' ships, taking back the gold of productive men, and waging his part of the war on irrationality—she is content to wait for his return without fear of disaster or abandonment, and simply focuses on pursuing her own values. After Dagny asks how she can live through such a thing, Danneskjöld answers simply:

> She can live through it, Miss Taggart, because we do not hold the belief that this earth is a realm of misery where man is doomed to destruction. We do not think that tragedy is our natural fate and we do not live in chronic dread of disaster. We do not expect disaster until we have specific reason to expect it—and when we encounter it, we are free to fight it. It is not happiness, but suffering that we consider unnatural. It is not success, but calamity that we regard as the abnormal exception in human life (696).

It is this brief statement, along with two images, that movingly reflect the sense of tranquility this couple has earned. The images are mentioned in passing, and convey almost mundane activities that others might take for granted in the course of a day: The first is of them walking together in the moonlight, side by side; the second is of them preparing for their return to the world, each consumed by a personal task, but breathing the same air. He is reading a book of Aristotle, and she is preparing her stage makeup. Simple, but profound, given what has come before such moments, and one understands viscerally the price they have paid to arrive at such peace.

It is the power of Rand's ability as a storyteller that conveys so much meaning with so few words and images. Here are two people who revel in the sight and presence of one another, and one's imagination can extrapolate to understand the kind of bond they share.   One senses there was no conflict in them coming together—no battle of wills or mistaken premises. They simply are—and are perfect together.

One cannot imagine them conquering one another, or needing to bring the other to his knees; such acts would seem out of place and character for each. The battles are outside, and so Ragnar and Kay have achieved respite in one another's company.

As Rand's presentation of romantic love often includes stark representations of conquering and conflict, her description of these two lovers is a refreshing change, and one that demonstrates a picture of love as peaceful and serene—a sanctuary where the heroic may come for rejuvenation of the soul. In the battle for rationality and the pursuit of values, one could say that such imagery is the ultimate expression of love—as it ought to be.

Reference

Rand, Ayn. 1957. *Atlas Shrugged.* New York: New American Library

Chapter 27

Beyond the "Stillborn Aspiration": Virtuous Sexuality in *Atlas Shrugged*[1]

Susan Love Brown

Introduction

Sexuality in Ayn Rand's novels always involves a woman with multiple male sex partners, almost never within the bonds of wedlock, and almost always in defiance of the values of the world around her. Rand takes pride in presenting these liaisons as noble and virtuous in a world of "stillborn aspiration" in which physical joy and pleasure are desired but not pursued.[2] In her presentation of Dagny Taggart and her lovers, Rand carefully constructs her argument about the nature of sex and the possibility of sexual virtue not tied to the conventions of marriage or religion but strongly connected to one's personal aspirations, achievements, and values. Sexuality in *Atlas Shrugged* (1999) represents a departure from the sexual relationships of her earlier heroines, Kira Argounova and Dominique Francon, rendering a more complete expression of virtuous sex than in *The Fountainhead* (1951) or *We the Living* (1996). In this paper, I compare the three sexual relationships of Dagny in *Atlas Shrugged* with their structural counterparts in Rand's earlier novels to demonstrate Rand's increasing sophistication in her presentation of sex, the curtailment of sadomasochism and perversion, and how important a comprehensive philosophy was to her portrayal of virtuous sex.

In a journal entry dated 4 May 1946,[3] "Philosophical Notes on the Creative Process" (478–82), Rand notes: "In my own case, I seem to be both a theoretical philosopher and a fiction writer. But it is the last that interests me most; the first is only the means to the last; the absolutely necessary means, but only the means; the fiction story is the end" (479). For Rand, the writing of fiction was the priority, and it is fair to assume that her earlier work did not necessitate the depth of philosophical thought about sex that was entailed in *Atlas Shrugged*. But as early as 6 October 1949, Rand had written in her journal an extended analysis of the relationship between sex and morality (608–10). She noted:

> The twisted element of truth here is that sex has to be a high spiritual base and source, and that without this it is an evil perversion. But the actual relation of sex and spirit is

not the way they believe: they believe that sex is evil as such, and that the spiritual aspects of marriage serve to redeem or excuse it, or make it a pardonable weakness which has no tie with and is opposed to the spiritual elements of the relationship. They do not suspect the essential, unbreakable tie between sex and spirit—which is the tie between body and soul. (609)

Here, Rand has eliminated the mind-body problem from the realm of sexuality, and from this she concludes: "On the right philosophical premise about sex, on my premise, it is a great compliment to a woman if a man wants her. It is an expression of his highest values, not of his contempt" (609).

In her attempt to define the virtuous boundaries of sex, Rand was ahead of her time. But as time went on, Rand refined her view of sex and continued to talk about it in public forums. For example, in her essay, "Of Living Death (II)," Ayn Rand noted:

Sex is a physical capacity, but its exercise is determined by man's mind—by his choice of values, held consciously and subconsciously. To a rational man, sex is an expression of self-esteem—a celebration of himself and of existence. To the man who lacks self-esteem, sex is an attempt to fake it, to acquire its momentary illusion. (2)

In her interview with *Playboy*, Ayn Rand stated:

A sexual relationship is proper only on the ground of the highest values one can find in a human being. Sex must not be anything other than a response to values. And that is why I consider promiscuity immoral. Not because sex is evil, but because sex is too good and too important.

For Rand, then, as expressed in "Of Living Death (II),"

the romantic love which we often associate with sex is an emotion possible only to the man (or woman) of unbreached self-esteem: it is his response to his own highest values in the person of another—an integrated response of mind and body, of love and sexual desire. Such a man (or woman) is incapable of experiencing a sexual desire divorced from spiritual values. (2)

It is significant that Rand saw herself as a fiction writer first, and that her skill at developing plot and drama were present from the beginning in her novels. But the principles of sexuality that Rand articulates so clearly were not as well developed in her first two novels; thus, the sexual relationships in those books became problematic from a philosophical, though not necessarily a novelistic, point of view. In *We the Living* and *The Fountainhead*, the portrayal of sex is dramatic but ambiguous and even perverse in relationship to Rand's broader themes and her eventual philosophy. While Rand relied on her skills as a writer in constructing her novelistic plots and structuring her novels, it is clear that she had not yet developed a comprehensive view of sexuality in her early works. Instead, she offered relationships tainted with sadomasochism that becomes so extreme that it prompts charges of rape from her readers, and with a naïve tendency toward "love at first sight." In order to see that this is so, it is necessary to examine the sexual relationships between the heroine and her lovers in these earlier novels. Let us begin by comparing, for example, the first sexual experience of Dagny Taggart and Francisco d'Anconia to that of Kira Argounova and Leo Kovalensky in *We the Living.*

First Love and A Priori Wisdom in *We the Living*: Kira and Leo

In *We the Living*, Rand's first novel, the young heroine, Kira Argounova, is all of eighteen years old when she has her first sexual encounter with Leo Kovalensky. Rand's treatment of sex in this instance stands out because of its love-at-first-sight motif.[4] The sexuality as portrayed here is definitive in terms of Rand's position that it is a positive force in Kira's life. However, there is no reason for Kira to be attracted to Leo, except on the basis of his looks and her association of them with certain notions that appeal to her. While one might point to Kira's naiveté and romantic notions as excuses that do work novelistically, they reveal the lack of a precise understanding of virtuous sex on Rand's part. The virtue is taken for granted, rather than demonstrated.

Kira is a young woman bent on becoming an engineer—a young woman who doesn't care what she wears, doesn't notice her own hunger or any pain, forgets to pick up the rations that sustain her family, and does not care about love. However, when she first lays eyes on Leo Kovalensky, she knows his character immediately without speaking to him and without any experience of him. When Leo runs across her in a street filled with prostitutes and mistakes her for one, she plays along, because she is taken in by his looks: "His mouth, calm, severe, contemptuous, was that of an ancient chieftain who could order men to die, and his eyes were such as could watch it" (61). Apparently, this kind of personality appeals to Kira, but it is based purely on appearances. Leo has said nothing.

Rand writes, "Kira leaned against a lamppost, looking straight at his face, and smiled. She did not think; she smiled, stunned, without realizing that she was hoping he would know her as she knew him" (61). But how could Kira know Leo? In the dialogue that follows, Kira learns that Leo is a heavy drinker and has the desire to go down "as far as you can drag me" (62). When Leo finds out that Kira is not a prostitute after all and asks her why she deceived him, her reply is: "I liked your face."

Now, while one might argue that in fact eighteen-year-old girls might be just this naïve, and while Rand even has Leo scold Kira for having taken such a chance, the fact is that Kira's attraction is based solely on Leo's looks. While she will get to know him before she actually sleeps with him, one cannot help but think that the model that Rand has presented here is one of impulsiveness designed to have a dramatic effect but hardly based on mutual values, since such values cannot be known.

Further development of the character reveals Leo's possible virtues, but there is nothing other than Kira's first impressions to initially reveal this virtue. The unmistakable recognition of a value without any other evidence but the eyes leads the reader to conclude that Kira possesses some mystical power to discern a good man just by looking, or she is very lucky. Neither case supports Rand's later philosophical views, and neither supports a sexuality based on knowledge and, therefore, value.

Kira is willing to go with Leo based on nothing more than a brief encounter—an encounter apparently laden with significance that the reader cannot grasp and must take on faith. (And, because of the romantic and dramatic nature of the writing, the reader is mostly willing to do this.) Rand hints that Kira would have been willing to sleep with Leo that night had he not uncovered her ruse and saved her from herself. Kira has a baseless wisdom. The recognition of values without prior experience is one feature of first love in *We the Living*. In her journal on *We the Living* (initially called *Airtight*), Rand says of Kira:

> Her love for Leo—the concentrated strength of all her will to live. He is, to her, the symbol of everything she wants and the meaning of life as she sees it. Therefore, her indifference to others, the clarity of her mind that leaves her cool to many useless emotions and affections, her straightforwardness—these lead her to an all-absorbing passion, almost unbearable for a human being. (51)

Yet, it is difficult to see from what this passion arises, and why it is symbolized in Leo, primarily because it precedes the reader's knowledge of his character.

Such instant recognition of value in a lover is typical of some of Rand's early stories,[5] and it need not be taken too seriously as anything other than a device for bringing two people together dramatically in her fiction prior to her working out in detail the philosophy needed to create deeper characterizations. But in looking back, we can see how far Rand had come, both philosophically and as a fiction writer, by the time she wrote *Atlas Shrugged*. Her own view of the role of sex in human life has grown more sophisticated by the time she portrays the relationship between Dagny Taggart and her first lover, Francisco d'Anconia.

First Love Revisited: Slug and Frisco Celebrate Life

The love affair between Dagny Taggart and Francisco d'Anconia firmly establishes the connection between sexual attraction and values and asserts the virtue of sex as a result. Unlike Kira and Leo, Dagny (Slug) and Francisco (Frisco) have known each other over a period of years during which each discovered his or her values through experience. They grew up together, playing, exploring, and learning, and they grew together, valuing the productive work that would become the focus of their lives, cementing the commonality of their aspirations and achievements—the ultimate basis of their sexual attraction. In the recounting of their childhoods leading up to their first sexual experience, Rand establishes the basic foundation of the physical pleasure that comes from recognizing a value in another person (90–104). But the possibility of Dagny's sexuality is invisible to those around her, precisely because it is based on the aspirations and achievements that she has in common with her lovers, first of all Francisco, and because it does not occur to others that a passion for one's work could be translated into sexual desire.

Dagny's own mother comments about her relationship: "Dagny and Francisco d'Anconia? ... Oh no, it's not a romance. It's an international industrial cartel of some kind. That's all they seem to care about" (102). But her mother finally realizes Dagny's sexual power when she sees her daughter dressed for her coming out party. Still, she never fathoms the reason for Dagny's disappointment after the party—her failure to find any young men of value, young men who match her own passion for life and for pleasure.

It is following this disappointment and a fierce tennis match in which Dagny wins over Francisco that Rand positions their first sexual encounter. The combination of their childhood adventures, Dagny's disappointment in the young men at her party, and the fierce physical match prepare the reader for the first sex scene in the novel and for the particular model of sex that Rand delineates throughout the rest of the book.

It is significant that this scene of first sex takes place in the rising sunlight of a new day after Francisco has spent the night with Dagny at her job barely talking to her, only waiting, symbolizing the dawn of a new set of passions—a new experience of sexual awakening. Rand sets the scene in nature, in the woods, with "no traces of human existence around them" (107). Thus, this first experience of sex is intensely private, intensely natural, and intensely physical. And, in spite of talk of submission and ownership, which Rand divides evenly among them, Francisco's words—"We had to learn it from each other"—indicate an equally new experience for both of them.

In her journal entry of 11 February 1947, Rand notes that the relationship of Slug and Frisco is "their celebration of life," that it involves "complete innocence," and that they are "both incapable of the conception that joy is sin" (552; see also *Atlas Shrugged* 109). Indeed, they keep their relationship a secret "as a thing that was immaculately theirs, beyond anyone's right of debate or appraisal" (109). Rand imbues virtuous sex with a kind of sacredness not to be tainted by the less wholesome views of others. But, more importantly, in this account of first sex, Rand establishes a connection, through the lives of her characters, between their values and their desire for one another—a connection not found in the similar portrayal in *We the Living* and *The Fountainhead*.[6]

But the consequences of a more thoughtful theory of sexuality do not end here. In *Atlas Shrugged*, Rand also largely overcomes two problems that assert themselves so boldly in *The Fountainhead*. First of all, she overcomes the sadomasochistic tendencies found in both Dominique Francon and Howard Roark —tendencies that can only be a response to less than admirable values or total psychological confusion. It is not possible to portray sex as a virtue when it is tied to distinctly unvirtuous (one is inclined to say vicious) actions, such as appear in the hatred and destructive actions of Dominique Francon toward Howard Roark and his work or in his rape of Dominique, engraved invitation or not. That relationship contrasts sharply with Dagny Taggart's two mature sexual relationships: with Hank Rearden and the final one with John Galt.

Besides reemphasizing the importance of sex as a response to values in the relationship between Hank Rearden and Dagny Taggart, Rand also takes the trouble to reinforce the voluntary nature of such relationships. And in establishing what a relationship might look like if based on the response to one's highest value —the relationship between Dagny Taggart and John Galt—she moves away from the coldly calculated sex of Howard Roark to the strong and powerful desire of John Galt that ultimately makes him vulnerable. Both of these relationships are an advance over the one between Dominique Francon and Howard Roark.

Sadomasochism, Who Needs It? Dominique Francon and Howard Roark

Sadomasochism was a problem for Rand in her first two novels. The equation of passion and violence in *We the Living*, however, is relatively minor compared to its appearance in *The Fountainhead*, where it finds its expression in the perverse attitudes and behavior of Dominique Francon and in the attraction of Howard Roark to them. The perverseness of sexual desire in this novel is so strong that it outweighs even the possibility of seeing sex as an act of virtue. While it clearly shows that sex is a response to values, the values to which Dominique Francon and Howard Roark are responding are distorted by their twisted psychologies.

According to Robert J. Stoller, "... perversion is the result of an essential interplay between hostility and sexual desire ..." (1975, xi). "The hostility in perversion takes form in a fantasy of revenge hidden in the actions that make up the perversion ..." (1975, xi). This definition describes almost perfectly Dominique Francon's character. In the sequence of scenes leading up to Dominique's first sexual encounter with Howard Roark, Rand draws a very clear picture of Dominique's personality: she seeks pain and destruction, and, as Stoller would have predicted, "To create the greatest excitement, the perversion must also portray itself as an act of risk taking" (1975, 4). Such is the nature of the actions that Dominique takes to attract the attention of the worker in the quarry, who happens to be Howard Roark.

Waking up to the sound of explosions, Rand states: "It was the sound of destruction and she liked it" (204). Not only does this anticipate Dominique's complicity in the destruction of Cortlandt later in the novel, but of her general desire to destroy anything of beauty or worthiness, less she feel enslaved by it. This, we find, includes sexual attraction. Scene by scene, Rand constructs a portrait of Dominique as perverse. After first setting eyes on Howard Roark, Dominique "thought she had found an aim in life—a sudden, sweeping hatred for the man" (201). She is attracted by what she assumes is Roark's lowly place, compared to her elevated one, and she desires him precisely because she loathes him (206).

Returning again and again to the quarry, Dominique taunts Roark and is taunted by him, and finally maneuvers him to her bedroom. Rand informs us: "She found a dark satisfaction in pain—because that pain came from him" (204). When Roark finally appears in her bedroom and rapes her, she experiences no pleasure, only pain. Rand is explicit about the nature of the act:

> It was an act that could be performed in tenderness, as a seal of love, or in contempt, as a symbol of humiliation and conquest. It could be the act of a lover or the act of a soldier violating an enemy woman. He did it as an act of scorn. Not as love, but as defilement. And this made her lie still and submit. (217)

Following this event, Dominique is most moved by the fact that, "I have been raped ... I've been raped by some redheaded hoodlum from a stone quarry" (219).[7] It is from this fact—that fact that the act caused her great pain and was performed by a man so beneath her—that finally gives her pleasure. "... she had found joy in her revulsion, and in her terror his strength, that was the degradation she had wanted and she hated him for it" (219).

It is clear that Rand had not yet worked out the foundations of virtuous sex, although the relationship of Dominique Francon and Howard Roark does give us a clue to sex as a response to values, only the values she portrays in *The Fountainhead* are not the kind that lead to virtuous sex but to the very degradation she portrays. The sexual relationship between Dominique Francon and Howard Roark does not live up to Ayn Rand's later philosophy in general or to her claim that sex can be virtuous. One could argue that Dominique's sexual debauchery is related to her confusion about the nature of the world, as Rand does, but the sex in *The Fountainhead* is so confused psychologically that only perversion results.

Contrastingly, in *Atlas Shrugged*, Rand deals with another character, Hank Rearden, who is confused about the relationship between desire and morality. However, doing so once she has thought out in more detail the true nature of sexuality in human life, she presents the case of Hank Rearden in a more comprehensive way, letting the reader accompany him on his journey of discovery.

Dagny and Hank: The Chain of Sexual Misunderstandings

Building on the foundation she has laid with the story of Slug and Frisco, Rand demonstrates the excitement and sexual tension that arises when two mature people find their values reflected in another, even when they may understand the basis for the feelings. Initially, the relationship between Dagny and Hank is a business relationship. But as each struggles against those who seek to stand between them and their achievements, they are drawn closer and closer together. Unlike Dominique and Howard Roark, who work against each other, Dagny and Hank surge forward until their achievements not only parallel each other like railroad tracks but become one and the same achievement, culminating in the running of the John Galt Line.

Hank Rearden's invention of Rearden Metal and Dagny's need and regard for Rearden Metal is symbolized in the bracelet that Hank made initially for his wife, Lillian, but which comes into Dagny's possession in a fair trade with Lillian for a diamond bracelet, which Lillian sees as more valuable and Dagny as less valuable than the metal bracelet, illustrating in one gesture their different values and their differing valuation of Hank Rearden himself.

Hank Rearden had felt a desire for Dagny from the time he first saw her, but his secondary response is one of guilt. He even experiences a moment of self-hatred over this desire, which he suppresses (563). While Rand does not totally divest this novel of her sadomasochistic bent or of her perversion (she describes the act of sex as "an act of hatred"—257), she does have Hank ask, "You want it?" and has Dagny answer, "Yes," establishing clearly the voluntary nature of the sex between them. This act constitutes "a single loyalty: their love of existence ... a single sensation of such intensity of joy that no other sanction of one's existence is necessary" (252).

Rand very cleverly builds up the sexual tension between Dagny Taggart and Hank Rearden in her description of their ride on the first running of The John Galt Line, thus tying their rising desire with the glory of their achievement. "She opened her eyes and saw that Rearden stood looking down at her. It was the same glance with which he had looked at the rail" (241). The tension mounts as the looks pass back and forth between them interspersed with images of smooth speed as the countryside passes before them—looks intermingled with the exhilaration each feels at the moment by moment thrill of the great engine moving at top speed across the tracks of Rearden Metal.

Following their initial sexual experience, Rand cleverly contrasts the increasing demands upon Rearden, as he loses control of his business, with his increasing understanding of his attraction to Dagny and his previous mistaken understanding about sex and morality. The learning experience of Hank Rearden is cleverly intertwined with Dagny's search for the maker of the engine that runs on kinetic energy.

The vacation that Hank and Dagny take together represents not only the search for John Galt, but the search for the answer to the mystery that Hank is just beginning to solve with regard to his own feelings. This love affair is a "learning experience" for Rearden. Although Rand refers to Rearden's "sadistic" touches, she actually manages to keep sadomasochism to a minimum. When, at one point, Rearden sinks into a depression because of the threats to his business, he emerges from it with a new understanding:

> What he knew, what he had discovered tonight, was that his recaptured love of existence had not been given back to him by the return of his desire for her—but that the desire had returned after he had regained his world, the love, the value and the sense of his world—and that the desire was not an answer to her body, but a celebration of himself and of his will to live. (378)

Rand's most explicit statement about sex comes when Hank Rearden visits Francisco d'Anconia in the Wayne-Falkland Hotel, never suspecting that Francisco is Dagny's first lover. Francisco tells him that "sex is not the cause, but an effect and an expression of a man's sense of his own value" (489). He further tells Rearden, "Love is our response to our highest values and can be nothing else" (490).

Hank Rearden's education is the result of experience, but that experience allows him to tap into the positive values that were always a part of him. It does not require Rand to miraculously convert a sadomasochist into a loving woman, as it does with Dominique. Just as he learns the value of his own abilities and achievements to the world, he learns about the connection between his values and his desire. Rearden's education and Dagny's search lead both to the man in whom both of their ideals reside: John Galt. Whereas Hank Rearden had to learn to trust his own sexual instincts as a reflection of his deepest values, John Galt already possesses this knowledge.

Sex as the Best Within Us: Dagny Taggart and John Galt

In the person of John Galt, Rand creates the man for whom sex is a total reflection of his values, and his values are a reflection of the highest morality in the world of *Atlas Shrugged.* The object of his desire is Dagny Taggart, whom Ayn Rand has set up as his most difficult conquest. But note, the difficulty of this particular conquest is not framed in the sadomasochistic way of the brutal physical conquest of Dominique Francon by Howard Roark. Nor is it directly in response to a concrete achievement of which Dagny is a part, like the building of The John Galt Line that led Dagny to Hank Rearden. This conquest, while symbolized by the achievement of the engine, is one of values tied to abstract ideals—Galt must conquer Dagny through her acceptance of his ideas. The difficulty of the conquest arises from the very thing that Galt values in Dagny the most—her devotion to her work, her pride, and her absolute conviction that she can make her railroad run under any conceivable conditions.

Galt has had to put off acting on his desire for Dagny until his work on the strike was almost complete. But Galt, unlike Howard Roark, almost gave in to his desires and finally does so, even at the risk of his own life.

Once again, Rand prepares the reader for Dagny's response to Galt. Galt is the first name mentioned in the novel, and it is the pursuit of Galt that occupies Dagny, even though she does not know it. When she finally meets John Galt after she has crashed in Galt's Gulch, she has the opportunity to meet him and to learn that he is the inventor of the engine, and that he has used this knowledge to protect the valley and its inhabitants. The fact that she broke through his defenses through sheer guts marks her as a match for him. John Galt embodies the greatest scientific achievement in human history, as well as the man with the most integrity, and the most abstract ideals.

Rand allows the reader to discover, along with Dagny, the kind of achievement that would warrant a desire this worthy. As Dagny uncovers the story of Twentieth Century Motors and the engine abandoned there, and as she fights against the unknown man who is depriving the world of its most talented people, Rand lays the foundation for the discovery by Dagny of her own greatest value. The engineer in her appreciates this invention, compelling her to search for its maker, as he, one by one, deprives her of all her possible sources of discovery and yet leads her inevitably to himself.

Dagny is, in many ways, the opposite of Dominique, who wallows in pessimism, while Dagny is described by Rand in her journal entry of 18 April 1946 as too optimistic, "thinking that men are better than they are ..." (424). But it is this hopefulness, which Rand describes as an "error" that makes her John Galt's biggest challenge and, therefore, his biggest conquest among the talented people in the world.

The first sexual encounter between Dagny Taggart and John Galt takes place in an abandoned railroad tunnel on burlap sacks. Dagny, sensing the presence of Galt among the workers, walks into the tunnel knowing he will follow her. Rand has prepared the reader for this moment throughout the novel. Dagny knows a good deal about John Galt, and he knows about her from his talks with Eddie Willers. There is no question, then, that each lover knows exactly what the other represents. In many ways, like Dagny and John, the reader has also been waiting for this moment.

But why place this scene deep in an abandoned tunnel?

> These tunnels, she had once thought, were the roots of the city and of all the motion reaching to the sky—but they, she thought, John Galt and she were the living power within these roots, they were the start and aim and meaning—he, too, she thought, heard the beat of the city as the beat of his body. (956)

Rand's description of Dagny's sexual experience casts it as the literal embodiment of her values: "... conscious of nothing but the sensations of her own body ... her most complex values by direct perception ... so her body now had the power to translate the energy that had moved all the choices of the life, into immediate sensory perception" (956). This scene is at once more abstract and more concrete than the sex scenes that preceded it.

In *The Art of Fiction* (2000), Rand stated that abstractions must be presented in concrete form in fiction (13). In this scene from *Atlas Shrugged*, Rand connects the dots for the reader, moving between Dagny's body and her mind—"it was only a sensation of physical pleasure, but it contained her worship of him, of everything that was his person and his life ..." (956).

After consummating their desire, Dagny and Galt talk for a long time about the past and about Galt's labor for Taggart Transcontinental. Once more, Rand contrasts the height of Galt's achievement (the invention of the engine) with the lowly work with which he has supported himself for the past ten years. Structurally, Dagny and Galt parallel Dominique and Roark in their stations in life: a wealthy woman opposed to a lowly laborer, and the fact that this is but an illusion. Yet, in the case of Dagny and Galt, Dagny is not fooled by Galt's position as Dominique is at first with Roark. She does not resent Galt's existence the way Dominique does. She does not try to harm Galt the way Dominique attempts to harm Roark. In formulating the epitome of virtuous sex in the persons of Dagny and Galt, Rand uses the same structural device but without the erotic hatred in *The Fountainhead*.

Conclusion

Rand's portrayals of sex in her novels prior to *Atlas Shrugged* were dramatic enough but wanting because of her association of pleasure and pain and her diving into the depths of perversion. While part of this can be attributed to Rand's own personal take on sexuality, another part can be attributed to the fact that she had not yet worked out a consistent view of the relationship between pleasure in one's sex life and pleasure in life itself. Once this discovery was made, its effects shown through in *Atlas Shrugged*, making the novel and its heroes ahead of their time.

In her depiction of the ideal man and his relationship with his ideal woman, Rand at last produced the model of sex as virtue, as response to the highest values that humans hold. For this and other reasons, *Atlas Shrugged* is Rand's greatest fiction achievement. In spite of some very antiquated notions about sex as conquest, Rand's philosophy of sex constitutes a genuine contribution to an understanding of how sex—removed from a context of sinfulness to which religion and mundane morality had condemned it—can be seen as the virtuous consequence of one's highest values.

Notes

1   In this paper I deal only with Rand's views of sexuality and not with her views on gender, although there is a connection between the two. For my thoughts on Ayn Rand and gender, see Brown (1999).

2   Ayn Rand, *Atlas Shrugged*, 368. Hank Rearden tells Dagny: "I wouldn't hold a stillborn aspiration I'd want to have it, to make it, to live it."

3   All journal entries cited in this paper refer to *Journals of Ayn Rand* (1999).

4   Some might probably object to this particular label and argue that it was the recognition of values at work here. No doubt. But the inexplicability of the basis for that recognition is what I am calling attention to. As a dramatic device, it has its uses, but in the context of developing a comprehensive view of virtuous sex, it gives the reader nothing much to work with.

5   See Ayn Rand, *The Early Ayn Rand* (1984).

6   Ironically, in *The Fountainhead*, the reader knows the admirable characteristic of Howard Roark—his love of his work, his talent, his integrity—before Dominique, who is physically attracted to Roark and seemingly for all the wrong reasons, but also based on some perception of his worth—again, without any real knowledge. But Rand does inform the reader of Roark's worth, so that they know what is coming. However, this still does not account for Dominique's prescience. In any case, Dominique's motivations are so perverse as to confuse the issue of virtuous sex.

7   Rand's claim that the rape in *The Fountainhead* was "rape with an engraved invitation" is disingenuous in the light of her published journals. In an entry that describes Howard Roark and his attitude about sex, Rand states: "It is primarily a feeling of wanting her and getting her, without great concern for the question of whether she wants it. Were it necessary, he could rape her and feel perfectly justified" (96).

References

Brown, Susan Love. 1999. Ayn Rand: The woman who would *not* be President. *Feminist Interpretations of Ayn Rand*. Edited by Mimi Reisel Gladstein and Chris Matthew Sciabarra. University Park: The Pennsylvania State University Press: 275–98.

Rand, Ayn. [1936, 1959] 1996. *We the Living*. 60th Anniversary Edition. New York: Signet.

———. [1943, 1952] 1993. *The Fountainhead*. 50th Anniversary Edition. New York: Signet.

———. [1957] 1999. *Atlas Shrugged*. New York: Plume/Penguin.

———. 1968. Of Living Death (II). *The Objectivist* 7, no. 10 (1–6) (October).

———. 1984. *The Early Ayn Rand*. New York: New American Library.

———. 1999. *Journals of Ayn Rand*. Edited by David Harriman. New York: Plume.

————. 2000. *The Art of Fiction: A Guide for Writers and Readers*. Edited by Tore Boeckmann. New York: Plume.

Stoller, Robert J. 1975. *Perversion: The Erotic Form of Hatred*. New York: Pantheon Books.

PART 7
Characterization

Chapter 28

The Price of Passivity: Hank Rearden's Mind-Body Dichotomy

Virginia Murr

Of all the heroes in Ayn Rand's *Atlas Shrugged*, Hank Rearden is the most capable innovator and producer. With amazing foresight and ingenuity, Rearden has catapulted the steel industry into the future. Even the great Francisco d'Anconia is honored to work as the lowest hireling at Rearden Steel. Rearden's business success stems from his devotion to a moral code that is based on self-interest, reason, and justice. Even though Rearden is subconsciously motivated by this producer's morality, he does not consciously recognize this value-system as a moral code. Instead, he accepts a mind-body dichotomy that reveres the mind and condemns the body as a measure of his moral worth. According to this looter's morality, moral stature is achieved through self-sacrifice, humility, and suffering. By not identifying the nature of the standards that the world judges him by, Rearden believes that he has no choice but to condemn his own standards and desires. The split between Rearden's mind and body fills his life with contradictions and internal struggles. It is not until Rearden loses virtually every value in his life that he begins to reject the morality that has turned him into a self-made victim.

Since his youth, Rearden has understood the necessity for a strict adherence to reality and the essential fact that in order to succeed in life, one must act upon rational self-interest. Never doubting "the nature of the world or man's greatness as its motive power and its core," Rearden entered the world of productivity with a deep, abiding respect for mankind (348). Rearden's success is proof of his boundless capacity to think and act. From ideas generated through his identification of reality, rational capacity, and evaluative judgment, Rearden creates previously unimaginable technologies. There is no compromise in the formula that Rearden uses to create his masterpiece, Rearden Metal. Adhering to rigid principles of right and wrong, Rearden knows that every number, every ingredient must be exact if he is to succeed. Any violation in his standards for production would be an inconceivable, fatal error. Therefore, Rearden's mills are the grand result of the achievement of his mind, and Rearden Steel is a tangible expression of his core values.

With an unforgiving dedication to productive excellence, Rearden has achieved the American Dream of becoming a self-made man. Rearden takes enormous pride in his achievements. He even makes a bracelet out of the first heat of Rearden Metal as a gift for his wife. As he examines the bracelet, Rearden remembers all of the physical and spiritual energy poured into that single piece of jewelry: "It had taken ten years to make that bracelet. Ten years, he thought, is a long time" (35). The pride that caused Rearden to produce that bracelet is bound within the spark of life that electrifies him every time he goes to his mills.

The spark of life that Rearden experiences at work is non-existent in his personal life. Even though he gives complete financial support to his mother, brother, and wife, they incessantly berate him as a selfish materialist. Rearden's brother, Phillip, refuses to earn a living, but he openly castigates Rearden for his wealth. Rearden's mother demands that he give Phillip a job, and denounces him as a monster for refusing. Even during his childhood, Rearden's mother would tell him that "he'd grow up to be the most selfish creature on God's earth" (42). According to the looter's code, Rearden's family is morally superior to him and his selfish achievements. This is particularly true for Lillian, Rearden's wife, who sarcastically condemns him as an antisocial, ascetic Puritan who knows no love except for his work. The litany of damnations periodically makes Rearden question by what standard his family condemns him. After some thought, however, Rearden allows his benevolent premise that all men love life to blind him to the possibility that anyone could be capable of conscious evil. Rearden secretly tells himself that he must be at fault for not being able to understand his family, so it would be unjust to judge them as harshly as he judges himself. Instead of condemning his family's seemingly irrational attacks on him, Rearden excuses their behavior as a twisted form of love and affection.

Attempting to atone for his inability to understand his family, Rearden accepts responsibility for providing them with happiness. Rearden persistently caters to his family's whims by sharing his wealth and time with them. Not only does Rearden listen to his family's denunciations of him, he even begins to agree with their assessments. Sanctioning the standards they hold him to, Rearden believes that "if his family called him heartless, it was true" (123). Against his better judgment, Rearden gives his brother money that ends up going to a non-profit organization set out to destroy producers like himself. Preferring to be at work, Rearden rushes home to be with Lillian for their anniversary party that ends up being a gathering of the intellectually inept social elite. Although Rearden would never have allowed these people into his mills, he gives Lillian the right to allow them into his home. Even though his personal life is continuously inexplicable even to himself, Rearden continues to withhold his judgment against everyone else.

Rearden's brand of justice is unyielding. Determined to show himself no mercy, Rearden even judges his pride in his work on the looter's premise that pride is selfish and, therefore, immoral. Knowing that humility is a moral ideal, Rearden deprives himself full expression of the pride he feels in his professional achievements. He shows no sign of indignation when Lillian tells him that the Rearden Metal bracelet he made specifically for her is no more valuable than a piece of train track. Later, while watching the first heat of Rearden Metal being poured for Taggart Transcontinental, Rearden tells Dagny that the two of them are a couple of blackguards because they "haven't any spiritual goals or qualities. All we're after is material things. That's all we care for" (87). In a simultaneous exhibit of a subconscious acceptance of the producer's morality, however, he continues to produce, he continues to feel pride, and he refuses to give up his productive standards, even for his family. The result of this paradox is Rearden's decision to trade suffering for the right to his pride.

Accepting the looter's view that the body is a hindrance to one's mind, or soul, Rearden refuses to cater to whimsical material indulgences. In Rearden's estimation, luxury items sought for pleasure are "miserably senseless" (345). Believing that man's mind is the sole value of humanity, Rearden accumulates wealth rather than spending it on items that would bring him pleasure. Even though he denies himself the pleasure of material luxuries, Rearden indulges his family's desire for parties and trinkets in an attempt to bring them a measure of happiness. Rearden wrongly assumes that the members of his family desire to be happy.

As a part of the material world, Rearden believes that sexual desire and the things of the body must be transcended if he is to partake of the higher human soul. According to Rearden, "desire was wholly physical, a desire, not of consciousness, but of matter, and he rebelled against the thought that his flesh could be free to choose and that its choice was impervious to the will of his mind" (152). He believes that indifference to his body will prevent him from being carried away by his innate physical desires. Morality, according to Rearden, includes the ability to ignore the physical desires that plague every man. Believing that he has submitted to the irrational desires of his body when he begins a sexual relationship with Dagny Taggart, and never willing to commit a wrong without paying the penalty for it, Rearden condemns himself to a shame-filled existence.

Rearden doesn't merely damn himself, however. He also condemns Dagny for her willingness to give in to her sexual desires and her obvious exuberance for their relationship. Rearden's "hatred of his own desire had made him accept the doctrine that women were pure and that a pure woman was one incapable of physical pleasure" (153). Before their physical relationship, Dagny was, to Rearden, the epitome of intelligence, action, and achievement. He had respected her, and he showed her his respect by treating her as an equal. After their first sexual encounter, however, Rearden lashes out at her in shame and disgust, telling her: "You're as vile an animal as I am" (238). The mere fact that Rearden is the vehicle by which Dagny has given in to her base desires creates even more guilt within him. Dagny may provide him with understanding, pleasure, and happiness, but all of these are immoral according to the looter's version of morality, which holds man's body as low and physical pleasure as degrading.

Rearden's guilt continues to increase every time he is forced to face his wife. To Rearden, Lillian is the goddess of physical control, completely untarnished by vulgar lust. She considers sex to be "the most undignified pastime" she has ever known (153). When Rearden would enter her room for copulation, "he would find her reading a book. She would put it aside, with a white ribbon to mark the pages. When he lay exhausted, his eyes closed, still breathing in gasps, she would turn on the light, pick up the book and continue her reading" (153). To Rearden, Lillian's disgust with sex is the result of her moral purity. Comparatively, Rearden sees himself as a beast driven by animalistic urges.

Rearden's devotion to his wife is a result of his homage to the institution of marriage, not to Lillian as an individual. From early in his youth, Rearden had built up the image of a wife as an Aristotelian whole that would complement the greatness within himself. It is this image imprinted on Rearden's mind when he thinks about his marriage. Yet, Rearden cannot even bring himself to like, let alone love, this woman who is his wife. Acknowledging that his feelings for Lillian are forced, Rearden repeatedly tells himself: "[Y]ou're guilty—no matter what [Lillian] does, it's nothing compared to your guilt" (286). As well, according to tradition, if he is to enjoy sex at all, it is supposed to be with his wife. His sexual relationship with Lillian, however, is strictly a matter of physical release for him. Instead of finding pleasure in the act, he must pay a price. He pays with his dignity.

Regardless of the pain he must endure as a result, Rearden is determined to continue his affair with Dagny; it is the most intensely pleasurable relationship he has ever known. In exchange, Rearden willingly cedes all rights to his self-esteem to Lillian, who he generously believes has pure motives toward their marriage. What Rearden can't see is that Lillian has devoted her life to destroying Rearden's spirit. Knowing her own moral inferiority, Lillian has decided to commit spiritual homicide in an attempt to take Rearden's moral superiority as her own. She almost achieves her goal by manipulating Rearden's reality and turning his virtues against him. When Lillian discovers that Rearden is having an affair, she happily assumes that her tactics are working and that Rearden has chosen some anonymous floozy as his mistress. With predatory perception, Lillian begins to feed on Rearden's weakness—his guilt. She tells her husband, "I want you to face, in your own home, the one person who despises you and has the right to do so" (399). Unbeknownst to Rearden, his moral superiority has made him easy prey.

When Lillian discovers that Rearden's affair is with Dagny instead of a lowly chorus girl, she panics and demands that Rearden end his affair. Lillian knows that Rearden's love for Dagny is the culmination of his true character, and that an affair with someone of Dagny's merit and integrity will lead Rearden to the same realization. If this happens, Lillian's game is up. Unaccustomed to Rearden's newfound self-esteem, Lillian struggles to keep him in her talons. In desperation, she says, "I own your life! It's my property. My property—by your own oath. You swore to serve my happiness. Not yours—mine!" (489). Finally glimpsing the true Lillian, Rearden begins to see that his marriage is a charade, not a sacred institution. When Rearden refuses to end the affair, Lillian realizes that she has lost her battle for Rearden's soul.

Lillian makes one more attempt to hobble Rearden by informing the people of political pull about his affair with Dagny. Rearden's guilty secret has now become a weapon against him and everything he has achieved. Thrilled finally to have some dirt on the saintly Rearden, the government immediately sends a man to him with proof of the affair as blackmail for the rights to Rearden Metal. As Lillian suspected he would, Rearden grants the government the rights to Rearden Metal in order to protect Dagny from disgrace. Having damned the best thing in his life as the most heinous, Rearden opened the door and allowed the parasites to devour his soul.

With his trial, Lillian's meltdown, and his family's impotent attempts to guilt him into forgiveness, Rearden is finally able to see the tragic waste of time he has gifted to the people who want to hurt him the most. Rearden realizes that Lillian had identified his true value from the very beginning of their relationship, but her motive was to destroy that value in order to raise herself up in her own image. The family that Rearden had supported his entire life expected him to suffer for his ability and kindness. Meting out his own brand of justice, Rearden files for divorce from Lillian and moves out of his own home, leaving his family to fend for themselves. When the government blackmails him to obtain the rights to his metal, Rearden sees that even the government recognizes his value and is willing to destroy him for its own benefit. Instead of standing by while the government pilfers his life work, Rearden decides it is time to join the strike and leave the looters without the benefit of his productive mind. Rearden's final realization is that conscious evil does exist—in the form of a morality that would punish his virtues and encourage his vices.

Rearden's essential error was not realizing that his standards, desires, and emotions were derived from his rational mind. Giving words to this realization, Rearden says, "I damned the fact that my mind and body were a unit, and that my body responded to the values of my mind" (521). As Francisco points out to Rearden, the material world is dependent upon the human spirit. Nature is one constant entity—an entity of inseparable body and mind, and its purpose is the achievement of one's happiness. Rearden could never have become wealthy without the materials he produced. These materials could never have been produced without the ideas from his rational mind and his ability to bring these ideas into reality. Therefore, the money Rearden earned is unequivocally tied to his spirit as an expression of his greatest virtues.

The same mind-body integration holds in sexual relationships. Reason generates ideas that are intended for action. Action, however, requires an assessment of reality. For example, Rearden lost his desire for Lillian when he realized that her puritan attitude was soul-deep. However, from the moment he saw Dagny working, Rearden was intensely aroused. This arousal was a reaction to not only her physical appearance, but to her intelligence, integrity, and self-confidence as well. Only when Rearden's body reacted to the values his mind perceived in Dagny was he ready to act. Therefore, Rearden's physical desire for Dagny is a direct result of his spirit. Rearden's "desire was not an answer to her body, but a celebration of himself and of his will to live" (352). Without conscious acknowledgment, Rearden's mind had been driving his sexual interests his whole life.

Having come full circle, Rearden is able to identify what his subconscious knew all along—that his professional standards and values are a moral code. Without acknowledging his subconscious devotion to the producer's morality, Rearden had unwittingly accepted the looter's morality and condemned himself to a lifetime of misery. Instead of taking pride in his achievements, enjoying the wealth he earned, and reveling in the pleasures of romantic love with a woman he respects, Rearden accepted suffering as penance for his virtues. Rearden perpetuated the looters' illusion of a world order that held their morality supreme and the producers as their slaves. Rearden respected the subjective, destructive evaluations of his destroyers, thereby making himself a "slave of their impotence" (420).

Every man must think and actively stand by the principles his reason has determined to be true. It is not enough, as Rearden discovered, to accept a moral code that one either does not believe in or has yet to understand. Rearden had not wanted to believe that men could consciously try to destroy life, but reality tells no lies. It is this epiphany that leads Rearden to the "final certainty that his life was his, to be lived with no bondage to evil, and that that bondage had never been necessary. It was the radiant serenity of knowing that he was free of fear, of pain, of guilt" (913). In the end, Rearden may have lost his company, his family, and his romance with Dagny, but after identifying the nature of his enemies and rejecting the guilt he had never deserved, Rearden has regained the most essential value that he had lost along the way—himself.

Chapter 29

Hugh Akston, the Role of Teaching, and the Lessons of *Atlas Shrugged*

Ken Schoolland and Stuart K. Hayashi

As an associate professor of economics and political science at Hawaii Pacific University, I (Ken) took special notice of the two academicians figuring most prominently in *Atlas Shrugged*. They are philosopher Hugh Akston and physicist Robert Stadler, who both taught at Patrick Henry University at the same time.

The two represent different philosophical approaches to human relations. Each perspective has found its way into the academic discourse, though one is far more popular than the other.

Akston has confidence in the human ability to reason, and so concludes that people must interact with one another accordingly. Thus he advocates free enterprise, as rational adults are competent to make their own decisions for themselves when entering into voluntary agreements.

Dr. Stadler, contrariwise, sees mankind as congenitally incapable of rational thought. He sees humans as simply "mindless animals moved by ... greedy, grasping, blind, unaccountable feelings" (Rand 1957, 1037). He resultantly infers that people "cannot be reached by rational argument" (ibid.) because the "mind is powerless against them" (ibid., 182). Thus they must be controlled through brute force, for civilians "understand nothing else" (ibid., 183). "Believe me," he insists, "there is no other way to live on earth" (ibid.).

The consequence of Stadler's paradigm is that it is he himself who gives up on using his own mind, and that his threatening force on innocent people to receive tax money to pay for his work—for which he intended to make puppets out of other human beings—is exactly what makes him the biggest puppet of all. Seeking to rule others, Stadler transforms himself into a tool and eventual slave of a government run amok.

To shield himself from acknowledging the ethical status of his misdeeds, he hides behind the excuse: "What can you do when you have to deal with people?" (ibid., 761).

Well, actually, Akston has yet another foil—Professor Simon Pritchett, who takes over as chairman of Patrick Henry University's philosophy department following Akston's retirement (ibid., 129). He summarizes his epistemology as "Reason, my dear fellow, is the most naïve of superstitions" (ibid.) and his politics as "we must control people in order to force them to be free" (ibid., 128).

Stadler denounces Pritchett as an "incredible creature" (Rand 1957, 184) and "disreputable mediocrity" (Rand 1957, 327), but it is fitting that Pritchett was an honored guest at the press conference at which Stadler unveiled the horrible Project Xylophone to the public, for, as much as Stadler tries to hide it from himself, he and Pritchett are of the same league (ibid. 761).

If Stadler did not implicitly share Pritchett's unbelief in reason, he himself would not have abandoned rationality by using the state as an apparatus to extort money from taxpayers. Stadler's acceptance of Pritchett's politics could only have resulted from a partial embrace of Pritchett's epistemology—an epistemology that divorces any link between the abstract theory that Stadler worships and the practical day-to-day concerns he refrains from thinking about.

Ultimately, Akston's premises provide the philosophic building blocks for a free society, while the assumptions of Stadler and Pritchett lay the foundation for statism.

The Gift of Prized Students

Despite their differences, both Akston and Stadler shared three particular ace pupils whom they treasured. In a way, the two professors competed for the hearts and minds of these individuals.

"Akston and I were a little jealous of each other over these three students," Stadler tells Dagny Taggart (ibid., 184). "I heard Akston saying one day that he regarded them as his sons. I resented it a little ... because I thought of them as mine ..." (ibid.).

Those three "sons" were Francisco d'Anconia, Ragnar Danneskjöld, and John Galt.

As a teacher of thirty years, I can relate to Akston's situation. I, too, have been fortunate to know some magnificent students. Each of them challenges the establishment just as Akston's triumvirate did. And much like those three pupils, my own prized students had and have "the kind of intelligence one expects to see, in the future, changing the course of the world" (ibid., 184).

These students of mine—my own personal "Galt's Gulch" of intellectual titans, if you will—include Gerhard "Geo" Olsson, Marie Gryphon, Talifaitasi "Tali" Satele, Robert Winston Posegate III, Bruce Weyhrauch, Nicki Moss, West Craske, Rick Lenning, and Misho Ognjanovich. And, of course, another person to add to that list is none other than this chapter's co-author, Stuart K. Hayashi. Together, these individuals have formed an informal organization in Honolulu called the Reason Club, of which I am the faculty adviser. It is named "reason" in honor of both the Reason Foundation and Ms. Rand herself.

Even if one or more of them becomes a "second-assistant bookkeeper somewhere" (ibid., 185), he or she will remain formidable and fascinating.

In one of his better moments, Stadler eloquently worded the way that I feel about my own great pupils: "[T]hese three were the kind of reward a teacher prays for. If ever you could wish to receive the gift of the human mind at its best, young and delivered into your hands for guidance, they were the gift" (ibid., 184).

When Hugh Akston reminisces to Dagny of the time he spent with his three "sons," I feel as if he is talking about my own experiences with the Reason Club. I first became familiar with my prized students in a manner similar to Akston's experience:

> I remember the day when I saw the three of them for the first time. ... At the end of the lecture, John got up to ask me a question. It was a question which, as a teacher, I would have been proud to hear from a student who'd taken six years of [my subject]. It was a question pertaining to Plato's metaphysics, which Plato hadn't had the sense to ask of himself. I answered—and I asked John to come to my office after the lecture. He came—all three of them came—I saw the two others in my anteroom and let them in. I talked to them for an hour—then I cancelled all my appointments and talked to them for the rest of the day. (ibid., 731)

Substitute the name "Plato" with "John Maynard Keynes" or "Noam Chomsky," and it sounds like Ayn Rand wrote that section after observing first-hand a scene straight out of my life.

The bond I formed with my best students then mirrored the one Akston had found with his own triumphant trio:

> We would sit just like this, in my back yard, on the nights of early fall. ... I had to work harder on those nights than in any classroom, answering all the questions they'd ask me, discussing the kind of issues they'd raise. ... I lost my sense of time—you see, when they were there, I always felt as if it were early morning and a long, inexhaustible day were stretching ahead before us. (ibid., 732)

Likewise, the student visionaries of my circle pelt me with their own tough questions on philosophy. Indeed, they, like Galt, strive for clarity and logical understanding of the universe they inhabit.

I also see remarkable parallels in the bravery and self-confidence displayed by Akston's three "sons" and that of my prized pupils.

When Francisco happened upon Lillian Rearden's party, where Dr. Simon Pritchett prattled on with his usual philosophy, d'Anconia mentioned having been a student of Akston's.

Disapproving of Akston, Pritchett asked Francisco derisively, "May we take it that you are an example of the practical results of his teachings?"

"I am," Francisco answered proudly (ibid., 138).

I see the same moral courage in the members of the Reason Club. There were a few occasions on which a few colleagues of mine unprofessionally "expressed" some disdain for me—naming me specifically in their classes—on account of my differing opinions with them with respect to political economy. When some of my students expressed disagreement with these professors, these students told me that the irritated professors asked them if they were in Schoolland's class. Fortunately, these students are no more intimidated by such professors' disapproval than Francisco was by Pritchett's.

Furthermore, these bright youths behave like Francisco and Ragnar, not only in their relation to their mentor, of course, but also in their relationship with the world they communicate with ... a world that, at present, seems to be more taken with Stadler's worldview than that of Akston and myself.

Real-life Robert Stadlers and Their State Institutes of Indoctrination

I identify with Akston on that count as well. Just as he had a friendly rivalry with Dr. Robert Stadler over their "three sons," I find myself in my own rivalry, not so friendly, for the hearts and minds of most of the world's college students against an academic and cultural establishment that has the same authoritarian attitude toward the human race that Dr. Stadler does.

At least Akston had only one Robert Stadler and one Simon Pritchett to compete with. I sometimes feel as if the bulk of the pedagogical mainstream is the Dr. Stadler I must face.

Sadly, I come across thousands of students who have apparently been instructed and indoctrinated by Professor Pritchetts for much of their years in school (not only in college, but from kindergarten on to the twelfth grade) as they repeat that they are not capable of rational thought, and thus cannot possess any responsibility for their actions, which means that they need some government of elitist "experts" like Stadler to dictate over them.

I see Pritchett's kind at work every day. Rand's description of the lecturers who perish in the Taggart Tunnel disaster describe a great many scholars I have met:

> The man in Roomette 2, Car No. 9, was a professor of economics who advocated the abolition of private property, explaining that intelligence plays no part in industrial production, that man's mind is conditioned by material tools, that anybody can run a factory or a railroad and it's only a matter of seizing the machinery. (ibid., 567)

> The man in Bedroom, A, Car No. 1, was a professor of sociology who taught that individual ability is of no consequence ... and that it's masses that count, not men. (ibid., 566)

Students often come to class having such ideological quackery instilled in them, so it is no surprise that they share Dr. Stadler's prejudice that human beings are congenitally bad and therefore need government to make them good.

I sometimes worry that, upon receiving their diplomas, these young individuals, "fresh out of college" (ibid., 342) will enter the world with the same mindset as Tony "the Wet Nurse" when he was first sent by the State to baby-sit Hank Rearden at his mill in the position of Deputy Director of Distribution. "The Wet Nurse," being of uncritical mind, always

> spoke in flat assertions. He would say about people, "He's old-fashioned," ... "He's unadjusted," without hesitation or explanation ... He uttered nothing but uncertain opinions about physical nature—and nothing but categorical imperatives about men. (ibid., 342–3)

That trait is pervasive throughout a significant portion of the campus population.

Naturally, Prichettian teachings have a considerable effect on students who seek intellectual professions that require the dissemination of thoughts, feelings, and ideas—not only in the academy, but in politics, clinical therapy, social work, churches, and especially the media. The products of the aforementioned instructors are students who too often become opinion leaders in the mold of writer Balph Eubank, who utters platitudes like, "Men have lost all spiritual values in their pursuit of material production and technological trickery. ... So we ought to place a limit upon their material greed" (ibid., 130).

They also turn into drones like Bertram Scudder, editor of a magazine called *The Future* (ibid., 130), which is very similar to the real-life *Mother Jones*, *The Nation*, *In These Times*, and *The Progressive*.

> "When the masses are destitute and yet there are goods available," he says, "it's idiotic to expect people to be stopped by some scrap of paper called a property deed. ... One holds property only by the courtesy of those who do not seize it. The people can seize it at any moment. If they can, why shouldn't they? ... Right is whatever's good for society." (ibid., 132–3)

The catchphrases of such professors and other intellectuals in assorted media easily seep into the psyche of popular culture.

That is why, whenever he hears someone consider the long-term consequences of irrational government regulations, bureaucrat Cuffy Meigs retorts, "In the long run, we'll all be dead!" (ibid. 783, 879). He got that from a real-life Stadlerite intellectual.

The Robert Stadlers, who for centuries have fancied themselves as being more civilized than the unwashed masses, operate under a primitive credo no more sophisticated than that which Hugh Akston accurately ascribes to Dr. Pritchett: "there is no mind and might makes right" (ibid., 735).

The Wet Nurse is much like a twenty-one-year-old in our own era, for he "had no inkling of morality; it had been bred out of him by his college …" (ibid., 342).

Indeed, when I take an informal poll in my classes, "If there were no risk involved, would you pass a law increasing the price of everyone's food in exchange for your receiving one million dollars for this?" most of the students answer yes.

When I ask them why they would be so eager to exercise government force and burden American consumers in such a manner, the reply is not unlike that of the Wet Nurse: "there are no absolute moral standards. We can't go by on rigid principles …" (ibid., 343).

Yet, as *Atlas* unfolds, even the poor, befuddled Wet Nurse comes to see through the statist myopia that academia has implanted into his brain. And this occurs because of a long line of teaching that transpires throughout the novel.

The Mentors of Mulligan Valley

As a professor, I believe that one way to judge the effectiveness of a teacher is to see whether or not his own students go on to be great teachers as well. By this I do not mean that they must necessarily stand in front of classrooms and lecture for a living. What I do mean by "great teachers" is that people learn valuable life lessons from them regardless of their occupation or what social position they play when enlightening others, whether it is as a friend, employer, or parent.

I find it a testament to Akston's greatness that his three "sons"—Galt, Francisco, and Ragnar—make for great individualist teachers themselves. Perhaps this was because of, not in spite of, the fact that none graduated with an education degree or, perhaps more importantly, a Ph.D. from a "hallowed" government school.

That they are fantastic mentors is demonstrated in how they help industrialist Hank Rearden learn what is truly going wrong in his own private life and in the world at large, and to free him from the bromides he absorbed from his teachers and family so that he can finally experience an emotional and intellectual awakening.

Taking their lessons to heart, Rearden himself turns out to be a good teacher as he gradually helps the so-called "Wet Nurse" understand how the world really works.

The insight flowing from Akston down through the intermediaries of Francisco and then Rearden, eventually ending up in the mind of the Wet Nurse, is sort of an intellectual "trickle-down" effect of wisdom.

I am proud that my own prized former students are equally good teachers.

Just as Akston informs Dagny that he learned a great new "moral philosophy … from my own pupil" (ibid., 686), I myself have my own set of students who have taught me at least as much as I have taught them, sharing with me new insights and paradigms that I scarcely could have dreamt of when I myself had entered college as a young man.

And, as Francisco did with Rearden and Rearden did with the Wet Nurse, my prized pupils have set out to educate people about the nature and importance of liberty.

One such example of a fine former student of mine, who fights for freedom while making "no concessions" (ibid., 735–6), is Marie Gryphon.

She now works as a policy analyst for the Cato Institute and does her best to educate people about free enterprise.

In the *Seattle Times*, she elucidated on the importance of letting children recognize themselves as individuals, rather than merely some unit of some ethnic collective:

> The Seattle school district should recognize that it has a precious resource in this generation: these are the first Americans with no experience of racism as a culturally sanctioned attitude. ... Seeing themselves as "post race," these teens are more likely than prior generations to date interracially, and to have friends of other races. It would be foolish to convince these kids that race is a present, pervasive source of division in their generation, and more foolish still to allow authority figures to reduce them to racial statistics when making important decisions about their lives.

In that same spirit, my Lithuanian friend Virgis Daukas assists in the effort of spreading Akstonite rationality.

Once a proud Dane overheard Virgis say that the government should stop playing "Robin Hood" (or is that really "Sheriff of Nottingham"?) and let every individual keep his or her own money. The Dane chastised Virgis, "You make such a big deal out of spending your own money. Isn't that very selfish?"

Virgis replied, "Which is more selfish—me spending my money or you taking my money by force so you can spend it?"

Virgis apparently heeded the wisdom of John Galt:

> Why is it immoral to produce value and keep it, but moral to give it away? And if it is not moral for you to keep a value, why is it moral for others to accept it? If you are selfless and virtuous when you give it, are they not selfish and vicious when they take it? (ibid., 957)

"Taken by force?" the Dane yelled at my friend Virgis. "Never!"

Virgis shot back, "So what happens to the person who refuses to pay taxes?"

D—"It wouldn't happen."

V—"Suppose someone actually refused?"

D—"Well, he would be arrested!"

V—"And what if he resisted arrest?"

D—"Then, the authorities would take him to jail."

V—"How?"

D—"Well, they would come to his house and take him."

V—"And what if he resisted?"

D—"Then the man would be charged with aggressing against the police."

V—"The police come to take him and his money, yet you call the resister an aggressor?"

"Well," continued the Dane, "he's threatening the police."

"If you come to my home and take my money," Virgis asked him, "am I the aggressor if I try to stop you?"

D—"But the police are different from you and me."

V—"So it is OK for the police to rob me?"

D—"It is society's decision, you are part of society."

When asked the above questions by Virgis and my free-market pupils, people go in circles to avoid facing the obvious truth. The person who resists too much may be killed. It's that simple. Yes, every resistance to authority is an escalating crime, with the penalty rising in physical severity until the offender stops challenging the authority of politicians. The ultimate penalty for resisting authority is death. It seldom comes to that because everyone is well aware of the final consequence and they have been carefully conditioned not to think of it.

This form of self-evasion, John Galt told Akston and everyone else, is what is destroying the world. As Galt might have said it in his three-hour radio speech: "If I don't pay my taxes, what will happen to me? Blank out."

This explains the evasive responses Hank Rearden encounters whenever he points out that laws are ultimately enforced at gunpoint. "Why speak of guns?" one of three judges replies at Rearden's trial. "This matter is not serious enough to warrant such references" (ibid., 453).

When meeting with a government-appointed panel of looters, Rearden gets a similar reaction from one of those looters—the failed-banker-turned-regulator Eugene Lawson (ibid., 907).

The process whereby people "blank out" the fact that death is the final punishment for breaking a seriously-enforced law was aptly explained by former student Stuart K. Hayashi in the March 7, 2002 edition of hawaiireporter.com: "In 1776, philosopher-economist Adam Smith described the phenomenon of 'the Invisible Hand.' ..."

However, throughout history, the government's ever-present regulations have spawned yet another sociopolitical-economic phenomenon—one whose existence very few people are willing to acknowledge and one that is inherent in all laws enforced by the state.

Stuart calls this phenomenon "the Invisible Handgun." Because people evade the fact that laws are ultimately enforced through the threat of violence, he explains, the handgun remains "invisible."

"The physical threat behind the legislation," he observes, "remains hidden under" a psychological "veil" (ibid.). That is Stuart's attempt to teach people lessons as Francisco did when explaining the virtue of money to Hank Rearden and the guests at Cherryl Taggart's wedding reception.

Another great former student is Gerhard "Geo" Olsson. Like Ragnar Danneskjöld, Geo is a bright young Scandinavian who sees the "Invisible Handgun" and battles the immorality of a thieving State.

Some years prior to this writing, he took a survey of Honolulu residents, asking them if they were aware of the enormous sums of their tax dollars being wasted on federal farm subsidies and other favor-seeking businesses—favor-seekers whom Ayn Rand called the Aristocracy of Pull (ibid., 358, 382).

Only two Honolulu residents knew about this, and it turned out that they knew of it because they had already taken my economics class. When all the others surveyed admitted no knowledge of this government program, Geo informed them of its nature. And when he did, I felt a pride in him as, I am sure, Akston did in Ragnar.

And how could I forget Talifaitasi "Tali" Satele of American Samoa? Yet another past protégé, he has become something of a celebrity, writing many pro-free-market articles for American Samoa's sole newspaper. When he first started writing, his radical proposals for freedom drew sharp antagonism from readers. But as time progressed, more and more people began to catch on, and he has gained quite a bit of respect from those who see the logic in his arguments.

I sure hope that the readers and listeners of Marie, Virgis, Stuart, Geo, and Tali find them as persuasive as Rearden did d'Anconia.

All of these apostles for liberty are to be commended for taking action. Anyone who tells you that Ayn Rand's characters are unrealistic because no one is truly so bold would be proven wrong upon meeting any of my prized students.

Is There Hope for the Future?

Of course, to fight the good fight is not the same as winning it. Sometimes I wonder if the valiant efforts of my disciples are enough to sway an ignorant and close-minded populace toward the philosophy of freedom.

When I see how many more college-goers sanction statism, I grow worried about the future for my favorite pupils, just as Hugh Akston did about his:

> I know that the only times I felt fear were occasional moments when I listened to [my students] and thought of what the world was becoming and what they would have to encounter in the future. Fear? Yes—but it was more than fear. ... I thought that the purpose of the world's trend was to destroy these children, that these three sons of mine were marked for immolation. (ibid., 733)

But Akston still saw hope for his three "sons," and that strengthens my own confidence in the rationality of my students to triumph over academia's statist slogans. My heart lifts when Akston admits that his moments of dread over the future

> were only occasional moments. It was not my constant feeling. I listened to my children and I knew that nothing would defeat them. I looked at them, as they sat in my back yard … and I thought that in the name of any greatness that had ever existed and moved this world, the greatness of which they were the last descendants, they would win (ibid.).

That is why I find it reassuring that even the Wet Nurse—the young Deputy Director of Distribution so loyal to the doctrines of the statist university he graduated from—eventually learns about the importance of freedom from Hank Rearden. It first becomes apparent when the State plans to dictate over Rearden Metal.

The theft of Rearden Metal, of course, is made to look like a voluntary donation of capital from Rearden to the State, which is why the government compels him—at gunpoint—to sign a euphemistically-named "Gift Certificate" saying that he voluntarily authorizes the seizure of his private property (even though refusing to sign it would spell a death sentence for him).

"Mr. Rearden, don't sign the Gift Certificate!" the Wet Nurse pleads. "Don't sign it, on principle."

Here, it is clear that the Wet Nurse is beginning to understand, despite what university scholars taught him, that what he previously (ibid., 343) called "rigid principles" do exist.

Near the end, he even sees the folly of his original intention to micromanage Rearden's mill on the government regulators' behalf. "I want to get out of the Deputy-Director-of-Distribution racket," he eventually tells Rearden (ibid., 867).

What does he want to do now? "I want to quit what I'm doing and go to work. I mean, real work" in the private sector where people actually produce (ibid.).

Impressed, Rearden tells the Wet Nurse, "You *have* learned a great deal in the two years you've been here" (ibid., 867) (emphasis Rand's).

I feel that his example is representative of the student population at large— many youths swallow academia's statist clichés as gullibly as the Wet Nurse did, but they can wise up, too.

After having been raised since birth to believe in the morality of statism, the Wet Nurse breaks free of dogma, gaining real insight on philosophy, economics, and ethics from Hank Rearden, himself mentored by Francisco and Ragnar, who in turn received counsel from Hugh Akston.

Thus it seems to me that this was not only a moral triumph for the Wet Nurse, but ultimately one for his teacher, who happened to be his link in a chain of wisdom-transmission going all the way back to Akston. It demonstrates that the integrity of just a few determined educators like Akston can actually overpower years of conditioning by the Stadlerite statist establishment.

Another Renaissance: The Coming Revolution of Reason

Unfortunately, soon after finding enlightenment, the Wet Nurse is murdered by the government agents who sought to plunder Rearden's mill.

As he holds the Wet Nurse's body in his arms, Rearden finds himself tormented by the realization of how much brainwashing the educational establishment inflicted upon him before he deprogrammed himself. In many ways, Rearden realizes, the boy's killers were not only the "unknown thug who had sent a bullet through the boy's body" (ibid., 922) and "the looting bureaucrats who had hired the thug to do it" (ibid., 922) but also, to a large extent,

> the boy's teachers who had delivered him, disarmed, to the thug's gun—at the soft, safe assassins of college classrooms who, incompetent to answer the queries of a quest for reason, took pleasure in crippling the young minds entrusted to their care. (ibid., 922–3)

The Wet Nurse learned the truth, but not early enough to make great use of his new knowledge. The Wet Nurse's professors robbed him of all the time he could have otherwise spent living as a rational adult.

Fortunately, Akston believes that such a time will come when the Pritchettians will no longer be able to victimize the Wet Nurses, for one day society will eventually appreciate his philosophy of reason and freedom.

When Dagny Taggart first meets him (ibid., 314) and refers to him by a label commonly applied to him (ibid., 138)—"one of the last of the advocates of reason"—Akston responds that he likes to think of himself as possibly among "the first of their return" (ibid., 314).

I like to think of myself that way—not as one of the last advocates of laissez faire, but one of the first of their return. It is the mission of myself, and a number of my top students, to create a peaceful intellectual revolution in academia and the culture altogether. We seek to educate people about the need for free markets—and the consequences of living without them.

It is Akstonite educators who can help save the Franciscos, Reardens, and Wet Nurses of this earth from its Simon Pritchetts and Robert Stadlers.

How can we Akstonite educators fight our battle for freedom? Because the United States still has not fallen so deep into statism that free speech is outlawed and only one party rules, it is not yet time to shrug. So the best course of action to take against statism is to speak up. It is vital for us to think, to talk, and to act—especially when it is easier to do nothing.

Imploring all Akstonite educators to take heart in this quest, I leave you with these words from John Galt's climactic testament:

[A]im at becoming a rallying point for all those who are starved for a voice of integrity ... The political system we will build is contained in a single moral premise: no man may obtain any values from others by resorting to physical force. ...

Such is the future you are capable of winning. It requires struggle; so does any human value. ... Do you wish to continue the battle of your present or do you wish to fight for the world? ... Check your road and the nature of your battle. The world you desired can be won, it exists, it is real, it is possible, it's yours. (ibid., 991–3)

Reference

Rand, Ayn. 1957. *Atlas Shrugged*. New York: Signet. 1985 paperback edition.

Chapter 30

When the Train Left the Station, with Two Lights on Behind
The Eddie Willers Story

Robert L. Campbell

And I followed her to the station
with a suitcase in my hand. [repeated]
Well, it's hard to tell, it's hard to tell
when all your love's in vain.
All my love's in vain

When the train, it left the station
with two lights on behind. [repeated]
Well, the blue light was my blues,
and the red light was my mind.
All my love's in vain.

Robert Johnson

No one thinks that *Atlas Shrugged* is about Eddie Willers. I doubt that anyone has come away from reading the novel wanting to be Eddie Willers. Yet much of the action in the novel is related from his point of view, and Ayn Rand clearly intended the reader to care about his fate.

Rand insisted that the goal of her fiction was to present an "ideal man." To the extent that she succeeded in making him human instead of divine, *Atlas Shrugged* is about John Galt, a genius inventor, philosophical innovator, and earth-shaking political activist, who is so highly evolved as to be impervious to pain or fear or guilt. The novel's real protagonist, Dagny Taggart, though Galt has much to teach her, is entrepreneurially resourceful, philosophically insightful, and psychologically resilient in ways that Eddie Willers is not.

A long way from being an ideal man, Eddie Willers is sharply, perhaps excessively conscious of his limitations. John Galt has dined with him countless times in Taggart Transcontinental's underground cafeteria; Galt's first convert and top lieutenant, Francisco d'Anconia, has known Eddie since childhood. Though both are thoroughly familiar with his good qualities, neither extends an invitation to join them in Galt's Gulch, where the "men of the mind" find refuge while on strike against a society and a state that seek to punish them for their virtues. Neither makes a single effort to persuade him, one on one, to join the strike. Apparently this is because Eddie Willers seems unable to imagine a successful life without the Taggart Transcontinental Railroad—or without Dagny Taggart, the executive he has also known since childhood, and reported to for years. When Dagny is about to join the strike, and Taggart Transcontinental faces complete collapse, Eddie Willers goes down with the railroad—as he somehow always expected he would.

Yet it is through Eddie Willers' eyes that we see the opening scene of the novel (1–12). And his tragic exit, as the government-controlled economy—and the engine pulling the Taggart Comet—break down beyond repair (1160–67), carries far more emotional weight than the single page of exuberant planning for the future with which the novel actually ends (1167–8). From a complex story with many characters that spans over three and a half years, Eddie Willers is rarely absent for long.

Who exactly is Eddie Willers? The kind of person he is supposed to be can be established simply and quickly. When Francisco d'Anconia visits Hank Rearden, not long before Rearden is to go on trial for a transaction that the government has made illegal, he asks who Rearden expected to benefit from his invention of Rearden Metal:

> "Did you want to see it used by men who could not equal the power of your mind, but who could equal your moral integrity—men such as Eddie Willers—who could never invent your Metal, but would do their best, work as hard as you did, live by their own effort, and—riding on your rail—give a moment's silent thanks to the man who gave him more than they could give him?"
> "Yes," said Rearden gently. (453)

And of Eddie's high level of moral integrity there is never any doubt. Asked at age ten what he would do when he grew up, Eddie answered, "whatever is right." "He had kept that statement unchallenged ever since ... he thought it self-evident that one had to what was right; he had never learned how people could want to do otherwise; he had learned only that they did" (6).

His moral commitment is in evidence throughout the story. For instance, Eddie feels guilty because Taggart Transcontinental has benefited improperly from the Equalization of Opportunity Act, allowing him to delay payment on the rails that he has ordered from Rearden Steel. He feels this way, even though the Act is the work of the company's president, James Taggart, whose only real talents lie in cutting dirty deals and lobbying the government for special favors—and both Eddie and his boss, Dagny Taggart, have firmly opposed all of James Taggart's maneuverings (225–7).

Narratively, Rand needs Eddie as a spectator, often placing him on the scene because of his unerring sense of moral indignation. More rarely, she needs him to lend his moral approval, as when he is moved by Hank Rearden's courtroom speech (481).

But Eddie Willers' capacity for moral indignation often makes him seem naïve. "Eddie's eyes were blue, wide, and questioning; he had blond hair and a square face, unremarkable except for that look of scrupulous attentiveness and open, puzzled wonder" (8). When the government of Mexico nationalizes Francisco d'Anconia's San Sebastián mines, which turn out to be completely worthless, Eddie doesn't understand how Francisco could have made such a mistake (89). Dagny already senses that it wasn't. When Eddie shows Dagny the statement from the State Science Institute, which condemns Rearden Metal through innuendo, without citing data or providing any reasons to expect adverse consequences, "The words were forced out of him by the unbelieving, bewildering imagination of a child screaming in denial at his first encounter with evil" (183–4). "Quiet, Eddie... quiet," Dagny has to tell him. "Don't be afraid" (185). Warning Dagny of a raft of new government regulations in the works, Eddie says, "you'll think I'm insane, but they're planning to kill Colorado" (297–8); he cries out, "Dagny, by what right?" (299).

Yet as the vise keeps tightening on Taggart Transcontinental, Eddie becomes adept at detecting where each new regulation came from: who paid off whom, whose logs were rolled, which faction has stuck it to which other. When Dagny returns to Taggart Transcontinental for the last time, after her sojourn in Galt's Gulch, he catches her up flawlessly on the true meaning of the Railroad Unification Plan (838) and tears James Taggart's official explanation to pieces (841–2). But what he has learned comes at a terrible cost:

> She had never imagined what the face of Eddie Willers would look like in the process of aging, but she was seeing it now—aging at thirty-five and within the span of one month. It was not a matter of texture or wrinkles, it was the same face with the same muscles, but saturated by the withering look of resignation to a pain accepted as hopeless.[1] (837)

And the confrontation with James Taggart over the Unification Plan takes a further toll: "he looked like a man worn by fighting one more of the attacks of disgust which he was learning to endure as a chronic condition" (846).

Cherryl Brooks has learned the hard way that the man she married, James Taggart, isn't the hero she took him for. She doesn't mind when her husband compares her to Eddie Willers: "She looked at him, her eyes incredulously wide. 'Then they just made [Bertram Scudder] a scapegoat, didn't they?' 'Oh, don't sit there looking like Eddie Willers! Do I? I like Eddie Willers. He's honest'" (872).

And it is Eddie who tells her, in scrupulous detail, how Dagny Taggart really runs the railroad (880). But Cherryl cannot bear up under what she has learned; she is days away from committing suicide.

A few months later, Dagny is roped into appearing with the President of the United States, Mr. Thompson, at his planned television broadcast on the national emergency: "She came to the broadcast studio with James Taggart as a policeman on one side and Eddie Willers as a bodyguard on the other. Taggart's face was resentful and tense, Eddie's—resigned, yet wondering and curious" (1005).

After Galt cuts in and gives his radio address, the reactions of Mr. Thompson and other members of the power elite leave Eddie "with a look of so great an indignation that he seemed paralyzed—as if his brain were crying, 'It's evil!' and could not move to any other thought" (1074).

Eddie's recurring tendency to freeze in the face of evil reflects a deep theme in his life: the longing for security.

One summer, when Francisco d'Anconia has just ended his summer visit to the Taggart estate (he is 15; she is 13; Eddie is 11), Dagny wonders why she and Eddie both liked Francisco so much. Eddie's answer: "He makes me feel safe." Dagny's: "He makes me expect excitement and danger" (96).

And this need remains with him. When he was seven, the old oak tree on the Taggart estate made him feel safe (5–6). When he is 32, it's Dagny's presence that reassures him. "When they entered her office, when he saw her sit down at the desk and glance at the memos he had left for her—felt as he did in his car when the motor caught on and the wheels could move forward" (24). We are told that Taggart Transcontinental was "the only thing that was the meaning of his own life" (62). He sees his fate as bound up with it: "I'm not any kind of great man. I couldn't have built that railroad. If it goes, I won't be able to bring it back. I'll have to go with it" (63). Even when Dagny is so appalled by the imposition of Directive 10-289, which chains everyone to his or her job, that she quits for the first time, Eddie is too attached to the company: "I want to follow," he whispered. I want to quit, and … I can't. I can't make myself do it" (553).

Eddie's attachment to the company and to Dagny, and his complete candor with someone he feels he can trust, make him a useful source of information. On five pivotal occasions (62–3, 217–18, 438–40, 567–71, 651–3), Eddie speaks to a track laborer named Johnny something. The worker is his frequent dining companion at the cafeteria for Taggart Transcontinental employees, located underground. Each conversation supplies John Galt with crucial information about the contractors or suppliers that Dagny Taggart is relying on, so he can disrupt her plans by persuading them to go on strike. Each conversation also supplies Galt with crucial information about Dagny herself. Only by the fourth conversation does Eddie (who is charged with keeping Dagny's location secret after she has temporarily left the company) begin to wonder, "Why do you keep questioning me about her?" (567–71).

When John Galt finally goes public, jamming President Thompson's address to the nation so he can give his own speech in its place, Eddie is one of just three people in the room who recognize the voice: "Nobody glanced at Eddie Willers, but Dagny and Dr. Stadler glanced at each other" (1009). Galt will end up addressing the other two personally, but not Eddie.

After the speech, Eddie makes this admission to Dagny:

> I used to talk to him …[…] His face … Dagny, it didn't look like any of the others, it … it showed that he understood so much … I was glad, whenever I saw him there, in the cafeteria … I just talked … I don't think I knew that he was asking questions … but he was … so many questions about the railroad … and about you. (1076–7)

Although Dagny and Eddie used to call Galt "the destroyer" (e.g., 439), and he used the information he got out of Eddie to target suppliers and scientists on whom Dagny was relying, Eddie was right to trust him. Dagny is by now in love with Galt, and though she has not yet joined the strike no longer opposes it; she doesn't hold anything that Eddie has divulged against him. Meanwhile, Galt is going to have other things on his mind, in what remains of *Atlas Shrugged*, but so far as the reader knows, he never entertains another thought of Eddie Willers, or of what is likely to become of him.

Someone else uses Eddie, too, though she does it inadvertently. His personal loyalty to Dagny Taggart, reaching all the way back into their childhood, has long had more to it than meets the eye.

At 16, Dagny begins a love affair with Francisco d'Anconia (then 18). Their decision to hide the affair gets the author's effusive commendation:

> They kept their secret from the knowledge of others, not as a shameful guilt, but as a thing that was immaculately theirs, beyond anyone's right of debate or appraisal. She knew the general doctrine on sex, held by people in one form or another, the doctrine that sex was an ugly weakness of man's lower nature, to be condoned regretfully. She experienced an emotion of chastity that made her shrink, not from the desires of her body, but from any contact with the minds that held this doctrine. (109)

Rand is famous for insisting that everyone should judge and prepare to be judged. So it is odd to find her encouraging anyone not in danger of physical violence or grossly disproportionate punishment to seek an exemption from other people's appraisal. There is nothing to suggest that Eddie Willers subscribes to any moral condemnation of sex, or shares the unsanitary sense of life against which Dagny and Francisco are rebelling. But by hiding her love affair, even from a close and loyal friend like Eddie Willers, Dagny feeds his illusion that she is married to her job and involved with no one. It is easier to understand why, later on, Dagny conceals her affair with Hank Rearden, who is married and has internal conflicts about sex, but the results are the same.

In the chapter titled "The Face without Pain or Fear or Guilt" (633–53), a series of white-knuckled confrontations unfolds among the rivals for Dagny Taggart's love. She has loved Francisco d'Anconia; she loves Hank Rearden (though he is about to lose her); she will love John Galt. Francisco and Hank narrowly avoid a physical fight; Eddie learns about Hank when Dagny, about to leave on an urgent trip after the Winston Tunnel disaster, summons him to her apartment; John, in turn, learns about Hank from Eddie.

Of the four men who love Dagny, only Eddie is completely out of the running. Called to her apartment to make last-minute preparations for her absence, he feels an imperative not to remind her of failures or disasters; he even tries to cheer her up. "He wondered what was the matter with him: he thought it inexcusable that he should find his discipline slipping just because this was a room, not an office ... He did not permit himself to look at her again" (649).

But there is more:

> He knew what was wrong with him, he thought; he did not want her to leave, he did not want to lose her again, after so brief a moment of reunion. But to indulge any personal loneliness, at a time when he knew how desperately the railroad needed her in Colorado, was an act of disloyalty he had never committed before—and he felt a vague, desolate sense of guilt. (650)

Of course, this is not disloyalty to the railroad.

Then Eddie glances up and sees Hank Rearden's monogrammed dressing gown hanging on the back of an open closet door. "He felt a sense of embarrassment magnified to the point of physical torture; it was the dread of violating her privacy twice: by learning her secret and revealing his own" (650). Eddie has to lie ("for the first time in his life") so Dagny won't know why he is upset.

There is no escaping the awkwardness of the moment. But what makes Eddie's burden unbearable is his conviction that he has no right to tell Dagny how he feels about her.

When Eddie escorts Dagny to the waiting train, Rand's language is harder-boiled than Robert Johnson's, but the meaning is the same:

> When she was ready, he carried her suitcase to a taxicab, then down the platform of the Taggart Terminal to her office car, the last at the end of the Comet. He stood on the platform, saw the train jerk forward and watched the red markers on the back of her car slipping slowly away from him into the long darkness of the exit tunnel. When they were gone, he felt what one feels at the loss of a dream one had not known till it was lost. (651)

After he sees her off, that anonymous track worker is waiting for him in the cafeteria. And what Eddie couldn't admit to Dagny, he blurts out to John Galt.

> I grew up with her. I thought I knew her. [...] I don't know what it was that I expected. I suppose I just thought she had no private life of any kind. To me, she was not a person and not ... not a woman. She was the railroad. And I didn't think that anyone

would have the audacity to look at her in any other way. ... Well, it serves me right. [...] If the railroad was all she meant to me, it wouldn't have hit me like this. I wouldn't have felt that I wanted to kill him! (653)

While Dagny returns to Taggart Transcontinental for the last time, after her sojourn in Galt's Gulch, "Her office was like a historical reconstruction, restored and maintained by Eddie Willers" (838). Though Eddie had good reasons to banish the "socially conscious" magazines that a flunky of James Taggart had put on display, and equally good reasons to restore the portrait of "robber baron" Nat Taggart, there is another level of meaning, as almost always in *Atlas Shrugged*. Eddie is restoring and maintaining a shrine.

Still Dagny cannot know, consciously, of Eddie's love for her until he haltingly confesses it to her, just before leaving on a dangerous mission that they both know may be his last (1116). Otherwise, she might have thought she needed to do something about it.

Unrequited love had hit hard in Ayn Rand's own life. The first man she loved had not returned her feelings; his impact on her was so great that he became the model for Leo Kovalensky in her first novel, *We the Living* (Branden 1986). Written a decade before *We the Living*, Rand's first surviving short story, "The Husband I Bought," dwells in excruciating fashion on a woman's unrequited love for a man and her determination to never let him see what her love for him had cost her. And the story is filled with lonesome train imagery. Even Dagny's longing for the ideal man she has never met, and who seems beyond reach, out where the railroad tracks come together, is described without irony as "unrequited love" (634).

It is his hopeless love for Dagny that surrounds Eddie with such an aura of doom. Despite his apprehension and his premonitions, he never does anything to put his survival in jeopardy till he makes the risky trip to San Francisco, where the Taggart station has shut down amid civil unrest, to reopen the line and try to restore Taggart Comet service. Yet the novel's opening scene is a panorama of subtle decay and slowly spreading discouragement. Eddie tries to remember the saying, "Your days are numbered" (4, 12). He uneasily recalls the stout old oak tree on the Taggart estate that turned out to be hollow when lightning took it down (5–6).

After finally discovering Dagny's involvement with Hank Rearden, he confesses, "A year ago, I wouldn't have damned her for finding something she wanted. But they're doomed, both of them, and so am I, and so is everybody, and *she was all I had left*" (653, my italics).

His goodbye message to Dagny is, "wherever you go, you'll always be able to build a railroad. I couldn't. I don't even want to make a new start" (1116). Is that why he is taking a high-risk trip on behalf of an enterprise that, as he and Dagny are both in the best position to know, is already past saving?

When the locomotive of the eastbound Taggart Comet breaks down in the middle of an Arizona desert, and there is no one left to call for help, Eddie refuses to join the crew and the rest of the passengers, who are leaving with a train of covered wagons. He can't repair the locomotive (neither could Dagny Taggart; one wonders whether John Galt could have done the job, with the materials at hand). Still, he insists on staying with it. "He felt like the captain of an ocean liner in distress, who preferred to go down with the ship than be saved by a canoe of savages taunting him with the superiority of their craft" (1166). Crying "Don't let it go!" out loud, and addressing one plea to Dagny after another inside his mind, he throws his life away.

Kirsti Minsaas has argued that Eddie Willers is a "tragic character used in the service of social critique ... Eddie is a man who chooses his fate, first by loyally trying to save Taggart Transcontinental, and then, when he fails, by opting for certain destruction rather than survival in a society where he no longer belongs ..." (2000, 188).

But Eddie is not facing generations of secret police and concentration camps, or years of immiseration and warlordism. He throws his life away just as the looters' state is undergoing its final collapse. He throws it away when merely staying alive for a few more weeks or months would afford him the opportunity to escape to the better world that John Galt and the other "men of the mind" are setting out to build. A man of "limited vision and limited stature" doesn't deliberately make himself one of the last victims of dying collectivist regime. Unless ... he can't get over knowing that Dagny will never be his. At the end of "The Husband I Bought," the narrator fully expects to die soon, even though she is only in middle age, and nothing is wrong with her health. Eddie's final scene begins when the locomotive "stopped abruptly, for no visible reason, like a man who had not permitted himself to know that he was bearing too much" (1160).

If Eddie Willers is even slightly typical of those who have high moral integrity, but limited vision and limited stature, what are the implications?

First, he is a hereditary employee of Taggart Transcontinental; his father and grandfather worked for Dagny's father and grandfather (5). "It's touching—your devotion to Taggart Transcontinental," James Taggart cracks. "If you don't look out, you'll turn into one of those real feudal serfs" (10–11). He is told that he needs a hobby (12); nowadays the admonition would be to get a life. His apartment is an "empty cube of space" (651). In all, Eddie Willers is a company man, of a sort that has rarely been seen:

> Whenever he entered the Taggart Building, he felt relief and a sense of security. This was a place of competence and power. ... Taggart Transcontinental, thought Eddie Willers, From Ocean to Ocean—the proud slogan of his childhood, more shining and holy than any commandment of the Bible. From Ocean to Ocean, forever—thought Eddie Willers, in the manner of a rededication, as he walked the spotless halls into the heart of the building ... (6)

Nor does he have any life apart from the revered leader who embodies the organization. When he was 10 years old, "in a clearing of the woods, the one precious companion of his childhood told him what they would do when they grew up." (6) Dagny told him she was going to run the railroad (51).

Second, for a man who comes across as immature and dependent, Eddie Willers is able to accomplish an awful lot. He is Dagny's obvious choice to succeed her when she has to leave Taggart Transcontinental to found and operate the upstart John Galt Line, which will run trains to Colorado on new rails made of Rearden Metal. "He knows his work and mine. He knows what I want" (195). Would knowing what she wants, waiting for each detailed phone call so he could be Dagny Taggart by proxy, always be enough? During his stint as Vice President, were his options really just to be "a stooge for her—and that would be an honor"— or "a stooge for Jim Taggart" (218)? Could Eddie have successfully carried out all of the assignments that Dagny gave him without doing a significant amount of independent thinking?[2]

All of this matters because very few of those who read and admire *Atlas Shrugged* resemble John Galt or Francisco d'Anconia or Dagny Taggart. Their future accomplishments are unlikely to include revolutionizing physics or inventing a new financial instrument or climbing some other pinnacle of cultural creativity. Their virtues, advanced or outstanding though they might be, will almost certainly not include complete openness to joy, accompanied by complete imperviousness to pain, fear, or guilt. They will never become gods in human form—as, by a sober accounting, the heroes of *Atlas Shrugged* have.[3]

By contrast, many of those who read the novel could be like Eddie Willers, giving silent thanks, from time to time, to the inventors of the paper bag and the washing machine and the cell phone and the piano, not to mention the developers of formal logic. If readers don't want to be like him, it can't be because he has the greatest moral integrity without the greatest genius or entrepreneurial spirit. It must be because of some other baggage he's carrying.

One might take Eddie's status as a hereditary company man and his hopeless love for Dagny as mythic—for much of *Atlas Shrugged* consciously aims at being mythic. In which case, he would not constitute a reliable guide to the character and prospects of a moral man who does not stand at the pinnacle of human potential. But Ayn Rand intended her characters to be prototypical of whole categories of human beings. And precisely because he wasn't at or near the pinnacle, Eddie Willers wasn't nearly good enough, as far as she was concerned. In her journal entries for 4 July 1968, a mini-treatise on her deteriorating affair with Nathaniel Branden, she had this to say about her rival, Patrecia Wynand:

Originally, he said that [Patrecia] represented his "Eddie Willers," i.e., an average person who had good premises although she was not all philosophical or intellectual. Then, he said this estimate of her had changed: that she was an unusual person who, in some way, reminded him of himself in his childhood ... (Quoted in Valliant 2005, 326, with Valliant's comments removed.)

From Rand's point of view, this meant that Patrecia was beneath him, no more deserving of his love than Eddie was of Dagny's. Because she thought of herself and Nathaniel Branden as Objectivist heroes (on the level of Howard Roark or John Galt), he would have to be throwing himself away on a woman who was merely at the level of Eddie Willers.[4]

Indeed, one has to wonder whether Ayn Rand expected her followers to be like Eddie Willers. Suppose there is a tiny band of Objectivist heroes, there are a lot of people like Eddie Willers—and there are no significant human possibilities in between. Does it follow that a person with "good premises" who has not achieved true greatness needs to be attached to an organization, whose leader has attained true greatness? Will the average good person even be drawn to love a truly great one, with no expectation of being loved in return? Confusions between the mythic and the real can have real consequences.

Notes

1   The injustice of the political system and the accelerating breakdown of the railroad are not the only sources of Eddie's pain. See below.

2   On this point, I agree with Nathaniel Branden (1998), who not only finds Eddie immature and dependent, but questions whether someone with his mindset could have been an effective "right-hand man" for a railroad's Vice President for Operations.

3   "However much [Rand] argued that she wanted to project a rational moral ideal, an ideal held strictly within the bounds of the achievable, it is doubtful whether this is, in fact, what she gave us. In her portraits of both Howard Roark and John Galt, she moves, in my view, beyond the world of rational heroics and into a world where the hero has become a god, engaging in risks without true danger and facing an evil impotent to harm him" (Minsaas 2000, 196). Minsaas notes that Rand's heroes practice a sort of halfway Stoicism, transcending their anger and fear and hatred, but not their joy. Eddie himself tries but fails to attain this halfway transcendence. I share Minsaas' doubts as to whether real human beings can practice halfway Stoicism. If Nussbaum (1994) is right, anger and pain and fear cannot be overcome without overcoming passionate love as well.

4   There was, of course, more going on here. Nathaniel had been concealing his affair with Patrecia for over 4 years, and Rand apparently still half-believed that Patrecia was in love with Nathaniel, but not vice versa. Her evaluation of Patrecia grew much more negative when she more fully appreciated the threat that the younger woman posed (Valliant, 2005).

References

Branden, Barbara. 1986. *The Passion of Ayn Rand: A Biography*. Garden City, New York: Doubleday.

Branden, Nathaniel. 1998. Questions and answers: 7 June 1998. Online at: http://www.nathanielbranden.com/catalog/articles_essays/QA-98june7.html.

Johnson, Robert. 1990. Love in vain. *Robert Johnson: The Complete Recordings*. Columbia Legacy C2K 46222 [CD]. (Originally recorded in 1937.)

Minsaas, Kirsti. 2000. The role of tragedy in Ayn Rand's fiction. *Journal of Ayn Rand Studies* 1(2), (Spring): 171–209.

Nussbaum, Martha C. 1994. *The Therapy of Desire: Theory and Practice in Hellenistic Ethics*. Princeton, New Jersey: Princeton University Press.

Rand, Ayn. 1957. *Atlas Shrugged*. New York: Random House. (Hard cover edition.)

———. 1984. The husband I bought. *The Early Ayn Rand: A Selection from Her Unpublished Fiction* (6-31). Edited by Leonard Peikoff. New York: New American Library. (Story written in 1926).

Valliant, James S. 2005. *The Passion of Ayn Rand's Critics: The Case Against the Brandens*. Dallas, Texas: Durban House.

Chapter 31

In the Beginning was the Thought:
The Story of the Wet Nurse

Jomana Krupinski

Tis writ, "In the beginning was the Word."
I pause, to wonder what is here inferred.
The Word I cannot set supremely high:
A new translation I will try.
I read, if by the spirit, I am taught.
This sense, In the beginning was the Thought.

Goethe, Faust

As Goethe so eloquently points out, the beginning of any creation is the thought of that creation. Thus, the act of thinking is the most productive and lucrative human deed. But what would happen if the world's greatest thinkers withheld, by force, necessity, or simply by their own choice, all of their greatest achievements and potential creations from the rest of the world? What if these thinkers refused to think, and doers refused to do? Ayn Rand's apocalyptic novel, *Atlas Shrugged*, addresses the terrifying reality of a world whose lawmakers become infected with the ideas that capitalism means greed and that philanthropy is the highest moral commandment. However, those successful businessmen and women who disagree with this current social thought struggle against officials who inundate them with mandate after mandate intended to destroy capitalistic culture.

The legendary John Galt is the leader of the rebellious defenders of capitalism, and he outwardly rebukes those who are not intelligent enough to notice that by following the philanthropic premises that the new lawmakers proclaim, they are destroying the world. If they would just stop to think rationally, something he does not believe they are capable of, they would see their own fallacies in their logic. Having the intelligent ability to reason and analyze is what he holds as his highest value, and Galt states that " ... man's only moral commandment is: Thou shalt think" (1018). He vehemently, and rightfully, believes that "Thinking is man's only basic virtue, from which all others proceed" (1017).

Because the lawmakers of Galt's society have proclaimed self-sacrifice as the ultimate moral premise, people faithfully follow, for fear of appearing selfish. Image and reputation are extremely important, and no one would dare be so uncivilized as to put greed over the needs of others. However, the irony lies in the fact that the actions they take to appear self-sacrificial are the most selfish deeds they can perform. If they were truly concerned about the good of humanity, they would admit that they understand that to celebrate the capitalist culture of America is morally right, and they would then extinguish their proclamations that greed is selfish. This "greed" is what feeds the country, supports the economy, and allows for everyone's way of life. However, the complexities of this style of thinking are understood only by a select few, and the rest obediently and unquestionably comply with the "expert" officials who make the laws.

Nonetheless, many people of Galt's society seem to struggle between what their rational minds tell them (albeit so subconsciously that they barely understand why) and what they are told to believe. In Garet Garett's book, *The Driver*, he states that "Naïve trust in the power of words to command reality is found in all mass delusions" (89). He makes this assertion after describing an instance when American government mandated that gold and silver are equal. Not one person spoke up about the mere fact that the amount of precious metal in a silver dollar was in reality worth only half as much as that in a gold dollar. Facts or no facts, the word of the government was law. However, people instinctively knew the truth of the situation, and the result was that they horded the more valuable gold while trading in their silver coins for gold ones, nearly wrecking the financial system.

This same kind of event is taking place in Galt's world. The unintelligent officials of the government hold a similar power over society, and the ensuing mass delusion is a testament to humanity's complacency in simply accepting law without question, despite the fact that every synapse of their subconscious minds is firing out a warning against the illogical. Unfortunately, there are only a few in Galt's society who recognize this and are willing to speak out against what is irrational, no matter what authority is involved. One of these people, a man named Tony—nicknamed the "Wet Nurse"—is symbolic of this struggle between his inherent, moral sense of what is right versus what is wrong.

The Guiltless Man

The boy known as the Wet Nurse is probably the most dynamic of all the characters. In his beginning role as Hank Rearden's Deputy Director of Distribution, he is the epitome of the Washington boys' "yes-man." Recently graduated, he spouts the irrational ideals of those professors and officials who claim that "… there are no absolute standards. We can't go by rigid principles, we've got to be flexible, we've got to adjust to the reality of the day and act on the expediency of the moment" (363). However, he is a bit too green to realize that it is precisely this inconsistency, along with the lack of logical premises that lead to logical conclusions that will eventually ruin the world.

The Wet Nurse does not make a good first impression on Hank Rearden. Rearden sees him as a boy with "no inkling of any concept of morality; it had been bred out of him by his college; this had left him an odd frankness, naïve and cynical at once, like the innocence of a savage" (362). In fact, this lack of morality is evident when the Wet Nurse offers to "make arrangements" with his friends in Washington to hand out more Metal to anyone Rearden chooses. Although the boy seems to admire Rearden, he doesn't know the man well enough to realize that his eagerness to please him will not be effective by using the tactics of the men in Washington, which unfortunately, is the only thing he knows.

Eventually, however, one begins to see the Wet Nurse evolving and thinking, using his rational mind to break free of his formal "training." After Rearden's trial, the boy is impressed. The fact that he admires and supports Rearden is surprising, given his previous display of loyalty to his education and the men in Washington. Nonetheless, the boy openly begins to wonder about Rearden's way of thought. He asks: "Mr. Rearden, what's a moral premise?" Rearden answers, "What you're going to have a lot of trouble with." Ignoring the wisecrack, the boy laughs and says "What a beating you gave them, Mr. Rearden!" And Rearden tells him that the thing that makes him so sure that it was they who took a beating, and not himself, was called a moral premise. This is the beginning of the shift in the boy's loyalties.

When conditions begin to worsen for Rearden, the Wet Nurse, who originally wanted to make deals for him with the Washington men, offers to undermine their authority by faking the books to help Rearden Metal stay afloat. This betrayal takes Rearden off guard and he asks why the boy would do such a thing. The Wet Nurse answers, "Because I want, for once, to do something moral" (555).

This is the turning point for the boy: this is where he steps out of his static, obedient following and becomes a dynamic free-thinker. Rearden recognizes this breakthrough, "realizing through how many twists of intellectual corruption upon corruption this boy had to struggle toward his momentous discovery" (555). Concerning the signing of the Gift Certificate, the boy adamantly pleads with Rearden not to sign it. Rearden spurs him on: "I won't sign it. But there aren't any principles." The boy recites what his teachers had taught him: "I know there aren't. I know that everything is relative and that nobody can know anything and that reason is an illusion and that there isn't any reality. Morals or no morals, principles or no principles, just don't sign it—because it isn't right!" (555).

Without even realizing why he is right, the boy recognizes that something in his subconscious mind is urging him toward what is moral, teaching him to dispel what is illogical and irrational. He is symbolic of many members of his society, who realize that something about their lives is not quite right, pleading silently with their eyes for help to anyone who is intelligent enough to figure out what they are incapable of consciously knowing. But the point is that they do know in a very primitive, survival-driven part of their brains. They simply can't wrap their minds around it, much less articulate it in a way that illuminates its fallacies.

Moving closer and closer toward enlightenment, the Wet Nurse begins to embody the thing that the unintelligent minds fear most: a man who "knows the real issue ... knows the things which must not be said—and he is not afraid to say them. He knows the one dangerous, fatally dangerous weapon. He is our deadliest adversary" (548). This description given by Dr. Ferris describes only one kind of person: "the guiltless man." He continues with a final, foreshadowing point: "... save us from the man who lives up to his own standards. Save us from the man of clean conscience. He's the man who will beat us" (548).

The Martyr

In his final act of loyalty, the Wet Nurse blatantly refuses to aid in the governmental staging of a revolt to give the appearance of infuriated employees rioting against Hank Rearden. Instead, he runs out of the office to spill the story to the police, the newspapers, or anyone he can find, hoping to release word that the riot is staged. But as the boy attempts to escape the uprising, he is shot and left for dead. However, he struggles to stay alive just so he can be sure that Rearden will get his message. And when Rearden finds him, the boy learns an important lesson, even as his death draws nearer. He asks, 'Mr. Rearden, is this how it feels to ... want something very much ... very desperately much ... and to make it?' Rearden confirms his feeling, and later, when Rearden calls the boy by his real name, the boy smiles and says "Not Non-Absolute anymore?" Rearden replies, "No, not any more. You're a full absolute now, and you know it" (992). This is the final affirmation that the boy has made a dynamic transformation from Washington 'yes-man' to the owner of a free-thinking, rational mind.

The Wet Nurse's death scene is one of mixed emotions, multiple meanings, and utmost significance. It is, at the same time, a touching tribute to the Wet Nurse's compassion for and loyalty to Rearden, as well as a deeply saddening and even angering moment of needless loss—the death of an innocent boy in a battle not his own. As the boy lay dying, he grapples with the greatest questions of his time, at last finding the answers in Rearden's arms, a moment filled with a father-and-son-like quality. In an act of heroic nobility, the boy says to Rearden, "How long was I to keep from sticking my neck out? Till they broke yours? And what would I do with my neck, if that's how I had to keep it?" (990).

Sadly, in his death, the boy finally understands and has the courage to say aloud what his subconscious has always been telling him: "... it's crap, all those things they taught us ... all of it, everything they said ... about living or ... dying ... But they said there are no values ... only social customs ... No values!" (991–2). Bringing his hand to his chest, and opening his eyes slightly wider, he whispers to Rearden, "I'd like to live, Mr. Rearden. God, how I'd like to!" (992). And as he dies, he looks at Rearden's face, " … he looked at that which he had not known he had been seeking through the brief span of his life, seeking as the image of that which he had not known to be his values" (994). The legacy of the Wet Nurse is ultimately his effect on Hank Rearden. Rearden's anger at the boy's death, his love for the boy's loyalty, and his admiration for the boy's heroic actions will release a cascade of emotions that pervade decisions made from that moment on.

In a way, the death of the Wet Nurse symbolizes the destruction of an old school of rational thought, having seemingly been bred out of the zombie-like citizens of Dagny Taggart's world; however, it also (paradoxically) symbolizes the birth of a new era led by a different sort of thinkers. After Galt's speech to the world, many people return to their logic and reason for survival, but they are too little too late—the irrational looters have reached a pinnacle beyond which the inertia of their actions cannot be stopped. Just as the Wet Nurse realizes the truth of his transformation in his final moments, so do those who realize that their world is being destroyed before their eyes. Despite how much they frantically attempt to grasp for the rational "fix" to their mistakes, the damage done by the looters is irreversible. Although the Wet Nurse and others have opened up their rational capacities once more, they are met only with destruction. However, this very same destruction will remove the illogical thinkers and unintelligent lawmakers from their roles as leaders, causing new leaders to step up and begin to rebuild under a different and intelligent regime.

Hence, the Wet Nurse, who begins as an inexperienced boy without an original thought, eventually gives his life for an idea that he rightfully earns, through years of struggling with the inconsistencies of his education and grappling with his subconscious intelligence. This idea, born of reason and logic, allows him to be true to himself and loyal to his employer, Hank Rearden. But the ingredients that turn this naïve boy into a seasoned man of reason are acquired only through "judgment to distinguish right and wrong, vision to see the truth, courage to act upon it, dedication to that which is good, [and] integrity to stand by the good at any price" (177). The inexperienced boy who was once known as the Wet Nurse, died as Tony, the man of reason—a martyr to Rearden, Galt, and all who recognize that the ruling values of life are reason, purpose, and self-esteem, and that all great achievements simply begin with an intelligent thought.

Chapter 32

The Destruction from the Nihilism Train: The Cherryl Brooks Story

Jennifer J. Rhodes

> Then the headlight she had felt rushing upon her, hit its goal—and she screamed
> in the bright explosion of the impact—she screamed in physical horror, backing
> away from him. (839)

In Ayn Rand's *Atlas Shrugged*, individuals like Dagny Taggart, Hank Rearden, Francisco d'Anconia, and John Galt are heroes because they stand up against those who want to live by the rules of an altruist-collectivist society. These heroes are triumphant because of their productivity, achievement, and virtues. They have great minds and intellect. These champions get ahead in a capitalist society through their hard work and productiveness, compared to the altruist looters who "get ahead" in business only through their political connections.

Cherryl Brooks is Rand's hero-worshipper. Working in a dime store, Cherryl escaped the slums of her hometown where she was told that it was her duty to be productive and support her lazy family. She believed that if she did not get away, she would "rot all the way through, like the rest of them" (249). She sought the idea of New York City as her way to succeed in the American Dream. While working in the dime store on the day of the first successful run of the John Galt Line, she meets James Taggart. Cherryl mistakenly believes that it's James who deserves the compliments for the John Galt Line victory. She admires that the papers say that he did not want to take credit for his accomplishment; James does not correct her, and she mistakenly believes that he is a hero.

When asked by Jim if she is indeed a hero worshipper, she rhetorically asks him if there is anyone else to look up to (248). She has a high regard for achievement and those individuals who reach it. Unfortunately she does not realize that Jim is not a virtuous hero. Jim makes several comments that support his beliefs in Kant's phenomenal world and the social primacy of consciousness. This runs counter to the Objectivist beliefs that Cherryl possesses. Cherryl believes that she is subordinate to Jim the Hero, and that these seemingly contradictory remarks only show that she will have to learn about true heroism.

For example, Jim elucidates that unhappiness is a virtue that makes a man great (253). This is a prime statement of altruism, the code of the looters and moochers. Cherryl believes that she misunderstood, considers the statement, and happily replies:

> It's great of you, Mr. Taggart, to think that your own achievement isn't good enough for you. I guess no matter how far you've gone, you want to go still farther. You're ambitious. That's what I admire most: ambition. I mean, doing things, not stopping and giving up, but doing. I understand, Mr. Taggart … even if I don't understand all the big thoughts. (253)

James realizes that Cherryl sees him as a hero, and he laughs, thinking how it's a joke on her (254). James takes interest in Cherryl because she is a hero-worshipper, although he does not want to explore himself to understand the deeper meaning of his attention.

Jim takes Cherryl to several social events, introducing her as his date that works at the dime store. She believes that Jim is a wonderful person because he doesn't hold her modest status "against her". Jim believes that businessmen should have a sense of social responsibility; unfortunately, Cherryl fails to realize that she is a form of this to him (367). After coming home one night, he proposes to her. Cherryl realizes that there is no romanticism in his request, especially since the setting is outside her poor apartment complex in her filthy neighborhood.

Before her wedding, a sob sister warns her, "… There are people who'll try to hurt you through the good they see in you—knowing that it's the good, needing it and punishing you for it. Don't let it break you when you discover that" (370). Cherryl had no idea that any individual would be so ignoble to do such a thing, let alone that this person would be her future husband. James Taggart is Rand's nihilist, a person who seeks the destruction of the good, including good people like Cherryl Brooks. Even though he refuses to realize this for himself, this is the ultimate reason for his evil, political ways and for marrying her. In fact, this is the reason why he hates and privately wants to annihilate heroes like Rearden, Francisco, and his productive sister; because he cannot kill the heroes, he seeks to destroy the hero worshipper. James voices his hatred of Dagny to Cherryl, and because she believes that Dagny stands for everything that Cherryl despises in the world, Cherryl confronts her. She vows to protect Jim, the hero, against Dagny and those who have made his life so miserable; unfortunately Cherryl does not realize that Jim is miserable because he is a nihilist.

However, within a year of their wedding, it's Cherryl who becomes miserable. Cherryl tries harder and harder to try to understand her husband, but as she gets more knowledge, the enigma becomes bigger. He hates her inquiring and watchful ways of how she looks at him. She fails to understand his cowardly ways. When Cherryl starts to realize that Jim might not be genuine in his business practices and that he is receiving nothing for this, she starts feeling confused and trapped (813).

When she could not envision what his motive might be, "she felt only that the headlight moving upon her had grown larger" (813).

She turns to the ethical Eddie Willers for the truth about Jim because she knew that Eddie had been Jim's childhood friend. The moral "common man" told her strictly the truth without any opinion and emotion. She learned that her suspicions were indeed true; Jim did not run the Taggart Transcontinental Railroad, and the John Galt Line was the result of his sister, Dagny, whom she had believed to be her enemy.

When she confronts Jim, he verbally degrades her. He claims that he married her because he loved her, but something still irks Cherryl. She has lost the awe she had once for Jim and has become a doting, lifeless wife. Now she just pities him and privately decides to continue to try to understand him in an attempt "to learn to understand the things that had destroyed her" (819).

When Cherryl asks him what he wants from her, she learns that he desires to be loved by her but not on her terms. He calls her a gold-digger of the spirit: "You didn't marry me for my cash—but you married me for my ability or courage or whatever value it was that you set as the price of your love!" (821)

She cannot believe that he expects to be loved, a love that is causeless and unearned. She's appalled that he believes in altruism:

> You want handouts, but of a different kind. I'm a gold digger of the spirit, you said, because I look for value. Then you, the welfare preachers ... it's the spirit that you want to loot ... You want unearned love. You want unearned admiration. You want unearned greatness. ... Without the necessary of being anything. Without ... the necessity ... of being. (821)

She feels the desire to leave. Now the world seems a little bleaker and she runs to the true hero, Dagny. Cherryl apologizes to Dagny about her error, and her erroneous confrontation at the wedding. Cherryl finds out that Dagny has the same Objectivist beliefs and values as she does. Because of this, they have a true bond as in sisterhood; however, it is not through the sanctity of marriage because Cherryl believes that her marriage to Jim is now immoral (824). Dagny gives some refreshing perspective and advice that Cherryl had expected from James when she first met him and expected him to be a true hero. For instance, Dagny tells her that she can live in the world by remembering that she places nothing above the verdict of her mind. The most important advice that Dagny gave was "the knowledge that my life is the highest of values, too high to give up without a fight" (827, emphasis mine).

When she returned to her home, Cherryl finds Jim and Lillian Rearden together. What strength she had gained from talking to Dagny, she had then lost. She could not find any explanation. "She had always thought that evil was purposeful, as a means to some end; what she was seeing now was evil for evil's sake" (836).

Cherryl again confronts Jim and it's a vicious fight. She again asks him why he had wanted to marry her in the first place. She is horrified that he wanted their love to be alms. She finally reaches the conclusion when she realizes that he married her because she was trying to become a better person (839). It's then that the train hits Cherryl hard; she learns that Jim is a nihilist. He wanted to destroy her because she was good, a hero-worshipper. In truth, Jim cannot kill the hero, so he seeks to obliterate the hero-worshipper.

She runs away, trying to escape. It's the words of a social worker that drive her too far. "… if you stopped living for your own enjoyment, stopped thinking of yourself and found some higher …" (843). This statement is the exact opposite of Dagny's advice about the highest value which is one's life. Cherryl commits suicide, "with full consciousness of acting in self-preservation" (843) because she cannot think about living in that kind of world.

Clearly, in all rationality, Cherryl should have realized that Jim is not the hero that she once worshipped. After she talked with Eddie, she knew that it was truly Dagny who was in charge of the railroad and was the productive achiever of the family. She had found her hero, and she knew that there were others out there, like Hank Rearden, who had earned his profits from his metal.

Finding out that there are nihilists out there should not drive anyone to destroy his or her life. Because Cherryl should still see that Dagny was an achiever and a hero is enough to say that Jim did not destroy her completely. Cherryl's values and virtues and beliefs in ambition could have helped her survive the reality that there are nihilists in the world.

Instead of giving up her life, Cherryl Brooks should have listened to Dagny, realizing that her life is the highest value. She could have left Jim and with the help of Dagny, revive herself back to the bright, ambitious woman that she was before she met him. It would take time, but now with the knowledge that nihilists exist, she could use that to steer clear of those people. She could have gone back and been productive in business and life.

What can someone do if they find that the world is turned upside down? People like James Taggart are not worth giving up one's life over, nor are the knowledge that people like him exists. Anyone who has been through intense struggle can always find strength inside himself or herself.

"… The knowledge that my life is the highest of values, too high to give up without a fight." Although she took her life "in an act of self-preservation," with true realization, she could have put up a fight to live. Cherryl Brooks could have turned from a hero-worshipper into a hero. With her ambition, she could have achieved greatness with hard work in business. The virtuous, productive businessmen and women are the heroes in our capitalist society. It's the heroes that believe in themselves and their achievements that are impressive. Because of her Objectivist beliefs, Cherryl should have been able to survive the hit from the nihilism train, just like the "great minds" and our heroes, Dagny, Francisco, Rearden, and Galt.

PART 8
History

Chapter 33

Atlas and "The Bible": Rand's Debt to Isabel Paterson

Stephen Cox

Ayn Rand acknowledged a crucial debt to only one of her contemporaries: Isabel Paterson. The inscription in Paterson's advance copy of *The Fountainhead* reads, "To Pat—You have been the one encounter in my life that can never be repeated— Ayn—April 25, 1943" (Branden 1986, 177). Those words came true; Rand would never find another mentor. But the full significance of the words, the full extent of Paterson's influence on Rand's thought and work, is only gradually coming to light. I would like to suggest that one of the most important examples of that influence is the vision of human action on which *Atlas Shrugged* is based.

If I am right, *Atlas Shrugged* can be called a Patersonian novel, in roughly the same sense in which *Les Miserables* can be called a Christian novel. To say this is not to deprive Ayn Rand of any credit rightly due her. Isabel Paterson did not write *Atlas Shrugged*, any more than Jesus wrote *Les Miserables*. Yet when one examines the role of Paterson's ideas in Rand's novel, one gains a better sense of the richness of Rand's intellectual and literary relationships, and her personal relationships, too.

Who was Isabel Paterson? That question is asked less frequently now than it was in 1986, when Barbara Branden's *The Passion of Ayn Rand* drew the attention of Rand's readers to a friendship that Rand acknowledged but grew reluctant to advertise.[1] It may be helpful, however, to review some basic facts about Paterson and her acquaintance with Rand.[2]

Isabel Paterson (1886–1961) was a distinguished writer and critic, one of the most visible literary personalities of America in the 1930s. She was an accomplished and sometimes a best-selling novelist, but her fame was largely dependent on the column of literary news and commentary that she wrote for *Books*, a nationally circulated journal of the *New York Herald Tribune*. The column ran for twenty-five years (1924–1949), proof of Paterson's success in projecting her ideas in an entertaining and challenging way. She was an incomparably vivid writer, devastatingly learned and witty; a master of both the formal and the colloquial styles; and a brilliant aphorist (Cox 1993). She was a student of almost everything, and she was never afraid to announce what she knew. She had none of the conventional intellectual's defensive reticence and ambiguity. She "taught them as one having authority, and not as the scribes" (Matthew 7:29). She said that she expected people to "listen to the facts" from her (Paterson 1931).

During the 1930s, Paterson was chiefly engaged in telling the facts about problems of history, philosophy, and politics. She was the literary world's most vocal critic of Franklin Roosevelt's New Deal, which, to her disgust, entailed a vast expansion of state power. Called a "conservative," she was actually a radical libertarian, opposing all activities of government except the prevention of force and fraud. Unlike many other critics of Roosevelt, she had not developed her ideas simply in reaction to the policies of the Democratic regime. She had vigorously attacked the Republican administrations of the 1920s, considering them exponents of intrusive and therefore ruinous government.

Rand's friendship with Paterson dates from late 1940 or early 1941, when Rand, recognizing Paterson's role as a leader of the libertarian Right, asked her to join an organization for the intellectual defense of individualism. Paterson refused; she was, as she said, neither a "signer" nor a "j'iner" (Paterson 1941). But she liked Rand, and soon she was inviting the younger woman to long conversations in her office at the *Herald Tribune* and her home in Connecticut. Rand was emphatically an individualist, but she knew relatively little about American traditions of individualism and was not well educated in political and economic theory. She eagerly embraced Paterson's ideas, dissenting only—though very definitely—from her belief in God.

May 1943 saw the publication both of *The God of the Machine*, Paterson's book about politics and history, and of Rand's breakthrough novel *The Fountainhead*, which Paterson's column helped to publicize to an initially unresponsive heartland America. Before the novel's success was assured, the two women had an important telephone conversation. Paterson urged Rand to write a nonfiction account of her ideas. Rand declined, maintaining her right to "strike" against a world that refused to interest itself in its own welfare. But "that"—the idea of the strike—"would make a good novel," she added. The phone conversation was the genesis of *Atlas Shrugged* (Branden 1986, 218).

In late 1943, Rand left New York for California. During the next few years she and Paterson corresponded, often at great length. Paterson used her contacts in the railroad industry to help Rand with her research for *Atlas*. It was Paterson who arranged for the trip in which Rand had the supremely exciting adventure of driving a major passenger train (Cox 2004, 304).[3] In mid-1948, Rand invited Paterson to visit her in Los Angeles, and Paterson reluctantly agreed. It was an unfortunate visit. Rand had tired of her role as junior partner in the relationship, and neither woman could keep from quarreling with the other. The friendship was permanently broken. Yet by 1948 Paterson had given Rand much that she could use. Not only had she provided a political and economic education; she had also communicated—in conversation and correspondence, and in *The God of the*

Machine—a picture of human action that dominates the organization of *Atlas Shrugged*.

Rand's response to Paterson's work was an especially intense example of a common phenomenon, the reproduction of a vivid picture of the world by a writer who has been impressed by it at some important stage of his or her education. The whole western tradition of storytelling has been impressed by the Homeric conceptions that influenced it during its first period of artistic self-consciousness. The idea of a world that appears to revolve around the acts of a single hero, the idea of an all-inclusive work of art devoted to evoking that world as strongly as possible, the idea that everything in such a work must be fitted to everything else, no matter how long and various the work may be, the idea of beginning a narrative in medias res, at some particularly interesting point in the sequence of events— these are the ideas that Virgil, Milton, and every other writer in the epic tradition derived from the *Iliad* and the *Odyssey*. And these are the ideas that other Western authors appropriated from the epic tradition when they began adapting it to the demands of contemporary reality and produced the novel. Margaret Mitchell did not need to pass an exam on Homer to get the idea of opening *Gone With the Wind* in medias res, or to organize her picture of the American Civil War around the adventures of a single heroine, paralleled by the adventures of similar and contrasting characters. All she needed (but that was quite a lot) was the knowledge of a certain set of artistic conceptions, which she could get from the Homeric poems either at the first or at the fiftieth remove.

Rand uses the same conceptions. But it is not just aesthetic ideas that organize a work of art. Other dominating ideas may be social, political, or metaphysical; and their source may be either general or highly specific and personal. Few psychological novelists have studied the works of Freud, but few have escaped the general influence of his dominant (indeed domineering) vision of the human mind. Walt Whitman exemplifies a more intimate kind of intellectual influence. For him, Ralph Waldo Emerson was a "Friend and Master," an "original true Captain" (Whitman 1856, 346, 358), and he was proud to think that his poetry was enacting Emerson's vision of the world. In reality, few people have differed from each other as much as Whitman and Emerson, but the important thing for Whitman was the conception of life that he derived from Emerson and accepted as authoritative.

Western literature's greatest monument of authority, both general and specific, is the Bible; and it was specifically as a Bible that Rand saw Paterson's work. Writing to Paterson's editor at the G.P. Putnam company, she pictured *The God of the Machine* as a comprehensive guide to truth, a book that would "answer [its readers"] every question and tell them everything they want to know about Americanism—philosophically, historically, economically, morally"; it would do "for capitalism what the Bible did for Christianity" (Rand 1943, 103, 102). Yet the Bible is not just a big book that can tell you all the things you "want to know." An encyclopedia—or, from Rand's point of view, the works of Aristotle—might also fit that definition. *The God of the Machine* was more, in Rand's opinion: it was "a document that could literally save the world—if enough people knew of it and read it" (Rand 1943, 102).

Rand's choice of an evangelical vocabulary—her emphasis on "sav[ing] the world," on winning people's minds to a saving belief, and on using a special book to do it—adds an important dimension to the concept of literary influence. The Christian Scriptures were not intended simply to express ideas; they were intended to get people to believe in those ideas, and to believe "unto salvation" (Luke 1:1–4, Romans 1:15; see also John 12:47). That, according to Rand, was the function of *The God of the Machine*. Like the early Christians, she thought that "[i]t takes a book to save or destroy the world" (Rand 1943, 102).

But how would this particular book—"the greatest book written in the last three hundred years" (Rand 1943, 102)—accomplish that purpose? It would do so by providing a comprehensive, fundamental, and shaping view of an individualist society: "*The God of the Machine* ... is the first complete statement of the philosophy of individualism as a political and economic system. It is the basic document of capitalism."

"No historical movement has ever succeeded without a book that stated its principles and gave shape to its thinking" (Rand 1943, 102). Capitalism formerly lacked a book that could impart a "shape," but it has "the book now" (Rand 1943, 102).

No one who knows Rand's work will mistake her meaning here. She is not praising Paterson's work merely for its ability to influence or "shape" public opinion, perhaps in some subjective or arbitrary manner. The "shape" she wants to see imparted to capitalist thinking is one that accurately reflects the shape of human action in a capitalist society. She found it in *The God of the Machine*. What was it?

The ideas for which Paterson argues are as complex as the economic and political system she expounds. But like Adam Smith before her, she begins with simple observations about the tendency of human beings to "truck, barter, and exchange one thing for another" (Smith 1976, 25). Suppose that you hold in your hand a twenty-dollar bill, and I hold in my hand a copy of my latest book. You would (I hope) be pleased to have that book, just as I would be pleased to have your twenty-dollar bill. Each of us wants what the other one has, so we can exchange one object for the other. If we do so, we will each end up with something we consider more valuable than what we possessed before. We will each increase our wealth, by means of our circuit of exchange.

Extend that circuit, bring more people into it, find a larger diversity of goods and a larger diversity of buyers, sellers, and producers, and many more opportunities will exist for the enhancement of wealth. Extend the circuit over the whole earth, and you will create a market in which all people can find the goods they want and, simultaneously, find encouragement to make and sell the goods that other people want, for the price that other people are willing to pay. The longer the circuit of production and exchange, the more producers connect with the circuit and locate buyers for their goods, the more individual desires will be gratified, and the more individual talents will be developed.

That may still sound simple. But to safeguard the "long circuit" of production and exchange, many institutional provisions must be made. Social and political institutions must be developed to maintain free exchange and confident investment—such institutions as objective law and limited government. According to Paterson, government does not directly produce wealth; its role is not to stimulate human action but to inhibit it, either usefully, by preventing force and fraud, or destructively, by attempting to regulate (i.e., to obstruct) free enterprise. Government that is not properly limited produces either a drain on the circuit or a "short circuit," as meddlers clothed with the force of (nonobjective) law come between buyers and sellers, disrupting their communication, inhibiting their trade, and preventing them from investing their resources in extensions of the circuit of commerce. Characteristically, such a government taxes productive enterprise in order to do more than protect the enterprise itself. Aspiring to its own "productive" role, the state extracts resources from the provision of things that people want and are willing to pay for and diverts them to projects that people are not willing to pay for; i.e., projects that are not economically worthwhile.

In Paterson's phrase, government even at its best is an "end appliance": it does not generate creative "energy" on its own; it merely uses energy, whether to protect private lives and property or to build monuments to itself in the form of conscript armies, welfare schemes, building programs, or whatever else (Paterson 1993, 82). The concept of energy brings us to the heart of Paterson's system. In her terms, advanced civilization is a circuit in which human energy is continually being "stepped up" (or, one might say, traded up) by the application of more effective methods of production and exchange (Paterson 1993, 57). In only two centuries, the "long circuit" has enabled humanity to trade exclusive reliance on the power of muscle, wind, and falling water for the virtually unimaginable power of electric generators, jet engines, and the worldwide computer network (the best contemporary image of Paterson's "circuit").

Clearly, the twenty-first century has at its disposal millions of times more useful energy than the early nineteenth century. What was the source of humanity's ability to liberate that energy? Paterson's answer is: the individual, creative mind. That is what devised the machines; that is what continues to generate the power behind the power (Paterson 1993, 130). Limit the individual mind by the contrivance of government, and you deplete the energy coursing through the long circuit. Limit it enough, and you destroy the circuit. One short circuit will follow another; power will leak away into nonproductive "end appliances," never to return; the great surge of energy will not flow again until someone learns how to rewire the circuitry.

That is exactly what happens in *Atlas Shrugged*. The novel describes an energy system that is rapidly degenerating. Government is constantly expanding; trade and communications are constantly shrinking. The visible representation of the process is the sequence of events that befalls America's railway system, a "long circuit" if ever there was one. Rand's heroine, Dagny Taggart, the vice-president for operations of the Taggart Transcontinental railroad, witnesses persistent interventions of government against private property and business. Law becomes a joke; long-range investment becomes nearly impossible; short circuits of the exchange process keep diverting productive energy to unprofitable destinations. Every intervention places some new obstacle between producers and consumers, until so many obstacles exist that production and trade all but cease along the course of the nation's disintegrating system of communications. No matter how hard Dagny tries to jury-rig the "circuits" of Taggart Transcontinental—repairing tracks to productive regions of the country, cutting tracks to less profitable regions, making wise investments, working around institutional interferences—she cannot compete with the government's obstructive regulations.

Finally she learns that to maintain the system, something more than hard work is necessary. The fundamental problem cannot be solved until the legal and political protections of the long circuit are put back in place—and the intellectual protections as well. As Paterson had argued, the circuit cannot be maintained unless people have the right ideas about how to do it (Paterson 1993, 53, 290–92). She discovers another thing. She learns in an especially convincing way that the great circuit's source of energy is the individual self. She meets John Galt, the ultimate individualist, who is also the ultimate embodiment of creative energy— the inventor of a machine that, like the creative inventions in Paterson's theory, turns nature's "static" energy into the "kinetic" energy that powers human action (Rand 1957, 355; compare Paterson 1993, 82, 161). Galt demonstrates to Dagny and other creative individuals that the long circuit of production and exchange is completely dependent, as Paterson had maintained it was, on the freedom of minds like their own. The last, contracted vestige of the circuit will fail when they stop their futile effort to maintain it under conditions of coercion.

The message is, essentially, to follow Paterson's advice about how to deal with the bad investments made by a badly engineered commercial system: "Let it all go." Don't repeat your mistakes, financial and intellectual, but start rewiring the system, using correct principles (Paterson 1932; 1993, 290–92). The method, as *Atlas Shrugged* describes it, is for productive people to withdraw from the larger economy and resume free trade among themselves, rebuilding the long circuit, step by step, with the aid of objective rules, "real money," and all the other things that Paterson thought were required. In the Galt's Gulch section of the novel, we see the circuit reestablished; at novel's end, we see it preparing to re-extend itself over "the ruins of a continent" (Rand 1957, 1168).

Paterson has often been criticized for her allegedly obfuscatory use of an "engineering metaphor"—energy, circuitry, and so on (Buckley 2004, 47; Doherty 2005, 50; Rothbard 1993, 33–4). But *Atlas Shrugged* suggests that the "metaphor," if that's what you want to call it, isn't far from reality. A railroad is literally a circuit of trade and production. It can be expanded or contracted; it can also be cut off, short-circuited, ruined, when the political and economic conditions for its maintenance are destroyed. Energy—"motive power" (Rand 1957, 63)—is literally required to run a railroad; and the source of this energy is the creative mind of the individual. *Atlas Shrugged* shows in vast detail how Paterson's ideas literally work.[4]

One of the "details" involves Paterson's concept of long-distance breakage. On 30 November 1943, soon after Rand began planning *Atlas Shrugged*, Paterson wrote her about a recent conversation with former President Herbert Hoover. Although Paterson had no high opinion of Hoover's intelligence, she was happy to find that he understood *The God of the Machine* and could "apply" at least one of its ideas. Hoover noted that when controls are forced on an economy, "something is bound to break"—perhaps not "at the point where the controls are apparently imposed," but somewhere (Paterson 1943). This idea is constantly present in the plot conflicts of *Atlas Shrugged*. While Taggart Transcontinental spends its money building a worthless line at the behest of political meddlers, a neglected rail splits on another, profitable route, cutting the flow of transport and causing businessmen to start deserting the railroad—one of the first episodes in a history of difficulties at point A entailing disasters at point B (Rand 1957, 55). Such episodes continue for 1100 pages, until Taggart Transcontinental's bridge across the Mississippi, the last crucial connection in the circuit of private enterprise, is destroyed by a government project, a final "end appliance" that has somehow gotten out of hand. At that moment, people in far-off New York know that they themselves are "doomed" (Rand 1957, 1137–38). They finally grasp Paterson's idea: even the greatest cities live, not because they are geographically well situated or have large, well-educated populations, but because they are part of the long circuit of production and exchange (Paterson 1993, 3–14; compare Rand 1957, 806).

According to both Rand and Paterson, the real reason for the destruction of the long circuit is not that too many bridges have collapsed but that too many of the circuit's vital human connections have disappeared. In *Atlas Shrugged*, Midas Mulligan's retirement from banking and Hugh Akston's retirement from teaching don't immediately destroy either finance or education, but "something is bound to break" somewhere. And that, again, is exactly what happens.

This is but one of many similarities that anyone who reads *Atlas Shrugged* can find between Rand's conception of the world and Paterson's. My concern in this essay has been with the two authors' basic picture of human action, not with such things as their agreement about the literary potential of the Atlantis myth (Rand 1957, 701) or even their agreement about large political issues.[5] Anyone who wishes to pursue such topics will find much to say. About the picture of human action, Rand herself had something more to say, in an essay she wrote in 1964, seven years after the publication of *Atlas* and sixteen years after the sundering of her friendship with Paterson.[6] The occasion was a new edition of *The God of the Machine*. Rand no longer calls it a Bible, yet it remains for her "a sparkling book, with little gems of polemical fire scattered through almost every page, ranging from bright wit to the hard glitter of logic to the quiet radiance of a profound understanding" (Rand 1964, 43). The essay warns against just one major aspect of Paterson's thought, her belief in God. But it also registers a literary complaint. Rand is concerned that *The God of the Machine* has not "fully demonstrated" Paterson's ideas:

> To be fully demonstrated, such a theory would have to define the exact social-political equivalents of the engineering concepts it uses. This, unfortunately, Mrs. Paterson has not done: she uses the literal terms of mechanical engineering in regard to political systems, thus creating the impression of a merely metaphorical discussion.
>
> But it is obviously not intended as a metaphor ... As it stands ... it has to be regarded as a hypothesis, which is suggested and left undeveloped. (Rand 1964, 42)

In fact, *The God of the Machine* uses plenty of "social-political equivalents." It carefully describes the ways in which energy is "circuited" with the help of "real money," "payment of debts," "private property," and so on (Paterson 1993, 62). It offers lengthy discussions of the ways in which Western tradition and law and the architecture of the American constitution provide for the protection of individuals and their creative endeavors. But Rand's reference to "literal terms of mechanical engineering" is revealing in several respects. First, it demonstrates that Rand herself is no longer as interested in architectural or "engineering" images as she was in her own book, *The Fountainhead*. Second, it illustrates a curious hesitancy about deciding what is "literal" and what is "metaphorical" in *The God of the Machine*: the "impression" of metaphor, she says, is actually created by Paterson's "literal" terms. Third, it evinces Rand's belief that Paterson's apparent "metaphors" deserved a fuller development in real-life terms—the same terms that she provided in *Atlas*, a book that successfully "demonstrated" her mentor's "hypothesis." She herself never says that explicitly, either in *Atlas*, which almost entirely avoids direct citation of real people, or in the alternately admiring and condescending tribute that she accorded "Mrs. Paterson's" achievement in 1964. Yet the evidence is clear in *Atlas* itself.

It is equally clear that Rand's use of the ideas she derived from the "one encounter" that could "never be repeated" does nothing to lessen her own literary achievement. Although Rand was capable of accepting Paterson's advice on literary questions (Rand 2000, 162–3), she had a very different approach to plot, style, and character development from that of her mentor.[7] Neither of the two great individualists could be mistaken for the other. Each was fully herself, in both a literary and an intellectual sense. Paterson did not write and could not have written *Atlas Shrugged*, just as Rand did not write and could not have written any of Paterson's novels, or *The God of the Machine*. Long before Paterson encountered Rand, she prophetically remarked that "[o]ne genius is about all a house will hold" (Paterson 1935). Rand showed, nevertheless, that one genius can still learn from another's blueprints.

Notes

1 Rand recommended Paterson's work to her friends (Cox 2004, 334, 408–409) and, after Paterson's death, reviewed it for her journal *The Objectivist Newsletter* (Rand 1964); see below, note 6. But no one who read that review, or Rand's authorized biography (Branden and Branden 1962), would be able to guess the significance that Paterson had in her personal life.

2 The following summary is based on Cox 2004. For the Paterson-Rand relationship, see especially Chapters 14, 19, and 24.

3 Railroads are a constant theme in Paterson's life and writing. The first words she spoke were prompted by the movement of a railroad train. Much of her youth was spent in railroad towns. As a young woman she worked for R.B. Bennett, attorney for the Canadian Pacific Railway. *The God of the Machine* (165–72, 222–3, 226–7) includes important discussions of railroad development.

4 It is worth noting that Paterson's ideas are the important ones, not those of Rose Wilder Lane, who incorporated ideas about "energy" in her own book of 1943, *The Discovery of Freedom*. Lane's ideas on this topic are sketchy and appear to be indebted to Paterson herself (Cox 2004, 284–6, 396–7).

5 Paterson was fascinated with myths of Atlantis, which appears with emphasis in both *The God of the Machine* (53) and her novel *The Golden Vanity* (173). One of the books she kept in her reference library was a well-used copy of James Bramwell's *Lost Atlantis* (author's collection). For some other Paterson-*Atlas* connections, see Cox 2004, 303.

6 Rand's essay, which originally appeared in 1964, was republished, with her approval, as the introduction to Bea and Robert Hessen's 1983 edition of *The God of the Machine*. Her approval demonstrates her continuing admiration for Paterson's work.

7 The evidence appears at large in their works. It is also indicated by Paterson's belief that *Atlas* was a great accomplishment although one with which she had a good many disagreements—philosophical, certainly, but undoubtedly stylistic and rhetorical as well (Branden 1986, 177; Cox 2004, 351, 358). Paterson probably felt that Rand, like some other people, "suffer[ed] from the delusion that a thesis makes a novel" (Paterson 1935).

References

Bramwell, James. 1938. *Lost Atlantis*. New York: Harper and Brothers.

Branden, Barbara. 1986. *The Passion of Ayn Rand*. Garden City, New York: Doubleday.

Branden, Barbara, and Branden, Nathaniel. 1962. *Who Is Ayn Rand?* New York: Random House.

Buckley, William F., Jr. 2004. The dynamic IMP. *National Review* 56 (13 December): 46–7.

Cox, Stephen. 1993. The significance of Isabel Paterson. *Liberty* 7 (October): 30–41.

———. 2004. *The Woman and the Dynamo: Isabel Paterson and the Idea of America.* New Brunswick New Jersey: Transaction Publishers.

Doherty, Brian. 2005. Our forgotten goddess. *Reason* 36 (February): 46–52.

Lane, Rose Wilder. 1943. *The Discovery of Freedom: Man's Struggle Against Authority.* New York: John Day Company.

Paterson, Isabel. 1931. Turns with a bookworm. *New York Herald Tribune "Books"* (1 February): 15.

———. 1932. Letter to Garreta Busey, c. 16 July. Isabel Paterson Papers. West Branch, Iowa: Herbert Hoover Presidential Library.

———. 1934. *The Golden Vanity.* New York: William Morrow.

———. 1935. Turns with a bookworm. *New York Herald Tribune "Books"* (21 April): 18.

———. 1941. Turns with a bookworm. *New York Herald Tribune "Books"* (15 June): 10.

———. 1943. Letter to Ayn Rand, 30 November. Isabel Paterson Papers. West Branch, Iowa: Herbert Hoover Presidential Library.

———. 1993. *The God of the Machine.* New Brunswick New Jersey: Transaction Publishers. (Original work published in 1943.)

Rand, Ayn. 1943. Letter to Earle Balch, 28 November. *Letters of Ayn Rand.* Edited by Michael S. Berliner. New York: Dutton, 1995, 102–104.

———. 1957. *Atlas Shrugged.* New York: Random House.

———. 1964. Review. *The God of the Machine.* Isabel Paterson. *The Objectivist Newsletter* 3 (October): 42–3.

———. 1983. Introduction. *The God of the Machine.* Isabel Paterson. Palo Alto, California: Palo Alto Book Service, i–v.

———. 2000. *The Art of Fiction: A Guide for Writers and Readers.* Edited by Tore Boeckmann. New York: Plume.

Rothbard, Murray N. 1993. Machine politics. *Chronicles* 17 (December): 33–5.

Smith, Adam. 1976. *An Inquiry into the Nature and Causes of the Wealth of Nations.* Edited by R.H. Campbell, A.S. Skinner, and W.B. Todd. Oxford: Clarendon.

Whitman, Walt. 1856. *Leaves of Grass.* New York: Fowler and Wells.

Chapter 34

A Note on Rand's Americanism*

Douglas J. Den Uyl

In my book on the *Fountainhead* I make the following claim: "by the time we get to *Atlas Shrugged*, however, America has completely abandoned her essential principles. In that novel America has drifted so far from its individualist roots that the protagonists must abandon it for their own ideal society" (Den Uyl 1999, 106). I want to explore this claim a little further, not necessarily because I have come to change my mind, but rather to be clearer on what the claim might mean with respect to Rand's view of America. I suppose that one obvious question is whether there is a continuum between the novels or a break between them. It's possible that Rand held the same vision of America in both novels, but simply grew more pessimistic about America's prospects in the intervening years. I shall call this the "standard" reading of Rand.

The alternative reading we might label the "radical" reading of Rand. On this reading, Rand abandons her Americanism of the *Fountainhead*. Although *Atlas* is set in America, Rand effectively advocates a political order that is new and only partially reflective of the essential nature of America. The radical reading would hold up "Galt's Gulch" as the model of the ideal social and political order. The main problem with the standard reading is that it opens Rand up to a comparison between her ideals and the realities of America, both politically and culturally. If there is any divergence, the question is raised as to what point Rand's vision is a new vision altogether and not a return to Americanism? The radical reading, in contrast, faces the problem that Rand seems to explicitly deny it. She does not endorse the radical reading and often in her non-fiction works seems quaintly patriotic.

If I have a thesis at all, it would be that Rand's thoroughly integrated vision of the moral and political, through her conception of individualism, is both her salvation and her undoing. *Atlas* is a positive expression of the moral centrality of the individual and of the fundamental role individual genius plays in social advancement. It is also, in the political character of Galt's Gulch, a depiction of a society organized around the primacy of individual liberty. These two are related, but not identical issues. Believing that they are the same issue distorts one's understanding of America.[1] By the same token, the conflation is both inspirational and even necessary, as we shall see.[2]

Let's first begin with our starting premise which is that in the *Fountainhead* Rand is unabashedly and optimistically pro-American. We can remind ourselves of all this in these words from Roark at his trial:

> Now observe the results of a society built on the principle of individualism. This, our country. The noblest country in the history of men. The country of greatest achievement, greatest prosperity, greatest freedom. This country was not based on selfless service, sacrifice, renunciation or any precept of altruism. It was based on a man's right to the pursuit of happiness. His own happiness. Not anyone else's. A private, personal, selfish motive. Look at the results. Look into your own conscience.

Apart from the direct and obvious references to America, notice that although there are appeals to results, the passage argues in terms of an essential nature that explains those results. The essential nature of America is the principle of individualism which is defined in terms of the renunciation of altruism. The pursuit of one's own happiness is the ultimate good. The appeal to happiness is clearly an allusion to the Declaration of Independence and is taken by Rand to be connected to the renunciation of altruism. That renunciation is found at the depths of the American soul, and notice how Rand appeals to that when she appeals to conscience at the end of the passage.

The appeal to conscience is, of course, necessary for the movement of the plot, since the jury will have to look within themselves to decide Roark's fate. But that appeal is significantly more than just a plot device. In context, it serves the function of saying that Americans generally, if they look deeply within themselves, will discover that individualist core to which Roark refers. The Americans to which Rand is referring are not just the ones in the novel itself. There is every sense that the reader is being called upon to judge Roark as well.

We find, then, in *The Fountainhead* a strong sense of optimism about America. That is a different tone than one gets from *Atlas*. We begin in uncertainly with "Who is John Galt," and Dagny seems isolated and alone in a way Dominique is not. Moreover there is an ominous dark mood throughout that hangs over the whole novel. Something is deeply wrong with the world and America in particular. Both novels have a "happy" ending, but in the *Fountainhead* that ending occurs within a functioning world, whereas in *Atlas* the price of happiness is the world itself. In considering these differences is the dark tone a sign of a significant change in opinion for Rand about the state of the American soul or the nature of America?

Consider, in this connection, the trial of Hank Rearden. Rearden's trial was not dissimilar to Roark's, but there is a significant and notable difference— Rearden's fate is not decided by a jury, but rather a panel of judges. That difference, I believe, says a good deal about where Rand has moved with respect to

America. The judges find Rearden guilty, but in doing so present to the reader a position Rand expresses directly elsewhere, namely that a culture's understanding of itself is a function of the elites in the position to articulate it (Rand 1982, 252). The first thing, then, to notice about Rearden being tried by judges is just that—the group is an educated elite body and not a "jury of one's peers." The people observing the trial, however, are a different matter. They are similar to Roark's jury—that is, they represent the "average" sort of person in the US. Rearden is found guilty, but his exchange with the judges is such that he wins the arguments and embarrasses the judges. The scene is written in such a way that the people observing are clearly on the side of Rearden, much as Roark's jury was finally on his side. There may be some question as to whether the observers are like Roark's jury or whether their pleasure in Rearden's triumph is just small minded satisfaction in seeing the judges turned into fools. But the natural reading still seems to me to be one where the people are more admiring of Rearden than cynical. The scales, then, seem to tip towards continuity with the *Fountainhead*.

We might also want to think about Eddie Willers as well, for he is arguably the single character most representative of "the common man" or the "ordinary" American. If Willers is Rand's common man, he too seems isolated and alone. The "common man" with the appropriate sensibilities about what is essential to America seems less prominent in *Atlas* than in the *Fountainhead*. Nevertheless, Willers in the end tries to keep the railroad going in spite of the collapse of everything. His sacrifice for this cause could be interpreted as demonstrating the inability of those with less talent to do what those with more can do, and no doubt that is part of Rand's point. But the spirit represented by Willers in trying to keep things going is the spirit of individualism that marks the American character for Rand. As she puts it:

Initiative is an "instinctive" (i.e., automatized) American characteristic; in an American consciousness, it occupies the place which, in a European one, is occupied by obedience (Rand 1982, 254).

In a non-fiction essay, Rand gives us a clue as to how to allow for the spirit of individualism while accounting for its absence at the moral and cultural level. Basically, as we saw in the case of Rearden's trial, individualism is latent in the general population, but unarticulated or criticized by the intellectual elites. This leads Rand to characterize Americans and the problem of America in the following way:

Values which one cannot identify, but merely senses implicitly, are not in one's control. One cannot tell what they depend on or require, what course of action is needed to gain and/or keep them. One can lose or betray them without knowing it. Today the American person is like a sleepwalking giant torn by profound conflicts. (When I speak of "the American people," in this context, I mean every group, including scientists and businessmen—except the intellectuals, i.e., those whose professions deal with the humanities. The intellectuals are a country's guardians.)

Americans are the most reality-oriented people on earth. Their outstanding characteristic is the childhood form of reasoning: common sense. It is their only protection. (Rand 1982, 256–7, 258)

In her non-fiction writing, and the *Fountainhead*, Rand expresses her faith in the American people's "common sense." Yet *Atlas*, by contrast, seems a good deal more ambivalent about it. In the *Fountainhead* one feels that the intellectual class is still struggling to win over the souls of the ordinary people. There is a close "community" feel in the *Fountainhead* that is absent from *Atlas*. It is not necessarily that the intellectuals have won the people over to collectivism in *Atlas*, but rather that the people have been abandoned by the elites altogether. The culture has been wrested from them and their instincts ignored. Perhaps in order for the world to collapse as it does in that novel, common sense would have to disappear. For this reason we should probably tilt towards the non-fiction attitudes expressed by Rand. On that basis, Rand never really becomes increasingly more pessimistic about the inherent individualism or common sense of the American people.

Finally we need to look at Rand's depiction of Galt's Gulch. Virtually all the characters of the novel with individualistic sensibilities and convictions retreat into it. Here individualism reigns supreme and some of the optimism found in the earlier novel is found here as well. The mere contrast with the outside world does not necessarily signify a change in opinion about the centrality of the United States or what it stands for, though it may signify the distance between what it stands for and what it has become. After all, Galt's Gulch is located in the heart of the United States, and Rand could have put it anywhere in the world. On the other hand, Rand's approach to values is universalistic, and the global political perspective could suggest that focusing on Rand's Americanism is too narrow and off the mark. Rand's journal entries support this argument (Rand 1997, 390). She describes her project as being concerned with "the world" and has few references to the United States in particular.

Is Rand, through *Atlas*, offering a new order that may resemble America but is nevertheless meant to be substantially different from it? The standard reading would answer "no," and I believe that is the correct answer. There is perhaps a good deal of evidence that could be cited in favor of this conclusion, but one very simple bit of evidence from the novel seems to me both sufficient and decisive:

A small brick structure came next, bearing the sign: Mulligan Mint. A mint?' she [Dagny Taggart] asked. "What's Mulligan doing with a mint?" Galt reached into his pocket and dropped two small coins into the palm of her hand. They were miniature disks of shining gold, smaller than pennies, the kind that had not been in circulation since the days of Nat Taggart; they bore the head of the Statue of Liberty on one side, the words "United States of America—One Dollar" on the other, but the dates stamped upon them were of the past two years.

"That's the money we use here," he said. "It's minted by Midas Mulligan."

"But ... on whose authority?"

"That's stated on the coin—on both sides of it." (Rand 1957, 727)

From this little section of the novel, it seems rather difficult to conclude that Rand believes Galt's Gulch is a radical departure from what is central and essential about America. There are, significantly, "no laws ... no rules, no formal organization of any kind" (Rand 1957, 714) to be found in Galt's Gulch, so the "authority" that backs the gold coins is one of the spirit and conceptual nature of the United States, and not one of an extant political order or institution. The sense is that the members of the valley all see themselves as living in the true United States (or something close to it) and upholding its basic values.[3] There's no sense of individuals establishing a colony in an attempt to forge a new political order. Indeed, the feeling, as we see from the foregoing passage, is more one of recovery than innovation.

With the standard reading winning the day, we seem to be done with the question with which we opened. Rand did not change her mind about the nature of America or Americans between the two novels. To rest contented here, however, would be to move to conclusion much too quickly. There is still the question to be considered of whether Rand understands America correctly, and I think the answer to this must be "in part." Since I believe her understanding is in some important ways confused, a kind of small wedge for the radical reading ironically opens up. In the end, we shall see that the tension between the "radical" Rand and the "patriotic" Rand is an instructive one for all of us who think about liberty. But let us get into these issues by first reminding ourselves of Rand's Americanism by quoting from something Rand wrote during the era of the *Fountainhead*. Many such passages from later texts could also be cited, but this one has the advantage of coming from a piece aptly titled "Textbook of Americanism":

What is the Basic Principle of America?

The basic principle of the United States of America is Individualism.

America is built on the principle that Man possesses Inalienable Rights:

- that these rights belong to each man as an individual—not to "men"[4] as a group or collective;
- that these rights are the unconditional, private, personal, individual possession of each man—not the public, social, collective possession of a group;
- that these rights are granted to man by the fact of his birth as a man—not by an act of society;
- that man holds these rights, not from the Collective nor for the Collective, but against the Collective—as a barrier which the Collective cannot cross;

- that these rights are man's protection against all other men;
- that only on the basis of these rights can men have a society of freedom, justice, human dignity and decency (Rand, 1998, 83).[5]

What one notices most about this passage is how it slides from individualism to rights. These two conceptions are, or at least can be, rather different things. One could, of course, say that what is being referred to here is political individualism which could be described as the view that rights are moral norms only applicable to, and descriptive of, individuals. While that may be true enough, we would then have to say something about the relevance of the individualism of the novels, that is, of Rand's depiction of heroic individuals such as Howard Roark or Dagny Taggart. That sort of individualism is rather different from the political individualism just posited. If, on the other hand, "individualism" is understood "morally" through depictions of people like Howard Roark and Dagny Taggart, then we would need to say something of what politics, if any, is implied by the approbation of that sort of individual. However much the two may be connected—and much of the point of what Rand writes is to try and draw that connection—they are nonetheless rather distinct issues.[6] And it is the blurring of that distinction that both distances Rand from what America is all about and brings her right to the center of it!

Once again, Galt's Gulch gives us an important window into the issue. We know already from what we cited above that there are no rules, laws, or formal organizations of any kind there. That context elicits the following perplexing response from Judge Narragansett when asked by Dagny what he is doing in Galt's Gulch and whether he is practicing his profession. The Judge responds as follows:

> "The law, Miss Taggart?" said Judge Narragansett. "What law? I did not give it up—it has ceased to exist. But I am still working in the profession I had chosen, which was that of serving the cause of justice. ... No, justice has not ceased to exist. How could it? It is possible for men to abandon their sight of it, and then it is justice that destroys them. But it is not possible for justice to go out of existence, because one is an attribute of the other, because justice is the act of acknowledging that which exists. ... Yes, I am continuing my profession. I am writing a treatise on the philosophy of law. I shall demonstrate that humanity's darkest evil, the most destructive horror machine among all devices of men, is non-objective law." (Rand 1957, 737)

This passage is problematic on a number of levels. First of all it lends some significant support to the radical reading. Through the Judge's description we are given the real possibility of a community of human beings who live together without law and government—namely Galt's Gulch itself. The Judge does not argue that he is drafting laws for Galt's Gulch or that someone should do so. Galt's Gulch can apparently continue quite well without any legal or political institutions, and the Judge shows no concern that it cannot so function. Of course, Rand later rebuts the possibility of an anarchical society in a well known non-fiction essay entitled "The Nature of Government." But that essay never refutes the possibility of a Galt's Gulch, only its feasibility in a world such as our own (Rand 1967, 329–37).[7] Rand could, of course, be saying that we should not take Galt's Gulch as a real community and thus that the fact that the Judge is not designing laws for it is not a sign of anything. But the simple answer to this is, why not? They are depicted as living together and have been for some time. Moreover, at that stage of the novel it is not certain how long they will continue to do so. It would seem that if a society without government were not possible or desirable, the Judge would be scribbling away furiously to get some sort of system of rules in place.

The significance of all this is that Judge Narragansett could not, in fact, practice his profession as a judge, though he could, of course, be a legal philosopher as he so describes himself in the passage cited.[8] That the "law does not exist" is a kind of double entendre, since on the one hand Galt's Gulch has no laws and on the other the kind of law that respects the objective understanding of justice has ceased to exist in the outside world.[9] But Judge Narragansett is still not a judge in either place. It is not even clear how he serves the cause of justice in Galt's Gulch, since those present presumably already live by "objective justice" and know quite well what it requires of them. His work would therefore have to consist in articulating in his treatise what is perhaps only implicit in the members of the community of Galt's Gulch. Yet it is not at all clear why the community in Galt's Gulch needs the articulation? There are no laws present by which to consider the divergence of the legal rules from a strict adherence to objective justice, and the characters of the individuals who live there do, in any case, fully exhibit the principles of objective justice.

The Judge could be writing the treatise for the day in which they all return to the world, but if that is so, then why hold it back from that world now? It would be a bizarre theory of justice indeed if people had to be made ready to receive it or that it was held back to teach them some kind of lesson! Actually, there is a way in which the people are being "made ready" for objective justice and already being taught a lesson about it, namely the collapse of the world. The collapse is presumably what happens when "objective justice" is ignored in a social/legal order. Nevertheless, the theory of justice—on the view that Judge Narragansett is its articulator—would be precisely what should be given to the outside world, however dim the chances of it receiving a positive reception from the elites. Indeed, the only sense Judge Narragansett's work makes, either as a judge or an articulator, is in the outside world. Imagine analogously Rand circulating her own novels only privately among a small group. What purpose could be served in that?[10]

I mention the role of the Judge and his remarks in this situation because he might be the natural person to look to for an understanding of how to combine political and moral individualism. Not only does one receive no help in this regard from the Judge's comments, but one begins to see something about the nature of Galt's Gulch that is a source of the confusion in Rand's conceptualization of individualism. What we discover is that the institutions of political individualism, namely the institutional instantiation and protection of individual rights, are handled in Galt's Gulch not by people like Judge Narragansett and the institutions associated with his profession, but rather by two other factors: character and technology. The internal order of the society is maintained by the characters of the people living there. The external liberty of the society as a whole is maintained by the technology that keeps Galt's Gulch from being discovered and invaded. In this respect, the hard work of setting up political institutions in real social orders is completely by-passed in Galt's Gulch, and the by-passing ends up, as a result, obscuring what government and law are all about, especially as it might relate to America.

Like America itself, Galt's Gulch can plausibly be considered a "liberal" social order. A liberal social order is one that leaves people generally free to pursue their own ends and to associate with whom they please. Yet it is the basis for liberalism as imagined in Galt's Gulch, and generally provided in Rand's novels, that needs to be called into question and distinguished from the kinds of arguments more appropriate to political theory.

It is useful here to think of liberalism as being traditionally defended from two main perspectives.[11] The first I shall call a "values" perspective that sees liberalism in terms of the instantiation of certain values among the citizens of the liberal order. For many, the most familiar form of this defense would be the encouragement of toleration and autonomy. In general, this form of liberalism "describes a set of standards or principles by which a community or society should live. A community is a liberal society if its institutions uphold or honor the values which make it liberal" (Kukathas 2001, "Two Concepts" 98).[12] The values defense is generally internalist in nature, since the liberal order is achieved through the development of the character, culture, and morals of the individuals found under its purview.

The values approach is rather different from what I shall call the "diversity" perspective. On the diversity way of defending liberalism the main focus is that people have diverse interests, values, and life goals, and in order to avoid conflict we allow maximum possible freedom under institutions set up for adjudicating disputes and to prevent abuses of power. The diversity defense cares little about what people are like, what values they have, whether their souls are constituted like that of Wesley Mouch or Hank Rearden. This defense is therefore structural and procedural. It focuses on the equal distribution of rights, political mechanisms for their respect, and procedures for the resolution of disagreements and violations of rights. As long as people do not violate one another's rights, whether they are tolerant of each other or autonomous matters very little.

In today's world, the battle between these approaches is usually fought between welfare state type contemporary liberals who seek to promote the "liberal virtues" of toleration and autonomy and classical liberals or libertarians who want to refer only to rights and minimal government intrusion. Of course, each side often has their own correlate positions with respect to values and diversity. More importantly for our purposes, however, is the fact that these two approaches can be found within perspectives that share the same political conclusions. That is our point here with Rand vis à vis others in "the movement." Thus, the value and diversity approaches to liberalism can be considered archetypically distinct and, as foundational paradigms, irreconcilable.[13]

Recall again, therefore, the passage we cited from the "Textbook on Americanism." At best this passage slides between individualism as a value defense to individualism as a diversity defense. In fact, however, it looks to me mostly like a value defense. That is, the argument is of the type that because individualism—of the non-altruistic non-exploitative type—is the correct value to possess, we value liberty for its power to secure, protect, and express that individualism. The novels especially, seem to be generally pushing this same line. The importance of liberty politically is depicted as a function of the kind of people it will not only allow to flourish, but encourage to flourish.

The problem with this approach to establishing a liberal order is that liberty also protects those who are not interested in heroic individualist life-styles. Indeed, the more diversity of ends one allows, the less heroic individualism seems to have to do with the defense of liberty. It may be true that Rand is trying to show us a deep and abiding connection between political individualism (liberalism) on the one hand and moral/cultural individualism on the other. But even if that connection is deep and abiding, it does not follow that the defense of liberalism should be made in light of it. It may be that the defense of liberalism depends as much on considering the lifestyle of the altruistic monk who lives for his religious order as it does the heroic individuals depicted in Rand's novels. To do this we would need to understand that the value of political individualism is of a different type and ontological stature than is the value of heroic individualism. That discussion must be left for elsewhere.[14] But it is easy enough to see now that if someone could show a deep and abiding connection between liberty and flourishing monasteries,[15] that would go very little distance in dissuading those of us who admire heroic individualism from coming to its defense.

America is a country, at least in its political conception of itself, much more in line with the diversity approach than the value one.[16] Liberty—and we must not forget equality too—were important because we were a diverse nation. True we had anti-Federalists and elements of Jefferson that worried about the moral "independence" of the citizens in an extended republic. But still, what generally won the day was the idea that we were a diverse people of different backgrounds, life plans, abilities, and aspirations. We not only needed to design institutions to protect and secure that diversity, but we also needed to design them such that they would not depend upon people being of a certain type or character in order to function. All this is well known, but almost equally glossed over or confused in Rand's novels and much of her non-fiction work. We should not mind the conflation of arguments, because we know that the Roarks and the Reardens could not survive in a collectivist authoritarian state. But proving that negative does not in and of itself make the positive case for liberty or show that they are even the same sort of case.

Despite these criticisms, Rand does correctly identify that political individualism is American. She also correctly identifies that moral or cultural individualism is American as well. From Western films to the "Robber Barons," heroic individualism is very much a part of the American soul and American culture. Moreover, heroic individualism and political liberty are good bedfellows, even if they are not necessarily Siamese twins. Part of Rand's genius certainly lies in her ability to make us see and value their connection. Yet because of what I'm calling her confusion or conflation of political and moral individualism, Rand is blinded to their distinctness and this in itself could be a source of pessimism. For it is conceivable that genius could decline faster than liberty (or not arise as quickly), and the reverse holds as well. The state may, for example, become more intrusive and yet genius still flourishes. That seems to be the case today, for as the state has become more intrusive than it was almost 50 years ago when *Atlas* was published, genius has still managed to flourish, especially in the areas of technology and medicine. Of course, at the limit, both would have to perish together, and there may be many points of mutual encouragement; but the connection between them socially is not so symmetrical as someone like Rand would like to suggest. This actual asymmetry could be a great source of pessimism for someone who has put these two or three components so tightly together in her novels and non-fiction writing. It is paradoxical, though nonetheless worth consideration, that when one calls for the collapse of the world and it does not collapse, increased pessimism rather than relief or optimism seem to be the result. Atlas should have shrugged long ago, but we are still here and, in many ways, better off than we were in 1957. Nevertheless, I do not want to conclude by focusing on the negative side of the "conflation" of individualisms, but more on their positive connection as Rand herself does, for here I think a novel like *Atlas Shrugged* has contributed something of inestimable value as well as provided an important lesson for all theorists of liberalism.

Nobel laureate and economist James Buchanan has written the following:

> Creating a new vision, a new soul for liberalism, is our most important task now. I am not here suggesting that attention should be limited to the design of all-inclusive political packages. Politics, for the most part, proceeds in piecemeal fashion, one step at a time. What I am suggesting is that we ... focus on the vision, the constitution of liberty, rather than merely on pragmatic utilitarian calculus that shows liberalism to

yield quantifiably better results than politicized economies. … We need to preserve, save, and recreate that which we may, properly, call the soul of classical liberalism. (Buchanan 2002)

The soul of the classical liberal for Buchanan is "the individual's desire for liberty from coercive power of others … [and] the absence of desire to exert power over others " (Buchanan 2002). This sounds remarkably close, at least in political terms, to "I swear by my life and love of it that I shall never live for the sake of another man nor ask another man live for mine." Moreover, Rand also points out that "the 'practical' justification of capitalism does not lie in the collectivist claim that it effects 'the best allocation of national resources'" (Rand 1967, 20). Indeed, in many important respects what Buchanan is calling for is provided exactly by the work of Ayn Rand. Through her novels and non-fiction writing she offers us a "new vision" and a "new soul" for liberalism.

Yet in saying all this about Rand being the quintessential soul crafter of classical liberalism and beacon of American liberty, we are brought to a realization that is both important for liberalism and somewhat problematic. The recapturing of the soul of classical liberalism (or just "liberalism" as I would prefer to use the term) seems only possible from the values perspective, and not the diversity perspective. This is first of all because "visions" are in essence appeals to internal values in a way that systems, structures, or rules are not. These latter things are thought to follow from, and be determined by, values and visions, not the other way around (though they can, of course, eventually be incorporated into a value structure). Secondly, people are generally both moved by and moved towards values that are their own. An abstract conception of compossible rights and universal negative rules of conduct may be worth our allegiance, but they are not very instructive about what I (or you) should be like as we live our lives. Thus their power to move us is less than, say, Rearden's power as an exemplar for one's conduct. Finally, liberalism is not a philosophy of life but a political philosophy and thus necessarily of more limited scope than a complete philosophy of life such as Rand offers in *Atlas* and elsewhere. If, therefore, we want to save the soul of classical liberalism, we must adopt the values approach to its defense. If, however, we want to understand it, something closer to the diversity approach must prevail.

The problem for liberalism is now apparent. Liberalism is a doctrine that issues in strictly political conclusions, but cannot as we have just seen, sustain and capture adherents without a strong and compelling values orientation. The dominance of the values orientation in turn threatens not only the diversity defense, but the whole idea that liberalism is limited to being a program of political principles, rather than a philosophy of life. The conflation of the political with the moral and cultural, exhibited now in the dominance of the values approach, has its own negative side of deconstructing the value of real cultural and moral diversity. That danger though real is, I believe, a risk that must be taken. For what is possible for human beings under liberalism is something that can be, as we see with Rand's work, dramatically and forcefully represented. We must therefore, for the liberty we value, also value and nurture efforts which give it soul. They are necessary if liberalism is to survive.

But as philosophers have known since antiquity, what moves the world may not map exactly on to the rarified and subtle nuances of thought suitable to philosophical truth. This asymmetry is, for the most part, denied or not acknowledged by Rand.[17] But the truth of it manifests itself either by issuing in a state of persistent pessimism about the world around one, or in a small but deep sense of "tragedy" that the path from philosophical principle to practical action is a long, twisted, and obstacle ridden one with no smoother alternative. I, for one, find the "tragic" path more conducive to the enjoyment of living, but its danger is a pessimism (or equally problematic, an enthusiasm) that comes from seeking to obliterate the distance between philosophy and life. Ayn Rand, through *Atlas Shrugged* and other works, leaves no such distance. The price of no distance is the confusion or conflation in ideas that has been mentioned.[18] But we have also now seen that some confusion or conflation may be precisely what inspires others to the right causes and principles. Perhaps the living we enjoy today is due precisely to people like Rand who lived as if the distance does not exist. Because of them, philosophy is repeatedly called upon to return and pay homage to life itself. *Atlas Shrugged* is such a clarion call to philosophy—and to life.

Notes

* I thank Douglas Rasmussen and Jonathan Fortier for helpful comments on earlier drafts of this paper.

1   The option developed by myself and Douglas Rasmussen of disassociating substantive morality from politics is not a choice with which Rand provides us. Our position is in many ways inspired by her, but it understands that politics is not morality writ large and does not depend on shared articulations of the good or what is right for its justification (see below). See our *Norms of Liberty* (Rasmussen 2005) (henceforth NOL). Because we do not package morality and politics the way Rand does, idealism in the social sphere is not necessarily a sign of a failed political order, nor is the desired political order necessarily accompanied by the right moral or cultural vision.

2   It should be noted that Douglas B. Rasmussen and myself, as discussed at the end of NOL, do believe liberty and excellence are connected, and even connected due to what is essential to each. However, they are distinct and maintaining that distinction is what keeps a theory from confusion and ultimately pessimism. The distinction allows for each part to be built separately and at different rates, even if they are mutually reinforcing and their telos is one of unity.

3   In this respect it is worth noting—and I thank Jonathan Fortier for pointing this out to me—that a number of the American Founding Fathers saw themselves as upholding the "true" English liberty that had been lost in the 1660—1750 period. The ambiguity

about whether the US is a radical or "conservative" revolution is a nice analogue to my argument here.

4   I should inform any young readers that Rand means by "man" and "men" here simply individuals. She is not talking about "males."

5   Although "Textbook on Americanism" was written in the 1940s, the citation is from the most recent and available source of which I am aware.

6   The point is not a logical one simply. There have been movements in history that argued that we needed a strong state to protect the creative genius of certain individuals both from external enemies and from democratic hoards from within. Indeed, this was part of a principled German opposition to liberalism and the Weimer Republic by such notables as Wilhelm von Humbolt and Thomas Mann. I am not agreeing with the position, only pointing to the existence of an alternative political philosophy enamored of individualism in this moral sense.

7   In fairness, Rand does say that it is not only the immorality of people that gives rise to government and laws. She also says that "even a society whose every member were fully rational and faultlessly moral, could not function in a state of anarchy [without government]; it is the need of objective laws and of an arbiter for honest disagreements among men that necessitates the establishment of a government" (334). Immorality and disagreement are apparently the two reasons for government in Rand's view, but there are neither in Galt's Gulch. For why law, at least, might be necessary even if there were no disagreements, see Rasmussen and Den Uyl, NOL, Chapter 12.

8   Rand allows for the possibility of "many errors and many disagreements" in the implementation of objective law (Rand 1967, 334). That complexity is not even hinted at in the comments of the Judge. Again, if objectivity required law and government, one would have thought this complexity would have given even more of a need to quickly establish the laws of Galt's Gulch. There is, however, custom in the world of the Gulch (the use of gold for money), and the connection between custom, law, and moral individualism is an even more complex topic.

9   Of course, Rand equivocates on "law" in the passage. Law as objective justice cannot cease to exist as stated that it has in the opening part of the passage.

10 Works of art are hidden away by Wynand and others in the *Fountainhead* on the grounds that their beauty should not be exposed to the unappreciative. Maybe an argument might be offered along the same lines for a novel, but I frankly find it difficult to make much sense of it in such a case.

11 The following distinction owes its origins to Chandran Kukathas who, in an interesting series of articles, draws an analogous distinction between two sorts of defenses of liberalism. His own views, in the end, are quite different from my own, especially in the last article cited below. There are, in addition, many subtleties involved in the distinction and relationship between the two approaches I mention that cannot be addressed here. They are versions of the relationship between the moral and the political. That relationship is fully discussed in NOL. To examine Kukathas' approach to the distinction see: (2001, "Two Concepts," 86–97); (2001, "Two Constructions"); and (2003, "Ethical Pluralism," 55–85); and see also his (2003, *The Liberal Archipelago*).

12 On this same page, Kukathas credits William Galston with formulating a similar distinction. Kukathas holds that his two concepts of liberalism cannot be reconciled

while Galston hopes that they can. Our own position, hinted at below, is that there cannot be a transcendental solution that obliterates the distinction, but there might be some reason to believe that a distinction is not a separation. By the same token, without making a broader "transcendental" move towards an integrated philosophical framework, Kukathas is correct to see the distinction as an irreconcilable opposition. See the epilogue to NOL.

13 Kukathas asserts the irreconcilability of the various versions of these two approaches in all the essays cited above. In taking liberty or liberalism as a baseline goal of a political and social order, I would agree. However, once one begins to ask about the relationship between morality and government, the appropriate nature of government, the nature of rights, the sociality of human beings, and other such necessary questions one sees that neither of these alternatives gets at the heart of liberalism which, precisely because of its being grounded in human values, holds that the protection of the possibility for value realization is the only legitimate role for government and the defining principle of rights. This we develop in detail in NOL.

14 Obviously, I would once again refer to *Liberty and Nature* and NOL.

15 By the way, this is not so fanciful an assertion as it might seem. The freest nation on earth has also been the most religious, so maybe there's a connection. Or maybe the connection is as great between those two as it is that liberty will spawn heroic individuals.

16 I am speaking here with respect to political philosophy. To point to America being (e.g.) filled predominantly with "white Christians" as an argument against diversity is a cultural issue and not one about the basic design or rationale of its institutions.

17 Rand's failure to acknowledge this asymmetry is due to her tendency to adopt an ethical rationalism that does not fully appreciate the importance of individual differences and thus fails to consider the role of practical wisdom in determining moral obligations. More fundamentally, this failure is also a result of her tendency to identify logic and ontology. See Douglas B. Rasmussen's contribution to this volume.

18 Yet that confusion or conflation is itself a testimony to the doctrine of tragic distance between what moves the world and what philosophy may require. For, to recognize confusion or conflation is to recognize what is confused or conflated and thus to recognize what is distant.

References

Buchanan, James. 2002. Saving the soul of classical liberalism. *Wall Street Journal*. (January 1).

Den Uyl, Douglas. 1999. *The Fountainhead: An American Novel*. New York: Twayne Publishers.

Kukathas, Chandran. 2003. Ethical pluralism from a classical liberal perspective. *The Many and the One: Religious and Secular Perspectives on Ethical Pluralism in the Modern World*. Edited by Richard Madsen and Tracy B. Strong. Princeton, New Jersey: Princeton University Press.

_____. 2003. *The Liberal Archipelago: A Theory of Diversity and Freedom*. Oxford: Oxford University Press.

_____. 2001. Two constructions of libertarianism. Unpublished F.A. Hayek Memorial Lecture, Austrian Scholars Conference, Auburn Alabama, 2001.

_____. 2001. Two concepts of liberalism. *Liberalism classical and modern: New perspectives*. Edited by J. Espada, M. Platter and A. Wolfson. Lexington: Lexington Books.

Rand, Ayn. 1998. Textbook on Americanism. *The Ayn Rand Column*. New Milford Connecticut: Second Renaissance Books.

_____. 1997. *The Journals of Ayn Rand*. Edited by David Harriman, New York: Dutton Books.

_____. 1982. Don't let it go. *Philosophy: Who Needs It*. Indianapolis: Bobbs-Merrill.

_____. 1967. What is capitalism. *Capitalism: The Unknown Ideal*. New York: Signet Books.

_____. 1957. *Atlas Shrugged*. New York: Random House.

Rasmussen, Douglas B. and Den Uyl, Douglas J. 2005. *Norms of Liberty*. University Park: Pennsylvania University Press.

_____. 1991. *Liberty and Nature*. La Salle, Illinois; Open Court.

Chapter 35

The Non Fictional Robert Stadlers: Traitors to Liberty

Walter Block

Introduction

Dr. Robert Stadler was one of the villains[1] of Ayn Rand's Atlas Shrugged (1957). He plays a relatively unimportant role in Atlas Shrugged. If he disappeared altogether from the book, the story would have rolled on pretty much as it did with his presence. Yes, one or two other minor characters would have had to have been scratched as well (e.g., the young aspiring scientist who was disappointed by the Great Man), Dagny would have been spared yet another experience of perfidy and cowardice and someone also would have been required to create the equations which lead to the X weapon, but other than that little else hangs in the balance.

However, in the real world it is almost impossible to overestimate the importance of Dr. Robert Stadler. This is because he plays the role of the man who full well "knows better," and yet, rejecting the exquisite insights with which he has been blessed, turns his coat, bites the hand that feeds him, and renounces truth and justice. His particular evil was that he knew better, but, nevertheless, still supported the intrusive government that plunders this semi fictitious society. It is one thing, from this perspective, for the average truck driver or waitress to support excessive government regulation of the economy, subsidies to its favorite "businessmen" and/or outright nationalization of large swatches of it. It cannot be denied they are blameworthy for voting for politicians who lead such dirigiste policies. But a harsher judgment is reserved for those who full well appreciate the hazards and, yes, immorality of these courses of action and yet still promote them. It is one thing for a layman to recommend eating poison mushrooms to the unsuspecting, out of ignorance. But it is quite another, and infinitely worse, for a botanist to do so.

Who, then, are the modern-day Robert Stadlers? These are the people who have publicly espoused economic freedom, who have been well taught these insights by masters of them, who have thereby garnered reputations for defending liberty and trade in on them, and yet, who, when push comes to shove, either jettison this philosophy entirely, or totally compromise it for power, prestige or out of just plain orneriness. In many cases they have been painstakingly taught the case for liberty and have given it the backs of their hands when they came to be in a position to champion it. In section II of this paper we make the claim that this applies to A. Alan Greenspan, B. Milton Friedman, C. Friedrich Hayek, D. Williamson Evers, E. Dana Rohrabacher to a greater or lesser extent. We conclude in section III.

The Robert Stadlers

Alan Greenspan

Exhibit "A" in this regard is surely Alan Greenspan. A long time associate of Ayn Rand herself, he made original and scintillatingly beautiful contributions to the freedom philosophy. He did so, most naturally, in the field of money, the life-blood of the economy. For example, he (1966) stated:

> An almost hysterical antagonism toward the gold standard is one issue which unites statists of all persuasions. They seem to sense—perhaps more clearly and subtly than many consistent defenders of laissez-faire—that gold and economic freedom are inseparable, that the gold standard is an instrument of laissez-faire and that each implies and requires the other. (96)

> When gold is accepted as the medium of exchange by most or all nations, an unhampered free international gold standard serves to foster a world-wide division of labor and the broadest international trade. Even though the units of exchange (the dollar, the pound, the franc, etc.) differ from country to country, when all are defined in terms of gold the economies of the different countries act as one—so long as there are no restraints on trade or on the movement of capital. (98)

> But the opposition to the gold standard in any form—from a growing number of welfare state advocates—was prompted by a much subtler insight: the realization that the gold standard is incompatible with chronic deficit spending (the hallmark of the welfare state). (100)

> This is the shabby secret of the welfare statist's tirades against gold. Deficit spending is simply a scheme for the 'hidden' confiscation of wealth. Gold stands in the way of this insidious process. It stands as a protector of property rights. If one grasps this, one has no difficulty in understanding the statist's antagonism toward the gold standard. (101).

Were any fair and judicious commentator to have read these writings of a relatively young man, and then be told that such a person would maintain his principles and later become the Chairman of the Board of Governors of the Federal Reserve System, he would reject such a supposition outright. For to be chairman of the fed is to work with and promote the U.S. dollar fiat currency, but this is anathema to the gold standard. There is only one possible way to reconcile these two seemingly irreconcilable positions: if the man took the job with the express purpose of undermining from the inside the U.S. dollar and placing this country on the gold standard. What better position to do this than from not only within the bowels of the beast, but as its very head?

In the event however such a hypothesis must be rejected out of hand. There is simply no evidence that Greenspan, lo these many years, has been tirelessly destroying our fiat currency from within, based on his position as head of the fed. Not even his most vociferous critics (Rothbard 1987; Block 1999; Blumen 2002; Swanson 2004) have made any such point. The evidence is all exactly in the opposite direction: he has been doing his level best to defend the present system, illegitimate from his own (earlier) perspective. The disinterested observer would have no choice but to conclude that the later Greenspan has turned traitor to the ideals of free enterprise he had earlier espoused.

Milton Friedman

Milton Friedman (1974, 1978, 1980, 1998; Friedman and Stigler, 1946; Friedman and Friedman, 1962, 1984) too, claims to be, and is widely seen to be, a strong advocate of the free enterprise system, even a radical champion of it. If there were any one short summary in this regard, it might well be the motto "free to choose." Not only was this the title of one of his books (1980), it was also the designation of his highly regarded and award winning PBS television series (http://www.freetochoose.com/).

My reaction? "Free to choose," indeed.

In his retirement, Friedman has chosen to focus on one of his many initiatives, school vouchers, with his Milton and Rose D. Friedman Foundation (http://www.friedmanfoundation.org/). Yes, the parents of school-aged children will be "free to choose," but their choices will be limited to public schools, and private ones approved of by the statist authorities. Would the Department of Education sanction an educational institution that taught the virtue of "altering and abolishing" the government? This is very much to be doubted. More likely, such schools would be characterized as "terrorist" and their owners hunted down. Nor would schools promoting Communism, Nazism, polygamous nor incest marriages between consenting adults. Our "hate crimes" laws would put paid to schools guilty of racism, sexism, heterosexism or lookism. What, then, of the freedom to choose any of these educational experiences?

Further, the vouchers supported by Friedman will be financed out of tax revenues. What will happen to the freedom to choose of those without children, or those opposed to education entirely, or those who for any other reason would not "choose" to spend their monies in such a manner? Friedman admits he is only trying to free up consumer choice, not it's financing, but the lover of liberty would surely do both.[2]

Milton Friedman played a strong role in promoting the voluntary military during the years of the Vietnam war (North 2003; Rumsfeld 2002). Superficially, this would appear to be entirely compatible with his self styled adherence to liberty. For what could be more emblematic of freedom than hiring soldiers to fight, rather than drafting them?

But a moment's reflection will show that this claim is more apparent than real. For, if we grant that the U.S. had no business in Viet Nam in the first place—that fifth rate country never threatened us—and that the voluntary military is much more economically efficient than the draft and would thus enable our runaway government more leeway to pursue its evil goals in that far corner of the world,[3] the Friedman's championing of the voluntary military in that context yields a far different and very insidious interpretation: that he was trying to aid and abet warmongers, or was at the very least remiss in not shielding himself from such. The libertarian cannot favor the draft, of course. But this does not at all mean he has to promote the voluntary military either. The proper manpower tactic for an aggressive imperialistic war mongering country is no soldiers at all—to be stationed abroad.

A similar interpretation may be placed upon his (1998, 119–23) withholding tax plan. Now this, surely, is incompatible with economic liberty (Twight 2004). Given that the government takes far more than its proper share of the GDP, any scheme that makes it easier to pay taxes strengthens this evil institution. And withholding does this with a vengeance. For if the entire year's tax bill is due from the citizen in April, it is far more likely to engender a firestorm of protest than if the employer withholds much smaller amounts week by week. In the latter case, it is both less noticeable and painful to pay. Sometimes, even, if too much is withheld over the course of a year, the government actually returns some of the taxpayers' money to him in April. What could better take the winds out of the sails of the tax protesting movement than that? Friedman's (1998, 106) excuse is once again war. We were fighting World War II at the time, and the last thing the government needed was disruption of the monies accruing to the public treasury.

There are two things wrong with the defense. First of all, this conflagration was fought to a great degree because of that madman, Hitler. But this maniac's rise to power stemmed from the economic disarray due to the German hyperinflation in the 1920s. And this tragedy, in turn, resulted from the treaty of Versailles, the last vicious and depraved act of World War I, one that the U.S. was completely unjustified in waging. So we see that Mr. Free to Choose once again aligns himself with U.S. foreign military adventurism. What of the "choice" of its victims?

Secondly, at least if Friedman had the decency to urge that income tax withholding be eliminated after World War II, when the supposed emergency justification for it had ended, it would be easy to forgive him his transgressions. Instead, we have had to wait for almost 50 years (1998, p. 123) for him to express regret for this episode: "We gave next to no consideration to any longer-run consequences. It never occurred to me at the time that I was helping to develop machinery that would make possible a government that I would come to criticize severely as too large, too intrusive, too destructive of freedom. Yet, that was precisely what I was doing... withholding would have been introduced had I been involved or not. The most I accept blame for is helping to make it more efficient than it otherwise might have been."

By far the lion's share of Milton Friedman's contribution to economic theory concerned money and monetary policy. And here he exemplifies the little girl with the curl: "when she was good, she was very, very good; when she was bad, she was horrid."

Here again, this Nobel Prize winning economist (1960, 4) starts out on very good footing:

> The (classical) liberal is suspicious of assigning to government any functions that can be performed through the market, both because this substitutes coercion for voluntary cooperation, in the area in question and because, by giving government an increased role, it threatens freedom in other areas. Control over monetary and banking arrangements is a particularly dangerous power to entrust to government because of its far-reaching effects on economic activity at large—as numerous episodes from ancient times to the present and over the whole of the globe tragically demonstrate.

Here, "free to choose" really is the guiding motif. Voluntarism vs. coercion, historical examples showing the perfidy of government, it is on the basis of just such statements that Friedman's reputation as a defender of liberty, markets and free enterprise was based.

However, as is his wont, Friedman (1962, 40, emphasis added) takes it all back:

> The fundamental defect of a commodity standard (read gold standard) from the point of view of the society as a whole, is that it requires the use of real resources to add to the stock of money. People must work hard to dig gold out of the ground in South Africa— in order to rebury it in Fort Knox or some similar place. The necessity of using real resources for the operation of a commodity standard establishes a strong incentive for people to find ways to achieve the same result without employing these resources. If people will accept as money pieces of paper on which is printed 'I promise to pay— units of the commodity standard,' these pieces of paper can perform the same function as the physical pieces of gold or silver, and they require very much less in resources to produce.

But this is highly problematic. Freedom to choose vanishes, vanquished by a stronger enemy: economic efficiency. No sooner are we offered a ringing endorsement for justice, but that we have shoved in our faces abject surrender. What happened to "freedom to choose?" Why should, arguendo, efficiency trump freedom? Friedman vouchsafes us no answer to these crucial questions.

In point of fact, we need not give up real wealth in order to attain freedom. Rather, the two go hand in hand. In general, those countries that are more free are richer, not poorer (Gwartney 1996). In this specific case, the gold would be dug up and buried elsewhere in any case, since it has great value in non-monetary uses. Only the additional amount, stemming from this use would be withdrawn from the earth under a gold standard. However, in the view of the market participants, this extra quantity can be more than justified as a sort of insurance policy against, among other things, government perversion of the money supply. We know this from the fact that whenever people have been free to choose their monetary medium, apart from some few cases of silver, they have invariably chosen gold.

Friedrich A. Hayek

Hayek also deserves a place on this list of scholars who have turned their back on free enterprise. He, too, either did know better, or should have known better. After all, he had as his (informal) teacher none other than Ludwig von Mises, a veritable giant of liberty. How and in what ways did Hayek "leak?" Let us count the ways.

Hayek (1948, 1976, 1990) is no more of an advocate of the people's choice gold standard than is Friedman. Instead, he favors the "ducat,"[4] an amalgam or basket of several fiat currencies. Although Hayek is an avowed opponent of "constructivism," it is difficult to see why the ducat does not qualify in this regard.

As well, he (1944) compromises on a whole host of issues. For example, Hayek accepts as legitimate maximum hours legislation and government welfare for the poor (1944, 37), antitrust (1967, 177; 1948 [1972], 110–11), laws based on quelling externalities (1944, 38), that is, outright nationalization, or subsidies for businesses with positive neighborhood effects such as "sanitary and health measures" (1948 [1972], 111), and outright socialized medicine (1944, 120–21). Hayek (1994, 112–15) is even weak on such policies as the minimum wage law and the Tennessee Valley Authority. While Hayek does indeed oppose rent control he (1981, 183–5) also counsels against eliminating it too quickly, lest markets become disrupted. But this means that landlords and tenants must suffer under this enactment after we have the power to eliminate it. Is there any difference in principle between this and slowly eliminating slavery when we could do so immediately since this, too, would serve as a challenge to the market process?

Williamson Evers

Williamson Evers studied (informally) with perhaps the greatest libertarian theorist the world has ever known, Murray N. Rothbard. The former was even a confidant of the latter. More than that, Evers made several brilliant and original contributions to the edifice of libertarian theory (1977a, 1977b, 1978a, 1978b, 1978c). They were made several decades ago, in the early days of the modern libertarian movement, but they are today as original and fresh as the day they were penned.

Evers has also written a series of books and articles on education, all from a libertarian perspective. As well he was editor in chief (1976–1980) of the sometime libertarian Cato Institute's Inquiry Magazine, and managing editor (1986–1991) of the always libertarian Journal of Libertarian Studies (http://www-hoover.stanford.edu/BIOS/evers.html).

And, yet, what do we find? This former libertarian aided and abetted foreign military imperialistic adventurism of the U.S.: Evers took an active role in promoting American educational initiatives during the undeclared Iraq war (Hoover 2003, Evers 2004)!

Stated Raimondo (2004) about this unsavory episode:

> It's funny, but Bill Evers used to be one of those libertarians who went around giving everyone else a purity test, and he often found them wanting. Back in the good old days, he used to write a column for Libertarian Vanguard, the newspaper of the Radical Caucus, called "Brickbats and Bouquets," in which he handed out kudos and judo chops to those that, in his view, deserved them. The ideologically pure were praised, and the deviationists were denounced in no uncertain terms. How fitting that he—the self-appointed enforcer of libertarian political correctness turned apostate, who makes Judas Iscariot look like Horatio at the bridge—should now be the recipient of one of the biggest brickbats of all time.

And in the view of Garris (2004):

> I got involved with the libertarian movement in 1972. One of the first libertarians I met and quickly became friends with was Bill Evers. In 1973 I initiated a faction fight in California's Peace and Freedom Party (which I had been active in for a few years) between libertarians and socialists. By 1974 we had won a statewide primary fight and took control of the legal structure of the Party.
>
> Bill Evers was one of the intellectual guiding lights for our successful faction. He co-wrote the 1974 platform of the California Peace and Freedom Party, which was unabashedly libertarian and specifically Rothbardian. Later that year, Murray Rothbard changed his earlier position and joined and endorsed the young Libertarian Party (LP).

At the 1975 national LP convention, Murray Rothbard and Bill Evers rewrote the party platform. The essential hardcore elements of the Rothbard-Evers platform continue today, partly due to LP rules which make it extremely difficult to change platform planks ...

> When Bill ran for Congress in 1982, he called for withdrawal of all US forces from around the world. He even made a point of calling for the abolition of the Marine Corps, in a challenge to his opponent, noted antiwar Republican (and ex-Marine) Paul McClosky.
>
> I don't know when Bill became pro-war, but I understand that he was a strong advocate of the invasion of Iraq, egging on the Stanford College Republicans to support the war.

Murray Rothbard is undoubtedly spinning in his grave at the enormity of this betrayal, but Robert Stadler must be cackling with glee.

Dana Rohrabacher

When I first met him, Dana Rohrabacher was a staunch member of the libertarian movement. He played guitar at some of the meetings, and was known as the "libertarian troubadour." He is correctly described by Canizares (2000) as follows: "In the mid-1960s, Rohrabacher forged his own political views as a libertarian activist in Orange County, California."

And how did this young man, immersed in the niceties of libertarian theorizing, turn out? As yet another candidate for the Robert Stadler award.

Says Canizares (2000): "He is a strident advocate for supremacy in space, a philosophy shaped along a winding road from libertarian activist to White House speechwriter in the Reagan administration." This, indeed, is the initiative for which he is most noted.

But how can it be libertarian to advocate spending taxpayer money on space exploration? Surely, only private initiatives in this direction are compatible with the libertarian philosophy.[5] Now that the market has arrived on the scene, can we expect Rohrabacher to call for the dismantling of NASA? So far, this has not occurred.

Conclusion

Would I rather live in a society organized according to the philosophies of such men as have been criticized above, rather than, say, politicians such as Al Gore, Bill or Hillary Clinton, John Kerry, Michael Dukakis, John, Robert or Ted Kennedy, or, on the other side of the aisle, those like Richard Nixon, Ronald Reagan, Gerald Ford, Rudy Guliani, Arnold Schwarzenegger, and George Bush (either of them)? To ask this question is to answer it. Of course, the views of the philosophical turncoats discussed above are vastly to be preferred to those of any recent office holder or politician likely to take high office. But this is very much beside the point of the present essay. Our objective in the present examination is to ferret out the modern day Robert Stadlers. He was a fictional character, a scholar, who had at one time embraced the insights, moral and practical, of the free society, and then, later, turned against them. Greenspan, Friedman, Hayek, etc., all fit this bill. If we are determined to identify those whose careers most closely parallel that of Stadler, let the chips fall where they may, this primordial fact cannot be denied, no matter how disappointing it may be to some. I, too, share this regret. These men were, and are still to some extent despite their transgressions, my heroes. I cannot help myself from rooting for them when they debate those who are avowed and explicit enemies of economic freedom and laissez faire capitalism. And yet, and yet, despite myself I feel compelled, by logic and the facts of the matter, to see them as the Robert Stadlers they are. It simply does not matter that the vision they espouse is much more nearly congruent with a fully free society than that favored by 97 percent of the population, and articulated by its leaders.

It would be one thing if a Friedman or a Hayek defended or justified their various market socialist schemes merely as a means toward the end of full free enterprise. Then, I could criticize their strategies, while agreeing with their ends. This would be akin to Greenspan becoming head of the fed, in an attempt to destroy it from within. In such as case, the "hearts" of Friedman, Hayek and Greenspan would be in the right place, and they would not deserve inclusion on the list of Robert Stadlers.

However, I know of no such proviso in any of the writings of any of these authors. Friedman, for example, simply states that the man of good will embrace school vouchers, or the 3 percent rule for the fed, or the voluntary military, etc., and goes on from there to defend them per se, not as a means toward the goal of true liberty. Would that matters were otherwise, he would not have been included on this list.[6]

Notes

1   I am writing from a position of strict anarcho-libertarianism. This perspective animates my criticisms. As we know, the Randian position on foreign wars and big space programs is different than the Rothbardian. I follow the latter, not the former.

2   To be fair to Milton (and Rose) Friedman, there are occasions where he (they) come close, but do not quite state, at least not clearly, that they favor vouchers only as a first or interim step in the direction of full separation of education and state. For example they opine (Friedman and Friedman, 1980, 161–3):

"This plan would relieve no one of the burden of taxation to pay for schooling. It would simply give parents a wider choice as to the form in which their children get the schooling that the community has obligated itself to provide. The plan would also not affect the present standards imposed on private schools in order for attendance at them to satisfy the compulsory attendance laws."

"We regard the voucher plan as a partial solution because it affects neither the financing of schooling nor the compulsory attendance laws. We favor going much farther. Offhand, it would appear that the wealthier a society and the more evenly distributed is income within it, the less reason there is for government to finance schooling."

"Our own views on this have changed over time. When we first wrote extensively a quarter of a century ago on this subject, we accepted the need for such laws on the ground that 'a stable democratic society is impossible without a minimum degree of literacy and knowledge on the part of most citizens' [footnote omitted]. We continue to believe that, but research that has been done in the interim on the history of schooling in the United States, the United Kingdom, and other countries has persuaded us that compulsory attendance at schools is not necessary to achieve that minimum standard of literacy and knowledge."

"We realize that these views on financing and attendance laws will appear to most readers to be extreme. That is why we only state them here to keep the record straight without seeking to support them at length. Instead, we return to the voucher plan—a much more moderate departure from present practice."

I owe these cites to B.K. Marcus and Mateusz Machaj.

3   The draft led to protests which eventually ended our undeclared war over there.

4   According to some interpretations, he favors this type of money only as a temporary measure. For a critique of the Hayekian "ducat" see Rothbard (1981–1982), Block (1996, 1999).

5   On private space travel, see David, 2004; also http://www.space-travel.com/; Huebert and Block, unpublished.

6   Friedman describes himself as a "small 'l' libertarian" (small "l" to distinguish himself from a large "L" member of the Libertarian Party). I have no power, nor desire, to read anyone out of the libertarian movement. The more members there are, the better, as far as I am concerned. However, we do have to have some standards. The libertarian name, capitalized or not, is an honorific. Not everyone who claims it deserves it.

References

Anderson, William L. 2002. Trouble with vouchers. *The Free Market*. Auburn, Alabama: The Ludwig von Mises Institute (September). Online at: http://www.mises.org/fullstory.aspx?control=507&id=73.

Block, Walter. 1969. Against the volunteer military. *The Libertarian Forum* (15 August): 4.

———. 1996. Hayek's road to serfdom. *Journal of Libertarian Studies: An Interdisciplinary Review* 12, no. 2 (Fall): 327–50. Online at: http://www.mises.org/journals/jls/12_2/12_2_6.pdf.

———. 1999. The gold standard: A critique of Friedman, Mundell, Hayek, Greenspan. *Managerial Finance* 25, no. 5: 15–33. Online at: http://giorgio.emeraldinsight.com/vl=4558845/cl=18/nw=1/rpsv/cw/www/mcb/03074358/contp1-1.htm; http://www.mises.org/etexts/goldcritique.pdf.

Blumen, Robert. 2002. Greenspan: The mind of God, or merely omniscient? *The Free Market* (9 September). Auburn, Alabama: The Ludwig von Mises Institute. Online at: http://www.mises.org/fullstory.aspx?control=1044.

Canizares, Alex. 2000. 'California dreamin': Congressman Dana Rohrabacher's vision of space. (19 May). Online at: http://www.space.com/peopleinterviews/rohrabacher_profile_000519.html.

David, Leonard. 2004. Brave new world? Next steps planned for private space travel. (6 October 2004.) Online at:
http://www.space.com/news/beyond_spaceshipone_041006.html.

Evers, Williamson M. 1977a. Toward a reformulation of the law of contracts. *The Journal of Libertarian Studies* 1, no. 1 (Winter): 3–14.

———. 1977b. Social contract: A critique. *The Journal of Libertarian Studies* 1, no. 3 (Summer): 185–94.

———. 1978a. The law of omissions and neglect of children. *The Journal of Libertarian Studies* 2, no. 1 (Winter): 1–10.

———. 1978b. Rawls and children. *The Journal of Libertarian Studies* 2, no. 2 (Summer): 109–14.

———. 1978c. Kropotkin's ethics and the public good. *The Journal of Libertarian Studies* 2, no. 3 (Fall): 225–32.

Evers, Bill. 2004. An Iraqi education: A firsthand report on postwar school reconstruction. *The Wall Street Journal.* (25 January). Online at:
http://fairuse.1accesshost.com/news1/evers.html.

Friedman, Milton, and Stigler, George. 1946. *Roofs or Ceilings? The Current Housing Problem.* Irvington on Hudson, New York: Foundation for Economic Education.

Friedman, Milton. 1960. *A Program for Monetary Stability.* New York: Fordham University Press.

———. 1974. *There's No Such Thing as a Free Lunch.* LaSalle, Illinois: Open Court.

———. 1977. *Friedman on Galbraith and on Curing the British Disease.* Vancouver, B.C.: Fraser Institute.

———. 1978. *Tax limitation, inflation and the role of government.* Dallas, Texas: The Fisher Institute.

Friedman, Milton, and Friedman, Rose D. 1962. *Capitalism and Freedom.* Chicago: University of Chicago Press.

———. 1980. *Free to Choose: A Personal Statement.* New York: Harcourt Brace Jovanovich.

———. 1984 *Tyranny of the Status Quo.* San Diego: Harcourt Brace Jovanovich.

———. 1998. *Two Lucky People.* Chicago: University of Chicago Press.

Fritz, Marshall. Alliance for the separation of school and state. Online at:
http://honested.com/edlib/.

Garris, Eric. 2004. The triumphant return from Iraq of the once-great libertarian. (15 January). Online at:
http://www.antiwar.com/blog/comments.php?id=P406_0_1_0.

Greenspan, Alan. 1967. Gold and economic freedom. *Capitalism: The Unknown Ideal.* Edited by Ayn Rand. New York: Signet: 96–101. Reprinted from *The Objectivist,* 1966.

Gwartney, James, Lawson, Robert, and Block, Walter. 1996. *Economic Freedom of the World, 1975–1995.* Vancouver, B.C.: The Fraser Institute.

Hayek, Friedrich A. 1944. *The Road to Serfdom*. Chicago: The University of Chicago Press.

———. 1967. *Studies in Philosophy, Politics and Economics*. New York: Simon and Schuster.

———. 1948 [1972]. *Individualism and Economic Order*. Chicago: University of Chicago Press.

———. 1976. *Choice in Currency: A Way to Stop Inflation*. London: The Institute of Economic Affairs.

———. 1981. The repercussions of rent restrictions. *Rent Control: Myths and Realities*. Edited by Walter Block. Vancouver: The Fraser Institute.

———. 1990. *Denationalization of Money*. Third edition. London: Institute for Economic Affairs.

———. 1994. *Hayek on Hayek: An Autobiographical Dialogue*. Edited by Stephen Kresge and Leif Wenar. Chicago: University of Chicago Press.

Hoover Fellow Williamson M. Evers Named Senior Education Advisor in Iraq. 2003. Hoover Institution Press Release. (12 August). Online at: http://www.hoover.stanford.edu/pubaffairs/Releases/2003/08evers.html.

Huebert, Jacob, and Block, Walter. Unpublished. "Privatizing Space."

Murphy, Robert. 2004. Profit, loss and Pluto. (14 October). Online at: http://www.mises.org/fullstory.aspx?Id=1644.

North, Gary. 2003. The Libertarian roots of the all-volunteer military. (20 December). Online at: http://www.lewrockwell.com/north/north235.html.

Raimondo, Justin. 2002. Who's afraid of Virginia Postrel? (8 April). Online at: http://www.antiwar.com/justin/j040802.html.

———. 2004. Bill Evers goes neocon. (15 January). Online at: http://www.antiwar.com/blog/comments.php?id=P407_0_1_0.

Rand, Ayn. 1957. *Atlas Shrugged*. New York, Random House.

———. [1969] 1988. Apollo 11. *The Voice of Reason: Essays in Objectivist Thought*. Edited by Leonard Peikoff. New York: New American Library: 161–78. Reprinted from *The Objectivist* (September).

Rothbard, Murray, N. 1981–1982. Hayek's denationalized money. *The Libertarian Forum* XV, nos. 5–6 (August-January): 9.

———. 1987. Alan Greenspan: A minority report on the new Fed Chairman. *The Free Market* (August): 3, 8. Found online at: http://www.mises.org/freemarket_detail.asp?control=267&sortorder=authorlast.

———. 1994. Vouchers: What went wrong? *The Free Market*. The Ludwig von Mises Institute (January): 1, 8.

Rumsfeld, Donald H. 2002. Lucky us: A tribute to Milton Friedman. *National Review Online* (31 July). Online at: http://www.nationalreview.com/nrof_document/document073102.asp.

Swanson, Mike. 2004. Alan Greenspan must go! (Fall). Online at: http://wallstreetwindow.com/greenspan.htm

Twight, Charlotte. 2004. Evolution of federal income tax withholding: The machinery of institutional change. *Cato Journal* 14, no. 3 (27 September). Online at: http://www.cato.org/pubs/journal/cj14n3-1.html.

Vance, Laurence M. 2004. Vouchers: Another central plan. (19 October). Online at: http://www.mises.org/fullstory.aspx?Id=1399.

Chapter 36

Atlas Shrugging Throughout History and Modern Life

Stuart K. Hayashi

Could Atlas ever shrug in reality?

Atlas Shrugged's title, of course, alludes to the famous figure of Greek myth. He was one of the original gods to reign over Creation. Along with them, he fought a war to quash a rebellion of "new gods" led by Zeus for control over the universe.

Once Zeus defeated his adversaries, he devised a unique punishment for each of them. He sentenced Atlas to hold the sky upon his shoulders for eternity. In our most popular images of Atlas, however, he is depicted carrying, not the heavens, but planet Earth, and that is the symbol relevant to Ayn Rand in her groundbreaking novel.

In it, copper magnate Francisco d'Anconia asks the innovative metallurgist-entrepreneur Hank Rearden,

> If you saw Atlas ... if you saw that he stood, blood running down his chest, his knees buckling, his arms trembling but still trying to hold the world aloft with the last of his strength, and the greater his effort the heavier the world bore down upon his shoulders—what would you tell him to do?
>
> 'I ... don't know,' Rearden confesses. 'What ... could he do? What would you tell him?'
>
> 'To shrug' Francisco answers simply. (Rand 1957, 429)

Atlas is not the only one who balances the earth with great effort. Metaphorically, so does Rearden himself, as well as other great industrialists.

Rand's thesis was that, just as Atlas kept the world afloat, as opposed to letting it crash into a "nether-ground" and shatter into a trillion shards, great industrialists and other men of intellect carry "the weight of the world" on their shoulders by maintaining and advancing the standards of civilization. The earth, as in the globe, depends on Atlas for its continued existence, just as "the world," meaning "society," depends upon "the men of the mind"—scientists, inventors, engineers, and entrepreneurs.

Yet holding up the planet is a burden for Atlas, just as Zeus intended. D'Anconia observed that even Atlas could only endure his task to a certain extent. If Zeus contributed to Atlas's burden by continually adding more weight to the globe, there would come a day when Atlas would become so exhausted that he would give up. He would shrug ... relieving himself of the alleged duty, letting the planet collapse into rubble.

By that same token, the thinkers of society can also cave in from exhaustion if overloaded with their own terra-bearing.

Hank Rearden certainly could relate. As with many real-life moguls, his ability to preserve civilization is shackled and hindered by the increasing weightiness of unnecessary government regulations and taxes on business.

It does not help any when the very "world"—society—that he saves from destruction ungratefully demands that he sacrifice even more of his happiness and life to serve it, even as it places obstacles preventing him from fully executing this very mission.

This phenomenon transpires everywhere on the globe, even in its freest nation—the United States.

So might Atlas ever shrug in America or abroad?

Ayn Rand vs. Academia's Real-life Simon Pritchetts

In the year 2000, Harvard University published an entire anthology in book form to deny the possibility. To make sure we all get the jab, the editors titled it *Does Atlas Shrug?* and then proceeded to answer, *No!*

Harvard's tome states that, if it were true that Atlas shrugs, then the economy should improve every time businesses or businesspeople receive a hefty tax cut, as it alleviates their constraints. If Atlas shrugs when the heaviness of the (tax) burden is greatest, the Harvard-published book postulates, then Atlas will do the opposite of shrugging (whatever that is) when the regulations are lightest.

On 15 February 2001 the leftwing *New York Times* published an op-ed by Jeff Madrick that cited the Harvard tome's anti-capitalist arguments.

"Robert A. Moffitt and Mark Wilhelm, economists at Johns Hopkins University and Indiana University," wrote Madrick, "found that high-income men did not work more hours in response to the especially generous tax cuts [made by President Ronald Reagan] in the 1980s."

Madrick added, "Austan Goolsbee, an economist at the free-market-oriented University of Chicago ... reports in *Does Atlas Shrug?* that incomes rose in the 1980s for high-income Americans for reasons distinct from tax incentives."

Madrick's analysis is shallow. To really judge whether Atlas can or does shrug in reality, one would have to look at the wider scope of history and culture.

Can one find an example of this among America's most accomplished corporate executives?

Billionaires Shrug Off Ayn Rand

As billionaire Theodore J. Forstmann observed in a report for Washington, D.C.'s Cato Institute, wealthy businesspeople tend to be incredibly dissimilar to Ayn Rand's heroes. This is not the fault of Rand, but of the billionaires, for few of them show more enthusiasm for free enterprise than they do the welfare state.

Going through *Forbes* magazine's 2006 edition of its noted list of the 400 richest Americans, I could only identify seven people who even remotely professed an ideological bias in favor of economic freedom and have shown consistency while espousing it.[1]

The list does contain a number of great entrepreneurs who have been unfairly persecuted for their success. However, if they are like Bill Gates, whose Microsoft Corporation was almost forcibly split in half by the federal government from 1998 to 2001, then they probably do not possess the spiritual courage any titan would need to withdraw from the world in the way a d'Anconia would.

For all the good he has done, Bill Gates would not be wise enough to go "on strike" against society even when it would be the truly moral option.[2] He has stated in public that he is familiar with Ayn Rand's writings. Only, he is not sharp enough to appreciate their full meaning.

Following a speech given at the Business School of Columbia University and New York University on March 24, 1999, when the antitrust suit against his company was still in progress, a student said to Bill Gates,

> Alan Greenspan, the Chairman of the Federal Reserve, came out [and] publicly stated [in 1966] that he felt that the philosophy behind the antitrust laws of the United States [was] based upon ... economic fallacy. And one of the people that influenced him was an author, Ayn Rand, [who] wrote ... *Atlas Shrugged*, which deals with antitrust laws in a way that seems very similar to what's going on today. And I was curious if you've read that novel? (Gates 1999)
>
> 'Yes,' Gates answered, 'I did read that.'

So did he then go on to express his appreciation of Ayn Rand and her ethical justification for *laissez faire*? God, no! He asserted,

> You don't even have to go as far as Greenspan, or *certainly not as far as Rand* to think that allowing businesses to keep innovating in their products, including supporting the Internet in their products, and providing those features without extra cost to users, you don't have to go very far at all to think that's a good thing. To me, you have to go about as far as common sense. And so, that summarizes my view on that topic. (Gates 1999) [emphasis added]

For Gates, that was the end of it. The billionaire could care less about the morality of the issue. For him, to break up the private property that is Microsoft is not some moral abomination. Rather, it is "common sense," in utilitarian terms, that the government's destruction of Microsoft would work against that of the "public interest" ... which conveniently coincides with Gates's.

The tycoon opted out of upholding his moral right to his private property as a result of his failure to grasp the existence of such rights. His outlook is utilitarian, which explains his bland reaction (or non-reaction) to Ayn Rand. Like many other "robber barons," he rejects the intellectual gift she gave him.

As Andrew Leonard observed on 29 January 1998 in the leftwing *Salon.Com*, "Bill Gates is a bleeding heart do-gooder liberal."[3]

It is less of a wonder, then, why Gates reacts so differently from *Atlas Shrugged*'s Hank Rearden, who faced a similar situation.

Just as its real-life counterpart did with Gates, the book's fictional federal government prosecuted (translation: persecuted) Rearden for the violation of morally illegitimate regulations over his own private property.

Gates' videotaped deposition for his own antitrust trial came across as evasive (Wasserman 1998), because Gates, lacking Ayn Rand's interpretation of ethics, was not fully confident that shareholders like himself had the rightful authority to exercise control over their own companies.

Gates would have done both himself and civilization a favor had he testified in the manner that Rearden did: fully confident of his right to his own business, as opposed to cringing before the altar of a pagan god called "the public good."

What Rearden said at his trial is what Gates should have but did not:

> I refuse to accept as guilt the fact of my own existence and the fact that I must work in order to support it. I refuse to accept as guilt the fact that I am able to do it and do it well. I refuse to accept as guilt the fact that I am able to do it better than most people— the fact that my work is of greater value than the work of my neighbors and that more men are willing to pay me ... It's not your particular policy that I challenge, but your moral premise. If it were true that men could achieve their good by means of turning some men into sacrificial animals, and I were asked to immolate myself for the sake of creatures who wanted to survive at the price of my blood I would refuse ... If it is now the belief of my fellow men, who call themselves the public, that their good requires victims, then I say: the public good be damned, I will have no part of it! (Rand 1957, 451–2)

Sadly, Gates will have part of it.

Yet while many of the other most prominent billionaires on the list[4] are also highly illiterate of Objectivism's economic wisdom, it remains true that there is great reason to believe Atlas does shrug. Often, the people who choose to shrug are not the ultra-rich, but rather ordinary and honest workers, many of whom may not even have heard of Ayn Rand. The fact that Atlas can shrug is illustrated in a famous economic model known as the Laffer Curve.

"T*" Does Not Only Stand for Taggart

With his notorious chart, Arthur Laffer, an economic adviser to former President Reagan, proved there are occasions on which the government can raise its revenues by reducing the tax rate.

That sounds counterintuitive at first. Before Laffer's day, many economists assumed there was a direct correlation between the tax rate and government revenue, which is to say a hike in tax rates would necessarily increase government revenue. But one can spot the absurdity of this presumption when one carries it to its logical end.

Let us say, hypothetically, that a national government can take in 100 billion U.S. dollars per year in revenue with a flat 25 percent tax on all income—from both individuals and private organizations. The Minister of Finance may then infer that if he doubles the tax rate to 50 percent, he can double the revenue to 200 billion dollars. In that same vein, if he triples the initial tax rate of 25 percent to 75 percent, then he can triple the revenue to 300 billion dollars. Taking this to its logical conclusion, quadrupling the initial tax rate of 25 percent to 100 percent should quadruple the annual revenue to 400 billion dollars.

Of course, it is silly to believe a flat 100 percent income tax could fetch so much money; it would be surprising if it got the government anything. If the State takes all of a person's income, he or she will have nothing left for him- or herself. This penalizes an individual for helping the economy through working at a business and selling services and products to other people. Most individuals would figure, "If my work doesn't get me anything for myself, why should I do it in the first place?"

Consequently, if a State raised its flat income tax of 25 percent to 100 percent, people would quit their jobs, businesses would stop selling any goods or services (all revenue from that would be confiscated anyway), and hordes of people would flock to a country with a government promising to treat them better.

Not even Bill Gates would put up with complete nationalization of all his income. Even he would find himself "shrugging" under these circumstances.

Hence, quadrupling the flat 25 percent income tax on all persons and businesses to 100 percent would not cause the $100 billion annual revenue to skyrocket, but would instead bring in revenue close to nil. Likewise, if the government reduced that tax rate from 100 percent to 25 percent, it would raise revenue from zero to ... well, higher-than-zero. It would result in fewer people moving away and would lead to people producing for the economy again.

At first, Laffer noted, when the State raises the tax rate from zero, there is some correlation between the rate of taxation and the rate of revenue. However, there comes a point between a tax rate of zero and 100 percent where, if the State raises the tax burden on producers any more—if it taxes Atlas's endurance too harshly—revenue will finally shrink as a result of businesspeople and workers reducing their own earnings, and therefore their own productivity to the economy, to avoid any further unnecessary financial penalty upon their labors.

And these labors are usually the result of all the mind power they put to work.

At this juncture, businesspeople feel as if they cannot support society or the State on their backs any longer, for both institutions have tortured them too much through taxing their strength excessively. Thus, the pressure proves too fatiguing for the businesspersons and they "shrug"—they reduce their own productivity or just plain quit.

Because they are no longer producing goods and services or the economy—or making any more money to support the State itself—these people have essentially gone on strike against society and the State.

Economists call that point "T*" (Income 1999–2003), but it is really "the point where Atlas Shrugs."

Let this phenomenon be known as the *Atlas Shrugged* Effect.

Atlas Shrugging Throughout History

This is more than mere theory; history confirms it. Borrowing quite a bit from economist Jude Wanniski's book *The Way the World Works*, as well as the writings of Thomas Gale Moore, Hawaii Pacific University economics professor Ken Schoolland explains the Laffer Curve to his students using the examples of eighteenth-century France and nineteenth-century Britain (1999).

Schoolland notes that in the late 1700s, King Louis XVI taxed the population of France at the average rate of 80 percent, leading to economic malaise. After King Louis's rule and Robespierre's Reign of Terror were deposed, Emperor Napoleon took over and cut the average tax rate to 25 percent.

That they could keep more of what they earned encouraged France's merchants to begin producing again, thus revitalizing the nation's economy. Though the income tax was lower, the income grew so much higher for everyone—to the extent that Napoleon's treasury swelled with great opulence. Unfortunately, Napoleon then squandered much of that wealth on his unwise and immoral attempt to conquer the rest of Europe.

Napoleon, thankfully, was put down by the British forces who, in turn, then slashed their own stifling taxes in the period of 1815 to 1851, particularly repealing the existing 173–454 percent tariffs on grain foods in 1846 (Anti-Corn http://tinyurl.com/5co9w) causing the Industrial Revolution to burn even more brightly with creative fire than before, enriching the empire[5] and filling up its treasury.

But as *Atlas Shrugged* warned, progress is not inevitable. It gradually comes to a halt when the State smothers it under tons of regulations and taxes.

One can argue the Ancient Greek, Roman (Clough and Rapp 1975, 37), Ming Chinese (Micklethwait and Wooldridge 2003, 6), and Islamic (Landes 1999, 399) Empires all reached their peaks when they were at their freest, while each of these civilizations gradually self-destructed as their bureaucratic government grew too overbearing and the taxation too stifling.

When Rome's gargantuan State collapsed upon itself and cast Europe into the Dark Ages, the average life expectancy and standard of living actually decreased to levels far below that of the Hellenistic Age (Bernstein 2000a, 75).[6]

Atlas also notoriously shrugged in this manner in the former Soviet Union, in Iran under the ayatollahs, and in Afghanistan under the Taliban.

In fact, academic economists James D. Gwartney and Robert A. Lawson (2004) and experts from the *Wall Street Journal* and Heritage Foundation (Miles et al. 2004) have shown there is a direct correlation between how consistently a national government abides by Ayn Rand's definition of economic freedom (largely inspired by John Locke's definition of natural rights) and how prosperous it is per-capita. Conversely, countries that are the most statist are the ones where Atlas shrugs most severely.

On a smaller scale and in a more modern setting, some large American corporations go on strike against this by moving their operations out of the United States and setting themselves up in places where they will face fewer hassles.

In all of the cases I have presented, however, one may argue that few of the businesspeople involved voluntarily quit their jobs. Merchants still existed when the Roman Empire exercised many oppressive laws, while the main reason people refrained from starting private utilities businesses in the former Soviet Union was that it was illegal to do so.

Are there any examples, then, of some entrepreneurs actually walking out on their own enterprises as a result of red tape strangling them too viciously?

"Brother, You Asked for It!"

One finds such instances in New York City's housing industry under rent control. Beginning in 1942, the city government passed a law forbidding any landlords from raising the rents on any apartments. This initially sounded beneficial to many tenants, but it was terrible for the most conscientious landlords.

Because of the inflation induced by the federal government's expansion of the money supply, all of the landlords' costs were in constant ascension. The capitalists who owned apartment buildings found themselves having to pay higher prices for electricity, plumbing, repairs, building upkeep, and security.

Because landlords were unable to raise their rents to catch up with the climbing costs, many of them found themselves going "in the red." A scrupulous landlord became caught in a bind. Either he had to cut his expenses, such as security and repairs, which would essentially result in lowering the quality of service to his tenants—or he would have to continue losing money until he inevitably went bankrupt.

Meanwhile, New York City's population growth in the ensuing decades heightened the demand for urban shelter. Yet, because the rent controls severely cut into the profitability of supplying urban housing, the supply of apartments dwindled. The outcome was a heartbreaking shortage.

As in the cases cited earlier, the Atlases who kept the urban housing market from crashing into pieces found even more tons of constraints stacked upon their backs, until they just gave up and resigned.

In the late twentieth century, it got to the point where some landlords eventually abandoned their own buildings outright. Leaving their grand multimillion-dollar investments behind was less financially risky than attempting the impossible task of running a great and profitable business without being able to pay for the maintenance of quality services.

How severely did Atlas shrug here? From 1972 to 1982, New York landlords abandoned an average of 30,000 apartments a year (Tucker 1990, 265). In other words, 300,000 apartments—almost two percent of all the apartments that were available in New York City in 1972—were left to rot away over a decade (Tucker 1990, 265). First the landlord walked away from the apartment building, refusing to take care of it, and so the tenants eventually left, too.

As Prof. Ken Schoolland describes the situation,

> Even the nice landlords had to cut back on repairs. When the buildings became uncomfortable or dangerous, tenants got mad and complained to the [government building] inspectors. The inspectors slapped fines on the landlords. ... Finally ... a decent [landlord] couldn't afford the loss ... anymore so he just up and left.
>
> "Imagine," Schoolland adds, "walking away from something that took a lifetime to build?" (2001, 27).

When ditching their own buildings, the landlords unknowingly sent a message to the politicians who constrained them and to the tenants who encouraged the regulation. It is the same one Francisco d'Anconia left the looters of *Atlas Shrugged* when he vanished into Galt's Gulch: "Brother, you asked for it!" (Rand 1957, 858).

These corridors of the "Big Apple" have degenerated into slums. Rent control created, in a microcosm, a breakdown of civilization and comfort in many areas of the city that now look just as bleak and decrepit as many parts of the United States did in *Atlas Shrugged* as the producers' "passive resistance" let communities disintegrate.

A walk down rent-controlled alleyways brings to mind the architectural conditions and overall grim ambience the character Eddie Willers observed of New York City in *Atlas*'s opening scene:

> The clouds and the shafts of skyscrapers against them were turning brown, like an old painting in oil, the color of a fading masterpiece. Long streaks of grime ran from under the pinnacles down the slender, soot-eaten walls. High on the side of a tower was a crack in the shape of a motionless lightning, the length of ten stories. A jagged object cut the sky above the roofs; it was half a spire, still holding the glow of the sunset; the

gold leaf had long since peeled off the other half. The glow was red and still, like the reflection of a fire: not an active fire, but a dying one which it is too late to stop. (Rand 1957, 12)

Adding to this decline is the sort of businessperson who gains prominence under heavy regulations. Moral individuals who take pride in their work have a difficult time operating in a statist economy mired in corruption, but looting louts do not.

When conscientious landlords vacated their own businesses, they left a vacuum in the housing market to be filled by unsavory hucksters who were willing to stay in the harsh economic climate because they did not mind providing tenants with cheap, inferior service.

When an ethical landlord had to cut back on repairs to stay in business, he felt a knack of guilt for refusing to fix anything broken in his tenants' apartment. This was no problem, however, for landlords who did not care about their tenants' well-being.

In a market free of price controls, many landlords compete with one another in supplying apartments. A greater supply of apartments makes it easier for everyone of every race to find adequate shelter. But corruption enters the picture under rent control, as the regulation-caused housing shortage gives unsavory landlords the opportunity to apply ethnic discrimination in the selection of tenants.

Indeed, unsavory wheeler-dealers thrive in such a system collapsing from over-regulation. *Atlas Shrugged* keenly dramatized the situation in which statism drives conscientious entrepreneurs out of an industry while rewarding its charlatans.

Productive entrepreneurs like Hank Rearden, who compete with one another by producing the best-quality product or service, become impotent in the face of shackling decrees, and are replaced in the steel industry by the likes of Orren Boyle, who instead compete with one another in terms of who can get the best favors from "protection"-selling politicians (Bernstein 2000b, 38–9, 41–2).

This also occurs with the socialization of banking, which leads Midas Mulligan to resign from his fellow men in disgust (Bernstein 2000b, 22) only to have his position filled by the buffoonish Eugene Lawson of the Community National Bank (Rand 1957, 295).

Yes, Virginia, Atlas Does Shrug

The matter of whether Atlas does shrug is one close to my heart, because the phenomenon seems to be occurring in my own home state of Hawaii. Since the late 1980s, my state has been consistently rated on numerous national surveys to be one of the worst for doing business (Schoolland 1999), as it is one of the most highly taxed and regulated, rivaling Massachusetts in its fiscal leftism (Schoolland 1999).

Naturally, many corrupt businesspeople have actually profited from the legislative jungle, receiving tax-funded contracts for government projects that should have been left completely to the private sector, while small businesses that have not succumbed to "playing the game" have been met with reprisals from the Democrat-controlled government for much of the 1990s (Slom 2000).

For Hawaii, this oppressive climate has resulted in a recession lasting over a decade (Schoolland 1999).

A new Republican gubernatorial administration, promising to end the corruption and the economic stagnation, took over in 2002. Now the state's executive branch tries to appear friendlier to private enterprise. Unfortunately, it does not roll back "Leviathan" as swiftly as it should.

And Hawaii's State Legislature continues to be dominated by "little Caesars" who share the belief of Wesley Mouch and Kip Chalmers that business must be curtailed for "the public's" benefit.

Yet these very same officials often have the nerve to publicly express their befuddlement over why Hawaii's economy performs so terribly and why so many corporations outside of my home state are afraid to make long-term investments here.

I have sometimes suggested to businesspeople that, when a state senator asks them why Hawaii's businesses earn much less than those on the mainland, they should reply as John Galt did in the book's climactic radio speech:

> We [entrepreneurs] required that you leave us free to function—free to think and work as we choose—free to take our own risks and bear our own losses—free to earn our own profits and make our own fortunes ... Such was the price we asked, which you chose to reject as too high. (Rand 1957, 989)

Of course, one may still wonder if there has ever been a case in history where people did not merely shrug subconsciously out of fear of being punished for pursuing their own creative ends, but because they, like John Galt, purposely went on strike against society in a highly deliberate and organized campaign to protest the claim that their lives and intellectual labors were the property of the State instead of themselves.

As John Galt said in his speech,

> I have done by plan and intention what had been done throughout history by silent default. There have always been men of intelligence who went on strike, in protest and despair, but they did not know the meaning of their action. ... Every period ruled by mystics [such as welfare-statists] was an era of stagnation and want, when most men were on strike against existence, working for less than their barest survival, leaving nothing but scraps for their rulers to loot, refusing to think, to venture, to produce, when the ultimate collector of their profits and the final authority on truth and error was the whim of some gilded degenerate sanctioned as superior to reason by divine right and by grace of a club. (Rand 1957, 975–6)

People have always gone "on strike, in protest and despair" against "gilded degenerate[s] sanctioned as superior to reason by ... grace of a club" but did any of them ever "know the meaning of their action"?

In 2003, there were such shrugging Atlases. In the Latin American nation of Venezuela, the largest labor union joined forces with the country's equivalent to America's Chamber of Commerce to go on a nationwide strike in all industries. This was to shut down the country's whole economy until the government called a referendum in which the dictatorial Marxist head of state, Hugo Chavez, would hopefully be cast out of office (Tracinski, 2003, 12–13).

In *The Intellectual Activist* magazine, Robert W. Tracinski wrote that he actually met Venezuelans participating in the strike who had actually read *Atlas Shrugged* and considered it an inspiration in their own crusade (20).

On 7 January 2003, Thor Halvorsson asked "Is John Galt Venezuelan?" in an online article covering the event.

The strike was successful in bringing about the referendum but, sadly, Chavez got away with rigging the new election. He thus remains in power and his repressive measures continue.

However, the nationwide strike in Venezuela was still an impressive one, and there may still come a day when Chavez or some other dictator will finally be defeated by such a work stoppage. In the meantime, Atlas has resumed shrugging in Venezuela the old-fashioned way—which is why, despite its fantastic oil reserves, the nation still suffers from privation.

When a book published by Harvard University asks, "Does Atlas shrug?" I look to current events and the past and answer yes. To those who maintain that Ayn Rand's classic is a mere far-fetched fantasy with no parallels in real life, I point to the many episodes of history demonstrating Ayn Rand's contention that the human mind cannot be coerced into creating wealth.

The next time Amtrak—the federal government's socialized version of Taggart Transcontinental—derails as a consequence of the State's ineptitude, and the next time you see prodigious managers and engineers flee an industry facing the encroachment of even more regulations, remember that you are witnessing the shrugging of Atlas in plain view.

Notes

1   Besides Forstmann, there are Cato Institute board members Rupert Murdoch (Fox News) and Frederick Wallace Smith (founder of Federal Express), publisher Richard Mellon Scaife (I include him because of his notable contributions to the Heritage Foundation and his leadership in the "rightwing conspiracy" against former President Bill Clinton), and Cato Institute cofounder Charles G. Koch, along with his brother, Reason Foundation board member David H. Koch and owner of the Dallas Mavericks, Mark Cuban.

I exclude Sun Microsystems CEO and cofounder Scott McNealy, Oracle Corp. founder Lawrence Joseph Ellison, and former investment banker Michael R. Milken, despite the first man professing to be a libertarian, the latter two's public acclaim for *Atlas Shrugged* and the last man's endorsement of the Rand-influenced satire poem *Tom Smith and His Incredible Bread Machine*. That is because, despite his own persecution at the hands of the State, Milken is a Democrat who has advocated that the federal government should extort money from taxpayers to finance disease research—research that would probably be conducted with greater competency in the private sector with private funding.

Meanwhile, McNealy and Ellison were only too eager to encourage the Clinton administration's attempt to obliterate Microsoft (Ellison even paid private investigators to find financial links between Microsoft and the pro-market organizations that defended it so that Ellison could publicly smear them).

To see *Forbes*'s list of America's 400 richest people, see http://www.forbes.com/400richest/, accessed 23 October 2006.

2   Attorney Michael Giorgino authored an enjoyable satire titled "Bill Gates Shrugs," for the April 2000 issue of *Liberty* magazine, in which Gates does morally defend his business conduct and goes on strike. Unfortunately, the Gates of real life is probably not as wise as the one portrayed in Giorgino's story, which can be read at http://www.angelfire.com/co2/RayThomas/shrug.html, accessed 23 October 2004.

3   When Washington state put on its ballot Initiative 602, which would reduce the amount of money the state confiscated in taxes, Gates donated $80,000 to the alliance working to fight against the initiative's passage, for Gates feared that such a tax rollback would mean that less government-stolen money would go to pay for the government's socialized school system (Leonard 1999). Gates's support for the regulation of gun ownership (Leonard 1999) also demonstrates that he does not comprehend the sanctity of private property rights.

4   Following Gates, the second and third-richest Americans—Berkshire Hathaway CEO and long-term investor Warren Buffett and Microsoft cofounder Paul Allen, respectively—are also "limousine liberals." Buffett's pet causes include nuclear disarmament for the United States (Louderback 2003), while Allen is an important contributor of campaign funds to the Democratic Party (Bickmeyer 2001).

Microsoft CEO Steven Ballmer, number eleven on the 2004 *Forbes* list, is also another life-long Democrat (Maxwell 2002, 216), while number twenty-four is George Soros—the great international speculator who is now most notorious for his far-leftwing activism and for championing a centralized regulation over global capitalism (Spath 2000).

The list also includes the welfare-statist, (il)liberal Republican (List, http://tinyurl.com/4s9re) Rockefellers and billionaire Ted Turner—a self-proclaimed "socialist at heart" (Auletta 2001; West 1999). John Galts they are not.

5   We have the Industrial Revolution to thank for the high standard of living we have today. Throughout the course of human history, from 10,000 B.C. all the way up to 1 A.D., the average human life expectancy was 20 years (Peron 2002). By 1800 A.D., it had only increased to 27 in the Americas (Peron 2002). This was true not only of American Indians but also of white settlers and blacks. Yet, the Industrial Revolution brought about an increase in American and European lifespans, in the period of 1800 to 1900, from 27 years (Peron 2002) to 47 (Stossel 2001).

While the human lifespan—and American lifespan—remained relatively stable for over 10 millennia (Peron 2002), the Industrial Revolution, in a single century, managed to boost the average American lifespan by over 73 percent.

Despite the horrible wars that occurred throughout the early twentieth century, the further advancement of industrialization again boosted the average American life expectancy from 47 years to 77 from 1900 to 2000 (Stossel 2001).

6   Naturally, life only began to improve for the West once the government finally shrank itself enough to give freethinkers and merchants some room to breathe, thus bringing about the Renaissance. Economics Nobel laureate Douglass C. North even says it was possible that the West did not return to the high standard of living it enjoyed in Rome's heyday until further shrinking of government power gave individuals the opportunity to use their minds to bring forth the Enlightenment and then the previously-mentioned Industrial Revolution (1981, 111).

References

Anti-Corn Law League. 2004. *Encyclopedia Britannica*. Cited 23 October. Online at: http://tinyurl.com/5co9w.

Auletta, Ken. 2001. The lost tycoon. *The New Yorker*, reprinted on Ken Auletta's Home Page. 23 April. Cited 23 October 2004. Online at: http://tinyurl.com/3sfjh.

Bernstein, Andrew. 2000a. *Cliffs Notes: Rand's Anthem*. Foster City, California: IDG Books Worldwide, Inc.

———. 2000b. *Cliffs Notes: Rand's Atlas Shrugged*. Foster City, California: IDG Books Worldwide, Inc.

Bickmeyer, Robert. 2004. Democrats are the real wealthy party. *The Daily Oakland Press*. Cited 23 October 2004. Online at: http://tinyurl.com/3jbmr.

Clough, Shepard B., and Rapp, Richard T. 1975 *European Economic History*. Revised edition. New York: McGraw-Hill, Inc.

Forstmann, Theodore. 1995. The paradox of the statist businessman. *Cato Policy Report* [online]. Cited 10 October 2004. Online at: http://tinyurl.com/6wrwy.

Gates, Bill. 1999. Speech at Columbia/NYU Business School. *Bill Gates's Web Site* Cited 10 October 2004. Online at: http://www.microsoft.com/billgates/speeches/03-24bizschool.asp.

Gwartney, James, and Lawson, Robert. 2004. *Economic Freedom of the World Annual Report*. Fraser Institute. Cited 24 October 2004. Online at: http://www.fraserinstitute.ca/shared/readmore.asp?sNav=pb&id=681

Halvorssen, Thor L. 2003. Is John Galt Venezuelan? American Enterprise Institute *Hot Flashes*. Cited 24 October 2004. Online at: http://tinyurl.com/59dym.

Income tax theories—the Laffer Curve—who pays how much? 1999–2003. *Virtual Economy Home Page*. Cited 10 October 2004. Online at: http://tinyurl.com/4b8et.

Landes, David S. 1999. *The Wealth and Poverty of Nations: Why Some Are So Rich and Some Are So Poor.* New York: W.W. Norton and Company.

Leonard, Andrew. 1998. Is Bill Gates a closet liberal? *Salon.* Cited 10 October. Online at: http://archive.salon.com/21st/ feature/1998/01/cov_29feature.html.

List of liberal U.S. Republicans. *The Free Dictionary.* Cited 23 October 2004. Online at: http://tinyurl.com/4s9re.

Louderback, Jeff. 2003. The real Warren Buffett. *NewsMax.* 19 August. Cited 23 October 2004 Online at: http://tinyurl.com/5g27q.

Maxwell, Fredric Alan. 2002. *Bad Boy Ballmer: The Man Who Rules Microsoft.* New York: William Morrow.

Micklethwait, John, and Wooldridge, Adrian. 2003. *The Company: A Short History of a Revolutionary Idea.* New York: The Modern Library.

Miles, M.A., Mitchell, D.J., Roll, R., Cartney, B.M., Beach, W.M., Eiras, A.I., Schavey, A., and Kim, A. 2004. *Index of Economic Freedom* Annual Report. The Heritage Foundation. Cited 24 October 2004. Online at: http://www.heritage.org/research/features/index/downloads.html.

Norberg, Johan. 2001. *In Defence of Global Capitalism.* Sweden: Timbro.

North, Douglass C. 1981. *Structure and Change in Economic History.* New York: W.W. Norton and Company.

Peron, Jim. 2002. The benefits of industry—we're living longer! Objectivist Center op-ed. Cited 23 October 2004. Online at: http://tinyurl.com/4rggj.

Rand, Ayn. 1957. *Atlas Shrugged.* New York: New American Library. 1985 paperback edition.

Schoolland, Ken. 1999. ECON 2015: *Principles of Macroeconomics* class. Hawaii Pacific University.

———. 2001. *The Adventures of Jonathan Gullible: A Free Market Odyssey.* third Revised American edition. Honolulu: Small Business Hawaii.

Slom, Samuel M. 2000. Governor in conspiracy to silence *Pacific Business News,* critics. *Small Business News* 25, no. 2 Cited 23 October 2004. Online at: http://www.smallbusinesshawaii.com/2000/Feb-2.html.

Spath, Stefan. 2000. The crisis of anti-capitalist George Soros. *Capitalism Magazine.* Cited 23 October 2004. Online at: http://www. capmag.com/article.asp?ID=723.

Stossel, John. 2001. *Tampering With Nature.* ABC News Special. Executive Producer Victor Neufeld. American Broadcasting Company. KITV-Hawaii Channel 4.

———. 2003. All worked up. *20/20.* ABC News. KITV-Hawaii Channel 4.

Tracinski, Robert W. 2003. The strike: Atlas shrugs in Venezuela. *The Intellectual Activist* 17, no. 2 (February): 12–20.

Tucker, William. 1990. *The Excluded Americans: Homelessness and Housing Policies.* Washington, D.C.: Regnery Publishing.

United States vs. Microsoft. Current Case. U.S. Department of Justice. Cited 23 October 2004. Online at: http://www.usdoj.gov/atr/ cases/ms_index.htm.

Wasserman, Elizabeth. 1998. Gates deposition makes judge laugh in court. *CNN.Com*. Cited 23 October 2004. Online at: http:// tinyurl.com/5etp9.

West, Andrew. 1999. "Capitalists" celebrate 50 years of communism in China. *Capitalism Magazine*. Cited 23 October 2004. Online at: http://www.capmag.com/article.asp?id=233.

Index